Study Guide to Accompany

David Shaffer's

DEVELOPMENTAL PSYCHOLOGY

Don Baucum

University of Colorado at Boulder

Brooks/Cole Publishing Company

Monterey, California

*To my son Van, now 5 years old,
who seems determined that I
understand developmental psychology
from his point of view.*

Don Baucum
January 1985

Brooks/Cole Publishing Company
A Division of Wadsworth, Inc.

Printed in the United States of America

10 9 8 7 6 5 4 3

BF721.54688   1985   155.4   84-12658

ISBN 0-534-02757-1

Cover Art: Maypole, Central Park, by William Glackens. Permission of the Fine Arts Museum
of San Francisco, Gift of the Charles E. Merrill Trust with matching funds from the de Young
Museum Society

Sponsoring Editor: C. Deborah Laughton
Cover Design: Katherine Minerva

CONTENTS

PREFACE

HOW TO USE THE STUDY GUIDE

Developmental psychology is an intriguing area of study. It cuts across most of the other areas of psychology, spanning any and all areas of human functioning from the perspectives of origins and change. Each of the many disciplines within psychology has its own methods and vocabulary, as does developmental psychology. Thus, whatever your background, you are faced with a complex task of interpreting, organizing, and summarizing. But it is a worthwhile and highly rewarding task through which you can achieve an overall understanding of people from many different points of view.

This study guide is intended to help you acquire developmental psychology, and it might also provide you with some ideas on how to go about studying other psychological disciplines. The study guide is based on two very general principles of learning which apply to any coursework you attempt: *organization* and *practice*. Whatever you study, a starting point is to organize the material in ways that enable you to understand it and to put it together as a whole, so that it makes sense for you. Then, with practice in using the material one way and another, you eventually achieve a level of mastery that allows you to do all sorts of important things such as understanding and predicting human behavior and also applying your knowledge to the taking of exams.

However, this study guide contains no shortcuts. It is not a substitute for the textbook. Instead, the exercises are constructed on the assumption that you have *already studied each chapter in detail*. In your initial reading of each chapter of the textbook, you should emphasize learning the basic concepts and vocabulary as you go, and you should pay special attention to understanding what you are reading - above and beyond simply memorizing the material. Given that, the study guide will help you fill in the gaps and get the overall picture, through organization and practice. In turn, the study guide will help you firm up your knowledge of the many details and points of view necessary to an understanding of what developmental psychology and people are all about.

This is the plan: Read and study the textbook a chapter at a time. Get an initial, working understanding of the material. Then settle into working through the study guide exercises with the textbook handy as a reference. The less you have to refer to the textbook as you go, the better you know the material. But you might need to go through the exercises more than once. Later, when you're preparing for an exam, make it a point to review the study guide exercises as one of your final steps. Each exercise is written with exam preparation in mind as well.

OVERVIEW AND KEY TERMS

Read carefully. Recall examples and discussion as you go, and define each key term.

This section of each chapter in the study guide summarizes basic concepts and vocabulary. However, it is written as an exercise to test your recall and understanding of the material, and detailed explanations and definitions are kept at a minimum. Thus each sentence serves as a compact set of "cues" for what you should remember and understand from the textbook. Vocabulary items are presented in a meaningful way, without elaboration. *You* provide the explanations and definitions yourself, as practice. Read this section carefully, a sentence or two at a time, pausing often to define words to yourself and think of examples along the way.

The major sections of each chapter are given. Chapter subsections are usually represented by paragraphs, as a guide for rechecking the textbook when you need to. Key vocabulary terms are always underlined, which allows you to scan quickly when reviewing the material.

Also note that this section will serve you well as a quick review in preparing for exams, since it provides a thorough summary. And throughout, every effort has been made to emphasize and interpret material in a way that is consistent with the textbook.

SELF-REVIEW

Fill in the blanks for each item. Check the answers for each item as you go.

In this exercise, major points and vocabulary are again summarized but with key concepts and terms omitted for you to fill in. Each item typically contains several fill-in-the-blanks, and the statements include cues to help you remember. However, unlike traditional programmed review, the study guide items do not provide all of the information you need. As before, it is assumed that you have already read and studied the textbook and at least made a start on learning the material. In addition, the items are not necessarily based on the same points covered in the *Overview and Key Terms* section.

The major sections and subsections of the textbook chapter are both given here, as a guide for referring back to the textbook. Many of the key terms appear as fill-ins, but other vocabulary and links to understanding are also left blank to provide a more thorough practice.

Writing in your answers will help, in part by giving you something to do beyond simply thinking about the material. Cover the margin answers as you start each page, then uncover them one at a time as you work. When you make a mistake, correct your written answer; taking the extra time to make corrections will also help you remember. In addition, whether right or wrong, take time to ask yourself why you chose a particular answer. Refer back to the textbook when you aren't sure.

Occasionally, more than one answer is given in the margin, and there will also be items for which you think of a different answer that is also correct. Psychology is like that. There are often many ways to say the same thing.

SELF-TEST I

Consider each alternative carefully. Then choose the best one.

The first of the two multiple-choice tests for each chapter contains 15 items. The emphasis is usually on general concepts and integration of the vocabulary with the material. It is intended as a sample of the many questions that might be posed. However, there are very few "gimmies," and most items use the vocabulary in a way that requires you to know it before you can get around to answering the question. The order in which the questions are presented parallels that of the textbook chapter, except that the items sometimes span several different sections.

To get the most out of the items, avoid using "process of elimination" and other such strategies you might normally apply to exams. The items are intended both as a practice test and as a learning device, which means that the "wrong" alternatives are also points that can help you understand the material. For each multiple-choice item, take the time to consider why the wrong alternatives are wrong, and when they are vocabulary items, pause to define them as well. This will also give you practice with the material.

Correct answers are given at the end of each study guide chapter. You may find it helpful to write your answers on a separate sheet of paper, which will allow you to go back and take the test again later. Also consider having a friend check your answers for you, which will make it less likely that you will automatically remember the correct answers the next time around. And when you don't know an answer, look it up in the textbook.

RESEARCH SUMMARY AND REVIEW

Using the textbook, review the research efforts indicated and write a summary of the important findings. Note the general purpose or context of the research.

Much of developmental psychology is based on logical lines of reasoning verified at key points by research. While you don't necessarily need to memorize names and dates, one of the more important skills you can acquire in any psychological discipline involves summarizing research efforts, extracting the important findings, and fitting data into the overall scheme of things. Although this exercise will help you learn the material through giving you something to do beyond thinking and memorizing, it will also give you practice that may help you in other psychology courses.

Research efforts for this exercise have been selected in accord with how much detail is presented in the textbook, so that you have something to summarize. Page numbers have been included; each page number corresponds to the *first* page upon which the research description appears.

Example summaries are given at the end of each study guide chapter. Your summaries will probably differ somewhat, but they should contain the essential features given.

SELF-TEST II

Consider each alternative carefully. Then choose the best one.

The second multiple-choice section contains 25 items constituting a different sample of the textbook material, in more detail. These items also incorporate the research to a greater extent.

As before, take the time to study the wrong alternatives as well as the correct ones. If you don't do well, go back and review both the textbook and the earlier sections of the study guide chapter before taking the test again. Correct answers are given at the end of each study guide chapter.

VIGNETTES

Consider the story, then answer each question using material from the textbook.

In this section "case study" situations are presented to give you more openended practice with the textbook material, and they have been written in accord with what you could reasonably know from the textbook. They reflect major points, lines of reasoning, and concepts from developmental psychology, and they contrast differing theories or points of view. The questions are suggestive of how you might interpret the situation described, to give you practice in integrating the textbook material in more or less real-life situations. And if you participate in class study groups, you might also find the stories useful as a forum for discussion.

Space for answering the questions is not provided, because of their possible length. It will be helpful, however, to write out your answers on notebook paper, since this will cause you to organize the material to a greater extent than simply thinking about it will. Answers can usually go a number of different directions, and thus the answers given at the end of each study guide chapter are mainly suggestive.

APPLICATIONS

Try each of the projects, noting answers to the questions as you go.

Where feasible, the projects go beyond the classroom and emphasize ways to apply the material in the outside world, again with the intent of giving you something to do other than simply sit and think and study. However, since you might or might not have access to children or special settings, many of the projects are hypothetical ones that might help you at some future date. And, as with the *Vignettes*, major topics and contrasting theories are emphasized. The projects too can serve as a forum for discussion groups.

Write down your answers here as well. Then compare them to the suggestive answers given at the end of each study guide chapter.

FINAL EXAM

At the end of the study guide a sample final exam is included, consisting of 80 multiple-choice questions (5 from each chapter). These are more general questions often summarizing major points and vocabulary, but some detail is included as well. As with the *Self-Tests*, you will also find it helpful to study the wrong alternatives as well as the correct ones.

Answers are given at the end of the *Final Exam* section.

CHAPTER ONE

INTRODUCTION

OVERVIEW AND KEY TERMS

Read carefully. Recall examples and discussion as you go, and define each key term.

THE CONCEPT OF DEVELOPMENT

Development is how organisms grow and change. Developmental psychology is the study of the physical, cognitive, emotional, and social changes that occur throughout the life-span. Child developmentalists focus on the period between conception and puberty.

Child development includes the prenatal period, infancy, and the toddler, preschool, and middle childhood periods. Adolescent development begins at puberty and continues to young adulthood. Although individual psychologists often focus only on one period in their research, development is a continual and cumulative process.

And, though a psychologist might study only a single aspect of development by itself, development involves all aspects of growth and change and thus requires a holistic perspective.

HUMAN DEVELOPMENT IN HISTORICAL PERSPECTIVE

Our conceptualizations of childhood and adolescence did not exist until very recent times. The ancient Spartans inspected infants to determine whether they would be allowed to live, and treated children harshly to toughen them into warriors. Infanticide was practiced into the Middle Ages, and children were treated as miniature adults on into the 1600s. There was no "bill of rights" for children such as that of Box 1-1.

In the 17th and 18th centuries, perhaps due to a renewed interest in the philosophical basis for human nature, a new look emerged and views of child care and education began to change. But the new look included differing points of view. Hobbes said that the child has original sin. Rousseau said that the child has innate purity and is an active, self-motivated learner. Locke said that the child is a passive tabula rasa. Such issues led to the recording of extensive baby biographies by 19th century educators and scientists such as Darwin, but these were hard to compare and were highly subject to observer bias, and few issues could be resolved this way.

Around the beginning of the 20th century, Hall devised the questionnaire method for studying children scientifically. Freud developed his psychoanalytic theory of development, based on extensive clinical interviews with adults. Thus Hall and Freud can be cited as the founders of developmental psychology. Theories such as Freud's describe and explain development, producing hypotheses that can be tested by observing people and collecting information. Thus Freud's theory has heuristic value.

1

The scientific method is used by modern-day psychologists to collect information and draw conclusions about how people develop. Although the scientific method comes in various forms, there are always the requirements that the researchers be objective and that their theories be supported by data. In turn, scientific understanding often depends on analysis of converging evidence, as discussed in Box 1-2.

Naturalistic observation is a valuable method that often uses time-sampling techniques to study behavior in everyday surroundings. Observer bias can interfere with scientific objectivity and thus must be carefully avoided, as through checking observer reliability. Another problem is that the observer's presence can cause people to behave differently. And in naturalistic observation it is difficult to determine what the actual causes of behavior are, as in the example of Charlesworth and Hartup's (1967) observational study of social reinforcement between nursery school children. Naturalistic observation often provides a starting point for research on causes.

In the interview method, the researcher asks child or parent a series of carefully selected questions. A structured interview makes it possible to compare answers directly because questions are asked in the same order. Although it is hard to know whether answers are honest and accurate, interviews can be designed to challenge children to answer accurately by posing problems. A variation of the interview method is the case study, in which an individual or case is assessed repeatedly and extensively through observation, testing, or interviews, as in Freud's work. Case studies are a rich source of information, although there are problems with accuracy and generalizability to other people, plus difficulties in comparing results from different cases. Another variation is the clinical method, in which the researcher asks varying questions according to how the person responds. This method yields protocols such as those of Piaget in his studies of cognitive development. Problems here include difficulty in comparing responses of different people, plus the increased possibility that the researcher's subjectivity can affect the results.

The experimental method is more objective and also allows the researcher to assess causes for behavior. Typically, the participants are sorted into groups who receive different treatments, thus establishing an independent variable. In turn, measuring the dependent variable shows the researcher whether the different treatments caused an effect. To be confident of the causes, researchers strive for experimental control, which includes treating the subjects the same in all ways other than the independent variable and also making the groups as much alike as possible through random assignment. These principles are illustrated in the Sprafkin, Liebert, and Poulous (1975) study of children's behavior toward puppies after watching *Lassie* TV programs. One recurring criticism is that laboratory experiments may be artificial, and so researchers often conduct field experiments in natural settings such as home or school, as in Friedrich and Stein's (1973) study of nursery school children's prosocial responses after watching *Mister Rogers' Neighborhood*. In contrast, quasi-experiments such as Cook and Campbell's (1979) citywide study of the benefits of children's watching *Sesame Street* take advantage of naturally occurring independent variables rather than experimentally controlled ones. But it is hard to assess causation versus correlation, as discussed in Box 1-3.

Measuring developmental "change" requires special research methods. Coates and Hartup's (1969) study of younger versus older children's ability to reproduce a model's behavior is an example of the cross-sectional comparison. But, as in Balte's (1968) argument that researchers have been mislead on changes in intelligence, factors other than developmental change can influence the findings in cross-sectional research. Some of these problems are eliminated in longitudinal comparisons such as the Fels study, but new problems are created. The same people are studied at different ages, thus allowing more of a look at individual differences in development; but such projects are costly and very time-consuming. Loss of subjects can produce a nonrepresentative sample. And there is the cross-generational problem that our world is continuously changing at the same time that the subjects are developing. Thus the <u>cross-sectional/short-term longitudinal comparison</u> combines the first two methods, as in the example of a program designed to reduce racial prejudice in children. This method saves time and money, and it also provides the clearest information about developmental change.

The generalizability of research findings across different cultures is also an issue, and thus <u>cross-cultural comparisons</u> assess whether findings are universal or culturally relative. Culture-specific patterns of behavior are also important to an understanding of child development.

ETHICAL CONSIDERATIONS IN DEVELOPMENTAL RESEARCH

In studying human development, the issue of <u>research ethics</u> is always present. With children in particular, the investigator must bear in mind that the child's rights come first, that the responsibility for maintaining ethical practices rests with the investigator, that the child must be informed and can refuse to participate at any point, that parental consent is required, and that no operation can be employed that may harm the child either physically or psychologically. When in doubt, and since it is always necessary to weigh the possible benefits of the research against the potential risks to the participants, research is typically reviewed and evaluated by professional committees in making a decision about whether to proceed. These considerations apply to all research involving human participants. But many questions remain as to what is ethical in research, as in the examples of whether children can be exposed to situations in which socially inappropriate behavior will occur, whether asking children about parental discipline is an invasion of privacy, whether children can be deceived in the course of research, whether naturalistic observation can occur without informing the participants, and whether verbal punishment can be used. An illustration of the reasoning employed in answering questions such as these is given in Box 1-4, in the context of studying aggressive behavior in children who had been abused by their parents.

SELF-REVIEW

Fill in the blanks for each item. Check the answers for each item as you go.

THE CONCEPT OF DEVELOPMENT

1. Growth and change in the individual's body, motor skills, mental or reasoning abilities, emotional expression, and patterns of social behavior are examples of _____ ; such change is studied by developmental _____.

development
psychologists

2. Three major concerns in studying child and adolescent development are (1) _____ the changes occur over time, (2) _____ the changes occur, and (3) why individual children _____ from each other.

how, why
differ

Human Development as a Continual and Cumulative Process

3. Development during childhood sets the _____ for adolescence and adulthood, which means that events during childhood play a role in forecasting the _____ of the individual.

stage

future

4. Human development is best described as a continual and cumulative _____, and the only constant thing is _____.

process, change

5. The five stages of childhood are the _____ period, _____, and the toddler, preschool, and middle childhood _____.

prenatal
infancy
periods

3

6. Adolescence begins with the onset of _____, and continues to young _____; the two general stages after young adulthood are _____ age and _____ age.

puberty
adulthood
middle, old

Human Development as a Holistic Process

7. The dominant theme in understanding development in the 1980s is to look at the whole child, known as the _____ perspective; although developmental psychologists often specialize in one or another aspect of development, it is important that we do not lose sight of the whole _____.

holistic

child or person

HUMAN DEVELOPMENT IN HISTORICAL PERSPECTIVE

Childhood in Premodern Times

8. In ancient times, children who seemed weak or unhealthy were often put to death through the practice of _____; and in medieval Europe, children started learning trades as early as age ___ and were in many ways treated as _____ adults.

infanticide

6, miniature

Origins of Modern-Day Views on Childhood

9. The idea of having children learn reading and writing and other such _____, as well as religious and moral _____, began in about the _____ century.

skills, values
17th

10. Hobbes viewed children as inherently selfish and bad, which was known as the doctrine of _____ _____; Rousseau saw children as inherently good, which was known as the doctrine of _____ _____.

original sin

innate purity

11. Locke argued that the child is a passive _____ _____ and that all knowledge, motives, and behavior are acquired through _____.

tabula rasa

experience

12. In the 19th century, philosophers, educators, and scientists such as Darwin observed the development of their own children and wrote _____ _____; however, because of the lack of a systematic approach and the possibility of observer bias, these did not yield useful _____ information.

baby biographies

scientific

Emergence of a Psychology of Childhood

13. Likely candidates as founders of developmental psychology are _____ for the questionnaire _____ and _____ for the development of psychoanalytic _____.

Hall, method, Freud
theory

14. A set of concepts and propositions about certain aspects of experience is called a _____; a specific prediction about behavior or development based on theory and tested by collecting data is called a _____.

theory

hypothesis

RESEARCH METHODS IN DEVELOPMENTAL PSYCHOLOGY

The Scientific Method

15. The basic attitude of the scientific method is that investigators be _____ and that their theories be based on _____ or _____ rather than mere opinion.

objective
observations, data

Applying the Scientific Method to the Study of Children and Adolescents

16. Rosenhan's (1970) interviews with civil rights activists

indicated that the more fully committed activists had parents
had parents who practiced the _____ that they preached,   altruism
and Midlarsky and Bryan's (1972) experiment indicated that
children were more charitable if they observed adults both
preach and _____ charity; these two studies provide an   practice
example of how _____ evidence helps us understand de-   converging
velopment.

17. Collecting data by observing people in their everyday surroundings is called _____ observation, and the way   naturalistic
in which this is done usually involves _____-_____   time-sampling
techniques; but problems are that observer _____ can influence   bias
the results and it is not possible to be sure of the _____   causes
of the behavior observed.

18. In the structured interview method, subjects are asked the
same _____ in the same _____, which allows the an-   questions, order
swers to be compared directly; in the case-study method, the
investigator prepares detailed _____ of one or more   descriptions
individuals and analyzes the results; and in the clinical method, subjects are asked _____ that vary according to   questions
how the subjects _____, with the goal of clarifying what   respond or answer
the subject has said or done.

19. In the experimental method, groups of participants are exposed to differing treatments to establish an _____   independent
variable, and the researcher measures the _____ varia-   dependent
ble to see if the treatments had an effect; to make the groups
the same except for the treatments, researchers use _____   random
assignment of subjects to groups.

20. Experiments conducted in natural settings are called _____   field
experiments, the goal being to maintain experimental _____   control
while extending research beyond the somewhat _____ set-   artificial
ting of the laboratory; research is also sometimes done outside
the laboratory when natural events cause two groups to differ
in an important way, as in the _____-experiment.   quasi-

Designing Research to Measure Developmental Change

21. One way of studying developmental change involves comparing
children of differing _____, as in the _____-_____   ages, cross-sectional
comparison; however, this approach yields little information a-
bout _____ differences.   individual

22. Researchers have also studied the same children over an extended period of time, as in the _____ comparison;   longitudinal
this approach is much better in assessing individual developmental _____, but it is prone to problems of nonrep-   differences
resentative _____ and is also costly and _____-consuming.   samples, time-

22. Perhaps the preferable way of studying developmental change
is the _____-_____/short-term longitudinal method,   cross-sectional
because it allows the researcher to assess individual _____   change
without problems of _____ samples and extend-   nonrepresentative
ed, costly research.

The Cross-Cultural Comparison

23. The value of studying children from different _____   cultural
backgrounds lies in determining what aspects of development are
_____ to all children, as well as discovering what as-   universal

5

pects of different cultures and their child-rearing practices
may cause children to _____ developmentally.   differ

ETHICAL CONSIDERATIONS IN DEVELOPMENTAL RESEARCH

24. Many experiments cannot be conducted with human participants, especially children, because of probable_____ or   physical
_____ harm; such experiments would be in viola-   psychological
tion of _____ _____.   research ethics

25. The primary responsibility for ethical research lies with
the _____ who conducts the research; in addition,   investigator
professional review _____ evaluate any possible harm   committees
in experiments and weigh the possible _____ of the re-   benefits
search against the potential _____ to the participants, to   risks
determine whether the research should be conducted.

26. As in the example of a researcher's attempt to develop a
structured interview to study the effects of child abuse, there
are often ethical questions involving invasion of _____,   privacy
use of naturalistic _____ without informed consent,   observation
and similar issues that are difficult to answer.

SELF-TEST I

Consider each alternative carefully. Then choose the best one.

1. Developmental psychology is concerned with identifying and explaining the changes people undergo throughout
     a. childhood
     b. adolescence
     c. adulthood
     d. all of the above

2. Although investigators may focus their research efforts on physical growth and development, or cognitive aspects of development, or psychosocial development, or other areas,
nowadays the developing person is viewed in terms of the
     a. holistic perspective
     b. learning and conditioning model
     c. psychoanalytic theory
     d. cross-sectional approach

3. In 1970, the White House Conference on Children took a child-centered position that
children have the right to
     a. grow in a society that represents the dignity of life
     b. grow up nurtured by affectionate parents
     c. be a child during childhood
     d. all of the above

4. The Spartans of ancient Greece had a view of children most consistent with the idea of
     a. innate purity
     b. the right to be a child during childhood
     c. children as miniature adults
     d. the right to grow up nurtured by affectionate parents

5. Locke's view of children as tabulae rasae characterized them as _____, whereas Rousseau's view of children as innately pure characterized them as _____.
    a. active, passive
    b. passive, active
    c. passive in both cases
    d. active in both cases

6. The primary impact of baby biographies such as the one written by Darwin was that
    a. comprehensive theories of child development emerged
    b. scientists had a good example of objective research on children
    c. data from different children could be compared directly
    d. human development became a topic worthy of scientific scrutiny

7. Which of the following is best for getting at the actual causes of behavior?
    a. naturalistic observation
    b. the clinical method
    c. the experimental method
    d. all of the above, equally

8. Which of the following allows for the best direct comparison of the participants' responses?
    a. structured interviews
    b. the clinical method
    c. the case-study method
    d. all of the above, equally

9. Of the following methods, which is the most prone to observer bias?
    a. structured interviews
    b. the clinical method
    c. the experimental method
    d. quasi-experiments

10. In an experiment, the results of differing treatments are determined by measuring the
    a. independent variable
    b. dependent variable
    c. both of the above
    d. none of the above

11. The early baby biographies were most similar to the
    a. structured interview method
    b. experimental method
    c. case-study method
    d. quasi-experimental method

12. If a researcher selects a single group of children and measures some aspect of their behavior as it changes from year to year, the researcher is using a
    a. cross-sectional comparison
    b. longitudinal comparison
    c. cross-sectional/short-term longitudinal comparison
    d. none of the above

13. Accurate information on individual differences in development can be obtained through the method called
    a. longitudinal comparison
    b. cross-sectional comparison
    c. both of the above
    d. none of the above

14. Loss of subjects in a study such as that of the Fels Research Institute can have the effect of
    a. producing a nonrepresentative sample
    b. making the research unethical
    c. making the study take much longer
    d. turning the study into an experiment

15. When there is a possibility of psychological harm in an experiment,
    a. the experiment is not conducted under any circumstances
    b. informed consent frees the researcher from responsibility for psychological harm
    c. a professional committee weighs benefits of the research against risks to the subjects, and makes a decision with appropriate safeguards
    d. the experiment is conducted if the researcher believes that it will yield benefits for humanity

RESEARCH SUMMARY AND REVIEW

Using the textbook, review the research efforts indicated and write a summary of the important findings. Note the general purpose or context of the research.

1. Rosenhan (1970), page 16: _____

_____

_____

_____

_____

2. Midlarsky & Bryan (1972), page 17: _____

_____

_____

_____

_____

3. Charlesworth & Hartup (1967), page 18: _____

_____

_____

_____

_____

4. Williams, Bennett, & Best (1975), page 19: _____

_____

_____

_____

_____

5. Sprafkin, Liebert, & Poulous (1975), page 22: _____

_____

_____

_____

_____

6. Friedrick & Stein (1973), page 23: _____

_____

_____

_____

_____

7. Cook & Campbell (1979), page 25: _____

_____

_____

_____

_____

8. Coates & Hartup (1969), page 26: _____

_____

_____

_____

_____

SELF-TEST II

Consider each alternative carefully. Then choose the best one.

1. Developmental psychologists study growth and change in behavior during
   a. the prenatal period
   b. the toddler period
   c. adolescence
   d. all of the above and more

2. Developmental growth and change occur during
   a. childhood
   b. adolescence
   c. adulthood
   d. all of the above

3. Adolescence begins with _____ and ends with _____ .
   a. grade school, high school
   b. puberty, high school
   c. grade school, young adulthood
   d. puberty, young adulthood

4. Human development is
   a. a continual process
   b. a cumulative process
   c. a holistic process
   d. all of the above

5. Western civilization's view that childhood is a special time and that children should receive education began
    a. in medieval times
    b. in the 17th century
    c. in the 19th century
    d. in the 20th century

6. The early baby biographies were examples of
    a. experiments
    b. case studies
    c. cross-sectional comparisons
    d. all of the above

7. Basically, the structured interview method was first developed by
    a. Sigmund Freud
    b. Charles Darwin
    c. G. Stanley Hall
    d. none of the above

8. The emergence of a psychology of childhood began with the work of
    a. G. Stanley Hall
    b. Sigmund Freud
    c. both of the above
    d. none of the above

9. Rosenhan's (1970) research on civil rights activists and Midlarsky and Bryan's (1972) experiment with children both indicate that children are more altruistic if their parents "practice what they preach" with regard to altruism; taken together, these studies provide an example of scientific reasoning based on
    a. cross-sectional comparison
    b. naturalistic observation
    c. converging evidence
    d. an ethical dilemma

10. Time-sampling is a technique most likely to be employed in
    a. naturalistic observation
    b. structured interviews
    c. laboratory experiments
    d. quasi-experiments

11. In the Charlesworth and Hartup (1967) study of positive social reinforcement among preschool children, it was found that
    a. older children dispensed more positive reinforcement
    b. all children reinforced members of their same sex more
    c. children who gave more social reinforcement also got more
    d. all of the above

12. According to Williams, Bennett, and Best's (1975) study of children's gender stereotyping in response to stories,
    a. children do not display gender stereotyping prior to adolescence
    b. 4th grade children display gender stereotypes, younger children do not
    c. 2nd grade children display gender stereotypes, younger children do not
    d. kindergarten children are already displaying gender stereotypes

13. The interview method generally works best with children when
    a. the researcher insists on precise, well articulated answers from participants
    b. the researcher poses problems and challenges children to display what they know
    c. the child's parents are present during the interview
    d. the children are aware of the most socially desirable way to respond

14. Freud's case-study method has limited usefulness because
    a. subjects may not report accurate information
    b. data on different subjects may not be directly comparable
    c. such information may lack generalizability to other groups of people
    d. all of the above

15. Piaget's work on children's intellectual development illustrates
    a. the structured interview method
    b. the case-study method
    c. the clinical method
    d. the experimental method

16. The different treatments imposed by an experimenter when testing a hypothesis represent the
    a. independent variable
    b. dependent variable
    c. reliability check
    d. random assignment

17. The potential benefits of TV-watching on intellectual and social development in children are supported by the research findings of
    a. Sprafkin, Liebert, and Poulous (1975) on children watching *Lassie*
    b. Friedrich and Stein (1973) on children watching *Mr. Rogers' Neighborhood*
    c. Cook and Campbell (1979) on children watching *Sesame Street*
    d. all of the above

18. The most important problem in interpreting the Cook and Campbell (1979) quasi-experiment on the the effects of watching *Sesame Street* was that
    a. no independent variable existed
    b. random assignment to groups was not possible
    c. no dependent variable existed
    d. no observer reliability checks were employed

19. The Coates and Hartup (1969) study of children 4-5 years old versus 7-8 years old reproducing an adult model's behavior after "describing" it or "passively observing" it is an example of the
    a. cross-sectional comparison
    b. longitudinal comparison
    c. cross-sectional/short-term longitudinal comparison
    d. cross-cultural comparison

20. Cross-sectional comparisons cannot
    a. be experimental
    b. yield information about developmental change
    c. yield information about individual change
    d. be ethically conducted

21. The Fels study that began in 1929 is an example of the
    a. cross-sectional comparison
    b. longitudinal comparison
    c. cross-sectional/short-term longitudinal comparison
    d. cross-cultural comparison

22. The cross-generational problem is likely in a
    a. cross-sectional comparison
    b. longitudinal comparison
    c. cross-cultural comparison
    d. all of the above

23. Benedict's belief that a person's behavior can only be understood within the context of his or her cultural environment is known as
    a. cross-cultural bias
    b. cross-sectional comparison
    c. generalizability
    d. cultural relativity

24. If you decided to test the effects of locking a group of children in an attic and feeding them through the door during the toddler period, your experiment
    a. would require informed consent by the children's parents
    b. would require review by a professional committee to determine benefits
    c. would require supervision by a medical doctor to prevent malnutrition
    d. would be grossly unethical and should not be conducted

25. In the final analysis, the responsibility for treating research participants fairly and protecting them from harm falls on the shoulders of
    a. ethics committees who weigh benefits and risks and make recommendations
    b. the investigator who proposes and conducts the research
    c. parents, teachers, and school officials who provide informed consent
    d. the federal granting agencies that fund psychological research

VIGNETTES

Consider the story, then answer each question using material from the textbook.

I. Mr. and Mrs. Williams told the researchers that their two children, Jack and Wilbur, were different from the very day each child was born. Jack almost never cried or put up a fuss, was quite affectionate, and always seemed curious in response to faces that appeared above his crib, even those of strangers. On the other hand, Wilbur was irritable from the outset and often cried for no apparent reason. He usually became upset when faces other than Mr. or Mrs. Williams' appeared above his crib, and he tended to avoid rather than seek interactions with people.

    1. Whose basic point of view about children is favored here, Locke's or Rousseau's? Why?

    2. From a different perspective, which child do you think Rousseau would pick as representative of all children? Which child might Hobbes pick? Why?

    3. From a research standpoint, how might the investigator go about obtaining this type of information from Mr. and Mrs. Williams?

II. Dr. Walker kept a thorough record of her child's behavior and progress throughout the first year of life, with careful attention to the sounds and noises her baby made that seemed to lead up to later language usage. She also kept notes on how her behavior affected her baby's vocalizing, in an attempt to learn how mother-child interactions might influence language development. Later, as a starting point in developing her own theory of early language development, she and her assistants replicated the project on several dozen other children by observing them weekly throughout the first year.

    1. What research methods were employed? What type of comparison was used?

    2. Why was the research conducted on additional children?

    3. If Dr. Walker observed that mothers' vocalizations to the child increased the rate of the children's vocalizations, would this mean that one "caused" the other? Why or why not?

III. A team of researchers set out to study aggressive behavior in preschool children (arguing, fighting, grabbing toys, and so on) in two different play settings, one where only large playground equipment was present and the other where only small toys were present. Their idea was that the children would share the playground equipment but would argue and fight more over the smaller, more personal toys. To test this hypothesis, the researchers carefully defined what would be considered aggressive behavior and used time-sampling procedures to observe the children from the edges of each play area. Indeed, the resulting observations verified the prediction that more aggression would occur when the children played with small toys.

1. What research methods were employed? Did small toys cause more aggression?

2. What might the researchers have done to ensure that their observations were accurate, and that all observers were recording the same behavior?

3. What ethical problems might arise in such a study?

APPLICATIONS

Try each of the projects, noting answers to the questions as you go.

I. As an illustration of the problems involved in observing behavior accurately, try the following exercises while watching a portion of *Mister Rogers' Neighborhood, Electric Company,* or *Sesame Street.* Define "prosocial behavior" very simply as an occasion on which one character (child or adult) is shown helping another character do something. Count each 5 seconds of helping as one occurrence--for example, a 15 second helping sequence would count as three occurrences. Observe the program for 5 minutes, tallying the occurrences of helping throughout.

1. Are there instances where you aren't sure that "helping" actually occurs? How might you improve the accuracy, and what might you do to check it?

2. Are there problems in missing a behavior while trying to record it? How might you solve these?

3. What other "prosocial" behaviors might you want to include in studying children's altruism?

II. Suppose you are an investigator trying to determine when gender stereotypes begin to appear with preschool children. You devise a short questionnaire as follows: What do mommies like to do best? What do daddies like to do best? What can mommies do better than daddies? What can daddies do better than mommies? Your plan is to tally the number of sex-role stereotypes in the children's responses.

1. How would you select children for a cross-sectional comparison?

2. How might you ask the questions? Could the order in which you asked them have an effect on the children's responses? Could the sex of the interviewer have an effect?

3. How would you decide when gender stereotypes begin to appear?

III. Redesign Application II for a longitudinal comparison.

1. How would you select children?

2. What effect might subject drop-out have on your results?

3. What effect might an increasing societal emphasis on sexual equality have during the course of your study?

Self-Test I

1. d	6. d	11. c
2. a	7. c	12. b
3. d	8. a	13. a
4. c	9. b	14. a
5. b	10. b	15. c

Research Summary and Review

1. Rosehan (1970): In the context of how child-rearing practices influence the develop-ment of altruism in children, it was found that the more fully committed civil-rights activists portrayed their parents as having practiced what they preached about helping people in need.

2. Midlarsky & Bryan (1972): Children who observed adults practicing charity with win-nings from a game of skill and "preaching" charity even on losing occasions were later more charitable themselves, indicating direct effects of adult behavior on children's altruism.

3. Charlesworth & Hartup (1967): In assessing age-related differences in social interac-tions, and also as an example of naturalistic observation, it was found that older pre-school children dispensed more positive social reinforcement to peers. In addition, all children reinforced members of their same sex more, and children who gave more social re-inforcement also got more in return.

4. Williams, Bennett, & Best (1975): As an illustration of cross-sectional research, and in the context of development of gender stereotypes, it was found that kindergarten, 2nd-grade, and 4th-grade children responded to story characters as "male" or "female" accord-ing to sex-role stereotypes, although an increase occurred between kindergarten and the 2nd grade.

5. Sprafkin, Liebert, & Poulous (1975): Watching *Lassie* TV programs had the effect of making 6-year-old children more likely to help and comfort crying puppies, indicating the potential prosocial effects of TV and illustrating the experimental method.

6. Friedrich & Stein (1973): In a field experiment, nursery school children who watched *Mister Rogers' Neighborhood* displayed more prosocial behaviors than children who saw other types of programming, indicating potential benefits of TV.

7. Cook & Campbell (1979): In a city-wide quasi-experiment, and as a study of the ef-fects of TV on general knowledge, it was found that children who regularly watched *Sesame Street* showed gains in comparison to children who did not watch the program.

8. Coates & Hartup (1969): As an illustration of a cross-sectional experiment, and to assess the role of verbal descriptions in the ability of children to reproduce a model's behavior from memory, it was found that 4-5-year-old children's ability to copy the model improved markedly if they had been instructed to describe the behavior while observing it; 7-8-year-old children spontaneously used description.

Self-Test II

1. d	6. b	11. d	16. a	21. b
2. d	7. c	12. d	17. d	22. b
3. d	8. c	13. b	18. b	23. d
4. d	9. c	14. d	19. a	24. d
5. b	10. a	15. c	20. c	25. b

Vignettes

I. (1) Rousseau's view is favored, at least with regard to Jack's "positive" inclinations. Locke's view might seem to be favored by Wilbur's behavior, with regard to more negative, unmolded behaviors, but Locke's idea of the tabula rasa rules out individual differences such as those between Jack and Wilbur. (2) Rousseau would pick Jack, in accord with the doctrine of innate purity. Hobbes would pick Wilbur, in accord with the doctrine of original sin. (3) A structured interview might be employed, with questions asked in a specific order to permit comparison between the children. A clinical interview would let the parents' responses determine the direction of the interview, and might yield data that would otherwise be missed. Either of these might be incorporated within a case-study approach, if the investigator also used testing or observation.

II. (1) Given that Dr. Walker did not try to elicit the specifics of language usage, the basic method is naturalistic observation within a longitudinal comparison. (2) The researchers would be interested in whether the original child's data generalized to other children. (3) Causality could not be inferred from this type of observation. For example, much of the baby's apparent responding to the mother could be entirely coincidental. Thus it would be necessary to experimentally vary the mother's vocalizations and other behaviors to see what effect this treatment would have on the child's language usage.

III. (1) The basic method is naturalistic observation; it is not a field experiment, because the researchers apparently did not arrange the play conditions or use controlled independent variables. Thus causes could not be determined here, and other factors within each play area might be reponsible. (2) Reliability checks would be made, by having different observers independently record the same behavior and compare their results. (3) Could the researchers ethically watch the children aggress against each other, without intervening when things got rough? Yet, intervening would void the results of their study. And, if they did not intervene, would they be implicitly teaching the children that aggression is acceptable? And, should they inform the children what was being observed? This would also void the study.

Applications

I. (1) An apparently simple definition such as "helping" can be very difficult to implement. At times you might decide that a character is simply interacting with another, and not really doing anything helpful. Also, it is possible to help someone by standing back and doing nothing to "interfere." Basically, you can improve accuracy by giving specific details of the behaviors in question, by using a second observer to assess reliability, and in this case videotaping the segment and observing it more than once. (2) Aside from having to pause and consider whether the behavior is or is not an instance of helping, you might also miss a behavior while looking down to record a previous one. A time-sampling procedure involving observing for 20 seconds, recording for 10 seconds, and then observing again would help. (3) Aside from helping, you might also include affection, use of positive social reinforcement, sharing without aggression, and behaving charitably toward other children.

15

II. (1) You would use different groups of children within each age range of interest, such as 3-year-olds, 4-year-olds, and 5-year-olds. (2) Order of the questions could have effects in unpredictable ways, and thus you might use the "mommie" questions first with half of the children and the "daddie" questions first with the other half. Posing the questions as "problems" to be solved by the children would help in getting them to give thorough answers. And, since sex of the interviewer might also have an effect in leading the children to give more "favorable" responses one way or the other, you might have half of the children interviewed by a male and the other half by a female. (3) Basically, you would have to decide in advance what number or percent of stereotyped responses would indicate a sufficient degree, since even the 3-year-olds might show some tendencies along these lines. Notably, the definition of what is and what is not a gender stereotype would not be easy either.

III. (1) For a longitudinal comparison, you would select one group of children at the beginning of the age range of interest, say 3-year-olds, and follow them with repeated testing for several years. (2) There are many ways in which a nonrepresentative sample might occur. Families who convey fewer stereotypes to their children might be more mobile, and thus more likely to move during the study. Or, families who emphasize gender stereotypes might be more likely to resent your questions of their children, thus removing their children from the study. And so on. Each time a child drops out, you would have to drop that child's data from the entire study. Thus you might wind up with data that reflect some children's development but are not generalizable to children overall. (3) As gender standards continue to change, for example, you might find that some children are directly affected and actually show less stereotyping with increasing age during a study that lasts several years.

CHAPTER TWO

THEORIES OF HUMAN DEVELOPMENT

OVERVIEW AND KEY TERMS

Read carefully. Recall examples and discussion as you go, and define each key term.

Ideally, a scientific theory is (1) concise, yet applicable to a wide range of phenomena, and (2) precise and capable of making explicit predictions. Theories are often revised or discarded, and there is nothing as practical as a good theory.

QUESTIONS AND CONTROVERSIES ABOUT THE NATURE OF HUMAN DEVELOPMENT

Developmental theorists differ on four basic issues: (1) They emphasize positive or negative aspects of children's character in accord with assumptions about human nature as good or bad; (2) in accord with the nature-nurture controversy, some theorists base development primarily on heredity, some on environment, and some on both in interaction; (3) on the activity-passivity issue theorists differ on whether children actively determine how society treats them or passively respond to society's treatment; (4) on the continuity-discontinuity issue, theorists differ on whether gradual increments or abrupt plateaus or change constitute development. In addition, continuity theorists focus on underlying processes, whereas discontinuity theorists focus on developmental stages. Box 2-1 presents a summary of these issues in the form of a test.

THE PSYCHOANALYTIC VIEWPOINT

Sigmund Freud's controversial psychoanalytic theory emphasized sexual urges. The theory was based on patients' life histories, using information gained by hypnosis, free association, and dream analysis as methods to assess unconscious motivation and conflicts between biological motives and the rules of society.

According to Freud, the newborn child is driven by two kinds of biological instincts: Eros, the life instincts, and Thanatos, the death instincts. Each of these produces psychic energy, which eventually divides among the three basic components of personality. The id is present at birth, and is unrealistic as it obeys the pleasure principle in investing psychic energy in objects intended to gratify instincts. Soon the ego emerges to control the id and gratify it according to the reality principle. Finally the superego develops as the child internalizes parents' moral standards. The superego strives for perfection and censors the expression of socially undesirable instincts. Sublimation occurs when the superego causes the ego to direct impulses from the id to socially acceptable outlets. Where id, ego, and superego are not balanced in terms of invested psychic energy, an unhealthy personality may result.

Repression occurs when conflicts are forced out of conscious awareness. Freud emphasized the sex instincts as a major life force, and a frequent source of conflicts. The sex instinct changes in character through maturation. The psychic energy of the sex instinct is called libido, and this shifts to different parts of the body as the child moves through psychosexual stages of development.

From birth to 1 year of age, the child is in the oral stage and libido centers on the mouth. Children suck, bite, and chew to gratify the sex instincts. In the anal stage from 1 to 3 years of age, libido shifts to the anal region and defecation becomes the means of gratifying sex instincts. In the phallic stage, from 3 to 6 years of age, libido moves to the genitals and gratification takes the form of self-fondling. Males develop sexual desires for their mothers, view their fathers as rivals, and experience castration anxiety in the Oedipus complex. Resolution of the Oedipus complex involves repression of incestuous desires and identification with the father. Females develop sexual desires for their fathers as a result of penis envy, and view their mothers as rivals in the Electra complex. This complex may simply fade away as the female matures and accepts reality.

Defense mechanisms of sublimation, fixation, and regression during the first three stages are discussed in Box 2-2. Next comes the latency period, ages 6 to 12, when libido is mostly channeled into schoolwork and play. Puberty brings the onset of the genital stage, characterizing the rest of the lifespan, in which libido is invested in activities related to courting, marriage, and reproduction.

Though Freud's theory may reflect his patients' sexually repressive culture, and though phallic-stage children generally don't know enough sexual anatomy to experience the Oedipus and Electra complexes, Freud's emphases on unconscious motivation and developmental stages are important contributions.

Erik Erikson retained much of Freud's theory but stressed the active-child view and the role of ego functioning to a greater extent, with motives stemming from culture and society rather than from sexual instincts. His eight stages of man focus on psychosocial crises experienced throughout the lifespan, including basic trust versus mistrust, autonomy versus shame and doubt, initiative versus guilt, industry versus inferiority, identity versus role confusion, intimacy versus isolation, generativity versus stagnation, and ego integrity versus despair, as presented in Table 2-1. Crises that are not resolved may cause problems later in life, as in the example of Scrooge. Erikson's theory does not give details on how to resolve the crises, however, and is thus primarily a descriptive theory of development.

Psychoanalytic theory is less popular today because it cannot be tested easily, and we have no clear way to measure psychic energy and other features of the theory.

THE LEARNING VIEWPOINT (BEHAVIORISM)

Behaviorism emphasizes scientific explanations of observable behavior and usually stresses the role of learning in development. Watson's radical behaviorism ruled out the study of mentalistic events and also described the infant as a tabula rasa, with development being a continuous process based on learning.

Classical conditioning is a type of learning in which a neutral stimulus comes to evoke behavior, as in the example of the ice-cream-truck bell. Operant conditioning involves learning that occurs because of the consequences of a behavior: A response followed by a reinforcer is more likely to occur again, and a response followed by punishment is less likely to occur again. Observational learning occurs through watching and imitating social models.

Social learning theory traces to Clark Hull. The neo-Hullians rejected psychoanalytic instincts and personality components and adopted the term habit to describe stable aspects of personality. The continuous acquisition of habits is motivated by primary drives which consist of biological needs, and also by secondary (or acquired) drives, such as the need for social approval, which are learned motives. Primary reinforcers reduce biological drives. Secondary reinforcers such as money reduce acquired drives. Dollard and Miller sought to explain personality development and socialization in these terms.

B. F. Skinner rejected the notion of primary and secondary drives, preferring to view motivation in terms of external consequences of behavior. But Skinner's radical behaviorism was in turn rejected by cognitive social-learning theorists such as Albert Bandura, who emphasized learning based on simple observation of behaviors in the absence of external consequences.

In recent years, the environmental determinism of the (radical behaviorists) has received less emphasis, and the cognitive social-learning theorists have emphasized reciprocal determinism in which children are actively involved in creating environments that influence their development. (*Piaget*)

The learning approach (1) has made contributions such as counterconditioning, (2) has provided much information on how children react to environmental influences, and (3) has emphasized scientific objectivity in the study of development. Criticisms include the oversimplified view of individual differences in heredity and maturation, and too little emphasis on cognitive determinants of development.

THE COGNITIVE-DEVELOPMENTAL VIEWPOINT

Jean Piaget emphasized the child as a constructivist: an active explorer oriented toward understanding the environment. From a background of zoology and epistemology, Piaget based his theory of cognitive development on his observation of the patterns of thinking displayed by children of differing ages.

Piaget's theory emphasizes equilibrium between one's thought processes and environment. The basic cognitive structure is the schema, which is an organized pattern of thought or action. Schemata develop from innate reflexes, as in the examples from Piaget's observations of his son Laurent. The child combines schemata into coherent systems of knowledge through intellectual functions called organization and adaptation. When a child adapts by incorporating new experiences into existing schemata, assimilation is occurring. When the child alters existing schemata to fit a novel experience, accommodation is occurring. These functions tend toward equilibrium, though constantly operating in reciprocal fashion to produce higher-order schemata.

Piaget describes four broad stages of intellectual development: (1) The infant begins in the sensorimotor stage with innate reflexes that eventually give rise to mental schemata. (2) By about 2 years of age, the child enters the preoperational stage and begins to use symbolism to represent and understand the environment. (3) By about 7 years of age, the child is much less egocentric and is capable of more logical thinking where concrete situations are involved, thus entering the concrete operations stage. (4) Hypothetical and abstract thinking appear by about 11 years of age in the stage of formal operations. Throughout, the idea is that development determines learning, and not vice versa. A discussion of how children's interpretations of rules depend on cognitive development is given in Box 2-3.

The study of social cognition traces to Piaget's work, and involves how children come to understand other people. Another of Piaget's contributions is the emphasis on how children's thought processes are very different from those of adults. Criticisms are that (1) Piaget ignored unconscious motivation, (2) that his stages may not by accurate, and (3) that he placed too great an emphasis on biological factors.

THE ETHOLOGICAL VIEWPOINT

Ethology places an even greater emphasis on biological bases of behavior, and focuses on innate behaviors thought to be a result of natural selection. Through naturalistic observation, ethologists look at what happens before and after innate critical behaviors. Crying, for example, may ensure that infants' needs are met and may also promote interactions that lead to emotional attachment. Learning interacts with innate behaviors to produce adaptation, as when the infant learns to discriminate familiar persons from strangers.

Contributions of ethology include specifications of the biological determinants of development, such as the idea that infants actively promote social encounters starting from birth. Motives such as altruism may also be inborn, as in Hoffman's argument that helping others is adaptive for the species, as discussed in Box 2-4. Criticisms of ethology are (1) that such theories are untestable, (2) that they serve only as post hoc explanations, and (3) that human innate responses are highly modified by learning.

A FINAL COMMENT ON DEVELOPMENTAL THEORIES

Among other differences, developmental theorists emphasize different aspects of development. Many developmentalists nowadays are theoretical eclectics, recognizing that each of the theories contributes to what we know about developing children and adolescents.

SELF-REVIEW

Fill in the blanks for each item. Check the answers for each item as you go.

QUESTIONS AND CONTROVERSIES ABOUT THE NATURE OF HUMAN DEVELOPMENT

1. Developmental theorists differ in viewing children either as inherently *good* or *bad*, and thus emphasize either *positive* or *negative* aspects of children's character.

good, bad
positive, negative

2. A second issue is the nature-nurture controversy; theorists differ in their emphasis on *heredity* and biological factors versus *environment* and learning.

heredity
environment

3. Nowadays, most theorists view development as a result of biological predispositions and environmental forces in *interaction*; however, theorists continue to differ on whether children determine how society treats them or whether children are extremely malleable in response to society, which is the *activity* - *passivity* issue.

interaction

activity - passivity

4. The continuity-discontinuity issue depends on whether we look at underlying processes, which appear to be *continuous*, versus what it is that is developing, such as intelligence or moral reasoning, which may appear *discontinuous*; in particular, discontinuity theorists focus on developmental *stages*.

continuous

discontinuous

stages

THE PSYCHOANALYTIC VIEWPOINT

5. One controversial aspect of Freud's psychoanalytic theory was the emphasis on *sexual* urges as determinants of child and adult behavior.

sexual

Overview of Freud's Psychoanalytic Theory

6. Freud's three basic methods of getting patients to discuss personal matters and reveal unconscious conflicts were *hypnosis*, *free* association, and *dream* analysis.

hypnosis, free, dream

7. Freud's view of the newborn child as a "seething cauldron" implies that the child's urges are inherently *bad*, and the child is "driven" by the life-sustaining instincts called *Eros* and the destructive "death" instincts called *Thanatos*.

bad or negative

Eros
Thanatos

8. At birth, psychic energy is invested in the *id*, which operates according to the *pleasure* principle and seeks immediate *gratification* of instinctual needs; next, the *ego* emerges as psychic energy is diverted to cognitive processes, and operates according to the *reality* principle in controlling impulses from the id; finally, the *superego* emerges as children internalize the moral

id
pleasure
gratification
ego
reality

superego

20

standards of their parents, striving for _perfection_.   perfection

9. When the superego causes the ego to channel impulses from
the id to socially acceptable outlets, _sublimation_ is   sublimation
said to occur; when conflicts are simply forced out of conscious awareness instead of being resolved, _repression_   repression
is said to occur.

10. Freud's psychosexual stages are based on maturation of the
sex instincts, which causes _libido_ to shift from one part of   libido
the _body_ to another.   body

11. In the _oral_ stage, libido centers around the mouth, in   oral
the _anal_ stage, libido shifts to the anal region, and in the   anal
phallic stage, libido moves to the genitals; severe con-   phallic
flicts in the psychosexual stages may yield arrested development called _fixation_, which impairs personality development.   fixation

12. Boys' sexual longings for their mothers and jealousy over
their fathers produce the _Oedipus_ complex; girls' sexual   Oedipus
envy of their fathers and jealousy of their mothers produce the
Electra complex.   Electra

13. A major problem with psychoanalytic theory is that if
phallic-stage children have difficulty recognizing sex differences in genital anatomy, it is unlikely that they could ex-
perience _castration_ anxiety or _penis_ envy, and the   castration, penis
Oedipus and Electra complexes would be unlikely as well.

14. Freud's main contributions were (1) the idea of _unconscious_   unconscious
motivation and (2) the view of development as occurring in
stages.   stages

Erik Erikson's Theory of Psychosocial Development

15. Erikson departed from Freud's emphasis on _sex_ instincts,   sex
instead stressing psychosocial life _crises_ that must be re-   crises
solved during _eight_ ages of man; instead of the id, Erik-   eight
son emphasized the _ego_, within a view that humans are   ego
rational, adaptive creatures who struggle to cope success-   rational
fully.

Psychoanalytic Theory Today

16. Since psychic energy cannot be _measured_, psychoanalytic   measured
theory is difficult to _test_, and thus psychoanalysts   test or verify
represent only a small _minority_ of child developmentalists.   minority

THE LEARNING VIEWPOINT (BEHAVIORISM)

17. In Watson's radical behaviorism, the infant is a _tabula_   tabula
rasa, and the building blocks of development are _learned_   learned
associations.

What is Learning?

18. Learning is a process that produces relatively _permanent_   permanent
changes in behavior or potential, as a result of _experience_   experience
or _practice_.   practice

19. The type of learning in which a previously neutral stimulus
comes to evoke some particular response is _classical_   classical
conditioning; in contrast, learning based on the consequences
of a response is _operant_ conditioning.   operant

20. Consequences which increase the probability of a a response are called _reinforcers_ ; consequences which suppress a response are called _punishers_.

reinforcers
punishers

21. Learning as a result of watching and imitating social models, even where consequences are not in effect, is called _observational_ learning.

observational

Theories of Social Learning

22. Neo-Hullians such as Dollard and Miller described personality development in terms of _habits_ that are learned in satisfying both _primary_ and _secondary_ drives.

habits
primary, secondary

23. Secondary reinforcers acquire their value through association with _primary reinforcers_ ; social approval is an example of a _secondary_ reinforcer.

primary reinforcers
secondary

24. Skinner rejected the notion of internal drives, proposing instead that behavior is motivated by _external_ consequences; but Bandura argued that _cognitive_ learning takes place without external consequences, through observation of models.

external
cognitive

Social Learning as a Reciprocal Process

25. The view of children as passive creatures molded by their environment is called _environmental_ determinism, which leads to Skinner's idea that _free will_ is merely an illusion; in contrast, the view that children are active in structuring the environment that in turn influences their behavior is called _reciprocal_ determinism.

environmental
free will

reciprocal

Contributions and Criticisms of Learning Theory

26. Contributions of the behaviorists include (1) treatments for undesirable _habits_, (2) a wealth of information on how children react to _environmental_ influences, and (3) an emphasis on scientific _objectivity_.

habits or behaviors
environmental
objectivity

THE COGNITIVE-DEVELOPMENTAL VIEWPOINT

27. Piaget's basic view was that the child is a curious, active explorer who _constructs_ reality through interpretations of the environment.

constructs

Origins of Piaget's Cognitive Theory

28. From a background of zoology and epistemology, Piaget originally went to work standardizing _intelligence_ tests, eventually becoming more interested in children's _incorrect_ answers than their correct ones.

intelligence

incorrect

Piaget's View of Intelligence

29. In Piaget's view, intelligence is geared toward harmony between thought processes and the environment, which yields _equilibrium_

equilibrium

30. "What" a child thinks is referred to as _content_, and is determined by an underlying _structure_; Piaget's basic structure is the _schema_, an organized pattern of thought or action.

content
structure
schema

31. According to Piaget, children enter the world with inborn _reflexes_, which are modified by experience into _schemata;_

reflexes, schemata

these early behavioral schemata later evolve into _mental_   mental
schemata.

32. Organization and adaptation are intellectual _functions_;   functions
complex higher-order schemata are formed through _organization_   organization
and _adaption_. adaptation.   adaptation

33. When a child adapts to a novel stimulus by employing an existing schema, _assimilation_ is said to occur; when a child   assimilation
alters a schema to fit a novel stimulus, _accommodation_   accommodation
is said to occur.

Stages of Cognitive Development

34. During the sensorimotor period, the infant (1) acquires a
basic sense of _self_, (2) learns _object_ permanence, and   self, object
(3) begins to acquire mental _schemata_.   schemata

35. The preoperational child (1) mentally represents the environment by using _symbolism_, (2) becomes more imagina-   symbolism
tive in _play_ activities, and (3) eventually becomes much less   play
egocentric and thus capable of taking others' point of view.   egocentric

36. During concrete operations the child begins to use logical
cognitive operations to understand objects and events; and   cognitive
during formal operations the adolescent becomes capable of
abstract thinking, including thinking about _thinking_   abstract, thinking
itself.

Piaget on Social Learning

37. Learning theorists view development as the _product_ of   product
social learning, whereas cognitive theorists view social learning as the product of _development_.   development

Contributions and Criticisms of the Cognitive-Developmental Viewpoint

38. Piaget's major contributions include (1) helping legitima-
tize _cognitive_ psychology, and especially (2) emphasizing   cognitive
that children are active explorers whose _thought_ processes   thought
are very different from those of adults; criticisms of Piaget
include (1) his ignoring of _unconscious_ motivation and   unconscious
(2) the variability in how and when children enter his developmental _stages_.   stages

THE ETHOLOGICAL VIEWPOINT

39. According to ethologists, there are biologically programmed behaviors in humans that evolved through Darwin's process of _natural selection_, and these behaviors interact   natural selection
with learning to influence development.

Contributions of the Ethological Viewpoint

40. In contrast to views of the infant as a tabula rasa, ethologists stress that infants are highly _social_ from birth,   sociable or social
and that infants have important inborn social _motives_; al-   motives
truism, for example, could be inborn through natural selection,
in that individuals who _help_ each other would be more likely   help
to _survive_ long enough to reproduce.   survive

Criticisms of Ethology

41. The idea of inborn motives, however, is basically not
testable and is difficult to attribute to evolutionary   testable

23

history except as a post hoc explanation.   history

A FINAL COMMENT ON DEVELOPMENTAL THEORIES

42. The various theories make different assumptions and emphasize different aspects of development; many developmentalists
nowadays take the best of each theory, and are thus *eclectic*.   eclectic

SELF-TEST I

Consider each alternative carefully. Then choose the best one.

1. Theories that do <u>not</u> accurately predict and explain new research findings
   a. have no value whatsoever
   b. violate the requirement that theories must be concise
   c. may still be valuable, through having stimulated the new research
   d. violate the requirements that theories must be precise

2. The issue of whether children are curious explorers or malleable recipients of environmental forces is called the
   a. question of original sin versus innate purity
   b. nature-nurture controversy
   c. activity-passivity issue
   d. continuity-discontinuity issue

3. The issue of whether development occurs in gradual increments or in abrupt stages is called the
   a. question of original sin versus innate purity
   b. nature-nurture controversy
   c. activity-passivity issue
   d. continuity-discontinuity issue

4. Eros and Thanatos are examples of
   a. phallic stage complexes
   b. sublimated impulses and urges
   c. instinctual sources of psychic energy
   d. internalized codes of conduct

5. The psychoanalytic theory of Freud placed major emphasis on
   a. sex instincts
   b. unconscious motivation
   c. fixation in psychosexual stages
   d. all of the above

6. Erikson's eight ages of man yield a theory of personality based on
   a. psychosexual adjustment
   b. psychosocial adjustment
   c. operant conditioning
   d. biological maturation

7. Who of the following would <u>least</u> qualify as a stimulus-response behaviorist?
   a. J. B. Watson
   b. Clark Hull
   c. Albert Bandura
   d. B. F. Skinner

8. The behaviorists of the 1980s tend to
   a. continue to emphasize the viewpoint of radical behaviorism
   b. be primarily psychoanalytic in their viewpoint
   c. accept the idea that heredity and maturation set limits on learning
   d. all of the above

9. The child is essentially passive and molded entirely by environmental forces in
   a. Erikson's psychosocial theory
   b. Watson's radical behaviorism
   c. Piaget's cognitive-developmental theory
   d. Bandura's social-learning theory

10. Which of the following theories emphasizes that the child is a curious, active explorer who is self-motivated to learn and understand?
   a. Skinner's operant conditioning theory
   b. Dollard and Miller's neo-Hullian theory
   c. Bandura's social-learning theory
   d. all of the above

11. The idea of continuous reciprocal interaction between child and environment throughout development assumes that children are
   a. curious, active explorers
   b. passively molded by environmental forces
   c. inherently negative
   d. inherently positive

12. Intelligence tests focus primarily on intellectual _____; Piaget's theory of cognitive development focuses on _____ and also on function.
   a. content, structure
   b. structure, content
   c. content, content
   d. structure, structure

13. When existing schemata are applied to a new environmental situation, _____ is said to occur; when schemata are altered to fit a new environmental situation, _____ is said to occur.
   a. accommodation, assimilation
   b. assimilation, accommodation
   c. assimilation, assimilation
   d. accommodation, accommodation

14. Piaget's work has had the effect of
   a. shifting the emphasis in the study of intelligence from content to structure
   b. helping make cognition an acceptable area of scientific study
   c. demonstrating that children's thought processes differ from those of adults
   d. all of the above

15. Ethologists, in their emphasis on innate responses which have adaptive significance, generally prefer to
   a. study behavior in its natural environment
   b. conduct laboratory experiments on behavior
   c. use hypnosis to assess instinctual and unconscious motivation
   d. conduct research on lower animals and not on humans

RESEARCH SUMMARY AND REVIEW

Using the textbook, review the research efforts indicated and write a summary of the important findings. Note the general purpose or context of the research.

1. Katcher (1955), page 50: _____

_____

_____

_____

_____

2. Weisberg (1963), page 58: _____

_____

_____

_____

3. Sagi & Hoffman (1976), page 69: _____

_____

_____

_____

_____

SELF-TEST II

Consider each alternative carefully. Then choose the best one.

1. A scientific theory is a set of concepts and propositions that should be
    a. concise
    b. precise
    c. both of the above
    d. none of the above

2. Watson's quotation "Give me a dozen healthy infants...and I'll take any one at random and train him to become any type of specialist I might select..." implies that development is
    a. based primarily on heredity
    b. based primarily on environment
    c. continuous
    d. discontinuous

3. The psychoanalytic method in which the patient talks about anything and everything that comes to mind is
    a. hypnosis
    b. free association
    c. dream analysis
    d. none of the above

4. Freud's emphasis on dream analysis was based on the idea that
    a. dreams give an indication of unconscious motives
    b. dreams represent habits and stable aspects of personality
    c. dreams come about through observational learning
    d. none of the above

5. The order in which Freud's three personality components appear as a result of the division of psychic energy is
   a. ego, id, superego
   b. superego, ego, id
   c. id, ego, superego
   d. ego superego, id

6. The _____ operates according to the reality principle, the _____ operates according to the pleasure principle, and the _____strives for perfection.
   a. id, ego, superego
   b. ego, id, superego
   c. superego, ego, id
   d. ego, superego, id

7. The superego develops as a result of the child
   a. learning the reality principle
   b. obeying the pleasure principle
   c. repressing conflicts involving sex instincts
   d. internalizing the parents' moral standards

8. Freud's psychosexual stages occur as a result of the maturing of the sex instinct and a shifting of _____ from one part of the body to another.
   a. libido
   b. Thanatos
   c. repression
   d. the Oedipus complex

9. The order in which Freud's psychosexual stages appear as the result of shifting of psychic energy is
   a. oral, anal, phallic, genital
   b. anal, oral, phallic, genital
   c. oral, phallic, genital, anal
   d. anal, oral, phallic, genital

10. In the dynamics of the Oedipus complex, the male child's fear that his father will castrate him because of the child's incestuous desires for the mother is resolved by
   a. repressing the incestuous desires for the mother
   b. identifying with the aggressor father
   c. both of the above
   d. none of the above

11. In the genital stage, libido is invested in
   a. preparing for a career
   b. forming friendships
   c. courting and marriage
   d. all of the above

12. Katcher's (1955) study found that phallic-stage children are inept at assembling dolls so that genitals match other parts of the body; this finding
   a. supports the idea of Oedipus and Electra complexes
   b. suggests that children experience castration anxiety and penis envy
   c. is consistent with the idea of Oedipus and Electra complexes
   d. disproves Freud's theory in all respects

13. The idea that the mother or primary caregiver can strongly influence personality development during early infancy as a result of how she responds to the infant's needs forms the basis for Erikson's stage of
   a. basic trust versus mistrust
   b. autonomy versus shame and doubt
   c. initiative versus guilt
   d. industry versus inferiority

27

14. Learning based on changes in behavior as a consequence of reinforcement and punishment is called
    a. classical conditioning
    b. operant conditioning
    c. observational learning
    d. accommodation

15. Primary drives are satisfied by _____ reinforcers, and acquired drives are satisfied by _____ reinforcers.
    a. primary, secondary
    b. primary, primary
    c. secondary, primary
    d. secondary, secondary

16. Which of the following best characterizes the view of neo-Hullian behaviorists such as Dollard and Miller?
    a. unconscious motives and instincts determine much of personality development
    b. personality consists of habits learned through drive reduction
    c. desirable and undesirable behaviors are learned through observation
    d. knowledge is acquired through organization and adaptation

17. Weisberg's (1963) study of infant babbling found that contingent social stimulation was the most effective in increasing the frequency of babbling; this implies that
    a. infants have an internal drive to babble
    b. infants cannot alter their behavior in response to reinforcement
    c. infants babble because of external stimuli babbling produces
    d. none of the above

18. Bandura's cognitive social-learning theory stresses the idea that
    a. behavior must be reinforced if learning is to take place
    b. drives must be satisfied if learning is to take place
    c. learning can take place through observation, without reinforcement
    d. learning tends toward cognitive equilibrium

19. Piaget's definition of intelligence as a basic life function is based on the idea of
    a. assimilation
    b. accommodation
    c. equilibrium
    d. none of the above

20. According to Piaget, the invariant order in which the cognitive stages occur from birth is
    a. sensorimotor, concrete operations, preoperational, formal operations
    b. sensorimotor, preoperational, concrete operations, formal operations
    c. preoperational, sensorimotor, concrete operations, formal operations
    d. preoperational, concrete operations, sensorimotor, formal operations

21. During the sensorimotor period, the child acquires
    a. a basic sense of self and others
    b. object permanence
    c. the first "mental" schemata
    d. all of the above

22. Egocentricity refers to Piaget's observation that preoperational children
    a. operate primarily according to the reality principle
    b. have strong habits which govern their own behavior
    c. think everyone has the same point of view as their own
    d. display a biological predisposition for survival of the fittest

23. During the stage of concrete operations, children tend to view rules as moral absolutes, which means that the children believe
    a. rules are arbitrary and can be altered to fit the situation
    (b.) rules cannot be altered or challenged, whatever the reason
    c. rules are not necessary where play is concerned
    d. rules are made to be broken

24. When an infant cries to get contact with an adult and to get satisfaction of basic
needs for food, etc., the ethological interpretation is that
    a. crying has been learned through conditioning and reinforcement
    (b.) crying is an adaptive behavior that has evolved through natural selection
    c. the child is in the oral stage and libido is invested around the mouth
    d. a crying schema is being accommodated to the demands of the environment

25. Sagi and Hoffman's (1976) finding that infants are "empathic" in responding to other
infants' crying indicates that
    a. crying occurs because it is reinforced
    b. empathy is not involved in altruism
    (c.) infants may be born with the capacity for empathy
    d. none of the above

VIGNETTES

Consider the story, then answer each question using material from the textbook.

I. Sandy was 18 years old and smoked two packs of cigarettes a day, every day. She had
been smoking since she was 15, having started at the same time some older friends of hers
started. When asked why she smoked, she said that it simply makes her feel good and
gives her something to do.

    1. What might Freud say about why Sandy smokes?

    2. What might Skinner say about Sandy's smoking?

    3. What would cognitive social-learning theorists such as Bandura emphasize?

II. Tommy was four years old and wanted to be "just like his daddy." He liked to dress
the same way as his father, and also insisted on dressing himself like his father did,
to the extent of tying his own shoelaces (or trying to) and such. Tommy also tried to
"fix" things like his father and mother did, though he often lost tools and occasionally
broke what he was trying to fix. Tommy's father and mother often talked about how proud
they were that Tommy wanted to be like his daddy.

    1. How would Freud explain Tommy's behavior?

    2. What might Erikson have to say on the basis of his psychosocial theory?

    3. What would the neo-Hullians such as Dollard and Miller probably say?

III. Rhonda and Samuel were fraternal twins, six months old. Their parents had often
observed that when either infant cried, the other one started soon thereafter. In all
cases, whichever parent was nearest to the children came quickly to comfort them, change
their diapers, feed them, or whatever was indicated, but the parents wondered if they
should be so responsive to the children every time crying started.

    1. What might Erikson tell the parents?

    2. What might Skinner say?

    3. How would an ethologist be likely to respond?

Try each of the projects, noting answers to the questions as you go.

I. Suppose, as a very simplistic account of Freudian psychoanalytic theory might, that the presence of phallic symbols in dreams indicates underlying sexual conflicts of one sort or another. A phallic symbol is generally any object shaped like a phallus, that is, a man's penis. Thus, the next time you have a dream you can remember in fairly good detail, count the number of phallic symbols that are present, and decide whether this indicates that you have unconscious conflicts about your sexuality.

    1. How would you know whether you have "a lot of" or "a few" phallic symbols?

    2. How would you interpret not having any phallic symbols in your dreams?

    3. How could you design a study to assess the relationship between phallic symbols in dreams and underlying sexual conflicts?

II. As the text notes, one reason for the popularity of Erikson's theory of psychosocial development is that it stresses conflicts *you* may remember, are currently experiencing, or can easily anticipate. In all likelihood, you are somewhere around the end of the stage of identity versus role confusion or the beginning of the stage of intimacy versus isolation. Consider the following:

    1. Do you have a basic sense of "Who am I"? What aspects of your family background, your college major, and your future goals are involved?

    2. How do you stand on intimate relationships versus feelings of isolation and loneliness? How do you satisfy implied "needs" for intimacy?

    3. With regard to questions 1 and 2, how would you define a "good" sense of self and "adequate" intimate relationships?

III. Here's a simple exercise you can perform the next time you find yourself in the company of a young child, say, in the age range from 1 to 3 years, to contrast the learning/conditioning view of development with Piaget's active-child/cognitive view of development. Simply observe some behavior that the child performs, and:

    1. Try to identify any external reinforcers the child is seeking.

    2. Try to describe the child's behavior in terms of assimilation, accommodation, and especially exploration for its own sake.

    3. Finally, make a decision about whether the environment shapes the child or the child shapes the environment.

ANSWERS

Self-Test I

1. c	6. b	11. a
2. c	7. c	12. a
3. d	8. c	13. b
4. c	9. b	14. d
5. d	10. c	15. a

1. Katcher (1955): A majority of children in the age range of 4 to 6 years made mistakes in trying to assemble dolls so that the genitals matched the other body parts, indicating confusion about genital anatomy at this age which in turn creates problems for Freud's theory of the phallic stage.

2. Weisberg (1963): Three-month-old infants received either social or nonsocial stimulation, in turn either contingent or noncontingent upon babbling behavior; babbling increased only in response to contingent social stimulation, indicating the effects of external social reinforcement on social behavior in the context of learning theory.

3. Sagi & Hoffman (1976): Infants less than 36 hours old were exposed either to another infant's cries, a computer simulation of infant crying, or no sound at all; infants who heard another infant's cries cried more themselves and were also more discomforted, supporting the ethological view that there is a biological basis for empathy.

Self-Test II

1. c	6. b	11. d	16. b	21. d
2. b	7. d	12. c	17. c	22. c
3. b	8. a	13. a	18. c	23. b
4. a	9. a	14. b	19. c	24. b
5. c	10. c	15. a	20. b	25. c

Vignettes

I. (1) Freud might note fixation in the oral stage, with a continuing excess need for oral gratification. (2) Skinner and other learning theorists might say that smoking in itself is a reinforcing event, with notes on how behaviors leading up to smoking are reinforced along the way; and, Skinner might look for external consequences of smoking that reinforce the behavior, such as escape from other situations, reinforcement from other smokers, etc. (3) Bandura's comments would be compatible with Skinner's, except for an emphasis on how smoking may have started through observational learning and imitation of friends, with or without reinforcement.

II. (1) Tommy's castration anxiety is causing him to resolve the Oedipus complex by identifying with his father. (2) Tommy has established reasonably good autonomy, and is in the stage of trying to resolve initiative versus guilt by acting grown up and seeking responsibilities. (3) Tommy has developed a strong acquired drive for social approval from his parents, and performs these behaviors because his parents provide secondary reinforcement through behaviors involved in being "proud."

III. (1) Continue to be as responsive to the children as possible, and be consistent, to establish a good sense of basic trust on the children's part. (2) Skinner's comments might be that the parents' attention reinforces the crying behavior, that the parents should decide whether they care about the crying as such, and if not, they should discontinue reinforcement for crying and reinforce some other behavior instead. (3) An ethological interpretation might be adaptive significance in satisfying needs and ensuring adult contact necessary to the forming of good emotional relationships, with notes on how the parents should continue to be responsive; comments on how one child's distress arouses empathy in the other might also be included.

Applications

I. (1) As it happens, almost any object that even remotely resembles a penis can be interpreted as a phallic symbol. This is one of the problems with this type of analysis, in that it is extremely subjective. Thus there are really not "norms" for presence of phallic symbols in dreams. (2) You could see this as absence of sexual conflicts, or as extremely deep repression of sexual conflicts. Take your pick. This indicates another problem in psychoanalysis, in that content of free associations, dreams, etc. can often be interpreted in directly opposite ways, again with much subjectivity. (3) You might objectively assess the presence of sexual conflicts and their degree, say, by questionnaire or by observation of behavior, and then devise a tight definition of phallic symbols to enable them to be counted and correlated against sexual conflict. Note that you would still not know what causes what.

II. (1) Your sense of self likely includes your sex and other personal characteristics such as size, motor abilities, attractiveness, etc. plus family characterisitics such as socioeconomic status, parents' occupations, racial or ethnic background, religion, and so on. You may also think of yourself largely in terms of being a "major" in some subject and a person headed for professional goals, marriage and family, life in a certain part of the country, etc. (2) People are generally lonely at least part of the time, and different people may have very different definitions of "intimacy"; thus how you are doing along these lines can probably only be answered in terms of your own personal satisfaction, which is one problem with Erikson's theory. Otherwise, people satisfy needs for intimacy in many different ways, through friends, lovers, school and work associates, and perhaps through brief interactions with acquaintances. Note that intimacy here may mean many things other than sexual interaction. (3) A definition here would consider your own needs and sense of personal satisfaction in some way that it could be compared to others, along dimensions such as happiness, self-fulfillment, and so on. This would necessarily be compared using a test of such factors, and a definition without such a comparison would be hard to defend.

III. (1) In this case, reinforcers are generally identifiable as any object or event the child moves toward, asks for, or otherwise displays an interest in; the test of a reinforcer here is whether the child will perform some other behavior in order to gain access to the supposed reinforcer. (2) In contrast, whatever the behavior you observe, you can think instead in terms of curiosity, exploration, and the child's basic desire to understand. Behaviors of young children often seem repetitive, as if practice and improvement are the goals, and with no identifiable external reinforcers present. Clues to assimilation are when the child tires of an object or action quickly, or when the child uses an object in some way more appropriate to some other object. Clues to accommodation are when the child looks "surprised" in response to some object or event, indicating that the child didn't expect what happened. (3) If a boy offers his mother a bit of his cookie and she praises him, you might interpret the praise as a reinforcer that has made the child more generous (given past instances of such reinforcement). Thus the environment shapes the child. However, it is also possible that the child has done nice things for others, actions that elicit praise from his companions. If so, he would be shaping the character of his environment, which would then influence his behavior. Over the long run, both of these processes will probably be operating in reciprocal fashion, so that the child behaves, influences the behavior of his companions, and so on, and the environment turns around through his companions' behavior and influences his own feelings, thoughts, and actions.

CHAPTER THREE

HEREDITARY INFLUENCES ON HUMAN DEVELOPMENT

OVERVIEW AND KEY TERMS

Read carefully. Recall examples and discussion as you go, and define each key term.

HEREDITY IN HISTORICAL PERSPECTIVE

In Aristotle's version of heredity, children inherited characteristics from fathers only. This view continued through Swammerdam's 17th century preformationist theory, in which the sperm cell contained a homunculus simply nourished by the ovum. Then the ovists argued that the ovum contained the homunculus fertilized by the sperm. In the 18th century, Wolff proposed that sperm and ovum unite to form a single cell which produces the embryo through epigenesis.

In the 19th century, Mendel inferred that heredity operates through characters that are transmitted across generations. Later called genes, these characters exist in pairs, and one member of each pair comes from each parent. Where members of the pair differ, one dominates the other. And in 1933, Morgan won the Nobel prize for his discovery of chromosomes in the nuclei of cells. Each chromosome contains thousands of genes. In the human body, each cell contains 46 chromosomes, arranged in 23 pairs.

PRINCIPLES OF HEREDITARY TRANSMISSION

Women begin periodic ovulation soon after puberty. Conception occurs when an ovum is fertilized by a sperm cell, thus forming a one-celled zygote. Ovum and sperm each contribute 23 chromosomes to the zygote.

The zygote grows through mitosis, which eventually produces the billions of cells a child consists of at birth. Each division produces new cells that exactly copy the genetic information present at conception.

Sperm and ova are special cells called gametes, produced through meiosis, with 23 unpaired chromosomes. During meiosis, millions of combinations are possible in the resultant 23 chromosomes present in the gamete. Thus each sperm and ovum is unique, and children of the same parents don't necessarily look alike (excepting monozygotic twins, as discussed in Box 3-1). The crossing over phenomenon adds further variability during meiosis: A pair of chromosomes may divide different from the way it was originally formed.

Through karyotypes it has been learned that the child's gender is determined by one particular pair of chromosomes. If this pair contains two X chromosomes, the child is female; if the pair contains one X and one Y chromosome, the child is male. Sperm cells containing a Y chromosome are more likely to fertilize the ovum, yielding a 60-40 male-to-female conception ratio. But males are more likely to be miscarried, which more or less equalizes the proportions of males and females born.

Genotype determines phenotype through the principle of genetic dominance. Many

33

traits are expressed through the interaction of alleles. Dominant alleles mask the effects of recessive alleles, as in the example of a brown-eyed allele dominating a blue-eyed allele and producing a person with brown eyes. Thus for many traits a person may be homozygous, having alleles that are the same in effect, or heterozygous, having differing alleles one of which dominates the other. A recessive trait can only appear as the phenotype if the person is homozygous for that trait. Examples of human dominant and recessive traits are given in Box 3-2.

Some alleles display incomplete dominance. An example is sickle cell anemia, in which the recessive sickle-cell allele is not completely masked. Some alleles display codominance, as in blood type AB, where alleles for type A and type B are both present. Sex-linked characteristics usually involve recessive alleles on the X chromosome. Red-green color blindness occurs more often in males because the male's Y chromosome cannot counteract the effects of an otherwise recessive X chromosome allele. Hereditary transmission also involves modifier genes, as in the case of pattern baldness. And the more complex human attributes such as intelligence and temperament are polygenic traits, which are determined by many genes as well as by environmental factors the person experiences.

CHROMOSOMAL AND GENETIC ABNORMALITIES

About one in seven newborns has a congenital defect. Many defects involve the sex chromosomes: In Turner's syndrome, the female is XO instead of XX, has physical abnormalities, and is sterile. In the poly-X syndrome, the female is XXX or more, is usually below average in intelligence, and is developmentally delayed. In Klinefelter's syndrome, the male has extra X chromosomes (e.g., XXY or XXXY), and develops some female characteristics at puberty. And in the supermale syndrome, the male is XYY, is taller on average, and is often below average in intelligence. Other defects involve the autosomes: In Down's syndrome (trisomy-21), an extra chromosome appears on the 21st pair, producing defects such as sloping forehead, short trunk and limbs, an "Oriental" eyefold, and mental retardation. In general, chromosomal abnormalities appear to be related to uneven segregation of chromosomes during meiosis. Also, the aging ova hypothesis attempts to explain why older mothers produce more children with congenital defects. But fathers' abnormal sperm cells contribute as well.

Many congenital defects, including cystic fibrosis and Tay-Sachs disease, occur due to the expression of recessive genes. Other defects result from genetic mutation. Some mutations may be adaptive, as in sickle cell anemia, which makes the person more resistant to malaria.

Genetic counseling focuses on detection and prevention of hereditary abnormalities. Prior to conception, methods include blood testing and karyotyping of parents, plus assessment of family history for incidence of disorders. Box 3-3 discusses the genetic basis for laws against marriage between close family members. Prenatal detection of some hereditary disorders is possible through amniocentesis, which involves karyotyping of fetal cells. A chorionic villus biopsy is an alternative method for extracting fetal cells. Ultrasound involves scanning of the outline of the fetus to detect gross physical abnormalities. Postnatal treatment of disorders such as phenylketonuria (PKU), Turner's syndrome, Klinefelter's syndrome, sickle cell anemia, cystic fibrosis, and diabetes is possible.

HEREDITARY INFLUENCES ON ABILITY, PERSONALITY, AND BEHAVIOR

Behavior genetics focuses on how heredity (along with environment) is involved in development. Within-species comparisons assess sucking, crying, smiling, and other behaviors displayed by all human infants. Selective breeding experiments with animals assess hereditary influences, as in the example of breeding maze-bright versus maze-dull rats. Family studies assess heritability as a function of degree of kinship (see also Box 3-1), noting that identical twins should be the most similar to each other, normal siblings the next most similar, and so on. Family studies also assess similarities between children and their natural or adoptive parents. Box 3-4 summarizes the use of correlation in assessing heritability and deriving heritability quotients.

It appears that heredity contributes to IQ, in that higher degrees of kinship involve higher correlations on intelligence test scores. But, especially with identical twins, children who are more similar may also experience more similar environments, and heritability of IQ may be overestimated. There is also an environmental component in IQ, since biologically unrelated children who live together may also show intellectual resemblance. While adopted children correlate more highly with natural parents than with adoptive parents, it has also been found that adopted children show significant correlations in IQ with other, unrelated, children in the home.

Specific aspects of personality such as temperament are also heritable. Identical twins show higher correlations in social responsiveness and other aspects of personality. At birth, Caucasian babies have been found to be more irritable than Chinese-American babies, also suggesting heritability. Early temperament patterns such as the "easy" versus the "difficult" versus the "slow to warm up" child may persist, although they can be modified by environment.

Personality traits such as introversion-extraversion display moderate heritability, as does empathic concern. But personality displays less heritability than IQ at each level of kinship. And Box 3-5 discusses how personality development might depend more on "nonshared" environmental aspects of the home than on those aspects of family life that children do share.

Studies of concordance rates for types of mental illness indicate heritability as well. Schizophrenia shows higher heritability as a function of greater degree of kinship as do disorders such as alcoholism, hyperactivity, manic-depressive psychosis, and various neurotic disorders. But these are inherited only as predispositions, and thus depend strongly on environmental factors if they are to appear in the individual. Box 3-6 describes the role of environmental triggers in interaction with genetic predispositions for mental illness.

ANOTHER LOOK AT THE NATURE-NURTURE CONTROVERSY

In resolving how heredity and environment interact to determine development, Stern's rubber-band hypothesis makes an analogy of genetic endowment being stretched to differing lengths by environmental forces. Another perspective is Gottesman's range of reaction principle, in which genotype sets upper and lower limits on the extent to which environment can affect phenotype. Individuals may also have relatively wide or narrow ranges of possible expression of the trait. Finally, traits may vary widely in canalization, some traits being affect by environment more than others. Observations of the effects of environment lead to ideas about creating optimal environments, but the same environment may have differing effects on different children. One possible reason is that the environments children prefer and seek out may depend in the first place on their genetic predispositions.

SELF-REVIEW

Fill in the blanks for each item. Check the answers for each item as you go.

HEREDITY IN HISTORICAL PERSPECTIVE

1. Aristotle's view of heredity was that children inherit traits, talents, and peculiarities from their *fathers*, and that   fathers
daughters or defective sons alike are *accidents* of nature.   accidents

35

The Doctrine of Preformationism

2. Swammerdam's 17th century preformationist theory was that each sperm cell contains an embryo called a _homunculus_; the ovists argued instead that the preformed embryo is in the mother's _ovum_.

homunculus

ovum

3. In 1759, Wolff observed the epigenesis of the _embryo_ from a single cell formed by the union of the father's _sperm_ and the mother's _ovum_.

embryo
sperm
ovum

Modern Genetic Theories

4. In 1865, after years of research on garden peas, Mendel reported that attributes are produced by characters we now call _genes_; these exist in _pairs_ to which each parent contributes one character, and one of the two genes is _dominant_ with regard to the attribute.

genes, pairs
dominant

5. Mendel also concluded that parents each produce _gametes_ which divide by the Law of _Segregation_ to set the stage for reproduction.

gametes
Segregation

6. Morgan discovered by 1933 that genes are grouped like beads on a string into _chromosomes_; later researchers discovered that normal humans have _23_ pairs of chromosomes, for a total of _46_.

chromosomes
23
46

PRINCIPLES OF HEREDITARY TRANSMISSION

Conception

7. When a ripened _ovum_ is penetrated by a _sperm_ cell, _conception_ occurs and the 23 chromosomes of each gamete unite to form the one-celled _zygote_ which may contain as many as 500,000 pairs of _genes_.

ovum, sperm
conception
zygote
genes

Growth of the Zygote and Production of Body Cells

8. The zygote divides repeatedly through the process called _mitosis_, duplicating the original chromosomes each time.

mitosis

Germ Cells and Hereditary Transmission

9. Male and female gametes contain only one member of each pair of chromosomes and are produced through the process called _meiosis_.

meiosis

10. During meiosis, segregation of chromosomes into gametes occures mainly by chance, yielding _millions_ of different possible gametes each of which is unique; further variability is added through the _crossing-over_ phenomenon, in that chromosomes often break and rearrange themselves.

millions

crossing-over

11. Identical twins are _monozygotic_ and genetically the same, with a kinship quotient of _1.00_; fraternal twins are _dizygotic_, with a kinship quotient of _.50_.

monozygotic
1.00
dizygotic, .50

12. The 23rd pair of chromosomes is _XY_ for normal males and _XX_ for normal females.

XY
XX

13. Two popular hypotheses as to why about 150 males are conceived for every 100 females are (1) that sperm bearing a Y chromosome can _swim_ faster and (2) that Y-bearing sperm are more resistant to _biochemical_ conditions in the uterus.

swim
biochemical

Patterns of Genetic Expression

14. What a person inherits genetically is called *genotype*,
whereas how a person actually looks, thinks, feels, or behaves
is called *phenotype*.

    genotype

    phenotype

15. Many characteristics are determined by a single pair of
genes; in turn, phenotype is determined by whether the alleles are either *dominant* or *recessive*.

    alleles or genes
    dominant, recessive

16. The allele for dark hair is dominant over the allele for
blond hair; thus, a person homozygous for dark hair will have
dark hair, a person heterozygous for dark hair and blond hair
will have *dark* hair, and a person homozygous for blond hair
will have *blond* hair.

    dark
    dark
    blond

17. Sickle cell anemia provides an example of *incomplete*
dominance; a person who is heterozygous for these alleles will
have some normal *red* blood cells and some sickled ones.

    incomplete

    red

18. Human blood types A and B are determined by alleles that are
codominant when paired, which yields blood type *AB*.

    codominant, AB

19. Red-green color blindness is an example of *sex*-linked inheritance, because this recessive allele is carried on the X
chromosome and is expressed much more often in the *male* sex
because there is no corresponding allele on the Y chromosome to
counteract it.

    sex-
    X
    male

20. Pattern baldness occurs more often in males because the
genes that cause androgen production also *modify* the recessive pattern-baldness gene and make it become *dominant*.

    modify
    dominant

CHROMOSOMAL AND GENETIC ABNORMALITIES

21. Approximately one out of every seven infants born has a
congenital problem or defect of some kind.

    congenital

Chromosomal Abnormalities

22. Turner's syndrome females are small, often with stubby fin-
gers and toes and a broad chest, due to having only one X
chromosome; "super" females are called *poly*-X and usually lag
both in physical and in *intellectual* development.

    X
    poly-
    intellectual

23. Klinefelter's syndrome males have extra X chromosomes and
may exhibit some female physical characteristics after entrance
into *puberty*; "super" males are genetically XYY and are
larger than normal males, but often are less *intelligent*
than normal males.

    X

    puberty, XYY
    intelligent

24. Down's syndrome, Klinefelter's syndrome, and the poly-X syndrome are more likely when the mother is *older*; one explanation is the aging *ova* hypothesis.

    older
    ova

Genetic Abnormalities

26. Cystic fibrosis, muscular dystrophy, PKU, and Tay-Sachs are
disorders carried by *recessive* genes; hemophilia may also
involve a recessive gene, or may appear through *mutation*.

    recessive
    mutation

27. Prenatal genetic counseling may involve karyotyping of fetal
cells obtained through *amniocentesis* or through the newer
technique called chorionic villus *biopsy*; in addition, the
outline of the fetus can be scanned by *ultrasound* to detect

    amniocentesis
    biopsy
    ultrasound

gross physical abnormalities.

28. Laws prohibiting marriage between close family members have
a genetic basis, in that the risk of inherited _defects_   defects
through the pairing of _recessive_ genes for defects is   recessive
greatly increased with inbreeding.

29. Phenylketonuria is a metabolic disorder involving a missing
enzyme; it can be treated by putting the child on a special   enzyme
diet.   diet

HEREDITARY INFLUENCES ON ABILITY, PERSONALITY, AND BEHAVIOR

30. Though behavior geneticists focus on _hereditary_ compon-   hereditary
ents of behavior, they also recognize the role of environment.

Methods of Assessing Hereditary Influences

31. Heritability can be studied through selective _breeding_   breeding
experiments with animals, as with Tryon's classic research on
maze-_bright_ versus maze-_dull_ rats; with humans, heritabili-   -bright, -dull
ty of traits and attributes is estimated by family _studies_   studies
that compare individuals of different levels of _kinship_.   kinship

32. Subtracting the correlation of a trait for fraternal twins
from the correlation of a trait for identical twins and then
multiplying by 2 yields the _heritability_ quotient.   heritability

Hereditary Contributions to Intelligence

33. Correlations between IQ test scores increase as the degree
of _kinship_ increases; this implies that the abilities meas-   kinship
ured by intelligence tests are _heritable_ to some extent.   heritable

34. If identical twins are treated more alike than are fraternal
twins, heritability estimates would be artificially _high_; but   high
in general, family studies indicate that intelligence probably
is _heritable_ to some extent, and that the influences of the   heritable
environment are also important.

35. Studies of Black children adopted by White families have
found that the Black children show _correlations_ of about   correlations
.30 with other children in the family, and also that the Black
children score _higher_ on IQ tests than comparable Black   higher
children who remain in disadvantaged environments.

Hereditary Contributions to Temperament and Personality

36. Selective breeding experiments with animals indicate that
basic _temperament_ characteristics such as activity level   temperament
and sociability are to some extent _heritable_.   heritable

37. Studies of human children generally indicate that tempera-
ment _traits_ such as activity level, social responsiveness,   traits or attributes
demands for attention, and irritability are more similar for
identical twins than for _fraternal_ twins, thus indicating   fraternal
heritability.

38. Although all inherited traits are subject to environmental
influences, traits involved in _temperament_ appear to be   temperament
more modifiable than intellectual traits.

39. People who are usually quiet and who avoid social contact
are called _introverts_, and people who are highly sociable   introverts
are called _extraverts_; generally, this trait is viewed as   extraverts
heritable.

40. People who are compassionate and interested in the welfare of others are said to be high in _empathic_ concern; this and many other traits are viewed as heritable.

empathic

Hereditary Contributions to Mental Illness

41. Mental illnesses such as schizophrenia often show higher _Concordance_ rates as a function of kinship, indicating a degree of heritability, although environmental _triggers_ are also necessary if the disorder is to appear in the individual.

concordance

triggers

ANOTHER LOOK AT THE NATURE-NURTURE CONTROVERSY

The Rubber-Band Hypothesis

42. The rubber-band hypothesis proposes that environmental experiences serve to _stretch_ genetic endowment to differing lengths for different persons, sometimes even reversing the effects of genetic _potential_.

stretch

potential

43. The range of reaction principle is that genetic endowment sets _limits_ on phenotypical development; it also implies that the range of possible phenotypes for a person with a high endowment is _wider_ than the range for a person with a lower endowment.

limits

broader or wider

Canalization

44. Attributes that are not easily modified by the environment are said to be highly _canalized_.

canalized

Can We Create Optimal Environments?

45. Optimal environments for development are hard to design because their effects may differ according to the person's genetic endowment and _predispositions_.

predispositions

SELF-TEST I

Consider each alternative carefully. Then choose the best one.

1. Preformationist theories were based on the idea that
    a. the sperm cell contains a homunculus
    b. the ovum contains a homunculus
    (c.) both of the above
    d. none of the above

2. Which of the following ideas is <u>not</u> attributable to Mendel?
    a. genes exist in pairs
    b. parents contribute genes equally to offspring
    c. within pairs of genes, one dominates the other
    (d.) genes are arranged in chromosomes

3. The uniqueness of the individual child is ensured because gametes may contain many different combinations of chromosomes, and also because particular genes are
    a. unpredictable in their effects on inheritance
    (b.) often recombined during the crossing-over phenomenon
    c. unrelated to heritability
    d. sometimes dominant and sometimes recessive

4. Inherited alleles constitute _____, and genetic dominance determines
_____.
   a. genotype, genotype
   b. genotype, phenotype
   c. phenotype, genotype
   d. phenotype, phenotype

5. The normal-vision allele dominates the allele for nearsightedness; therefore, if
both parents have normal vision but are heterozygous, the chances of producing a near-
sighted child are
   a. 3 out of 4
   b. 2 out of 4
   c. 1 out of 4
   d. 0

6. The allele for curly hair dominates the allele for straight hair; thus, if two curly-
haired parents produce a straight-haired child,
   a. one parent is homozygous, the other is heterozygous
   b. both parents are homozygous
   c. both parents are heterozygous
   d. parental genetic make-up cannot be determined in this case

7. Blacks who are heterozygous for sickle cell anemia have both normal and sickled red
blood cells; this illustrates the principle of
   a. genetic dominance
   b. genetic codominance
   c. incomplete dominance
   d. sex-linking inheritance

8. Females who display only a single X chromosome on the 23rd pair (i.e., XO) are examples of
   a. Turner's syndrome
   b. Down's syndrome
   c. Klinefelter's syndrome
   d. the XYY syndrome

9. Which of the following does not increase in likelihood as maternal age increases?
   a. Down's syndrome
   b. Klinefelter's syndrome
   c. diabetes
   d. the poly-X syndrome

10. Which of the following is not a recessive hereditary trait?
   a. cystic fiborsis
   b. phenylketonuria
   c. hemophilia
   d. Huntington's chorea

11. Heritability of intelligence primarily involves
   a. sex-linked genetic endowment
   b. polygenetic determination
   c. amniocentesis
   d. none of the above

12. The most basic cause of chromosomal abnormalities is probably
   a. uneven segregation of chromosomes during meiosis
   b. aging ova and sperm cells
   c. exposure to environmental hazards
   d. faulty homunculi

13. Generally, as the kinship quotient increases,
    a. correlations in IQ increase
    b. correlations in temperament characteristics increase
    c. concordance rates for mental disorders increase
    (d.) all of the above

14. Heritability of temperament or personality characteristics is usually found to be
    a. higher than heritability for IQ
    b. the same heritability for IQ
    (c.) lower than heritability for IQ
    d. too small to be of significance

15. The idea that heredity sets upper and lower limits on developmental potentials is called
    a. the rubber-band hypothesis
    (b.) the range of reaction principle
    c. canalization
    d. optimization

RESEARCH SUMMARY AND REVIEW

Using the textbook, review the research efforts indicated and write a summary of the important findings. Note the general purpose or context of the research.

1. Tryon (1940), page 99: _____

_____

_____

_____

_____

2. Scarr & Carter-Saltzman (1979), page 103: _____

_____

_____

_____

_____

3. Scarr & Weinberg (1977, 1983), page 103: _____

_____

_____

_____

_____

4. Freedman (1965, 1974), page 104: _____

_____

_____

_____

_____

5. Matthews, Batson, Horn, & Rosenman (1981), page 107: _____

_____

_____

_____

_____

SELF-TEST II

Consider each alternative carefully. Then choose the best one.

1. The idea that each of the father's sperm cells contains a tiny homunculus that is simply nourished by the ovum is attributable to
   a. Aristotle
   b. Swammerdam's preformationism
   c. the ovists' preformationism
   d. Wolff's observations of epigenesis

2. The aspect of Mendel's work that explains why a child might resemble one parent more that the other is that
   a. genes are transmitted unchanged from generation to generation
   b. attributes are determined by a pair of genes, one inherited from each parent
   c. within genetic pairs, only the dominant gene will be expressed
   d. gametes contain only one-half of the normal genetic information

3. The point in time at which the sperm cell penetrates the ovum is called
   a. ovulation
   b. conception
   c. ripening
   d. all of the above

4. The zygote divides and grows through
   a. mitosis
   b. meiosis
   c. both of the above
   d. none of the above

5. The basic process through which gametes such as sperm cells and ova are produced is
   a. mitosis
   b. meiosis
   c. crossing over
   d. mutation

6. Normal human cells contain
   a. 45 chromosomes
   b. 46 chromosomes
   c. 47 chromosomes
   d. 500,000 chromosomes

7. Dizygotic twins have a kinship quotient of
   a. 1.00
   b. .50
   c. .25
   d. 0

8. Gender is determined by
   a. X and Y chromosomes in the 23rd pair
   b. dominant and recessive alleles
   c. karyotypes
   d. environmental influences

9. The combination of an elongated X chromosome and a short, stubby Y chromosome yields
   a. a male
   b. a female
   c. either a male or a female, depending upon dominance
   d. a child with Klinefelter's syndrome

10. The principle of genetic codominance is illustrated by the case that a child who inherits an allele for blood type A and an allele for blood type B will have
   a. type A blood
   b. type B blood
   c. type AB blood
   d. type O blood

11. A sex-linked trait such as red-green color blindness occurs more often in males since
   a. the X allele cannot counteract the dominant Y allele
   b. the X allele cannot counteract the recessive Y allele
   c. the Y allele cannot counteract the dominant X allele
   d. the Y allele cannot counteract the recessive X allele

12. A male who develops some female secondary sex characteristics at puberty may be an example of
   a. Turner's syndrome
   b. the poly-X syndrome
   c. Klinefelter's syndrome
   d. the XYY syndrome

13. Which of the following is not a recessive hereditary defect?
   a. sickle cell anemia
   b. muscular dystrophy
   c. hemophilia
   d. Down's syndrome

14. Prenatal chromosomal abnormalities can be detected through
   a. amniocentesis
   b. ultrasound
   c. both of the above
   d. none of the above

15. Which of the following hereditary diseases cannot as yet be treated?
   a. sickle cell anemia
   b. Tay-Sachs disease
   c. phenylketonuria
   d. diabetes

16. The classic selective-breeding experiment of Tryon (1940) in creating maze-bright and maze-dull rats indicated that
   a. maze-learning ability in rats is highly heritable
   b. maze-learning ability in rats is primarily a function of environment
   c. maze-learning ability in rats is transmitted primarily by the mothers
   d. none of the above

17. Similarity between children on intelligence in spite of a kinship quotient of .00
   a. would support heritability interpretations if the children lived in the same home
   b. would support environmental interpretations if the children lived in the same home
   c. would support heritability and environmental effects in interaction
   d. none of the above

43

18. In the Scarr and Carter-Saltzman (1979) study of identical and fraternal twins, it was found that mistaken beliefs by the parents about their twins did not affect the degree of similarity between the twins on intellectual measures; this indicated that
    a. parents treat identical twins more similarly
    b. parents treat fraternal twins more similarly
    c. family studies overestimate heritability of intelligence
    d. family studies provide a reasonable estimate of the heritability of intelligence

19. Scarr and Weinberg (1977, 1983), in their studies of Black children adopted into middle-class White homes, found that
    a. the Black children showed a significant intellectual resemblance to other children living in the home
    b. pairs of unrelated Black children living in the same home showed significant intellectual resemblance to each other
    c. the Black children scored higher in intelligence tests than comparable Black children in less advantaged environments
    d. all of the above

20. In Freedman's (1965, 1974) research on social responsiveness in infants, higher similarity was found for identical twins; since neither the researchers nor the parents knew until after the study which twins were identical versus fraternal,
    a. the results were probably due to rating bias by the investigators
    b. the results were probably due to differential treatment by the parents
    c. the results were probably attributable to environment
    d. the results were probably attributable to heredity

21. Thomas and Chess' research on children classified as "easy," "difficult," or "slow to warm up" during infancy shows that
    a. genetically based temperament is long-standing and unmodifiable
    b. temperament is acquired during early child-rearing experiences
    c. temperament may be genetically based and modified by child-rearing experiences
    d. none of the above

22. In the Matthews, et al. (1981) study of middle-aged identical and fraternal twins, the heritability of empathic concern was supported by the finding that
    a. identical twins were more similar than fraternal twins
    b. fraternal twins were more similar than identical twins
    c. fraternal and identical twins all showed high similarity
    d. neither identical nor fraternal twins showed significant similarity

23. If the concordance rate for a particular type of mental illness were found to be higher for identical than for fraternal twins, the likely conclusion would be that
    a. the disorder is determined entirely by heredity
    b. the disorder is influenced by heredity
    c. the disorder is determined entirely by environment
    d. the disorder is influenced neither by heredity nor by environment

24. The rubber-band hypothesis states that
    a. genetic endowment can be stretched to different lengths by one's environment
    b. environmental influences are stretched to different lengths by heredity
    c. canalized attributes cannot be influenced by environmental forces
    d. none of the above

25. Due to differing genetic predispositions from child to child, optimal environments to enhance child development are
    a. already in effect in many parts of the nation for all aspects of development
    b. possible for intellectual but not personality development
    c. possible for personality but not intellectual development
    d. probably not possible, regardless of the aspect of development

Consider the story, then answer each question using material from the textbook.

I. Charles and Leona had two normal children, a boy and a girl, in the early years of their marriage when both parents were in their mid-twenties. In the years that followed, they practiced routine methods of birth control, planning to have no further children. Then, when Leona was 41 and Charles 42, Leona unexpectedly became pregnant again. Both parents were in good health, and there was no history of defective children in either of their family backgrounds. Yet, they wondered about their child-to-be.

  1. What might a genetic counselor tell them about their chances of having a Down's syndrome child?

  2. What methods might be employed to determine if the fetus is normal?

  3. What other types of defects might these tests detect?

II. Wilma and William were twins, but their parents noted consistent differences in temperament of the two children almost from the day the children were born. Wilma was not especially fond of strangers she encountered, and she cried often and expected to be fed on time or else. In contrast, William rarely cried, even when he wasn't fed on time, and he simply didn't pay much attention to new people one way or the other.

  1. Into what temperament categories would each child fit, in accord with research by Thomas and Chess?

  2. Would you expect the parents to treat Wilma and William differently as a result of differences in temperament? Why or why not?

  3. Are Wilma and William monozygotic twins? Why or why not?

III. Suzanne was 16 and her younger sister Ellen was 13. The two girls were as different as night and day. Suzanne was impulsive, often short-tempered, and generally hard to get along with from her parents' point of view, although she was very popular with other girls her age and had a number of close friends. Ellen was typically quiet, reflective, and much more interested in schoolwork and books, and she tended to stay to herself much of the time, except that she did enjoy spending time with her parents.

  1. How do the girls rate on the introversion/extraversion scale?

  2. In genetic terms, how would you explain to their parents that the girls could be so different in temperament?

  3. From an environmental perspective, what "nonshared" characteristics might be involved?

APPLICATIONS

Try each of the projects, noting answers to the questions as you go.

I. Sickle cell anemia is produced by a recessive gene. Suppose that both mother and father are found to carry this recessive gene, as a result of blood tests. Consider or compute the following:

  1. Are the parents normal, in terms of red blood cells?

  2. What are their chances of producing (a) a completely normal child, (b) a child with one recessive gene for sickle cell anemia, and (c) a child with sickle cell anemia?

3. During the prenatal period, could amniocentesis or a chorionic villus biopsy determine the child's status in this respect?

II. Assume that both parents are Jewish, in which case the probability of carrying the recessive for Tay-Sachs disease is about 1/30. Compute the following:

1. Determine the probability that their child will have Tay-Sachs disease if both parents carry the recessive allele.

2. Determine the probability that their child will have Tay-Sachs disease if the parents are first cousins, given that one parent carries this recessive allele and the other parent is unknown as to carrying the recessive allele.

3. Determine the probability that their child will have Tay-Sachs disease if the parents are unrelated and it is unknown whether either parent carries the recessive allele.

III. Given that the average correlation for IQ test scores between identical twins reared together is .87, versus .53 for fraternal twins reared together (Table 3-4), consider or compute the following:

1. What would be the heritability quotient for IQ test scores, as per Box 3-4?

2. For the identical twins, what would be the role of nonshared factors, as per Box 3-5?

3. Does the high average correlation for IQ between identical twins indicate that heredity is almost entirely responsible for the abilities they display? Why or why not?

ANSWERS

Self-Test I

1. c	6. c	11. b
2. d	7. c	12. a
3. b	8. a	13. d
4. b	9. c	14. c
5. c	10. d	15. b

Research Summary and Review

1. Tryon (1940): Maze-bright rats and maze-dull rats were selectively bred, and by the 18th generation the worst maze-bright performer was better at running mazes than the best maze-dull performer, indicating the role of heredity in cognitive abilities.

2. Scarr & Carter-Saltzman (1979): Identical versus fraternal twins were compared as to whether they believed they were identical versus fraternal; findings were that the belief did not affect the degree of intellectual similarity, lending support to heredity interpretations of intelligence.

3. Scarr & Weinberg (1977, 1983): Black children adopted into White families showed significant intellectual resemblance to the other children in the families; plus, where unrelated pairs of adopted children were placed in the same home, the adoptees showed significant resemblance to each other. Both findings suggest that environmental factors are important in the determination of intelligence.

4. Freedman (1965, 1974): Although neither the investigators nor the parents knew which

pairs of twins were monozygotic or dizygotic, monozygotic twins showed greater resemblance in social responsiveness during the first year of life, supporting heredity interpretations with regard to temperament and personality.

5. Matthews, et al. (1981): Middle-aged identical twins showed a significantly greater resemblance in empathic concern as compared to middle-aged fraternal twins, supporting heredity interpretations with regard to temperament and personality.

Self-Test II

1. b	6. b	11. d	16. a	21. c
2. c	7. b	12. c	17. b	22. a
3. b	8. a	13. d	18. d	23. b
4. a	9. a	14. a	19. d	24. a
5. b	10. c	15. b	20. d	25. d

Vignettes

I. (1) Statistically, the risk of a Down's syndrome child is 1 out of 65 for a mother in this age range, as compared to only 1 out of 1000 when the earlier children were born. (2) Amniocentesis or a chorionic villus biopsy would allow karyotyping, which could reveal the extra chromosome on the 21st pair if the child had inherited Down's syndrome. (3) Klinefelter's syndrome, poly-X syndrome, and the other chromosomal abnormalities could be detected.

II. (1) Wilma would be a "difficult" child, and William would be a "slow to warm up" child. (2) The parents would probably treat the children differently. For example, a deviation from the usual feeding time would produce much more protest from Wilma, which in turn might make the parents more careful about maintaining routines with Wilma. Similar effects might occur with diaper changes and later naptime routines. Throughout, the parents might form quite different expectations about the behavior and personality of each child, in turn leading to different child-rearing practices and corresponding effects on the children via "environment." (3) The twins are dizygotic, not necessarily because of the differences in temperament, but because monozygotic twins are identical in all respects including sex (the 23rd pair of chromosomes).

III. (1) Suzanne is on the extravert end of the continuum, and Ellen is more of an introvert. (2) The girls have only 50% of their genes in common (i.e., a kinship quotient of .50), and the particular genetic combinations present in each girl are also different. In sum, the parents are capable of producing 64 trillion different children. Also note that temperament and personality are polygenic, which means that different combinations of the same genes could still have different results. (3) The first-born child is typically reared somewhat differently and may also dominate the younger sibling. Such differences yield markedly different environments within the same home. The girls would also be in different grades at school, and perhaps different schools as well (see also Box 3-5).

Applications

I. (1) Incomplete dominance here would produce some sickled cells in the blood of each parent. (2) Given the incomplete dominance of the sickle cell allele, a completely normal child would have to inherit the normal allele from both parents. Thus, if S represents the normal allele and s represents the sickle cell allele, the four possible combinations are SS, sS, Ss, and ss. Only the SS would be completely normal, and the probability is 1 out of 4. Chances are 2 out of 4 that the child will inherit a single sickle cell allele and thus be a carrier, and 1 out of 4 that the child will have complete sickle cell anemia. (3) Obtaining a sample which includes fetal red blood cells could detect this condition.

II. (1) Given *T* as normal and *t* as Tay-Sachs, combinations are *TT*, *Tt*, *tT*, and *tt*. Thus 1 child out of 4 would predictably have Tay-Sachs disease (and 2 out of 4 would be carriers of the recessive). (2) If one cousin carries the recessive, the probability is 1 out of 8 that the other does also. In turn, if both carry the recessive, chances are 1 out of 4 of producing a child with Tay-Sachs. Thus, the combined probability of these two events is 1/8 x 1/4 = 1/32 (see Box 3-3). (3) With no knowledge about the presence of a recessive in either parent, the probability for each parent is 1 out of 30, and if both parents do carry the recessive, the probability of a Tay-Sachs child is 1 out of 4. Combining these probabilities yields 1/30 x 1/30 x 1/4 = 1/3600.

III. (1) The estimated heritability quotient *H* = (*r* identical twins - *r* fraternal twins) x 2; thus *H* = (.87 -.53) x 2 = .68, as described in Box 3-4. (2) Nonshared environmental effects = 1 - *r* identical twins; thus nonshared effects = 1 - .87 - .13, as described in Box 3-5. (3) For one thing, a correlation does not indicate whether the overall abilities are "high" or "low"; it simply indicates that the identical twins turn out to be similar on the abilities measured. But this similarity could occur anywhere within the range of reaction principle. In other words, environment is still a major factor. Although identical twins may not be treated identically, they still live in the same home environment and thus share at least some of the characteristics of that environment that relate to intellectual abilities. Such characteristics include access (or lack of access) to stimulating materials, language usage of parents, problem-solving abilities and concepts modeled by parents, and so on.

CHAPTER FOUR

PRENATAL DEVELOPMENT AND BIRTH

OVERVIEW AND KEY TERMS

Read carefully. Recall examples and discussion as you go, and define each key term.

Prenatal development occurs within the mother's uterus, which is an environment in the sense that it has impact on the unborn child. In particular, the protection afforded the child by the womb depends upon factors such as the mother's age, health, emotional state, nutrition, and a variety of other factors.

FROM CONCEPTION TO BIRTH

Prenatal development spans about 266 days in three phases: the germinal period, the period of the embryo, and the period of the fetus.

In the germinal period, after conception, the zygote moves toward the uterus and begins successive divisions to form the blastula, which is comprised of the blastocyst and the trophoblast. The blastula undergoes implantation in the uterus, marking the end of the germinal period. Only about 1 out of 4 implantations are successful.

The implanted blastula secretes a hormone that prevents menstruation, and the period of the embryo proceeds. The trophoblast develops into (1) amnion, which fills with amniotic fluid to suspend and protect the embryo, (2) yolk sac, producer of initial blood cells for the embryo, (3) chorion, which surrounds amnion and embryo and which is covered in part by villi that attach to the uterus to form the placenta, and (4) allantosis, which develops into the umbilical cord and placental blood vessels. Oxygen and nutrients pass the semi-permeable placental barrier on through a vein in the umbilical cord to the embryo. Carbon dioxide and wastes pass out of the embryo through umbilical arteries on through the placental barrier to the mother. The blastocyst develops into the embryo's ectoderm, mesoderm, and endoderm, which differentiate into various structures and organs. Milestones include formation of heart and blood vessels by the 3rd week, heartbeat and blood circulation by the 4th week, eyes with corneas and lenses by the 5th week, a rudimentary skeleton by the 7th week, and overall rapid development of the brain during the 5th through 8th weeks. In general, the first month is the period of the most rapid growth, the first two months are critical in terms of spontaneous abortions, and the period from the 2nd through the 8th week marks the sensitive period of high susceptibility to teratogens that can pass the placental barrier and produce birth defects.

The period of the fetus begins with the 3rd month. Just prior, during the 7th and 8th weeks, sexual development began as the indifferent gonad appeared, in turn to develop as testes or ovaries depending upon presence or absence of a Y chromosome. In the 9th and 10th weeks, a male fetus's testes produce hormones to develop a male reproductive system; otherwise, a female reproductive system develops. By the end of the 3rd month the fetus is moving, can swallow and digest and urinate, and is clearly male or female although only 3 inches in length. The first trimester is the period through the end of the 3rd month.

The second trimester begins with the 4th month. By the end of the 4th month the fetus is 8-10 inches long, is capable of vigorous kicks, and has a heartbeat detectable by
stethoscope. By the end of the 5th month, the fetus is about 12 inches long and has a
heartbeat audible by placing one's ear on the mother's abdomen. By the end of the 6th
month, the fetus is 14-15 inches long, weighs about 2 pounds, and can hear the mother's
heartbeat and other noises outside the uterus. The age of viability is typically reached
by 24 to 28 weeks, prior to which survival is unlikely outside of the uterus.

The third trimester begins with the 7th month. During this period, weight typically
increases to 7½ pounds or more, length to 19-20 inches or more. By the 9th prenatal
month, the fetus typically adopts the head-down "fetal" position. Uterine contractions
during the 9th month help move the fetus into position for childbirth.

ENVIRONMENTAL INFLUENCES ON PRENATAL DEVELOPMENT

Maternal age is related to the neonate's chances of survival. Mothers under age 20
and first-time mothers over age 35 face greater risks for themselves and for their children. The parity effect involves greater risk with more pregnancies (i.e., more than
four). Increased risk is also associated with the mother's emotional state, especially
where anxiety, depression, or ambivalence about pregnancy are present.

Malnutrition increases risks of congential defects and infant mortality, especially
if mother and fetus are malnourished during the third trimester. Effects on intellectual
development may not be permanent, depending upon intervention after malnutrition.

Teratology is the study of prenatal and congenital defects that result from diseases,
drugs, chemicals, and other such hazards. The various organs and body structures have
differing critical periods of susceptibility. The period of the embryo is the most critical overall, but many birth defects are anytime malformations.

Teratogenic diseases of the mother are many. Rubella (German Measles) during the
first trimester can produce blindness, deafness, heart defects, and mental retardation.
Congenital syphilis can cause sensory defects and brain damage. Rh factor incompatibility occurs when an Rh negative mother has an Rh positive child, and any leakage of the
mother's blood antibodies into the fetus's blood stream can cause erythroblastosis and
birth defects such as cerebral plasy, mental retardation, or even death. Rhogam prevents
the build-up of antibodies in the mother's blood during succeeding pregancies. Other maternal diseases are listed in Table 4-2, along with their effects.

Many drugs taken by the pregnant mother can have adverse effects. An example is
thalidomide, a mild tranquilizer which caused severe structural deformities such as phocomelia, in which all or part of the limbs are missing. A partial list of drugs with
potentially serious effects is given in Table 4-3. Progesterone masculinizes female fetuses and overmasculinizes males. DES (diethylstilbestoral) increases the risk of later
cervical cancer in female offspring. Alcohol consumption during pregnancy can produce
fetal alcohol syndrome (FAS), with effects such as microcephaly, hyperactivity, developmental delay, and mental retardation. Tobacco may produce physical, intellectual, and
emotional deficiences, although some studies have found no such effects. The effects of
marijuana and LSD use are unclear. Use of heroin and other addicting drugs produces neonates who are addicted and tend to have negative temperament characteristics. Methadone,
in addition to addictive drug effects, increases the possibility that babies will become
victims of Sudden Infant Death Syndrome (SIDS).

Radiation, as in X-rays and cancer treatments, can produce serious birth defects.
Chemicals such as pesticides, and also various food additives, are suspected teratogens.
Even high altitude can be problem, through causing anoxia in the fetuses of nonacclimat-
ized mothers. However, sexual intercourse during pregnancy is not likely to cause harm.

As summarized in Box 4-2, ways to reduce the chances of an abnormal baby include genetic counseling, avoidance of exposure to diseases, no use of drugs except as prescribed,
and close attention to the mother's nutrition.

THE BIRTH PROCESS

Normal childbirth includes the first stage of labor, which begins with uterine contractions and ends with full dilation of the cervix, the second stage of labor, beginning with the fetus's movement through the cervix and ending when the baby has emerged, and the third stage of labor, in which the uterus contracts to expel the placenta. Factors in determining how difficult childbirth will be include the mother's attitudes, knowledge of childbirth, and preparation. The father's participation is also an aid to childbirth, in addition to fostering engrossment between father and child.

Natural childbirth traces to the work of obstetricians such as Lamaze, and involves preparatory exercises for the mother and avoidance of medication during labor and delivery. Father and mother attend classes, and the father is present as a "coach." Postpartum depression occurs with many mothers during the first week or so after childbirth. Gentle birthing derives from the work of Leboyer, and involves minimizing the trauma experienced by the child: The delivery room is dimly lit and quiet, the neonate is placed on the mother's stomach, and later the child is immersed in a warm bath to simulate conditions of the womb and ease the transition to life. Although gentle birthing is controversial, parts of the procedure are now routine. Other considerations in childbirth include effects on older children in the family, who may feel neglected. One solution is to involve older children in childcare.

Complications during childbirth can have long-range effects on the child. Anoxia can occur through damage to the umbilical cord or aftereffects of medication given to the mother, and oxygen deprivation can cause brain damage or death. Cerebral palsy may be a result. But mild anoxia has not been shown to have long-range effects. Breech birth increases the risk of anoxia. Cesarean section is employed when the fetus's position makes normal delivery impossible. Birth medications such as analgesics, anesthetics, sedatives, and stimulants can affect babies and make them sluggish and irritable during the first few weeks, in turn interfering with parental attachment. Such effects can last up to a year after birth. Box 4-3 describes medical procedures often used when birth complications occur, including in-utero monitoring, use of forceps, Cesarean sections, and use of isolettes.

Small-for-date babies and short gestation (preterm) babies are born low in birth weight (i.e., less than 5½ pounds). These children may have difficulty surviving and may develop respiratory disorders such as hyaline membrane disease. Isolettes improve the chance of survival, but preterm infants are less likely to experience good attachment. Long-term consequences of low birth weight are in turn less likely in stable, highly supportive homes than in unstable, disadvantaged homes. Postmature babies may experience malnutrition and anoxia, and thus physicians perform Cesarean sections or employ induced labor when a baby is seriously overdue.

The view that childbirth is an entirely natural phenomenon requiring no interference leads to the idea of home deliveries. Low infant mortality rates in countries such as Holland, where home delivery is popular, support this view. The other point of view, prevalent in England and the U.S., is that childbirth is a high-risk endeavor best conducted in a hospital because of possible last-minute emergencies. Birthing rooms in hospitals provide a compromise on this issue.

SELF-REVIEW

Fill in the blanks for each item. Check the answers for each item as you go.

FROM CONCEPTION TO BIRTH

1. Prenatal development includes the _____ period, the   germinal
period of the _____, and the period of the _____.   embryo, fetus

51

The Germinal Period

2. Early mitotic cell division of the zygote produces the blastula, which consists of the inner _____ and the outer _____.

> blastocyst
> trophoblast

3. The burrowing of the blastula into the uterine wall is called _____, which occurs within the first two weeks after _____; only about one blastula out of ___ achieves successful implantation.

> implantation
> conception, 4

The Period of the Embryo

4. The trophoblast differentiates into four structures: (1) the _____, which fills with fluid and protects the embryo, (2) the _____ _____, which temporarily produces blood cells for the embryo, (3) the _____, which eventually forms the placenta, and (4) the _____, which forms the umbilical cord and the blood vessels of the placenta.

> amnion
> yolk sac
> chorion
> allantosis

5. Nutrients from the mother pass the _____ barrier and are carried through the _____ cord to the embryo; this process is reversed for waste products.

> placental
> umbilical

6. The blastocyst differentiates into three layers: (1) the _____, which in turn becomes skin, hair, surface glands, and nervous system, (2) the _____, which forms muscles, bones, connective tissue, and circulatory and excretory systems, and (3) the _____, which forms the digestive tract, lungs, and other internal systems and organs.

> ectoderm
> mesoderm
> endoderm

7. By age 2 months, at the end of the period of the _____, the baby is about ___ _____ long and weighs about one-tenth of an ounce.

> embryo
> 1 inch

The Period of the Fetus

8. Just prior to the period of the fetus, a genital ridge called the _____ _____ appears; then, in males, the ___ chromosome triggers growth of testes, or in females, absence of the Y chromosome allows _____ to develop.

> indifferent gonad, Y
> ovaries

9. The fetus's heartbeat can be heard by placing an ear to the mother's abdomen by about the end of the _____ month, and by the end of the second trimester the fetus is about ___-___ inches long and weighs about ___ pounds, having now reached the age of _____ with a chance of surviving outside the womb.

> 5th
> 14-15
> 2
> viability

ENVIRONMENTAL INFLUENCES ON PRENATAL DEVELOPMENT

Maternal Characteristics

10. Risks of birth complications or birth defects increase markedly when the mother is under age ___ or over age ___, especially if the mother is having her first child.

> 20, 35

11. Whether due to the mother's age or depletion of the mother's reproductive system, women experience more birth complications if they have more than ___ children; this is the _____ effect.

> 4, parity

Nutrition

12. Research indicates that the effects of malnutrition are the most pronounced during the _____ trimester, although recovery after birth is good given that the child receives adequate nu-

> third

trition and a _____ environment.   supportive

Teratogens

13. Birth defects can result from teratogens experienced throughout prenatal development, as with _____ malformations; but   anytime
the most sensitive phase is the period of the _____, when   embryo
body parts and organs are developing rapidly.

14. Rubella is most dangerous during the _____ trimester;   first
syphilis is most dangerous from the _____ week onward; and the   18th
dangers in gonorrhea and herpes simplex are greatest at _____. birth

15. Rh incompatibility occurs when an Rh _____ mother has   negative
an Rh _____ child; the mother's blood builds up antibod-   positive
ies that attack and destroy the fetus's _____ blood cells, the   red
result of which is _____.   erythroblastosis

16. Thalidomide babies had a number of defects, including an absence of all of part of the limbs with the hands or feet instead
connected directly to the body; this is called _____.   phocomelia

17. Masculinization of female fetuses can be caused by the sex
hormone _____, and long-range effects such as cervi-   progesterone
cal cancer in female offspring have been associated with the mother's use of _____ during pregnancy; ironically, both sex hor-   DES
mones have been used to prevent _____.   miscarriage

18. Alcohol use during pregnancy can produce FAS, which is the
_____ _____ syndrome, with effects such as microcephaly,   fetal alcohol
_____ retardation, and motor and temperament disorders.   mental

19. Use of addicting drugs during pregnancy can produce neonates
who are also _____, as well as negative temperament   addicted
characteristics that interfere with emotional _____ be-   bonding
tween parents and child.

20. Because oxygen starvation can cause _____ in the fetus,   anoxia
some obstetricians recommend that pregnant women avoid _____   air
travel.

On the Prevention of Birth Defects

21. In spite of the many hazards during pregnancy, it appears
that about ___ % of all neonates are perfectly normal and that   90%
many of the others have relatively _____ defects that are   minor
temporary or correctable.

THE BIRTH PROCESS

22. Uterine contractions come at 10-15-minute intervals during
the _____ stage of labor; the baby is born during the _____   first, second
stage of labor; and the _____ is expelled during the   placenta
third stage of labor.

23. In prepared childbirth, labor and delivery are often easier
for the mother, and the father's presence both helps the mother
and fosters _____ between father and child.   engrossment

24. Prepared childbirth, as in procedures developed by _____,   Lamaze
includes relaxation and breathing _____, presence of   exercises
the _____ during labor and delivery, and minimal use of   father or coach
pain-killing _____ during the process.   medications

25. Leboyer's _____ _____ procedure includes   gentle birthing

53

keeping the delivery room dimly lit and _____ and avoiding
use of harsh procedures such as _____ the infant, in
each case designed to minimize birth _____.

quiet
spanking
trauma

Complications of Birth

26. Anoxia at birth can result from pinching or tangling of the
_____ cord, use of _____ medications with the
mother, or ingestion and lodging of _____ that blocks breathing; moderate to severe anoxia from these and other causes can
produce _____ damage or even death.

umbilical, sedative
mucus

brain

27. A child born feet-first is a _____ birth, and there is
an increased risk of _____; abnormal positionings of the fetus sometimes require birth by _____ section.

breech
anoxia
Cesarean

28. Medications given to the mother during labor and delivery
can affect the child's intellectual and motor _____
for anywhere from several _____ up to a full _____ after
birth.

development
weeks, year

Complications of Low Birth Weight

29. Infants who are born when due but who weigh less than about
____ pounds at birth are called _____-____-_____ babies;
infants who are small as a result of being born too early are
called _____-_____ or preterm babies; infants who
are born after their due dates are called _____ babies.

5½, small-for-date

short-gestation
postmature

30. Hyaline membrane disease, also called the _____
distress syndrome, is most likely with babies of _____ birth
weight.

respiratory
low

31. To aid with attachment and emotional bonding between parents
and infant, parents are now encouraged to touch and caress their
low-birth-weight infants while the infants are still being maintained in _____ or incubators.

isolettes

Postmaturity

32. Perhaps because the placenta becomes less efficient in maintaining the fetus, postmature infants have a slightly increased
risk of _____ and malnutrition, and it is sometimes necessary to _____ labor or perform a Cesarean _____.

anoxia
induce, section

Should You Have Your Baby at Home?

33. Those who favor delivery at home instead of in the hospital
argue that childbirth is a _____ process that usually requires no interference; those who favor hospital delivery argue
that complications and _____ requiring special treatment can arise; one compromise is the hospital _____ room.

natural

emergencies
birthing

SELF-TEST I

Consider each alternative carefully. Then choose the best one.

1. The correct order for prenatal developmental stages is
    a. germinal, fetal, embryonic
    b. germinal, embryonic, fetal
    c. embryonic, germinal, fetal
    d. embryonic, fetal, germinal

2. Beliefs such as that women who listen to music during pregnancy will have children who are interested in music or that pregnant women who are sexually active will have children who are sexually precocious are
   a. sometimes true
   b. sometimes false
   c. always true
   d. always false

3. The semi-permeable membrane that restricts passage of materials into the embryo or fetus is the
   a. placental barrier
   b. umbilical cord
   c. implantation
   d. indifferent gonad

4. Which of the following normally cannot pass the placental barrier?
   a. gases such as oxygen and carbon dioxide
   b. blood cells of the child and mother
   c. sugars, proteins, and fats
   d. teratogens such as viruses

5. Spontaneous abortion during the period of the embryo can result from
   a. an immature or malformed uterus
   b. abnormal implantation of the blastula
   c. genetic abnormality of the embryo
   d. all of the above

6. The correct order for the following "milestones" of the period of the embyro is
   a. eyes with corneas and lenses, heartbeat and blood circulation, basic skeleton
   b. basic skeleton, heartbeat and blood circulation, eyes with corneas and lenses
   c. heartbeat and blood circulation, eyes with corneas and lenses, basic skeleton
   d. eyes with corneas and lenses, basic skeleton, heartbeat and blood circulation

7. The age of viability begins soon after the end of the
   a. first trimester
   b. second trimester
   c. third trimester
   d. none of the above

8. Older mothers have a greater risk of birth complications and defects; this is also one possible explanation for
   a. the parity effect
   b. postpartum depression
   c. engrossment
   d. Rank's birth trauma

9. Generally, the unborn child is most sensitive to the effects of teratogens during
   a. the germinal period
   b. the period of the embryo
   c. the period of the fetus
   d. all of the above, about equally

10. The observation that babies of highly anxious mothers tend to be hyperactive, irritable, and irregular in their feeding, sleeping, and bowel habits may be due to
   a. genetically based temperament
   b. mother's heightened emotional state during pregnancy
   c. behavior of the previously anxious mother toward the baby after childbirth
   d. any of the above

11. Which of the following can potentially cause birth complications or defects?
    a. aspirin
    b. vitamins
    c. antibiotics
    d. all of the above

12. Which of the following primarily affects the baby during the birth process?
    a. gonorrhea
    b. hepatitis
    c. herpes simplex
    d. all of the above

13. Fetal or neonatal anoxia is possible as a result of
    a. mother's travel to high altitudes without acclimatization
    b. barbiturate use by the mother during pregnancy
    c. pinching of the umbilical cord during childbirth
    d. any of the above

14. Which of the following is not good advice for pregnant mothers?
    a. seek prenatal care with emphasis on teratology
    b. avoid all drugs except as essential and prescribed by a physician
    c. get vaccinated against viruses such as rubella during pregnancy
    d. allow weight gain to take its course, without severe diet restrictions

15. Generally, research indicates that the presence of fathers during labor and delivery
    a. distracts the mother and interferes with her concentration on childbirth
    b. is a major obstacle to effective use of medical personnel and procedures
    c. is hard to accomplish, in that most fathers prefer not to be present
    d. is supportive for the mother and aids in engrossment with the child

RESEARCH SUMMARY AND REVIEW

Using the textbook, review the research efforts indicated and write a summary of the important findings. Note the general purpose or context of the research.

1. Stein & Susser (1976), Stein, Susser, Saenger, & Marolla (1975), page 128: _____

_____

_____

_____

2. Zeskind & Ramey (1978, 1981), page 128: _____

_____

_____

_____

3. Lefkowitz (1981), page 137: _____

_____

_____

_____

4. Kendrick & Dunn (1980), Dunn & Kendrick (1981), page 144: _____

_____

_____

_____

_____

SELF-TEST II

Consider each alternative carefully.   Then choose the best one.

1. After conception, the zygote undergoes successive mitotic divisions until it forms the ball-like structure called the
    a. blastocyst
    b. blastula
    c. trophoblast
    d. implant

2. The trophoblast develops into the
    a. amnion
    b. chorion
    c. allantosis
    d. all of the above

3. The blastocyst develops into the
    a. ectoderm
    b. mesoderm
    c. endoderm
    d. all of the above

4. Structures that protect and nourish the unborn child develop from the _____, and the embryo itself develops from the _____.
    a. blastocyst, trophoblast
    b. blastocyst, blastocyst
    c. trophoblast, blastocyst
    d. trophoblast, trophoblast

5. The embryo's umbilical cord, along with the blood vessels of the placenta, develop from the
    a. amnion
    b. yolk sac
    c. chorion
    d. allantosis

6. "External" structures such as skin, hair, nails (and also the nervous system) are formed from the
    a. ectoderm
    b. mesoderm
    c. endoderm
    d. all of the above

7. The genital ridge, called the indifferent gonad,
    a. develops into ovaries in a Y chromosome is present; otherwise, testes develop
    b. develops into testes if an X chromosome is present; otherwise, ovaries develop
    c. develops into testes or ovaries depending upon how much the mother exercises
    d. none of the above

57

8. The period of the fetus begins
   a. at the end of the first trimester
   b. at the end of the 5th week
   c. at the end of the 2nd month
   d. at the end of the germinal period

9. By the time the fetus is 12 weeks old, it is about _____ long and weighs about _____.
   a. 1 inch, 1/10th of an ounce
   b. 3 inches, 1/2 to 3/4 of an ounce
   c. 14-15 inches, 2 pounds
   d. 20 inches, 7-7½ pounds

10. The fetus typically achieves the age of viability between
    a. the 16th and 20th weeks
    b. the 20th and 24th weeks
    c. the 24th and 28th weeks
    d. the 28th and 32nd weeks

11. According to Kessner's research, the period of least risk to the fetus or neonate in terms of the mother's age is
    a. 15-20 years old
    b. 20-30 years old
    c. 30-40 years old
    d. 40-50 years old

12. The research by Stein and her colleagues (1975, 1976) found that malnourishment during the third trimester as a result of war famine increase infant mortality; in turn, long-range effects on the infants who survived were that
    a. physical development was severely impaired
    b. intellectual development was severely impaired
    c. physical and intellectual development were impaired
    d. no impairments were found, presumably due to improved nutrition after the famine

13. Zeskind and Ramey's (1978, 1981) research on early intervention with fetally malnourished children indicated that
    a. corrective nutrition is important to intellectual development
    b. a supportive environment is important to intellectual development
    c. both of the above
    d. none of the above

14. With regard to sensitive periods for prenatal effects of teratogens, in general, the unborn child
    a. is sensitive only during the embryonic period
    b. is sensitive only during the fetal period
    c. is most sensitive during the embryonic period
    d. is most sensitive during the fetal period

15. Which of the following is least dangerous to the unborn child during the first trimester, in terms of the child's susceptibility?
    a. rubella
    b. syphilis
    c. X-rays
    d. progesterone

16. Which of the following involves mother's antibodies causing erythroblastosis in the embryo or fetus?
    a. rubella
    b. Rh disease
    c. toxemia
    d. toxoplasmosis

17. Phocomelia was observed in infants after pregnant mothers' use of
   a. thalidomide
   b. methadone
   c. LSD
   d. DES

18. Fetal alcohol syndrome (FAS) includes symptoms such as
   a. microcephaly
   b. heart malformations
   c. mental retardation
   d. all of the above

19. In the Lefkowitz (1981) study of long-term effects of maternal smoking on children, smokers produced children who, by 9-11 years of age, were
   a. physically smaller
   b. less intelligent
   c. less well behaved
   d. none of the above

20. Generally, sexual intercourse during pregnancy
   a. should be strictly avoided after the first trimester
   b. should be strictly avoided after the second trimester
   c. most often leads to sexual frustration for both parents
   d. is apparently not harmful unless unusual complications are present

21. Although neonatal hazards are many, more than ____% of all neonates are normal.
   a. 60%
   b. 70%
   c. 80%
   d. 90%

22. Delivery occurs during the second stage of labor, which typically lasts about
   a. ½ hour or less
   b. ½ to 1½ hours
   c. 1½ to 3 hours
   d. 3 hours or more

23. Gentle birthing is identified primarily with
   a. Grantly Dick-Read
   b. Fernand Lamaze
   c. Otto Rank
   d. Fredrick Leboyer

24. Natural or prepared childbirth typically does not include
   a. training in relaxation and breathing for the mother
   b. presence of the father during training, labor, and delivery
   c. avoidance of medications during childbirth
   d. a dimly lit, quiet delivery room

25. Kendrick and Dunn's (1980, 1981) research on how older children are affected by the birth of a child indicated that parents should
   a. shower the older children with as much attention as possible
   b. punish the older children if they appear jealous of the neonate
   c. incorporate the older children in neonatal care
   d. ignore jealous behaviors by the older children

VIGNETTES

Consider the story, then answer each question using material from the textbook.

I. Harriet and Al decided to have children soon after they were married, but, as it happened, it was nearly four years later that Harriet missed a period and allowed her hopes to rise. Because of the couple's excitement over the possibility, Harriet went to her obstetrician a couple of weeks later, and tests revealed that indeed she was pregnant. But, not long after that, Harriet's baby was "spontaneously" aborted.

   1. Describe possible natural causes for the spontaneous abortion.

   2. List possible teratogenic causes.

   3. By analogy to post-partum depression, what emotional effects would you expect Harriet to experience?

II. My former wife and I (DB) attended prepared childbirth classes, and I was present throughout labor and delivery of our son. I served mainly as a coach, helping her relax as much as possible during labor, including reminding her to control her breathing and not to "push" until it was time for delivery. Then, as our son was born, I stood near the head of the table and gave her as much emotional support as I could. She was conscious throughout, although she had been given minimal medication (because labor had been induced). Not long after my son's birth, I carried him down the hall to our room, experiencing one of the most profound and indescribably joyous emotional reactions I've ever known, especially when he opened his eyes widely and curiously and gazed up at me.

   1. Discuss my feelings in terms of "engrossment."

   2. What long-range effects might this experience have had on my interactions with my son?

   3. How might engrossment between my son and his mother have been affected if she had been given maximal medication prior to childbirth?

III. Janet looked forward eagerly to the birth of her first child, in spite of the physical changes she experienced in the long months of pregnancy and in spite of her fears that childbirth would not exactly be painless. At first, after an uncomplicated and conventional birth of a healthy daughter, Janet was elated and thrilled and convinced that it was well worthwhile. But within a few days whe began to feel extremely depressed and convinced that childbirth wasn't worth it after all, and she often found herself crying for no particular reason.

   1. What characteristics of Jane's prenatal outlook might dispose her to post-partum depression?

   2. After childbirth, what factors might be involved?

   3. What general approaches would be helpful for Janet in getting over her depression?

APPLICATIONS

Try each of the projects, noting answers to the questions as you go.

I. Suppose you have a friend who has just discovered that she is pregnant. Aside from wanting to know about the physical and emotional changes she will experience, she is also curious about the "milestones" at which she and her husband (and others) will be able to "detect" the child's presence and behaviors.

   1. Devise a list of milestones and when they can be detected.

   2. What behaviors might an obstetrician be able to detect, and when?

   3. Are there any behaviors by the unborn child that might indicate "boy" or "girl"?

II. Suppose you have a friend who is an expectant father and whose wife is highly interested in his participation in natural or prepared childbirth. However, whatever his reasons, he is highly reluctant and also sees no particular reason for his participation.

    1. What potential benefits for him might you describe?

    2. What potential benefits for his wife might you describe?

    3. What potential benefits for the baby might you describe?

III. The arguments in favor of hospital delivery (as opposed to home delivery) usually focus upon possible emergencies during childbirth that might require immediate attention and special equipment not available in the home. As an aid to understanding the issues involved, consider the following:

    1. What prenatal conditions of the child might indicate hospital delivery?

    2. What conditions of the mother might indicate hospital delivery?

    3. What complications at or around childbirth might indicate special treatment?

ANSWERS

Self-Test I

1. b	6. c	11. d
2. d	7. b	12. d
3. a	8. a	13. d
4. b	9. b	14. c
5. d	10. d	15. d

Research Summary and Review

1. Stein & Susser (1976), Stein et al. (1975): Dutch records revealed that malnourishment during war famine was associated with lower birth weights and also higher infant mortality, especially when it occurred during the third trimester; subsequent comparison of adults either exposed or not exposed to the famine as children indicated no general long-term effects of malnutrition, implying that children can recover given adequate nutrition and support after birth.

2. Zeskind & Ramey (1978, 1981): As an evaluation of the effects of socially supportive intervention with fetally malnourished infants, if was found that children who received supportive day care over the first 3 years of life fared better than those who only received nutritional and medical care by itself, with regard to measures of friendliness, self-assurance, and IQ.

3. Lefkowitz (1981): Children 9-11 years old were compared by whether their mothers had smoked cigarettes during pregnancy, and no differences between the children were found in terms of size, intelligence, achievement, being well behaved, or being popular with peers; thus the possibly harmful effects of smoking during pregancy were not verified.

4. Kendrick & Dunn (1980), Dunn & Kendrick (1981): Older children sought attention while mothers were caring for newborns, and it was later found that showering the older children with parental attention did not help in terms of how much they later played with the newborn; instead, simply not permitting the older children to brood or to elicit extra attention was more effective, indicating ways to work with older children in this respect.

1. b	6. a	11. b	16. b	21. d
2. d	7. d	12. d	17. a	22. b
3. d	8. c	13. c	18. d	23. d
4. c	9. b	14. c	19. d	24. d
5. d	10. c	15. b	20. d	25. c

Vignettes

I. (1) Natural causes include abnormal implantation of the embryo, burrowing of the embryo into a site incapable of sustaining the embryo (including malformation or immature development of the uterus), and genetic abnormality of the embryo. (2) Most teratogens could have this effect, given severe exposure and damage. The more likely ones are chicken pox, cytomegalovirus, hypertension, influenza, mumps, smallpox, hallucinogens, tobacco, and radiation. (3) Given the degree of enthusiasm indicated, Harriet might well mirror the effects of post-partum depression, perhaps especially if she comes to believe that something she did was responsible. Her symptoms would thus include depression, irritability, and generalized hopelessness and despair.

II. (1) I apparently became quite engrossed through significant involvement with the birth process, which perhaps aided emotional bonding of a sort that seemed very real to me then, as now. I will always remember the feeling I had when he first looked up at me, and I remember the experience vividly. (2) Through the sense of "belongingness" established in those first moments it is likely that participation helped me stay actively involved with my son. This is difficult to separate from what I might have done and felt anyway, given conventional childbirth, but it may have had a marked effect in making me feel directly responsible in helping him begin life. (3) She describes similar feelings during delivery and later while we were allowed to keep our son for an hour or so, and things might have been quite different had she been medicated. Notably, medications for the mother also affect the child, in terms of drowsiness, irritability, and unresponsiveness, which would have interfered with engrossment in these early moments.

III. (1) Predisposing factors include her enthusiasm and elation, which might in a sense "set her up" for subsequent depression. Other factors include possible medications administered during the birth process and perhaps absence of the father in accord with conventional childbirth. (2) After childbirth, factors might include others paying more attention to the infant than her, hormonal changes following childbirth, and perhaps (although not necessarily) minimal emotional support from the father. (3) General sorts of approaches include providing emotional support, encouraging her to talk about her feelings, and assurance that she is not unusual in having this kind of reaction. Discussions with other mothers who have experienced similar problems would also help.

Applications

I. (1) Milestones include kicks, by about 4 months, audible heartbeat by an ear placed to the mother's abdomen, by about 5 months, startle responses to loud noises, by about 6 months, and visibility of the fetus's hand, head, etc. pressing against the mother's abdomen, by about the middle of the 9th month. (2) The fetus's heartbeat can be detected by stethoscope by about 4 months, and various movements of the fetus can be detected by ultrasound scanning somewhat later. (3) No. Measures such as activity level and the like are unreliable.

II. (1) For the father, benefits include a more explicit knowledge of childbirth than he could gain any other way, a distinct sense of participation and involvement with the process of birth, a likely increased fascination with the newborn child, and also engrossment and early emotional bonding. (2) For the mother, benefits include emotional support at a time when she really needs it, assistance in helping her remember to relax, less probability that she will need medication, and a more positive, cooperative view of childbirth as a result of his participation. (3) Benefits for the child derive from benefits for father and mother, and include lack of side effects of medication if it is not used, lack of effects of maternal anxiety, and perhaps also a lessening of the overall birth trauma (see also the discussion of Leboyer's gentle birthing technique).

III. (1) Prenatal conditions that would serve as warning signs include abnormal positioning of the fetus, various indications of possible anoxia, postmaturity and other possible indicators for Cesarean section, premature birth and a need for isolette care, and a variety of prenatally detected birth defects that would place the infant at risk. (2) Postmaturity might also indicate the need for induced labor; other maternal conditions would include weakened or medically unsound physical health, presence of venereal disease, use of addictive drugs, and suspected exposure to teratogens. (3) Relatively unanticipatable conditions would include twisting or pinching of the umbilical cord, failure of the neonate to expel mucus, and subtler, undetected birth defects.

CHAPTER FIVE

THE PHYSICAL CHILD: SENSORY CAPABILITIES,
MOTOR DEVELOPMENT, AND GROWTH

OVERVIEW AND KEY TERMS

Read carefully. Recall examples and discussion as you go, and define each key term.

THE NEONATE

The Apgar test, given at birth, assesses heart rate, respiratory effort, muscle tone, color, and reflex irritability. The Brazelton Neonatal Behavioral Assessment Scale, given typically on the third day of life and repeated a few days later, measures 20 infant reflexes plus 26 social responses. Parents of sluggish or unresponsive infants can learn to elicit more favorable responses from their infants through Brazelton training, and parents of normal children can as well, as discussed in Box 5-2.

Infants are born with reflexes that help them adapt. Survival reflexes include breathing, rooting, sucking, and swallowing. Primitive "subcortical" reflexes include grasping, swimming, and stepping, plus the Babinski and Moro reflexes. At birth, primitive reflexes are diagnostic indicators of neurological wellbeing, although they disappear during the first year of life as the cerebral cortex develops.

At birth all sensory systems are functional but immature. Infants can see, but distance vision at birth is about 20/600, and visual acuity is poor because the lenses do not accommodate well. The pupillary reflex indicates sensitivity to brightness. And neonates can visually track a slowly moving target. Infants hear reasonably well and are startled by loud noises. Coordination between vision and audition is also present at birth.

The habituation technique can be used to determine how well infants can hear: The infant is habituated to a stimulus, and then the stimulus is changed to see if the infant can detect the change, as assessed by orienting, change in heart rate, and other behaviors. Neonates also display a preference for human voices. Other capabilities of the neonate include taste (sweet vs. salty vs. other tastes), smell (localization of odors and discrimination of mother's breast), touch, temperature, and pain.

Infant states of consciousness include regular sleep, irregular sleep, drowsiness, alert inactivity, waking activity, and crying. Neonates sleep about 70% of the time, in cycles throughout day and night separated by other states. Sleep time and number of cycles decrease gradually, until the infant is sleeping all night and taking short daytime naps by 3-7 months of age. At birth, REM sleep occurs during about 50% of sleep time, decreasing to 25-30% by 6 months of age and 18.5-25% by age 2 years. Autostimulation theory holds that the infant's higher percentage of REM sleep is due to a greater need for central nervous system stimulation at that age.

Sudden Infant Death Syndrome (SIDS) occurs during sleep. Causes are unknown. Clues are that SIDS occurs more often between 2-4 months of age, during winter, and with infants who have respiratory infections or irregular breathing patterns such as apnea. Thus it is possible that SIDS would occur in an infant whose innate survival reflexes are waning, if mucus happened to block nasal passages. An <u>apnea monitor</u> detects respiratory interruptions and sounds an alarm to awaken parents.

Neonates vary widely in crying and do so, on average, about 6-7% of their time. Abnormal or unhealthy babies have a high-pitched, aversive cry. Healthy babies have at least a hungry cry, a mad cry, and a pain cry, all distinguishable by mothers. Infants also use <u>fake cries</u> to attract attention. However, parental responsiveness to cries does not apparently teach the child to cry more; instead, responsiveness helps the infant develop trust and learn other modes of communication as well.

Soothing a fussy baby may require feeding or simply presenting a pacifier if the baby is not hungry. Rocking, humming, and other rhythmic stimulation may help, as may simply picking the baby up. Differences in irritability and soothability are present from birth.

MATURATION AND GROWTH

The infant's birth weight doubles by 4-6 months, triples by 12 months, and quadruples by 24 months. Growth rate is then slow and steady until the adolescent growth spurt, after which the stature of an adult is reached by the mid to late teens.

Body proportions change as a result of <u>cephalocaudal development</u> and <u>proximo-distal development</u>. Each trend is present throughout childhood.

Most bones are soft at birth. Fontanelles are soft spots in the skull that finally harden by about age 2 years. Most parts of the body develop more bones as development proceeds, as in the limbs, which allows better control. Skeletal development is largely complete by age 18. <u>Skeletal age</u> is a reliable indicator of physical maturation.

All muscle cells are already present at birth, though immature. Muscle development is cephalocaudal, occurring gradually through childhood, then accelerating during the adolescent growth spurt, with dramatic increases moreso for males than for females.

Brain development is rapid during infancy. At birth, brain weight is 25% of eventual adult weight, increasing to 75% by age 2 years and to 90% by age 5. Production of <u>neurons</u> and <u>glia</u> cells is most rapid from the prenatal period through the 2nd year after birth, a period called the <u>brain growth spurt</u>. At birth the more primitive brain stem and midbrain are the most highly developed areas. Primary motor areas and primary sensory areas mature next. Development of motor control is cephalocaudal, and the primitive reflexes disappear by about 6 months of age as the higher cortical centers assume control. <u>Myelinization</u>, produced by glia cells, insulates neurons and increases the efficiency of neural transmissions. The shorter attention span of preadolescents may be related to this normal lack of myelinization prior to puberty. <u>Multiple sclerosis</u> is a result of disintegration of the myelin sheaths around neurons. The cause is unknown.

<u>Cerebral lateralization</u> yields left-hemisphere centers for speech, hearing, motor fucntions, and some aspects of verbal processing and right-hemisphere centers for spatial functions, visual imagery, and tactile sensitivity. Functioning is integrated through the corpus callosum. Sensory areas are the first to specialize. Language areas are not fully specialized until after puberty.

MOTOR DEVELOPMENT

Development of motor abilities parallels nerve and muscle development. Milestones include (on average) sitting without support by 7.8 months, standing well alone by 13.9 months, and walking well by 14.3 months, in terms of ages when 90% of infants have mastered the skill. Ages for motor milestones are highly variable, but all children follow the same general sequence.

Manipulation of objects progresses from the palmar grasp at birth to the <u>ulnar grasp</u> by about 6 months of age to the <u>pincer grasp</u> near the end of the first year. Early visual-motor coordination is hit-or-miss, since it is visually "initiated"; but by 20 weeks of age or so, reaching becomes visually "guided." Blind children lage behind sighted children in developing reaching, and some never learn unless specially taught to use cues such as the sounds objects make.

Toddlers toddle because they are top heavy. Locomotor skills and fine motor skills alike improve rapidly during the preschool years, then more gradually during middle childhood. Boys and girls are nearly equal in physical abilities until puberty, and the differences that emerge during adolescence may be due to biology, sex-role socialization, or both.

PUBERTY - THE PHYSICAL TRANSITION FROM CHILD TO ADULT

The two major changes marking adolescence are the adolescent growth spurt and puberty. Puberty in girls is signaled by menarche, although ovulation may not begin until 12-18 months later. Puberty in boys is indicated by beginning pigmentation of pubic hair, plus other physical changes.

The adolescent growth spurt typically begins in girls from 7½-12 years of age, and in boys from 10½-16. Peak growth rate occurs about 1½ years after onset in girls and about 1 year after onset in boys. Weight increases first, then height, then musculature.

For girls, sexual maturation typically begins about age 11 with the formation of breast buds and beginning growth of pubic hair. During the height spurt, breasts grow rapidly and interna and external sex organs mature. Menarche typically comes about 2 years after the onset of breast development, at the end of the height spurt.

For boys, sexual maturation begins about age 11-11½ with enlargement of testes and scrotum and growth of unpigmented pubic hair. Penis growth follows, during the onset of the adolescent growth spurt, and boys enter puberty about when penis growth is complete. Facial hair, body hair, and the male voice change occur somewhat later.

For both sexes, large variability is present in age of sexual maturation. Onset of puberty has been occurring at younger ages over the past 100 years or so, perhaps due to improved medical care and nutrition. In general, adolescent growth is marked by concerns over attractiveness and physique, with possible byproducts such as anorexia nervosa as discussed in Box 5-3. Body type is a major concern, as with the implications of being an ectomorph, an endomorph, or a mesomorph. Mesomorphs tend to be viewed the most favorably. Body type and personality type could be genetically related, or it may be that body type creates self-fulfilling prophecies. Another personality factor is the timing of maturation, in that early maturers, especially boys, tend to gain social advantages that can persist. But timing of sexual maturation may be less important now that in years gone by.

CAUSES AND CORRELATES OF PHYSICAL GROWTH AND DEVELOPMENT

Biological predispositions interact with environmental influences to determine physical growth and development. Characteristics such as height and weight are heritable, and our genes regulate hormones which in turn affect growth. The hormone thyroxine is essential to brain and nervous system growth. The pituitary gland regulates this and other hormones such as the growth hormone (GH) during infancy and childhood. As adolescence approaches, the pituitary activates the adrenal gland, which in girls triggers the adolescent growth spurt and pubertal changes. Girls' sexual maturation results from estrogen and progesterone production by the ovaries at about the same time. In boys, the adrenal gland triggers production of testosterone by the testes, which in turn triggers the adolescent growth spurt and sexual maturation. For both sexes GH continues to be produced as a catalyst for the other hormones.

Environment also plays a significant role, nutrition being the most important factor. Prolonged malnutrition during the first 5 years of life can retard brain growth and physical development, although sort-term malnutrition can be compensated for by catch-up growth. Severe protein/calorie deficiency can cause marasmus, which includes a frail, wrinkled appearance, wasting away of body tissues, and probable intellectual impairment. Protein deficiency by itself can cause kwashiorkor, which includes thinning of hair, swelling of face, legs, and abdomen, and also skin lesions. Vitamin/mineral deficiency can retard growth and make children listless, irritable, and less resistant to disease. Overnutrition can also be a problem leading to obesity and medical complications. Overeating during childhood and adolescence causes extra fat cells to be added permanently. These and other factors such as activity level and glandular malfunction are discussed in Box 5-4.

Illness suppresses physical development temporarily and interacts with nutrition. Emotional stress and lack of affection can also retard physical development, and these factors are apparently involved in the failure-to-thrive syndrome and in deprivation dwarfism. It may be that emotional trauma inhibit GH production.

Modern infants reach physical milestones earlier than did infants in the 1930s, for example. One explanation is the secular trend hypothesis, noting improved nutrition and health care in recent years. Another is the practice hypothesis, noting that today's children have more toys to manipulate and are less often confined to cribs. Although earlier studies such as those of Hopi Indian children on cradleboards indicated little effect of motor practice, current thinking is that practice is extremely important. Research on infants deprived of opportunities to practice motor skills has found significant delays. Recent research also notes that placing the infant often in an upright position can facilitate and accelerate motor development.

SELF-REVIEW   *1-21-88*

Fill in the blanks for each item. Check the answers for each item as you go.

THE NEONATE

Is My Baby Normal?

1. The Apgar test, given within _1_ minute after birth and again at _5_ minutes after birth, assesses _heart_ rate, respiratory _effort_, _muscle_ tone, color, and reflex irritability; infants who score 4 or lower require immediate _medical_ intervention.

1
5, heart
effort, muscle
medical

2. The Brazelton Scale, given on the _3rd_ day of life and again 2 or 3 days later, assesses _20_ infant reflexes and _26_ social responses; an extremely unresponsive infant may have neurological _dysfunction_.

3rd
20, 26

dysfunction

3. An infant who appears socially sluggish on the _Brazelton_ Scale is at risk for not receiving as much parental attention and thus developing _emotional_ difficulties; parents of such infants can benefit from Brazelton _training_.

Brazelton

emotional
training

Capabilities of the Newborn Infant

4. Breathing, sucking, swallowing, and the eyeblink are examples of _survival_ reflexes necessary to beginning life; the more subcortical _primitive_ reflexes such as Babinski, Moro, swimming, and stepping may also have been important in our evolutionary history.

survival
primitive

5. Infant brightness discrimination is implied by the _pupillary_ reflex, although infant visual acuity is poor because the eyes do not _accommodate_ to bring objects into clear focus.

pupillary

accommodate

67

6. Infant audition is reasonably _good_ at birth, as assessed by the _habituation_ technique in which the infant becomes accustomed to a stimulus which is then altered slightly to see if the infant reacts.

good
habituation

7. Other neonate sensory capabilities, although perhaps immature, include touch, temperature, pain, _taste_, and _smell_.

taste, smell

Living with an Infant

8. Neonates sleep about _70_% of their time, and REMs occur during about _50_% of sleep time; overall sleep time and percentage of REM sleep gradually _decline_ over the first 2 years.

70%
50%
decrease

9. Autostimulation theory proposes that infants have more REM sleep as a way of stimulating higher _brain_ centers, thus compensating for the infant's tendency to _sleep_ so much.

brain
sleep

10. As many as 7-10 thousand infants in the U.S. each year die of _Sudden Infant Death_ Syndrome, in which the infant stops breathing during sleep; one theory holds that these infants usually display respiratory _apnea_ which is more likely to cause death during the transition from subcortical to higher cortical control at about age _2_ months.

Sudden Infant Death

apnea

2

11. Infants produce at least three types of cries: (1) the _hunger_ cry, which starts with a whimper and grows, (2) the more intense _anger_ cry, and (3) the _pain_ cry, which begins with a long shriek; by about 3 weeks of age, infants also begin to acquire attention-seeking, _fake_ cries.

hunger
mad or angry, pain

fake

12. Continuous rhythmic stimulation tends to _soothe_ a fussy baby, as does simply _picking_ the baby up.

soothe
picking

MATURATION AND GROWTH

Changes in Height and Weight

13. The two most rapid periods of physical growth after birth are (1) the _first 2_ years and (2) later during the adolescent _growth spurt_.

first 2
growth spurt

Changes in Body Proportions

14. Progressive growth and development in a head-to-tail direction is called _cephalocaudal_, and growth and development from the center of the body outward is referred to as _proximo-distal_; both trends are present from birth to the _adolescent_ growth spurt.

cephalocaudal

proximo-distal
adolescent

Skeletal Development

15. Soft spots in the infant's skull that gradually ossify into a single skull bone are called _fontanelles_; other parts of the body, however, develop _more_ rather than fewer bones as the body matures.

fontanelles
more

Muscular Development

16. Muscle development proceeds in a _cephalocaudal_ direction, although all of the muscle _cells_ are already present at birth; muscle development is gradual except during the adolescent growth spurt, when a corresponding muscle _growth_ spurt also takes place, especially in males.

cephalocaudal
cells

growth

Development of the Brain and Nervous System

17. From birth to about age 2 years, brain weight increases from about _25_% of eventual adult brain weight to about _75_%; with the inclusion of the third prenatal trimester, this period is referred to as the _brain_ growth spurt.

    25, 75

    brain

18. Glia cells yield a sheathing of individual neurons, a process called _myelinization_, which insulates the neurons and speeds the tranmission of impulses; disintegration of these sheaths is the basis for _multiple sclerosis_, which results in loss of muscular control and perhaps paralysis.

    myelinization

    multiple sclerosis

19. Specialization of the cerebral hemispheres, called cerebral _lateralization_, begins; first to specialize are the primary _sensory_ areas, whereas the speech centers are not completely specialized until _adolescence_.

    lateralization
    sensory
    adolescence

MOTOR DEVELOPMENT

Basic Trends in Locomotor Development

20. The ages at which children acquire basic locomotor skills in sitting, standing, and walking vary widely, but children follow the same general _sequence_.

    sequence

Other Motor Milestones

21. Manipulation of objects progresses from the relatively primitive _palmar grasp_ reflex to the claw-like _ulnar_ grasp to the thumb-and-forefinger _pincer_ grip during the first year of life.

    palmar grasp, ulnar
    pincer

22. Early visual-motor coordination is hit-or-miss and is thus referred to as visually _initiated_; by about 20 weeks of age, in-flight corrections are possible and reaching is visually _guided_.

    initiated

    guided

Beyond Infancy - Motor Development in Childhood

23. Walking and running in a straight line is possible by about age _3_ years; skipping and hopping on one foot are possible by about age _4_; some children can learn to ride a bicycle at about age _5_; and skills such as using household tools or playing games such as baseball are typically possible when the child is _8_ - _9_ years of age.

    3
    4
    5

    8 - 9

PUBERTY - THE PHYSICAL TRANSITION FROM CHILD TO ADULT

The Adolescent Growth Spurt

24. On average, girls begin the adolescent growth spurt around age _10½_, reach peak growth about age _12_, and return to a slower rate of growth about age _13_; in contrast, boys lag each of these ages by about _2_ - _3_ years.

    10½, 12
    13
    2 - 3

Sexual Maturation

25. On average, sexual maturation for girls begins about age _11_ with the development of breast _buds_; menarche occurs about _2_ years later, and ovulation first occurs about _1_ year or more after that.

    11
    buds, 2
    1

26. Sexual maturation for boys begins, on average, at about age _11_ with an initial enlarging of testes and scrotum; rapid penis growth occurs about _6_ months later, coinciding with the onset

    11

    6

of the adolescent *growth* spurt, and puberty is typically   growth
reached by about age *15* .   15

Psychological Impact of Adolescent Growth and Development

27. Attractiveness and physique are major concerns arising with
the entrance into *adolescence* and puberty; research indi-   adolescence
cates that children prefer the *mesomorph* type of body and   mesomorph
that children of this body type are more popular.

28. Another general finding is that boys who mature *earlier*   earlier
have social advantages that may persist into *adulthood* ; a   adulthood
similar situation occurs with girls, at least those who mature
early during *junior* high school.   junior

CAUSES AND CORRELATES OF PHYSICAL GROWTH AND DEVELOPMENT

Biological Mechanisms

29. Physical growth and development is determined by heredity
and environment in *interaction* , and characteristics such as   interaction
height and weight are highly *heritable*.   heritable

30. The master gland that regulates all of the other endocrine
glands is the *pituitary* ; one of its roles is to release   pituitary
small, regular amounts of *GH* to stimulate development of body   GH
cells during childhood and adolescence.

31. In females, the adolescent growth spurt is triggered by the
production of androgen-like hormones by the *adrenal* gland,   adrenal
and at about the same time the ovaries begin to produce the female hormones *estrogen* and progesterone to stimulate sexual   estrogen
maturation.

32. In males, the adolescent growth spurt is triggered by the
male hormone *testosterone* , which also stimulates sexual   testosterone
maturation.

Environmental Influences

33. The most important environmental influence on growth and development during the first 5 years of life is *nutrition* ; se-   nutrition
vere protein/calorie deficiency can lead to *marasmus* pro-   marasmus
tein deficiency by itself can lead to *kwashiorkor* , and var-   kwashiorkor
ious vitamin and mineral deficiencies can make children listless, irritable, and less resistant to *disease* .   disease

34. Retarded physical growth and development can also result
from too much stress and too little affection, as indicated in
the *failure - to - thrive* syndrome.   failure-to-thrive

35. Today's children reach motor milestones earlier than in days
past; an explanation based on improved nutrition and health care
is the *secular trend* hypothesis, and an explanation based   secular trend
on increased access to toys and less confinement in cribs is the
practice hypothesis.   practice

36. Studies of institutionalized orphans who had few toys and
who remained in their cribs most of the time favor the *practice*   practice
hypothesis.

*Answer question, then a (+) if centrally important concept,
and a (−) for less than central.*
1-21-88

SELF-TEST I

Consider each alternative carefully. Then choose the best one.

(−+−)1. On the Apgar test, a neonate with a slow heart rate, slow or irregular respiratory effort, strong muscle tone, pink body with blue extremities, and a weak cry would score
  a. 2
  b. 4
  c. 6
  d. 8

2. On the Brazelton Scale, an extremely unresponsive neonate with a low score would
(−)
  a. have need for parental Brazelton training
  b. have indications of possible brain damage
  c. both of the above
  d. none of the above

(+)3. Which of the following is not classified as a survival reflex?
  a. eyeblink
  b. rooting
  c. swimming
  d. swallowing

(+)4. Which of the following is accurate with regard to neonates?
  a. vision is present from birth, though somewhat blurred and fuzzy
  b. audition is present from birth, with a preference for listening to human voices
  c. soon after birth neonates can discriminate tastes of sweet versus sour
  d. all of the above

5. Infants are generally most susceptible to conditioning and learning during Wolff's
state of consciousness called
(−−−)
  a. drowsiness
  b. alert inactivity
  c. waking inactivity
  d. crying

(+)6. Which of the following decreases over the first few months of life?
  a. percentage of REM sleep
  b. percentage of time spent sleeping
  c. number of nap cycles per day
  d. all of the above

(+ +(+)7. Respiratory apnea is cited as a possible cause of
  a. Sudden Infant Death Syndrome
  b. failure-to-thrive syndrome
  c. marasmus
  d. kwashiorkor

8. A crying baby is likely to be
(+ +)
  a. mad
  b. in pain
  c. desirous of parental attention
  d. all of the above

+ +(+)9. The periods of most rapid physical growth and development after birth are
  a. the first 2 years and middle childhood
  b. early childhood and middle childhood
  c. the first 2 years and early adolescence
  d. early childhood and early adolescence

(+)10. Which of the following is present at birth?
   a. all of the brain cells the child will ever have
   b. all of the muscle cells the child will ever have
   c. both of the above
   d. none of the above

(+)11. The attention span of an infant may be shorter than that of an adolescent because
   a. the primary sensory areas of the cerebrum are the last to develop
   b. the cerebral hemispheres are not fully lateralized until puberty
   c. vitamin-mineral deficiencies are common among infants
   d. mylenization of the reticular formation is not complete until puberty

(+ +(+)12. Evidence for biological mechanisms in physical growth and development includes the findings that
   a. sequencing of motor skills development is consistent from child to child
   b. rate of maturation is a heritable attribute
   c. pituitary functioning controls physical growth and development
   d. all of the above

(−)13. Which of the following triggers the adolescent growth spurt in females?
   a. activation of the adrenal gland
   b. testosterone produced by the ovaries
   c. an increase in GH
   d. all of the above

14. A child who experiences short-term malnutrition of a relatively minor nature will
(− − −)probably, when diet later becomes adequate,
   a. develop marasmus or kwashiorkor
   b. experience catch-up growth
   c. be mentally but not physically retarded
   d. remain permanently smaller than normal

15. Overnutrition during infancy and during the adolescent growth spurt has the effect of
(−)   a. producing an excess of fat cells that remain with the body for life
   b. depositing fatty tissue temporarily with fat cells, causing them to swell
   c. both of the above
   d. none of the above

RESEARCH SUMMARY AND REVIEW

Using the textbook, review the research efforts indicated and write a summary of the important findings. Note the general purpose or context of the research.

1. Myers (1982), page 160: _____

_____

_____

_____

_____

2. Condon & Sander (1974), page 164: _____

_____

_____

_____

_____

3. Wolff (1969), page 168: _____

_____
_____
_____
_____

4. Ainsworth, Bell, & Stayton (1972), page 168: _____

_____
_____
_____
_____

5. Birns, Blank, & Bridger (1966), page 169: _____

_____
_____
_____
_____

6. Staffieri (1967), page 185: _____

_____
_____
_____
_____

7. Jones & Bayley (1950), Jones (1957, 1965), page 186:_____

_____
_____
_____

8. Gardner (1972), page 192: _____

_____
_____
_____

9. Dennis (1960), page 195: _____

_____
_____
_____
_____

SELF-TEST II

Consider each alternative carefully. Then choose the best one.

1. The Apgar test assessed infant heart rate, respiratory effort, muscle tone, color, and reflex irritability; an infant in need of immediate medical intervention would score
   a. 9 or higher
   b. 7 or higher
   c. 5 or higher
   d. 4 or lower

2. The Brazelton Scale is based on
   a. infant reflexes
   b. infant responsiveness to social stimulation
   c. both of the above
   d. none of the above

3. In Myer's (1982) study of parents who receiving Brazelton training,
   a. no benefits were found for parents of healthy, responsive children
   b. benefits were found for mothers but not for fathers of unresponsive children
   c. benefits were found for fathers but not for mothers of unresponsive children
   d. none of the above

4. Which of the following is most clearly related to modern-day survival?
   a. the rooting reflex
   b. the Babinski reflex
   c. the Moro reflex
   d. the grasping reflex

5. Presence of vision at birth is indicated by the
   a. Moro reflex
   b. stepping reflex
   c. pupillary reflex
   d. rooting reflex

6. In the habituation technique, an infant's failure to show a change in heart rate, respiration, orientation or the like following a change in the stimulus would indicate that
   a. the infant has clearly discriminated the stimulus change
   b. the infant apparently did not discriminate the stimulus change
   c. the infant did not enjoy the stimulus change
   d. the infant went to sleep during the experiment

7. In Condon and Sander's (1974) study of infant responsiveness to different types of sounds, it was found that
   a. infants respond more to English than to Chinese
   b. infants respond more to vowel sounds than to nonlanguage sounds
   c. infants respond more to natural language sounds than to any other sounds
   d. all of the above

8. In Wolff's description of newborn infant states of consciousness, REMs occur during
   a. regular sleep
   b. irregular sleep
   c. drowsiness
   d. alert inactivity

9. Wolff's (1969) study of young mother's responses to their infants' cries indicated that the mothers could
   a. distinguish hunger cries from fake cries
   b. distinguish pain cries from mad cries or hunger cries
   c. distinguish fake cries from mad cries or pain cries
   d. not distinguish among the various types of cries

74

10. Ainsworth, Bell, and Stayton's (1972) study of mothers' reactions to crying by their infants indicated that
    a. babies can easily be "spoiled" by too much parental responsiveness
    b. responsiveness to fake cries yields lack of infant confidence
    c. babies whose mothers were responsive to cries later tended to cry less
    d. all of the above

11. Birns, Blank, and Bridger's (1966) study of infant irritability
    a. supported the idea of individual differences in temperament at birth
    b. favored the idea of learned differences in temperament
    c. found that competent soothing techniques are effective with all infants
    d. demonstrated that pacifiers are superior to other techniques of soothing

12. Which of the following does not accelerate during the adolescent growth spurt?
    a. muscular growth
    b. sexual maturation
    c. brain development
    d. motor development

13. The motor development sequence of sitting, standing, and finally walking
    a. is consistent across all children
    b. occurs at the same ages for all children
    c. contradicts the cephalocaudal growth trend
    d. occurs with no apparent need for practice

14. The correct order for skills involved in the manipulation of objects is
    a. palmar grasp, pincer grasp, ulnar grasp
    b. pincer grasp, palmar grasp, ulnar grasp
    c. palmar grasp, ulnar grasp, pincer grasp
    d. pincer grasp, ulnar grasp, palmar grasp

15. Fraiberg's program of having parents talk to their blind children as they approach them and also to provide toys that make distinctive sounds had the effect of
    a. making blind children's motor development comparable to that of sighted children
    b. improving blind children's motor development, though they continued to lag
    c. improving directed reaching by blind children but not overall motor development
    d. none of the above

16. From puberty on, the increasing gap between male and female muscular ability appears
    a. due to males simply having more muscle than females
    b. due to differences in sex-role socialization
    c. both of the above
    d. none of the above

17. For boys and for girls, the peak period of growth during the growth spurt occurs
    a. prior to achievement of sexual maturity
    b. about the same time as achievement of sexual maturity
    c. after achievement of sexual maturity
    d. at no particular time with respect to sexual maturity

18. Typically, the onset of sexual maturation is indicated by _____ in girls and by _____ in boys.
    a. breast buds, enlargement of testes
    b. menarche, appearance of facial hair
    c. enlargement of the vagina, voice change
    d. ovulation, ejaculation

19. With regard to individual variability in sexual maturation,
    a. some girls achieve sexual maturity before others experience the onset of puberty
    b. some boys achieve sexual maturity before others experience the onset of puberty
    c. girls typically achieve sexual maturity before boys do
    d. all of the above

20. Generally, in our society, the more popular children with adults and peers alike are
    a. ectomorphs
    b. endomorphs
    c. mesomorphs
    d. none of the above

21. Whatever the reason, adolescents who have anorexia nervosa often have
    a. cold and unresponsive parents
    b. indifferent parents
    c. firm and overprotective parents
    d. uninformed parents with regard to nutrition

22. In the research efforts of Jones and Bayley (1950) and Jones (1957, 1965) on the timing of maturation in adolescent males, it was found that
    a. early maturers were more socially confident and successful in school, but the differences did not persist into adulthood
    b. late maturers were more socially confident and successful in school, but the differences did not persist into adulthood
    c. early maturers were more socially confident and successful in school, and the differences persisted into adulthood
    d. late maturers were more socially confident and successful in school, and the differences persisted into adulthood

23. In females, adolescence begins when the pituitary gland
    a. activates the adrenal gland to trigger the growth spurt and development of pubic hair
    b. activates the ovaries to produce estrogen and progesterone which in turn cause development of breasts, uterus, and vagina
    c. both of the above
    d. none of the above

24. Gardner's (1972) study of deprivation dwarfs hospitalized for observation and treatment indicated that these children suffered from
    a. malnutrition
    b. emotional deprivation
    c. both of the above
    d. none of the above

25. Dennis's (1960) studies of institutionalized orphas in Iran who received little opportunity for practice of motor skills indicated that physical maturation
    a. is sufficient by itself for motor development
    b. is necessary but not sufficient for motor development
    c. is not necessary but is sufficient for motor development
    d. is essentially unrelated to motor development

VIGNETTES

Consider the story, then answer each question using material from the textbook.

I. Sandra displayed normal reflexes at birth as assessed by the Brazelton Scale, but she was extremely irritable and cried at the slightest sound. Her parents' attempts to soothe her had little effect except to make her cry louder most of the time, which her parents found very frustrating. Holding and cuddling did little to help. And when not crying, Sandra often seemed apathetic to their attempts to interact with her.

    1. From the text discussion, in what ways might Brazelton training help?

    2. If Sandra's parents did not receive special training or otherwise figure out how to interact with her more effectively, would she be at increased risk for failure-

to-thrive syndrome? Why or why not?

    3. Similarly, given no improvement in parent-child interactions, would Sandra be at increased risk for deprivation dwarfism? Why or why not?

II. During most of his childhood, George was a bit on the pudgy side. But with the onset of puberty he became categorically fat. Dieting did not seem to help, although George readily admitted that he didn't take to diets very well. Eating was one of the few things he truly enjoyed. He did not date, he avoided sports that tended to get him out of breath, and his best social interactions with his classmates usually involved his telling of fat jokes about himself or otherwise making people laugh at him.

    1. From the text discussion of obesity, what factors might be involved in George's weight situation?

    2. Would George be an ectomorph, an endomorph, or a mesomorph? How might his class-mates respond to him from this point of view?

    3. What self-fulfilling prophecies might be operating in George's case?

III. Deborah was an "early bloomer," both in terms of when she began her adolescent *1-26-88* growth spurt and when she began showing unmistakable signs of sexual maturation. Thus, in the fourth grade, she was taller than any of her friends (boys or girls), her figure was quite womanly, and she had reached menarche. But she had come to regard her early changes as some kind of special ordeal vested upon her for reasons she couldn't imagine. Deborah's mother talked with her often about the changes, mentioning that she too had matured earlier than her friends, but Deborah still worried about being very different and perhaps being on the road to becoming very, very big and tall.

    1. At what ages would you deduce that Deborah's growth spurt and first signs of sexual maturation began? *8-10 yrs.*

    2. What genetic factors might be operating in the timing of Deborah's maturation?

    3. Why would Deborah be less than thrilled about early maturation? How might she feel later, say in high school? *Negative reinforcement of differences and self-esteem.*

APPLICATIONS

Try each of the projects, noting answers to the questions as you go.

I. Make a list of 10 people you know reasonably well who are in your own age range. Then rank them from 1 to 10, giving the lower scores to the "less popular" and higher scores to the "more popular" with respect to your overall opinions along these lines. Next, assign each person the label "endomorph," "ectomorph," or "mesomorph." Finally, add up the ranked scores separately for each physical type, and average each type.

    1. What type should score the highest? Why?

    2. What physical type are you? Is there any relationship between your rankings and your own physical type? Why might there be, and why not?

    3. Since you are at least of college age, would you expect any differences between your rankings and those of a grade-school child? Why or why not?

II. From the material discussed throughout the chapter, make a short list of things you might do as a parent to enhance your child's motor development over the first two or three years of life.

    1. What kinds of practice might you give the child during infancy?

2. What kinds of practice might you give the child during toddlerhood?

3. What role might your social interactions with the child play in motor development?

III. Again from the perspective of a potential parent, devise a short list of ways you might handle different types of crying displayed by your infant.

1. What does research indicate is best in response to fake cries?

2. Would you expect your techniques to work with all infants? Why or why not?

3. What effects might a highly irritable, hard-to-soothe infant have on your attitude toward childrearing?

ANSWERS

Self-Test I

1. c	6. d	11. d
2. a	7. a	12. d
3. c	8. d	13. a
4. d	9. c	14. b
5. b	10. b	15. c

Research Summary and Review

1. Myers (1982): Parents of healthy infants received Brazelton training and were later found to be more knowledgeable, confident, and satisfied with regard to childrearing, as compared to a control group who received not special training. Implications were that such training is effective with potentially any parents.

2. Condon & Sander (1974): Infants 2 days old displayed behavior indicating a tendency to synchronize movements to human speech but not to other sounds, which suggested that responsiveness to human language may be innate.

3. Wolff (1969): Relatively inexperienced mothers responded faster to pain cries than to hunger or anger cries from their infants, indicating that infant crying conveys different meanings at a very early age.

4. Ainsworth, Bell, & Stayton (1972): Over the first year of life, babies cried less if their mothers had a pattern of responding quickly to their cries, counteracting notions that parent responsiveness to crying creates "spoiled" babies.

5. Birns, Blank, & Bridger (1966): Hungry 2-3-day-old infants were made even more irritable, and it was found that soothing techniques were effective with some infants but not with others. The implications were that differences in temperament may be innate.

6. Staffieri (1967): Children 6-10 years old selected pictures, selected adjectives to describe the pictures, and designated popular versus unpopular classmates in each case in accord with an apparent preference for the mesomorphic body type, indicating the possible effects of physique upon social and personality development.

7. Jones & Bayley (1950), Jones (1957, 1965): As compared to early maturing boys, late maturers were found to be less socially skilled and less popular as well as more anxious and more confident, and the differences persisted into adulthood. Timing of maturation was thus indicated as a factor in personality development.

8. Gardner (1972): Where parents were emotionally unresponsive, children showed lags in physical growth and development in spite of adequate physical care, which indicated the

role of childrearing upon motor development and led to a beginning understanding of deprivation dwarfism.

9. Dennis (1960): Orphan children in institutional environments that did not allow practice of motor skills showed severe lags in motor development, emphasizing the importance of practice and lending support to the practice hypothesis.

Self-Test II

1. d	6. b	11. a	16. c	21. c
2. c	7. c	12. c	17. a	22. c
3. d	8. b	13. a	18. a	23. c
4. a	9. b	14. c	19. d	24. b
5. c	10. c	15. b	20. c	25. b

Vignettes

I. (1) Brazelton training might give the parents a wider variety of techniques to use in soothing Sandra and eliciting positive behaviors such as smiling, cooing, and so on. Any successes along these lines would help her parents in turn be more patient, thus aiding in the establishment of a good emotional relationship. (2) Without success in getting positive reactions from Sandra, the parents might come to view her as an "impossible" child. However, depending upon their patience, they might continue to try indefinitely and thus make progress sooner or later. Failure-to-thrive syndrome is more likely with a difficult child, but occurs only as a result of severe emotional deprivation. (3) As before, the quality of the parents' responses as well as the degree to which they might become unresponsive or emotionally cold toward Sandra is the issue; there is no guarantee that their behavior will reach this extreme, although the risk is somewhat increased.

II. (1) Overeating could be either a cause or a result, and it might or might not be related to George's problem in the first place. He could have learned overeating from his parents. Or he could be compensating for other things missing in his life. Or he may have inherited a tendency to be overweight. (2) George would be an endomorph, typically the least popular among schoolchildren. (3) One likely self-fulfilling prophecy is that he views himself as hopelessly fat and thus doesn't regulate his diet, which keeps him fat. Another is that he avoids exercise because he is fat, which prevents him from burning off the calories he consumes. Yet another is that teachers and classmates discourage him from athletics, which helps keep him fat. And so on. Also note George's incentive to remain fat and maintain his "popularity."

III. (1) Deborah would be about 10 years old in the fourth grade. Using menarche as the reference, she typically would have displayed breast buds and other signs of the onset of puberty about 2 years earlier, about age 8, and she would have begun the adolescent growth spurt just prior to that, about age 7½. She would currently be peaking in growth rate. (2) Research indicates that genetic factors in timing of maturation do occur, and the early maturation noted for Deborah's mother is consistent with this view. (3) As discussed in the textbook, research has sometimes found that early maturing females are less popular with schoolmates, although such effects are perhaps less likely nowadays. Later, Deborah's status would change markedly and she would have something of an edge over her female classmates.

Applications

I. (1) Mesomorphs would predictably score the highest, especially since research indicates that such differences can persist into adulthood in the context of early versus late maturing. Thus physique preferences might persist as well, although self-fulfilling prophecies might be involved. (2) You might well color your preferences a bit in accord

79

with your own body type, but this could go various directions. If you like your basic physique, you might favor others who are similar. On the other hand, if your wishbook includes some physical changes you would prefer to make in yourself, you might favor people who look like what you wish you look like. (3) A college population might contain a different mix of body types than the general population. Although self-fulfilling prophecies might ensure a good representation of mesomorphs at college, it is also possible that either the ectomorphs or the endomorphs who, as children, spent more time in intellectual pursuits might gain a share of the popularity in college. Your rankings might be quite different from those of grade-school children.

II. In addition to basic nutrition and health care, your list should include items involving good emotional attachment and ample practice with motor behavior. Practice includes allowing the child access to situations and toys which foster development of the more complex motor skills in particular. (1) During the first year, getting the child out of the crib would be especially important. Note the effects of early practice with the stepping reflex, and also the importance of placing the child in upright positions (often, but within reason). Incentives that might elicit head-lifting, moving around when in the crib, and directed reaching would also help. (2) Walking brings with it the opportunity for practice with a greater array of interesting objects (and greater dangers, too). Objects that can be assembled and disassembled might be helpful. And, in accord with the child's abilities at a given age, games that involve running, hopping, skipping, and jumping would help. Within limits, climbing would also be desirable. (3) Throughout, your responsiveness to the child's attempts to develop motor skills is a key factor, both in terms of development of musculature and basic physical growth (note the discussion of deprivation dwarfism).

III. Hunger implies feeding. Anger implies altering the situation that produced the anger, if this is reasonable, and also use of methods such as rocking, humming to the child, and simply picking the child up. Pain implies removing the source of the irritant. And fake cries imply attending to the infant and otherwise being responsive to emotional needs. The key is to learn to discriminate your infant's cries accurately and then respond accordingly. As noted, a pacifier doesn't help a hungry infant. Similarly, rocking an infant who has diaper rash will probably not be effective. (1) Ainsworth, Bell, and Stayton's (1972) research suggests that responsiveness in general fosters security and sets the stage of learning of other modes of communication, in each case reducing crying. So, where reasonable, you respond. (2) Birns, Blank, and Bridger's (1966) research indicates that some babies will cry sometimes no matter what you do. A particular technique might also be effective with some children but not with others, although some, such as rocking and humming to the infant, usually work well. (3) Aside from disrupting your life and frustrating you, an irritable infant can start you wondering about your worth as a parent, in turn setting the stage for less responsiveness to the child. Extreme unresponsiveness can have detrimental effects on many aspects of the child's development, as discussed throughout the chapter.

CHAPTER SIX

PERCEPTUAL DEVELOPMENT

OVERVIEW AND KEY TERMS

Read carefully. Recall examples and discussion as you go, and define each key term.

Sensation is the detection and transmission of information from receptors to the brain. Perception is the interpretation of sensory information.

THE NATIVIST/EMPIRICIST CONTROVERSY

Empiricists such as Locke and James believed that infants are born without abilities involved in discriminating between sensations and forming perceptions. Nativists such as Descartes and Kant believed that many perceptual abilities, including spatial perception, are innate. Current research favors the nativists, although infant perceptions are immature. Thus maturation and experience are also important.

VISUAL PERCEPTION IN INFANCY

Research by Fantz and colleagues using looking chambers has assessed infant visual abilities and preferences. Neonates can discriminate visual forms at birth, and they prefer stimuli with patterns. The also look more at human faces than at other stimuli, but this seems due to certain physical characteristics of faces rather than the fact of faces being "human." Infants from 4 days to 6 months of age have been found to prefer "face-like" and "scrambled face" stimuli bout equally, but they prefer both more than an unpatterned stimulus. One reason is contour: Infants search for and attend to targets with light/dark transitions. Another reason is visual complexity, and this preference increases over the first 2 months of life. A third reason is curvature, with this preference also appearing at about 2 months. Other clues to infant visual preferences are that infants younger than 2 months scan mainly the edges and contours of stimuli, whereas infants 2 months and older look more at internal features. And research using the Kanizsa stimulus indicates that infants do perceive form, as assessed by habituation techniques. The overall picture is that the infant's central nervous system is maturing rapidly over the first 2 months of life, enabling better visual acuity, and at the same time the infant is beginning to form perceptual schemata for familiar objects, which include curvilinear stimuli such as faces and mother's breast. Thus the contour and complexity of faces first capture the infant's attention, then the moving parts such as lips and eyes are more important, and by about 2 months of age the infant is interested in what the faces "mean." By 3 months of age infants can recognize their mothers' faces even from a photograph, and they can discriminate between different strangers. And over the first 6 months infants require less and less exposure time to discriminate faces and to remember them.

Spatial perception in neonates is limited by poor visual acuity and a lack of stereopsis, but monocular cues such as perspective, the density gradient, and interposition might still make spatial perception possible. The visual cliff apparatus is used to test infant depth perception, and infants younger than about 6½ months of age will not cross the deep side to reach their mothers. In addition, infants as young as 2 months old have been found to show changes in heart rate when placed directly on the deep side, suggesting depth perception. Other points are that 6-12-week-old infants have been found to display size constancy and that infants 6-20 days old can detect visual looming. But, regardless of the extent to which spatial perception is present at birth, it improves dramatically over the first year of life.

AUDITORY PERCEPTION IN INFANCY

Early auditory perception is indicated by neonates turning their heads toward sounds. As early as 3 days of age, infants may be able to recognize their mothers' voices. Neonates also respond specifically to language sounds and can tell the difference between vowels such as /a/ and /i/ at 2 days of age. And neonates 1 day old prefer music over random noise, indicating that this might even be a species-specific trait.

INTERSENSORY PERCEPTION

Cross-modal perception involves using one sensory modality to identify a stimulus familiar through another modality, as in the example of identifying a golf ball. Differentiation theorists such as Bower and Gibson believe that the sense are integrated at birth and gradually differentiate through learning. Thus cross-modal perception would be innate. Enrichment theorists such as Piaget believe that the senses are separate at birth, and thus cross-modal perception would be learned.

Studies of intersensory interaction favor differentiation theory. Infants seem to combine the effects of light and white noise as if only one sensory experience were involved. Some studies of intersensory incongruity also favor differentiation theory. Researchers have found that infants become frustrated when they reach for a virtual object and that infants are upset by visual-auditory discrepance involving their mothers' voices. Both findings favor sensory integration at birth. Studies of cross-modal perception have yielded mixed results, although the improvement of cross-modal perception over time favors enrichment theory. The balance of evidence favors differentiation theory, however: Infants gradually become more selective in attending and responding over the first year, as if senses were becoming more independent. The very gradual improvement of certain forms of cross-modal perception, as from vision to the kinesthetic sense, may be due to the senses not maturing at the same rate.

The dominance of vision over other senses develops gradually over the course of childhood. Children are less mislead than adults by conflicting visual cues. Vision also comes to dominate tactile sensation and other modalities, but not proprioception. In addition, the dimension of perceptual style known as field dependence/independence affects how well children deal with conflicting visual cues.

PERCEPTUAL LEARNING AND DEVELOPMENT IN CHILDHOOD

Attention involves tuning out distracting stimuli and concentrating long enough to detect or identify an object in question. Although 2-3-month-old infants will scan the internal features of an object, they are not as systematic as older children. Organized, exhaustive, and efficient scanning develops gradually over the first 6-7 years of life. Neonates are capable of selective attention, but it improves markedly with age. Attention span is very short during infancy and improves gradually throughout childhood and adolescence, perhaps due in part to myelinization of the reticular formation.

Form perception displays a developmental sequence. At 2-4 months of age, infants shift from being captivated by contour and complexity to paying more attention to moderate discrepancies in schemata. For example, a 4-month-old will prefer an unfamiliar face (moderately discrepant stimulus) to a scrambled face (highly discrepant stimulus). This representational stage continues through the first year, but then infants begin attending more to highly discrepant schemata. And a 2-year-old will prefer the scrambled face, as if trying to figure out why it is different. Another line of research indicates that older children are better at unmasking visual forms, as in the embedded figures test and in tests where the child must identify incomplete figures. Younger children also attend to object more as wholes, and do not pay close attention to an objects' parts.

Gibson's differentiation theory holds that perceptual learning is based primarily on discovering the distinctive features of objects, features that distinguish one type of object from another similar one. In learning to read, as discussed in Box 6-3, Gibson says children pass through three phases: (1) a story-telling phase, where content is not related to printed words, (2) a matching phase, where spoken words are roughly matched to symbols, and (3) a sound and letter recognition phase. Both the "whole-word" method and the "phonics" method of teaching children to read are effective, and many reading programs combine elements of each approach.

ENVIRONMENTAL INFLUENCES ON PERCEPTION

Neonates are capable of various types of perception, but learning and experience are important to the development of all perceptual skills. Development of the visual system requires visual stimulation. Research on chimpanzees reared in complete darkness indicates atrophy of the optic nerve, and chimpanzees reared in darkness except for brief daily exposure to unpatterned stimuli do not develop normal visual discrimination. These results are similar to effects of human cataracts. Research on kittens indicates that the visual cortex contains cells for vertical, horizontal, and oblique orientations of stimuli: Kittens reared with goggles that block specific orientations display abnormal development in the visual cortex. People who have visual astigmatisms may experience similarly altered development of visual-cortical cells. But impairments such as having only one functional eye can apparently be compensated for, since monocular individuals can use perspective cues for depth perception.

Experiencing movement is apparently necessary for development of visual perception, in accord with the movement hypothesis. Research on kittens found that those who only rode in a cart-like apparatus did not display depth perception, but later research indicated that "movement" need not be self-produced. The subject can remain stationary while the stimulus field moves and depth perception can develop normally.

Social and cultural experiences also influence development of perception. People in societies containing rectangular buildings and home furnishings detect horizontal and vertical shapes better than oblique ones, which is called the oblique effect. The carpentered environment hypothesis explains this in terms of visual experiences. But research across cultures is confounded with ancestry, since Oriental people typically show little or no oblique effect regardless of the environment in which they are reared.

Our expectations and perceptual sets in conjunction with our experiences determine what we see, as discussed in Box 6-4. Prior experience determines how we interpret two-dimensional pictures and drawings, in part because of what whe have learned to expect them to represent. Social values also influence perception, as in research in which words presented by tachistoscope were recognized better when they were in accord with the religious, political, social, and economic values of the subjects. And children from poorer homes tend to overestimate the size of coins, indicating that they attach greater value to money.

If the home environment includes domineering, demanding parents who insist on rigid adherence to rules, the child may be highly field dependent and more likely to be influenced by distracting stimuli in perceptual tasks. If parents are less restrictive and more willing to allow individual initiative, the child may be more field independent and less prone to perceptual distractions. Research using tasks such as the tilted room and the embedded figures support this theory, as do observations that farming and pastoral societies tend to produce people who are more field dependent as a probable result of the emphasis on cooperation.

Fill in the blanks for each item.   Check the answers for each item as you go.

1. The process by which information is detected and then transmitted to the brain is called _____; the brain's interpretation of this information is called _____.

sensation
perception

THE NATIVIST/EMPIRICIST CONTROVERSY

2. James' argument that the infant perceives the world as a blooming, buzzing confusion implies that the senses are innately _____, and that discrimination among sensory modalities is _____.

integrated
learned

3. The nativist argument of Descartes and later Kant is that perceptual discrimination is _____ and based on structural characteristics of the human nervous system.

inborn or innate

VISUAL PERCEPTION IN INFANCY

Pattern Perception

4. Infant visual discrimination and preferences have been assessed by the use of _____ chambers, as in the finding by Fantz that infants less than 2 days old discriminated and preferred _____ stimuli such as drawings of faces and bull's-eyes.

looking

patterned

5. Other research by Fantz and colleagues indicated infant preference for human _____, but not necessarily due to "human" qualities; instead, infants (1) react to light/dark transition, called _____, (2) react to the number of elements in the stimulus, called _____, and (3) by about 2 months of age prefer _____ such as that present in human faces.

faces

contour
complexity
curvature

6. Infant pattern preferences and visual scanning patterns begin to change at about ___ months of age, as the central _____ system matures and visual _____ improves; infants are also acquiring meanings for perceptual stimuli, i.e., forming perceptual _____.

2, nervous
acuity

schemata

Perception of Faces

7. By 3 months of age, infants still require time to make accurate discriminations between strangers' _____ and remember them; by 5-6 months, infants can discriminate the faces of strangers much more _____, and even with brief exposure are unlikely to _____ a face.

faces

quickly
forget

Spatial Perception

8. Prior to about 3½ months of age an infant's eyes do not converge, which means the infant does not exhibit _____; but depth perception is still possible through the use of perspective, interposition, and other _____ cues.

stereopsis

monocular

9. Infant depth perception can be assessed through use of Gibson and Walk's _____ _____ apparatus: Infants older than about ____ months typically will not cross the deep side, and younger infants who cannot crawl show changes that indicate the presence of _____ perception.

visual cliff
6½

depth

AUDITORY PERCEPTION IN INFANCY

Voice Recognition

10. Infants 1-3 days old can selectively change their rate of
sucking on a special _____ to produce recordings of   pacifier
their mothers' voices, indicating voice recognition.

Reactions to Speech and Language

11. From the second day of life, infants can discriminate /a/
versus /i/ _____ sounds, indicating that certain language   vowel
skills are _____ .   innate or inborn

The Sound of Music

12. Infants as young as 1 day old will change their rate of
_____ on a special pacifier to produce _____ instead   sucking, music
of nonrhymthic noise, indicating perhaps an inborn preference
for music.

INTERSENSORY PERCEPTION

13. Using one sensory modality to identify a stimulus familiar
primarily through a different modality is called _____-modal   cross-
perception.

Theories of Intersensory Integration

14. Bower and Gibson, in their belief that the senses are integrated at birth, are called _____ theorists;   differentiation
Piaget, in contrast, is characterized as an _____   enrichment
theorist because of his emphasis on senses being separate at
birth and integrated later.

Research on Intersensory Perception

15. Research in which neonates tend to "add" the effects of
light and noise favors _____ theory; research   differentiation
using illusory _____ objects favors differentiation theory,   virtual
because the neonates' expectations to feel what they see implies that the senses are _____ at birth, but these re-   integrated
sults are not always obtained; and research on cross-modal perception indicates that this ability may not appear until 4-6
months of age, which indirectly favors _____ theory.   enrichment

Another Look at the Enrichment/Differentiation Controversy

16. Differentiation theorists reconcile the conflicting evidence
by noting that the senses develop independently of each other
as they begin to _____ after birth, which means   differentiate
that (1) any and all _____ modalities improve, and (2)   sensory
accuracy, as in cross-modal perception, is limited by the
child's capabilities in the _____ developing modality.   slower

Sensory Dominance

17. In adults, _____ dominates most other sensory modalities, vision
the main exception being _____ with regard to   proprioception
cues for body position; children, however, are less dominated by
visual cues.

PERCEPTUAL LEARNING AND DEVELOPMENT IN CHILDHOOD

Development of Attention

18. Research indicates that even by 5 years of age children's

visual _____ is not very systematic, and perceptual judgments are often inaccurate; similarly, the ability to ignore distractions and employ _____ attention improves throughout childhood.

scanning

selective

19. Younger children also have much shorter attention _____, and improvement continues into early adolescence along with increasing myelinization of the _____ formation.

spans

reticular

Development of Form Perception

20. A 4-month-old child is likely to be interested in stimuli that are _____ discrepant for existing schemata, whereas a 1-2-year-old is more likely to prefer stimuli that are _____ discrepant.

moderately

highly

21. The ability to find hidden, _____ figures in drawings develops throughout childhood and into adolescence, as does the ability to recognize _____ stimuli with some of the lines missing; and older children are more likely to attend to the _____ rather than the "parts" of a stimulus.

embedded

incomplete

whole

22. Gibson's differentiation theory holds that perceptual learning is based on discovering the _____ features that identify objects, an example being that learning to read involves attending to the distinctive features of letters prior to learning their _____.

distinctive

sounds

ENVIRONMENTAL INFLUENCES ON PERCEPTION

What Kinds of Experiences Are Important?

23. Chimpanzees reared in total darkness exhibit _____ of the optic nerve that is irreversible; even with some exposure to unpatterned light, the chimpanzees still cannot discriminate _____ from squares.

atrophy

circles

24. Studies of kittens with vision-restricting goggles show abnormal development of the visual _____, and people who have visual _____ have comparable difficulties in perceiving lines in certain orientations.

cortex
astigmatisms

25. Studies of kittens also indicate that visual perceptual development requires _____ with regard to the stimulus field, although this movement need not be _____-produced by the organism.

movement
self-

Social and Cultural Influences

26. Cultural effects on perceptual development are suggested by the finding that Indians who lived in tepees could identify _____ stimuli better that peoples who live in rectangular structures, but this finding might also reflect heredity and is not necessarily attributable to the _____ environment hypothesis.

oblique

carpentered

27. Research findings in which people perceive "important" words better than "unimportant" words indicate that perception also depends upon _____ values; similarly, children from low-income homes tend to _____ the size of coins more than middle-class children do.

social or cultural
overestimate

28. People who are less distracted in their perceptions by contextual or background factors are said to be relatively field _____, and such people tend to come from homes in

independent

which parents were less restrictive and less _____-oriented; people who are likely to be distracted by irrelevant information are said to be field _____, and their parents tend to have been highly _____ and rule-oriented.

rule-

dependent

restrictive

29. Cross-cultural studies indicate that farming and pastoral societies, in their emphasis on obedience and _____, tend to produce field _____ people; in contrast, hunter-gatherer societies stress independence and _____-reliance and tend to produce field _____ people

cooperation
dependent
self-
independent

WHAT IS PERCEPTUAL DEVELOPMENT?

30. Although research on perception tends to emphasize differing aspects such as heredity, maturation, or various environmental _____, perception is actually a part of the overall _____ process of development.

experiences
holistic

SELF-TEST I

Consider each alternative carefully. Then choose the best one.

1. The basic process by which we interpret sensory input is
    a. sensation
    b. perception
    c. integration
    d. differentiation

2. Research by Fantz and colleagues on neonatal perception in looking chambers indicates
    a. that infants prefer to look at human faces because the faces are human
    b. that infants prefer to look at human faces because the faces are patterned
    c. both of the above
    d. none of the above

3. By about 2 months of age, infants prefer to look at stimuli which have
    a. contour
    b. complexity
    c. curvature
    d. all of the above

4. Which of the following involves perceptually "constructing" a triangle from an incomplete stimulus array?
    a. the Kanizsa stimulus
    b. the virtual objects
    c. the embedded figure
    d. the visual cliff

5. Generally, it appears that infants begin developing schemata for human faces
    a. within a few days of birth
    b. at about 1 month of age
    c. at about 2-3 months of age
    d. at about 5-6 months of age

6. Depth perception is apparently very poor or nonexistent in
    a. 1-month-old infants
    b. monocular infants
    c. illiterate adult laborers
    d. all of the above

7. Apparently, 1-2-month-old infants
   a. are capable of size constancy
   b. can detect visual looming
   c. respond to visual/auditory incongruities
   d. all of the above

8. Generally, within the first few days of life, neonates
   a. can recognize the sound of their own mothers' voices
   b. can distinguish between the vowels /a/ and /i/
   c. prefer music to nonrhythmic noise
   d. all of the above

9. Which of the following favors enrichment theory?
   a. studies of intersensory interaction
   b. studies of intersensory incongruity
   c. studies of cross-modal perception
   d. all of the above

10. Which of the following apparently does not improve or increase throughout childhood?
    a. selective attention
    b. attention span
    c. dominance of vision over audition
    d. dominance of vision over proprioception

11. As child get older, they perform better
    a. on embedded figures tasks
    b. in recognizing incomplete figures
    c. in attending to parts as well as the whole
    d. all of the above

12. The most important ability in learning to read is
    a. attending to distinctive features of letters
    b. forming perceptual schemata for objects
    c. stereopsis
    d. cross-modal perception

13. Children from lower-income homes tend to
    a. show the oblique effect
    b. perceive in ways that contradict enrichment theory
    c. overestimate the size of coins more than middle-class children do
    d. be unable to perceive depth in photographs

14. A field-independent person is more capable of
    a. overcoming conflicting visual cues
    b. finding objects embedded in a distracting visual field
    c. tolerating ambiguous situations
    d. all of the above

15. Child development is
    a. an enrichment process
    b. a genetic process
    c. a perceptual process
    d. a holistic process

RESEARCH SUMMARY AND REVIEW

Using the textbook, review the research efforts indicated and write a summary of the important findings. Note the general purpose or context of the research.

1. Fantz (1961), page 205: _____

_____
_____
_____
_____
_____

2. Fantz & Fagan (1975), page 206: _____
_____
_____
_____
_____

3. Fantz, Fagan, & Miranda (1975), page 206: ____
_____
_____
_____
_____

4. Maurer & Salapatek (1976), page 208: _____
_____
_____
_____
_____

5. Treiber & Wilcox (1980), page 209: _____
_____
_____
_____
_____

6. Campos, Langer, & Krowitz (1970), page 211: ____
_____
_____
_____
_____

7. Bower (1966), page 211: _____
_____
_____
_____
_____

8. DeCasper & Fifer (1980), page 214: _____
_____

_____

_____

_____

9. Aronson & Rosenbloom (1971), page 218: _____

_____

_____

_____

_____

10. Maccoby (1967), page 223: _____

_____

_____

_____

_____

11. Gibson, Gibson, Pick, & Osser (1962), page 227: ___

_____

_____

_____

_____

12. Held & Hein (1963), page 231: _____

_____

_____

_____

_____

13. Walk (1981), page 232: _____

_____

_____

_____

_____

SELF-TEST II

Consider each alternative carefully. Then choose the best one.

1. The basic process by which information is detected and transmitted to the brain is
   a. sensation
   b. perception
   c. integration
   d. differentiation

2. According to the nativist position on perception, such as that of Descartes and Kant,
   a. infants are tabulae rasae
   b. infants experience a blooming, buzzing confusion
   c. discrimination of sensory input is virtually entirely learned
   d. many perceptual abilities such as spatial perception are innate

3. Research efforts by Fantz and colleagues on infants in looking chambers indicate that, over the first 2 months of life,
   a. infants increasingly prefer patterned to unpatterned stimuli
   b. infants attend to progressively more complex stimuli
   c. infants gradually develop preference for curvature in stimuli
   d. all of the above

4. Maurer and Salapatek's (1975) research on visual scanning of human faces by 1-month-old versus 2-month-old infants indicated that
   a. younger infants attend more to contours, older infants more to internal features
   b. younger infants attend more to internal features, older infants more to contours
   c. younger and older infants alike attend more to contours than to internal features
   d. younger and older infants alike attend more to internal features than to contours

5. Changes in pattern perception over the first 2 months of life are probably due to
   a. maturation of the central nervous system
   b. early visual learning experiences
   c. both of the above
   d. none of the above

6. Kagan's research on perceptual schemata indicates that by 2 months of age infants
   a. prefer stimuli which are highly similar to existing schemata
   b. prefer stimuli which are moderately discrepant from existing schemata
   c. prefer stimuli which are highly discrepant from existing schemata
   d. have no particular preference in terms of similarity or discrepancy

7. In Treiber and Wilcox's (1980) study of infant form perception, accurate perception of the Kanizsa stimulus was indicated because the infants
   a. displayed no habituation to triangles
   b. displayed irritation in response to triangles
   c. apparently were habituated to triangles
   d. preferred triangles to human faces

8. The extent of infant spatial perceptual ability is evidenced by the research of
   a. Campos, et al. (1970) on infants placed on the deep side of the visual cliff
   b. Bower (1966) on size constancy with cubes placed at compensated distances
   c. Bower, et al. (1970b) on infant responses to visual looming
   d. all of the above

9. DeCasper and Fifer (1980) allowed infants to select either their mothers' voices or that of a female stranger by sucking on a special pacifier; recognition of mothers' voices was indicated by the infants
   a. increasing their rate of sucking to produce mothers' voices
   b. decreasing their rate of sucking to produce mothers' voices
   c. both of above
   d. none of the above

10. Research on infant responsiveness to music indicates that
    a. babies are not inherently musical, and music appreciation is learned
    b. babies generally prefer nonrhythmical noise to rhythmical music
    c. music appreciation may be a species-specific trait with humans
    d. music appreciation does not appear until college music appreciation coursework

11. Differentiation theory, such as that of Bower or Gibson, takes the view that
    a. the senses are integrated at birth
    b. the senses are separate and independent at birth
    c. intersensory interaction is not present at birth
    d. none of the above

12. Research such as that of Aronson and Rosembloom (1971) on intersensory incongruity often indicates that infants are upset by visual-auditory discrepancy; this favors
    a. enrichment theory
    b. differentiation theory
    c. both of the above
    d. none of the above

13. Persons proficient at using proprioceptive cues in Wilkin's tilted chair are
    a. cross-modally incongruent
    b. differentiated
    c. field dependent
    d. field independent

14. Research indicates that visual scanning, over the first 6-7 years of life, becomes
    a. more exhaustive
    b. more systematic
    c. more detailed
    d. all of the above

15. Maccoby's (1967) research on selective attention by children from kindergarten through the sixth grade while listening to two simultaneous voices indicate that
    a. selective attention improves over this age range
    b. at all ages children do better if they know in advance what to attend to
    c. both of the above
    d. none of the above

16. Myelinization of the reticular formation is apparently completed during
    a. early childhood
    b. middle childhood
    c. early adolescence
    d. early adulthood

17. Kagan's research on perceptual schemata indicates that by 2 years of age children
    a. prefer stimuli which are highly similar to existing schemata
    b. prefer stimuli which are moderately discrepant from existing schemata
    c. prefer stimuli which are highly discrepant from existing schemata
    d. have no particular preference in terms of similarity or discrepancy

18. Research on abilities involved in unmasking visual forms indicates that improvement occurs throughout childhood on
    a. embedded figures tests
    b. recognition of incomplete figures
    c. identifying parts as well as whole
    d. all of the above

19. Gibson's differentiation theory emphasizes the ability to attend to distinctive features of stimuli; based on the research by Gibson, et al. (1962), this ability is present
    a. by the end of the first 3 years of life
    b. at about the age children normally enter grade school
    c. at about the age children reach the fourth grade
    d. relatively late, at about the age children enter puberty

20. In the phonics method of teaching reading, children first learn to attend to
    a. whole words and their complete pronunciation
    b. pronunciation of separate syllables within words
    c. the sounds of individual letters within words
    d. none of the above

21. In Held and Hein's (1963) research, kittens either pulled a small cart through a visual field or passively rode; the results implied that
    a. self-produced movement is necessary for normal visual perceptual development
    b. the stimulus field must move for normal visual perceptual development
    c. either of the above
    d. none of the above

22. Walk's (1981) research on visual perception in kittens indicated that
    a. self-produced movement is necessary for normal visual perceptual development
    b. the stimulus field must move for normal visual perceptual development
    c. either of the above
    d. none of the above

24. Social and cultural effects on perceptual development are indicated by
    a. Annis and Frost's research on the carpentered environment hypothesis
    b. Hudson's research on three-dimensional perception by South Africans
    c. Bruner and Goodman's research on perception of coins by lower-income children
    d. all of the above

25. Field independent persons
    a. tend to come from less restrictive and less rule-oriented homes
    b. exist in greater numbers in hunter-gatherer societies
    c. traditionally are more likely to be male than female
    d. all of the above

VIGNETTES

Consider the story, then answer each question using material from the textbook.

I. At about age 2 years, Mike developed an enjoyment of being spun around and around in a swivel chair the family had in their den. He would often try to persuade his father or his mother to sit in the chair with him and spin again and again, to the point that his parent would become dizzy and more than a little nauseous. Yet Mike would plead for more and he never showed signs of anything except rapt enjoyment and amusement.

1. How is Mike's behavior consistent with the discussion of development of the kinesthetic sense?

2. Comment on the possible parallels between Mike's lack of unpleasant side effects and the discussion of verbal versus proprioceptive dominance.

3. At about what age would you expect Mike to start losing his nausea-free enjoyment of being spun around?

II. Marianne was born with a cataract that caused considerable clouding of the vision in the affected eye, although it did not altogether restrict the passage of light. Sadly, the cataract was not removed until Marianne was about 2½ years old. But at that point preliminary tests indicated a successful operation and good restoration of visual acuity.

1. If Marianne had been placed on the "shallow" side of visual cliff apparatus at about age 7-8 months, would she likely have crossed the "deep" side to her mother? Why or why not?

2. Drawing from Riesen's research on light-restricted chimpanzees, what effects on Marianne's future visual perception might the cataract have had?

3. Would these effects likely be temporary or permanent? Why?

III. Landana was a South American Indian girl whose people lived in the tropical rain forest and rarely ventured beyond the thick, dense foliage of the jungle. They were more or less isolated from the outside world, at least while Landana was young, and she did not see her first television or magazine photographs until her family took her along on a rare visit to the city when she was about 14 years old. And in the city that day, Landana felt quite thoroughly out of place, at least at first.

1. Given that Landana's people lived in wood and grass structures that were not rectangular in shape, would you predict that she would not display an oblique effect? Would this be genetic or environmental?

2. What effects on three-dimensional perception might you predict in Landana's case?

3. What characteristics of Landana's society would you assess in making a prediction about field dependence/independence?

APPLICATIONS

Try each of the projects, noting answers to the questions as you go.

I. Within a goal of knowing what to expect from a neonate the next time you encounter one, compile a list of visual and auditory perceptual abilities (and inabilities) that characterize children during the first few days of life.

1. How does neonate vision compare to audition? How might your interactions with a neonate be affected?

2. What types of sounds would you expect a neonate to prefer and attend to?

3. Speculate on what types of sounds infants might find soothing, versus stimulating or irritating.

II. As in *Application I*, compile a list of changes in perceptual abilities that have occurred by about 2 months of age.

1. How does vision compare to audition at this point?

2. What types of visual stimuli might the 2-month-old prefer and attend to?

3. Summarize the "cognitive" effects of these changes regarding perceptual schemata.

III. Toys for infants come in a dazzling array of designs, shapes, colors, and so on. From the perspective of giving your potential infant the kinds of toys that might aid perceptual development, consider the following:

1. Would a 1-month-old prefer toys that have contrasting shapes and colors, or toys that make interesting sounds? Why?

2. What characteristics of stuffed toy animals and human dolls might appeal to an infant during the first few months of life?

3. At about what age might an infant begin to benefit from puzzles and toys that contain objects of different shapes? What can you determine about the relative complexity of the shapes with regard to infant abilities in perception?

ANSWERS

Self-Test I

1. b   6. a   11. d
2. b   7. d   12. a
3. d   8. d   13. c
4. a   9. c   14. d
5. c   10. d   15. d

Research Summary and Review

1. Fantz (1961): Neonates were placed in a looking chamber, and it was found that they attended more to patterned than to unpatterned stimuli, although they did not show a preference for "face-like" versus "scrambled face" stimuli. Implications were that the preference for looking at faces depends upon various perceptual features.

2. Fantz & Fagan (1975): In assessing basic perceptual determinants of infant visual preferences, it was found that infants in a looking chamber preferred simpler stimuli at age 1 month but more complex stimuli at age 2 months and older.

3. Fantz, Fagan, & Miranda (1975): Further assessment of infant visual preferences indicated that the preference for curvature in stimuli does not appear until about age 2 months, providing further evidence that the preference for human faces as such is not inborn.

4. Maurer & Salapatek (1976): In assessing what infants attend to, it was found that 1-month-olds scan mainly the contours and boundaries of human faces, whereas 2-month-olds scan internal features more, also indicating that preference for looking at human faces as such is not inborn.

5. Treiber & Wilcox (1980): In assessing infant perceptual capabilities, it was found that as early as 1 month of age infants can perceive form in the Kanizsa stimuli, as indicated by the habituation technique.

6. Campos, Langer, & Krowitz (1970): Infants as young as 2 months of age detected cues for depth when placed on the deep side of the visual cliff, as measured by changes in heart rate, which indicated early infant spatial perceptual ability.

7. Bower (1966): In determining infant capabilities regarding size constancy, it was found that 6-12-week-olds could discriminate different-sized cubes even though the cubes were placed at distances which compensated to produce the same-sized retinal image.

8. DeCasper & Fifer (1980): As a test of neonates' ability to recognize their mothers' voices, it was found that 3-day-olds could learn to change their rate of sucking on a special pacifier to produce mothers' voices instead of that of a female stranger.

9. Aronson & Rosenbloom (1971): Infants 1-2 months old became disturbed when their mothers' voices were projected from a location other than where mothers were sitting, indicating early integration of sensory modalities and favoring differentiation theory.

10. Maccoby (1967): Selective attention in a situation where two voices were presented simultaneously was found to improve from kindergarten through the sixth grade, and all children performed better when told in advance which speaker to listen to; the basic purpose of the research was to assess age-related changes in selective attention.

11. Gibson, et al. (1962): In assessing age-related changes in perceptual abilities related to learning to read, it was found that 6-8-year-olds could detect distinctive features in transformed letter-like stimuli better than 4-5-year-olds.

12. Held & Hein (1963): It was concluded that self-produced movement is necessary to

normal development of visual perception in kittens, because those kittens who were passively transported through a visual field did not display visual perception comparable to that of kittens who were permitted to move.

13. Walk (1981): In contrast to Held and Hein (1963), in was found that kittens did display comparable visual perception even when not permitted to move, given that the stimulus was interesting enough to maintain the kittens' attention.

Self-Test II

1. a	6. b	11. a	16. c	21. a
2. d	7. c	12. b	17. c	22. a
3. d	8. d	13. d	18. d	23. c
4. a	9. c	14. d	19. b	24. d
5. c	10. c	15. c	20. c	25. d

Vignettes

I. (1) Since cross-modal judgments from vision to the kinesthetic sense develop slowly and are not very accurate until 10-11 years of age, it is also probable that the transfer of information to other bodily systems is not as efficient in young children. Similarly, the kinesthetic sense is not fully developed and young children may be able to tolerate more stimulation of this sort. As an adult, being "rocked" like an infant might well make you sick also. (2) Older children, and adults, depend more on proprioceptive cues. It is likely that the spinning chair is dizzying to Mike's father and mother for this reason as well. (3) By implication, around 10-11 years of age Mike's kinesthetic sense should start producing more "adult" effects. Also note that in the age range 8-17 children are paying more and more attention to proprioceptive cues when such information is inconsistent with their visual input.

II. (1) Other things equal, Marianne would probably have avoided the deep side on the basis of monocular cues for depth perception, such as linear perspective and density gradients. (3) Overall, we would predict few if any effects on Marianne's visual perceptual skills. She would have had the necessary information and practice through her good eye. And the cataract as described would probably have allowed sufficient light penetration to prevent atrophy of the optic nerve.

III. (1) The relative absence of rectangular structures might well rule out the oblique effect for Landana, although her presumed Oriental ancestry might also explain this result. Chinese peoples who live in cities do not show the oblique effect. (2) Research by Hudson (1960, 1962) indicates that she would either not perceive depth in photos or on TV or at least would not expect to perceive depth in such stimuli, although her perception of depth and distance relationships in the natural environment should not be impaired. (3) If Landana's people are agricultural, you would predict field dependent, also noting emphases on obedience, cooperation, and placing of group needs above those of the individual. If her people are hunter/gatherers, you would predict field independent on the basis of probable emphases on assertiveness, self-reliance, and independence.

Applications

I. Neonates generally hear much better than they see. For vision in the first few days of life, note scanning of the "bolder" boundaries and contours of faces, preference for "simpler" stimuli, minimal perceptual schemata, relatively poorly developed spatial perception (except for gross stimuli, as in visual looming), and also limitations on visual acuity. For audition in the first few days, note recognition of mother's voice, discrimination of basic vowel sounds, a preference for sound over silence, and an apparent preference for musical sound over random noise. (1) Thus audition is initially better developed in the neonate, implying that you will fare better with auditory than with visual types of interaction. (2) Neonates (and infants in general) prefer rhythmical sounds such as singing, humming, and orchestration. (3) The infant would probably find mother's voice soothing in itself, given a warm relationship between mother and child. Otherwise, music that infants "bounce" to would obviously not soothe them. Marches and rock 'n roll would likely have stimulating effects, whereas Muzak, rhapsodies, and lullabies would soothe. Predictably, if humans have a built-in responsiveness to music, then infants would be soothed by the same music adults find soothing.

II. Visual changes at or about 2 months of age include preference for more complex stimuli, scanning of more detailed internal features of faces, preference for curvature, increasing attention to moderately discrepant stimuli, beginnings of preference for human faces over other stimuli, detection of depth cues, and perception of size constancy, in each case in accord with an interaction between learning experiences and central nervous system maturation. In contrast, auditory changes involve more the refinement than the acquisition of perceptual skills and preferences, an example being the improvement of language-sound discrimination. (1) Although visual perception is rapidly improving over the first 2 months, it still is probably not as well developed as audition. One clue is that infants may require until 3 months of age to be able to discriminate faces and thus prefer to look at their mothers rather than strangers. (2) Infants begin to show preference for various stimuli present in human faces by this point, although another month or so typically passes before this preference is fully present. Also, moderately discrepant stimuli elicit more attending. (3) Infants are thus becoming more capable of learning through the visual mode, and the increasing speed with which infants can learn and remember different faces from about 2 months of age onward implies the beginnings of reliance on visual perception for perceptual learning.

III. (1) In accord with the summaries in *Applications I* and *II*, a 1-month-old infant may well prefer toys that produce interesting sounds, due to better auditory discrimination at this age. (2) At first, noise-making stuffed animals and human dolls would probably have better effect. From about 2 months of age on, "funny" faces, human-like appearance, and probably movement (self-movement of toys, and also movable limbs on toys) would be more appealing. (3) Basically, contrast between shapes would begin to intrigue the child more from about 2 months onward, and increasingly fine degrees of complexity in toys would be preferable through the first several years of life in accord both with visual perceptual development and fine motor development.

CHAPTER SEVEN

LEARNING AND DEVELOPMENT

OVERVIEW AND KEY TERMS

Read carefully. Recall examples and discussion as you go, and define each key term.

WHAT IS LEARNING?

Learning involves a relatively permanent change in the way an individual thinks, perceives, or reacts, as a result of experience (such as study, practice, or observation). Young children learn in at least three ways: (1) by repetition (or mere exposure), (2) by associations formed through conditioning, and (3) by observation of social models.

HABITUATION AND MERE EXPOSURE EFFECTS

Infants display familiarity with a stimulus through habituation, which is a simple form of learning. Prior to about 4 months of age, infants also dishabituate and begin responding anew to a familiar stimulus. As memory improves through maturation, 4-12-month-olds habituate more rapidly and are less likely to dishabituate. Older children, and adults, sometimes don't habituate to stimuli in the first place, instead displaying the mere exposure effect in which the familiar is preferred.

CLASSICAL CONDITIONING

As developed by Pavlov, classical conditioning is based on pairing of a conditioned stimulus (CS) with an unconditioned stimulus (UCS). Eventually, after repeated pairings, the CS alone will elicit a conditioned response (CR). The CR is similar to the unconditioned response (UCR) that is naturally elicited by the UCS. Thus a bell is paired with food, and eventually the bell alone will elicit salivation similar to the salivation elicited by food. Stimulus generalization occurs when stimuli slightly different from the CS also elicit a CR. Discrimination occurs when stimuli are too different from the CS to elicit a CR. Extinction refers to the gradual weakening of a CR when the CS is no longer being paired with the UCS.

Watson and Raynor exposed Little Albert to a white rat (CS) paired with a loud noise (UCS); the white rat alone eventually elicited fearful behavior (CR). Albert also generalized the fear to other white furry things. Prejudices may also be learned by classical conditioning. Positive counterconditioning involves pairing a pleasant UCS with a CS that has previously acquired aversive properties. Aversion therapy, as in treatment for enuresis, views bladder tension as a CS which is paired with an aversive UCS such as a buzzer to establish a CR of waking up. These and other procedures in counterconditioning are discussed in Box 7-1.

Infants as young as 2-3 days old can acquire conditioned responses such as sucking in response to a tone. Although few such reflexes can be conditioned during the first few weeks, classical conditioning may explain how infants learn the meaning of breasts, bottles, and the faces of caregivers.

OPERANT (INSTRUMENTAL) CONDITIONING

In operant conditioning the learner emits a resonse, and either pleasant or unpleasant consequences follow. Instrumental conditioning traces to Thorndike's work with
cats escaping puzzle boxes, although conditioning of "operants" was developed primarily
by Skinner. Pleasant, favorable consequences are called reinforcers. This can involve
presenting something desirable to the learner (positive reinforcement) or it can involve
taking away something the learner finds undesirable (negative reinforcement). Either way,
the operant behavior is strengthened. On the other hand, punishment involves unpleasant,
unfavorable consequences, with a result of suppressing or weakening behavior. This can
also be accomplished in two ways, either by presenting something the learner finds undesirable or by taking away something the learner finds desirable. These four possibilities are summarized in Box 7-2. Note in particular that negative reinforcement is not at
all the same as punishment. In general, reinforcement is more effective than punishment
in producing behavior change, perhaps because reinforcement specifies what the learner
should do and punishment does not.

Primary reinforcers satisfy basic, unlearned needs. Secondary reinforcers are conditioned through association with primary reinforcers. Money is a secondary reinforcer
because its value lies in exchange for primary reinforcers. But money is also a generalized reinforcer, as are praise, attention, approval, and respect. These acquire a value
of their own which lasts well beyond their relationship with primary reinforcers. One
very potent generalized reinforcer is parental approval.

Neonates can learn operant responses soon after birth, although many trials may be
required to learn a relatively simple response such as turning one's head to obtain milk.
Progressively fewer trials are required with older infants. But, early on, infants acquire behaviors that attract attention and nurturance, thus setting the stage for emotional attachment to caregivers.

Complex behaviors can be conditioned through shaping: Reinforcement is first given
for simpler behaviors, then successive approximations to the more complex behavior are
gradually instilled. Box 7-3 describes the work of Lovaas and associates on shaping social responsiveness in autistic children. Shaping can also be applied to language usage
beginning with simple sounds and working up to words and then sentences.

Timing of reinforcement is important in operant conditioning. Immediate reinforcement is the most effective, and delays of a few seconds can prevent learning in infants
perhaps because of their limited memory ability. Older children, and adults, mediate reinforcement delays better. Frequency of reinforcement is also important. Continuous reinforcement produces rapid learning, but partial reinforcement produces learning that is
more resistant to extinction. This partial reinforcement effect occurs in part because
the learner has difficulty being sure that reinforcement has been discontinued. Partial
reinforcement can be scheduled various ways, the basic types being (1) fixed-ratio (FR),
which produces steady responding and good resistance to extinction, (2) variable-ratio
(VR), which produces brisk responding and strong resistance to extinction because of the
unpredictability involved, (3) fixed-interval (FI), which requires a time period to pass
before a response can be reinforced, and (4) variable-interval (VI), in which the time
period before the response can be reinforced varies unpredictably. Real-world situations
involve many variations and combinations of such schedules, and both desirable and undesirable behaviors get reinforced.

The Premack Principle explains reinforcement by noting that any event or activity
that is probable for an individual can reinforce any other event or activity that is less
probable. Another issue in reinforcement is that some behaviors are intrinsically reinforcing, and the use of external incentives in such cases can actually undermine the behavior. Yet another issue involves the learned helplessness effect: Infants whose crying and cooing and the like have little effect on caregivers may simply stop trying and
become socially unresponsive. And the information value of stimuli, in conjunction with
development of control, is a factor in the effectiveness of reinforcers with children.

Most parents use punishment at least occasionally, especially where dangerous behaviors are involved. One way that punishment suppresses behavior is through classical conditioning of fear and anxiety with the behavior, in that the behavior becomes a CS. Thus punishment is more effective when it is administered early in the behavioral sequence, so that fear and anxiety stop the child early. Punishment after the fact is less effective. Intensity of punishment is also a factor, and if it is too intense it can create levels of anxiety that interfere with learning and can also make the child fear the person who administers the punishment rather than fear the act. Consistency is also important, in that erratic punishment can actually strengthen the behavior one is trying to suppress. Punishment is more effective when delivered by a warm and caring person, when accompanied by explanations as to why the behavior is wrong, and when used in conjunction with positive reinforcement for acceptable, incompatible behaviors.

Potential side effects of punishment include resentment and avoidance of the person who administers the punishment, and perhaps management problems when away from that person. One point is that punishment models aggressive behavior. Another problem is that habitual use of punishment can lead to child abuse. Such side effects are less likely with the response cost technique, which involves withholding or removing a pleasant stimulus the child would otherwise receive. Also useful is the time-out technique, in which the child is removed from an enjoyable activity whenever misbehavior occurs during that activity. Choice of punishment also reflects the type of offense and the way in which the child has responded to previous punishments. Finally, punishment can be bypassed by using the incompatible response technique, in which undesirable behavior is simply ignored and eliminated through reinforcement of alternative behaviors. Similarly, the self-instructional technique involves teaching children to remind themselves why certain acts are wrong and should be avoided.

OBSERVATIONAL LEARNING

In observational learning the child observes social models, makes mental notes, and later imitates. Bandura believes that a majority of our habits are learned through observation because it is efficient and allows for learning of highly complex behaviors (such as language) that are difficult to learn otherwise. Observation also explains how children learn novel behaviors that their models are not deliberately trying to teach them, in that it is not necessary for the child to perform the behavior at the time that learning is taking place and no "trials" or reinforcement are necessary. Bandura's classic experiment with preschool children watching an adult assault a Bobo doll and later imitating the behavior provided evidence for observational learning. Imitation of a model can occur long after observation, and Bandura proposes that children store symbolic representations in memory either in the form of images or of verbal labels. And children generally attend more to models who are warm and nurturant or competent and powerful, as well as models of the same sex, ethnic group, and so on.

Although neonates can imitate facial expressions, more complex imitation develops over the first year and beyond. Deferred imitation is possible by about 20-24 months of age, presumably through symbolic representation. Research indicates that 4-5-year-olds can use verbal representation to learn complex behaviors if they are instructed to do so, and by 7-8 years of age children are proficient at using verbal representation on their own in learning by observation.

Television affects children differently according to age. Infants up to about 18 months of age attend more to live models, and by about age 3 years children attend about equally to live and TV models. Preschool children attend more to the visual components of TV programs, whereas elementary-school children attend more to meaning and plots. Heavy exposure to TV violence is correlated with aggressive behavior in children. And commercial messages affect children as well. By age 3 years children can sing jingles for advertised products and they tend to believe the commercials and ask for the products. An understanding of the purpose of commercials comes later, at about 9-11 years of age, and skepticism about commercial claims appears at about 13-14 years of age. But how children respond to commercials also depends upon responses modeled by adults and peers. Otherwise, TV also has prosocial effects. And Box 7-5 describes how films and observational learning have been used to eliminate fearful reactions in preschool children.

COMPLEX PROCESSES IN LEARNING

More complex forms of early learning include acquiring concepts that guide behavior in novel situations the child encounters. An important aspect of all types of learning is the stimulus generalization principle, which allows us to respond to new situations without having to relearn what to do each time. Generalization allows the formation of habits, although these can be either good or bad. Infants and toddlers generalize primarily on the basis of physical characteristics of stimuli. Older children, and adults, generalize more in accord with how things are labeled or classified. Discrimination complements generalization, in that we also learn when not to respond a habitual way.

The "5 to 7" shift involves marked changes in the way children go about learning concepts in this age range. The Harlows' research on the "win-stay, lose-shift" concept demonstrates the effects of learning to learn, and this ability improves considerably in the age range of 5-7 years. Similarly, the ability to solve oddity problems, which involves learning to select stimuli that have not been reinforced, improves in this age range. Another improvement in conceptual skills is indicated by research on learning reversal shifts versus nonreversal shifts. Preschool children learn nonreversal shifts more easily, perhaps because partial reinforcement has occurred prior to the shift. In contrast, grade-school children learn reversal shifts more easily, indicating the use of mediators such as verbal labels as language and thinking become more interrelated.

The mediational hypothesis holds that older children use verbal mediators such as "odd" in solving oddity problems and "size" or "color" in solving reversal-shift problems. In the latter, for example, a nonreversal shift would be harder for the older child because it would require switching to a different mediator. Notably, preschool children perform better on reversal shifts if they are instructed to use verbal mediators, which indicates that they do not have a mediation deficiency. Instead, the younger children display a production deficiency in that they do not spontaneously use verbal mediators.

In contrast, Piaget's cognitive hypothesis argues that cognitive development is a prerequisite to language development and that children are first beginning to "think" about language in the age range 5 to 7. Whereas the mediational hypothesis implies that older children solve problems better because they use language mediators, Piaget says that children use language mediators because they can solve problems better. An example is the emerging sense of metalinguistic awareness. In addition, cognitive development away from the younger child's centration explains the "5 to 7" shift, in that the older children is better able to consider more than one aspect of problems.

SELF-REVIEW

Fill in the blanks for each item. Check the answers for each item as you go.

WHAT IS LEARNING?

1. Learning is a relatively *permanent* change either in behav-   permanent
ior or in behavior potential; three requirements are that (1)
the individual thinks, perceives, or reacts in a *new* way, (2)   new
the change is a result of *experience* instead of maturation   experience
or physiological damage, and (3) the change is relatively permanent as noted.

HABITUATION AND MERE EXPOSURE EFFECTS

Developmental Trends

2. When an infant stops attending to a stimulus, _habituation_
has occurred; infants younger than about 4 months quickly begin
responding to the stimulus again, however, which indicates that
dishabituation has occurred perhaps due to limited memory
abilities in this age range.

habituation

dishabituation

Mere Exposure and the Development of Positive Attitudes

3. Repeated exposure to a stimulus or situation does not always
lead to habituation in older children and in adults; instead, we
often develop favorable attitudes toward _familiar_ objects,
in accord with the _mere exposure_ effect.

familiar
mere exposure

CLASSICAL CONDITIONING

4. In the basic Pavlovian experiment on classical conditioning,
a _CS_ such as a bell is paired with the _UCS_ such as food, and
through repeated pairings the _CS_ alone becomes capable of eliciting the _CR_ of salivation.

CS, UCS
CS
CR

5. If a stimulus very similar to an established CS can also elicit the CR, stimulus _generalization_ is present; but if the
new stimulus is too different from the CS, no CR will occur, and
discrimination instead of generalization is present.

generalization

discrimination

Classical Conditioning of Emotions and Attitudes

6. In the case of Little Albert, a furry white rat was the _CS_
which came to elicit the _CR_ of fear or crying; to create this
learning, the researchers _paired_ CS and UCS and thus classical conditioning occurred.

CS
CR
paired

7. A therapeutic approach in which a pleasant UCS is paired with
a feared CS to eliminate that fear is called _positive_ counterconditioning; in contrast, undesirable behaviors such as enuresis can be eliminated by _aversion_ therapy.

positive

aversion

Can Neonates Be Classically Conditioned?

8. Classical conditioning of a _UCR_ such as sucking has been
demonstrated with infants as young as _2 - 3_ days old.

UCR
2 - 3

OPERANT (INSTRUMENTAL) CONDITIONING

9. For Thorndike's cats, pressing a lever was _instrumental_
in escaping a puzzle box and obtaining food; in Skinner's terms,
this would be called _operant_ conditioning.

instrumental

operant

Reinforcement and Punishment

10. A stimulus that strengthens a response is a _reinforcer_ ;
if something pleasant occurs following the response, _positive_
reinforcement is being used, and if something unpleasant is taken
away after the response, _negative_ reinforcement is being
used.

reinforcer
positive

negative

11. A stimulus that weakens or suppresses a response is called a
punisher; this can be arranged either by taking away something _pleasant_ or by presenting something _unpleasant_
as a consequence of the behavior.

punisher
pleasant, unpleasant

12. Stimulus events which strengthen behavior "naturally," in

the absence of prior learning, are _primary_ reinforcers; | primary
stimuli which acquire the power to reinforce because of their
previous association with primary reinforcers are thus called
secondary reinforcers. | secondary

Operant Conditioning in Infancy

13. Neonates are capable of learning _operant_ behaviors, al- | operant
though they may require many _trials_ before learning occurs. | trials

Shaping of Complex Behaviors

14. As in Lovaas' work with autistic children, complex behavior | shaped
such as language usage can be _shaped_ from simpler behavior by
reinforcing _successive_ approximations to the desired, more | successive
complex behavior.

Factors That Affect Operant Conditioning

15. In the everyday world, inconsistencies in events and situa- | partial
tions often yield only _partial_ reinforcement for behavior,
but it happens that partial reinforcement makes behavior more
resistant to _extinction_, especially if the reinforcement | extinction
occurs on a _variable_-ratio schedule. | variable-

Why Do Reinforcers Reinforce?

16. One way of looking at reinforcement is to note that any | high-, low-
high-probability behavior can be used to reinforce any _low_-
probability behavior, which is the _Premack_ Principle. | Premack

17. Behaviors that are enjoyable for their own sake are said to | intrinsically
be _intrinsically_ reinforcing; if external reinforcement is
added in such situations, the behavior may actually be weakened
unless the external reinforcement adds _information_ about | information
"correct" versus "incorrect" or the like.

18. If an infant's bids for parental attention often go unanswered, the infant may acquire an attitude of apathy and learned
helplessness with regard to control of the environment. | helplessness

Punishment: The Aversive Control of Behavior

19. Effective use of punishment involves pairing of the aversive
consequences, which constitute the _UCS_, with the beginning acts | UCS
in the sequence of the undesirable behavior; other points are
that (1) punishment should be regular and _consistent_ in re- | consistent
sponse to the undesirable behavior, (2) the person who adminis-
ters punishment should have a _warm_ relationship with the | warm
child, (3) explanations and _reasons_ why the behavior is | reasons
wrong should be included, and (4) alternative, desirable behav-
iors should be _positively_ reinforced. | positively

20. Punishment can also involve taking something pleasant away,
such as a toy or a privilege, as in the _response_-cost tech- | response-
nique, or the child can be removed temporarily from an enjoyable
activity as a consequence of misbehavior, as in the _time-out_ | time-out
technique; and ways of avoiding use of punishment altogether include reinforcing another behavior that prevents the misbehavior
from occurring, as in the _incompatible_ response technique. | incompatible

OBSERVATIONAL LEARNING

21. Bandura views observational learning as very important to
development because (1) it is more _efficient_ than simple | efficient

trial-and-error learning, (2) language and other _complex_   complex
behaviors probably can't be learned any other way, and (3) many
behaviors are learned by observation when the _model_ is not   model
actually trying to teach the child anything.

How Doe We "Learn" by Observation?

22. As indicated by Bandura's research on children watching
adults behave aggressively toward Bobo dolls, learning can take
place even though the child doesn't actually _perform_ the be-   perform
havior and even in the absence of _reinforcement_ for the   reinforcement
behavior; in addition, observing a model being punished for aggressive behavior may inhibit the children's _performance_   performance
of aggression but not their learning of how to aggress.

23. To span the delay between learning and performance, Bandura
hypothesizes that children use _symbolic_ representations of   symbolic
a model's behavior which are stored in _memory_.   memory

Developmental Trends in Imitation and Observational Learning

24. During the first year of life, infants can only imitate a
model who is actually _present_; by about 20-24 months, child-   present
ren become capable of _deferred_ imitation through the use of   deferred
mental images and verbal labels.

Television as a Modeling Influence

25. Responsiveness to TV models begins to increase at about _18_   18
months of age and peaks at about _3_ years of age; preschool   3
children are captivated more by _visual_ effects in programs,   visual
whereas older children attend more to _plots_ and motives.   plots

26. With regard to commercial advertising, young children tend
to _believe_ that the ads are honest and do not develop a bas-   believe
ic skepticism about commercials until _adolescence_.   adolescence

COMPLEX PROCESSES IN LEARNING

Generalization and Discrimination

27. A process important to all types of learning involves applying former learning to new stimuli and situations, as in stimu-
lus _generalization_; infants and toddlers are most likely   generalization
to generalize when the _physical_ aspects of stimuli are sim-   physical
ilar, whereas older children and adults, generalize more on the
basis of how objects and situations are _classified_.   labeled or classified

28. New situations sometimes require different responses, how-
ever, and thus generalization is complemented by _discrimination_   discrimination

Later Developments in Concept Learning: The "5 to 7 Shift"

29. Childrens' use of concepts in problem-solving changes during
the age range _5_ to _7_; one example is that children in this   5 to 7
age range become faster at discovering the "_win_-stay, _lose_-   win, lose
shift" concept in discrimination problems, another is that they
become more capable of solving _oddity_ problems in which one   oddity
of three stimuli is different, and another is that they find it
easier to learn _reversal_ shift discrimination problems.   reversal

30. One explanation of the "5 to 7 shift" emphasizes children's
greater use of private speech and verbal _mediators_ as they   mediators
reach this age range; thus they might use a label such as "_odd_"   odd
in solving oddity problems or a label such as "size" in learning

104

the relevant dimension prior to a reversal *shift* .   shift

31. Thus the mediational hypothesis says that older children
find reversal shifts easier because nonreversal shifts would require learning a new dimension and using a different *mediator*.   mediator

32. However, younger children do not have a mediation deficiency,
because they can be taught to use verbal *labels* in solving   mediators or labels
discrimination problems; instead, since they do not spontaneously
use mediators, they have a *production* deficiency.   production

33. The mediational hypothesis implies that learning to use language comes before learning to *solve* problems, whereas Piaget   solve
argued that learning to solve problems comes before learning to
use *language*; he thus attributes the "5 to 7 shift" to the   language
other *cognitive* advances taking place in this age range,   cognitive
which include acquiring *metalinguistic* awareness and also   metalinguistic
progressing beyond the highly focused *centration* that char-   centration
acterizes the thinking of younger children.

SELF-TEST I

Consider each alternative carefully. Then choose the best one.

1. Learning involves a change in behavior
    a. in which the individual thinks, perceives, or reacts in a new way
    b. as a result of experience rather than heredity, maturation, or damage
    c. of a relatively permanent rather than temporary nature
    d. all of the above

2. Younger infants, say, less than 4 months old
    a. habituate more slowly and dishabituate more quickly than older infants
    b. habituate more quickly and dishabituate more slowly than older infants
    c. habituate and dishabituate more slowly than older infants
    d. habituate and dishabituate more quickly than older infants

3. In Pavlov's basic classical conditioning experiment, the bell is the _____ and the food
is the _____.
    a. CS, UCS
    b. CS, CR
    c. UCS, CS
    d. UCS, UCR

4. If a previously conditioned subject still shows a CR to the original CS but does <u>not</u>
show a CR to a somewhat different CS, it is an example of
    a. stimulus generalization
    b. extinction
    c. discrimination
    d. prejudice

5. The idea that most human behavior depends upon its consequences is basically
    a. classical conditioning
    b. operant conditioning
    c. observational learning
    d. mere exposure learning

6. If a child normally gets to watch TV on Saturday morning and you take away this privilege as a result of misbehavior, you are using
   a. positive reinforcement
   b. negative reinforcement
   c. punishment
   d. classical conditioning

7. A good example of a secondary reinforcer is
   a. food
   b. escape from an aversive stimulus
   c. money
   d. none of the above

8. Within the first week of life, infants are capable of learning through
   a. classical conditioning
   b. operant conditioning
   c. both of the above
   d. none of the above

9. Lovaas' work with autistic children is best described as being based on
   a. classical conditioning and shaping
   b. operant conditioning and shaping
   c. classical conditioning and counterconditioning
   d. operant conditioning and counterconditioning

10. Punishment works best is
   a. it is delivered near the beginning of the undesirable behavior
   b. it is combined with reinforcement for alternative, desirable behavior
   c. it is consistent and occurs every time the undesirable behavior occurs
   d. all of the above

11. Bandura argues that observational learning is very important in development because
   a. learning by observation is more efficient
   b. many complex behaviors can't be learned without models
   c. it explains incidental learning, when models are not trying to teach anything
   d. all of the above

12. The way children learn about violence and aggressive behavior from watching TV is most similar to
   a. Bandura's research on modeled behavior toward Bobo dolls
   b. Skinner's research on operant conditioning of rats and pigeons
   c. Pavlov's research on conditioned salivation in dogs
   d. Premack's research on high- and low-probability behaviors

13. According to Bandura, observational learning mainly involves the child acquiring
   a. symbolic representations of behavior that are stored in memory for later use
   b. stimulus-response habits as a result of reinforcement
   c. associations between conditioned and unconditioned stimuli
   d. none of the above

14. Suppose you first teach children of different ages to pick a red stimulus instead of a green one, ignoring whether the stimulus is square or round; then, in a second phase, you reward the children for picking the square and ignoring color. This "shift" would be most easily learned, typically, by
   a. a 4-year-old child
   b. a 7-year-old child
   c. a 10-year-old child
   d. a college student

15. According to the mediational hypothesis, the "5 to 7 shift" occurs because
    a. children are acquiring metalinguistic awareness
    b. children are decentering
    c. children are using visual images more
    (d.) children are using verbal labels more

RESEARCH SUMMARY AND REVIEW

Using the textbook, review the research efforts indicated and write a summary of the important findings. Note the general purpose or context of the research.

1. Papousek (1961, 1967), page 252: _____

_____

_____

_____

_____

2. Lepper, Greene, & Nisbett (1973), page 257: _____

_____

_____

_____

_____

3. Homme, de Baca, DeVine, Horst, & Rickert (1963), page 258: _____

_____

_____

_____

_____

4. Watson & Ramey (1972), page 259: _____

_____

_____

_____

_____

5. Perry & Parke (1975), page 262: _____

_____

_____

_____

_____

6. Bandura (1965), page 265: _____

_____

_____

7. Stoneman & Brody (1981): _____

_____

_____

_____

_____

8. Bandura & Menlove (1968), page 272: _____

_____

_____

_____

9. Birch (1981), page 273: _____

_____

_____

_____

_____

10. Gollin & Shirk (1966), page 275: _____

_____

_____

_____

_____

SELF-TEST II

Consider each alternative carefully. Then choose the best one.

1. Generally, young children learn by
    a. repetition and mere exposure
    b. association through conditioning
    c. observation of social models
    d. all of the above

2. In Little Albert's case, the white rat was the ___ and the steel rod provided the ___.
    a. UCS, UCR
    b. UCS, CS
    c. CS, CR
    d. CS, UCS

3. To eliminate a phobia such as Little Albert's, you might find it effective to
    a. use positive counterconditioning, pairing white furry animals with food
    b. have the child observe social models petting white furry animals
    c. both of the above
    d. none of the above

4. In aversive counterconditioning for enuresis, the CS is _____ and the UCS is _____.
  a. bladder tension, the buzzer
  b. bladder tension, the wet sheet
  c. the buzzer, bladder tension
  d. the wet sheet, bladder tension

5. Thorndike's cats learned to escape the puzzle box in accord with
  a. operant conditioning
  b. classical conditioning
  c. the mere exposure effect
  d. observational learning

6. If a child normally goes to bed around 8:00, under protest, and you occasionally allow the child to stay up until 9:00 as a consequence for good behavior, you are using
  a. the response-cost technique
  b. the time-out technique
  c. the self-instructional technique
  d. reinforcement

7. One likely explanation of how parental approval continues to influence behavior even after the child becomes an adult is that parental approval is
  a. an unconditioned stimulus
  b. a generalized secondary reinforcer
  c. an incompatible response
  d. an extinguished response

8. Papousek's (1961, 1967) research in which infants learned to turn their heads at the sound of a bell to obtain a nippleful of milk was based on
  a. classical conditioning
  b. operant conditioning
  c. both of the above
  d. none of the above

9. In operant conditioning, reinforcement is more effective when
  a. it is delivered very soon after the response
  b. it is delivered on an intermittent schedule
  c. the reinforcer represents a high-probability behavior
  d. all of the above

10. Where intrinsically reinforcing behavior is involved, as in the study by Lepper, Greene, and Nisbett (1973), adding a noninformative external reinforcer will probably
  a. increase or strengthen the behavior
  b. decrease or weaken the behavior
  c. extinguish the behavior completely
  d. generalize the behavior to other situations

11. In accord with the Watson and Ramey (1972) study, the likely effect of putting a child in a setting that teaches that no control of what happens is possible will be to
  a. teach the child to try harder to achieve control
  b. temporarily suppress attempts at control in that situation
  c. permanently suppress attempts at control in that situation
  d. foster an attitude that the parent is a punitive agent to be feared

12. Punishment is a reasonable method of controlling behavior if
  a. it is delivered by a warm and affectionate punitive agent
  b. it is not cruel or unusual
  c. it is accompanied by explanations of the reasons for punishment
  d. all of the above

13. In Bandura's (1965) classic experiment on modeling and aggression, the "model-punished" group of children, in contrast to the "model-rewarded" and "no-consequences" ones,
    a. learned less about how to aggress, and were less likely to aggress
    b. learn the same about how to aggress, but were less likely to aggress
    c. learned less about how to aggress, but were more likely to aggress
    d. learned the same about how to aggress, and were more likely to aggress

14. Children generally imitate
    a. agemates or older children
    b. same-sex models
    c. models who are competent and powerful
    d. all of the above

15. Deferred imitation of a model who is not actually present typically appears during
    a. the first year of life
    b. the second year of life
    c. the third year of life
    d. the fourth year of life

16. A 5-year-old child who watches TV commercials is likely to
    a. ask for the products advertised
    b. sing along with jingles
    c. be captivated by visual effects
    d. all of the above

17. Children who watch prosocial TV such as *Sesame Street* and *Mister Rogers' Neighborhood*
    a. are likely to attend mainly to aggressive or violent portions
    b. are likely to enact some cooperative and helping behaviors
    c. may well acquire an attitude of learned helplessness
    d. will probably require extra incentives to stay awake

18. Bandura and Menlove's (1968) study of children watching films of other children interacting with dogs was based primarily on
    a. classical conditioning
    b. counterconditioning
    c. operant conditioning
    d. observational learning

19. Birch (1981) demonstrated that reinforcing children for selecting a low-probability snack makes it more likely that they will later select a nonreinforced snack from the same category; this is an example of
    a. discrimination
    b. shaping
    c. secondary reinforcement
    d. generalization

20. Learning-to-learn primarily involves
    a. conditioned habits to specific stimuli
    b. acquiring an ability to sit still in classrooms
    c. acquiring a concept relevant to solving a problem
    d. use of image mediators

21. Gollin and Shirk's (1966) research on children solving oddity problems favored
    a. the "5 to 7 shift"
    b. the idea that children use verbal mediators in problem solving
    c. concept learning, as opposed to conditioning
    d. all of the above

22. Suppose you reinforce a monkey for picking a yellow object instead of blue one, regardless of whether the object is large or small; after a number of trials with this problem, the monkey would later find it easier to shift to picking
    a. the blue object
    (b) the small object
    c. a red object from a different pair of stimuli
    d. any of the above with equivalent ease

23. In the preceding question (#22), a 10-year-old child would find it easier to shift to
    (a) the blue object
    b. the small object
    c. a red object from a different pair of stimuli
    d. any of the above with equivalent ease

24. With regard to the use of verbal mediators, preschool children
    a. cannot learn to use them at this age
    b. must be operantly conditioned to learn to use them
    (c) do not spontaneously use them, but can if instructed to do so
    d. spontaneously use them most of the time

25. Piaget's cognitive explanation of the "5 to 7 shift" would emphasize
    a. metalinguistic awareness
    b. decentering
    c. the role of language as a secondary issue
    (d) all of the above

VIGNETTES

Consider the story, then answer each question using material from the textbook.

I. One day Sammy's mother and he were playing in the den with the TV on in the background. Sammy wasn't paying attention to the TV and was more concerned with the "ducking and dodging" and mild sort of wrestling he was engaged in with his mother. At age 4 years, Sammy hadn't acquired much appreciation for the plot of the cowboy movie that was on TV. But, when a commercial for a new chocolate candy bar named "Friendsies" came on, he abandoned playing with his mother and watched raptly as a child a bit older than himself bought a Friendsie, walked outside the store, took a bite, and was immediately surrounded by attractive friends who smiled and laughed and asked the boy to come play with them.

    1. From a classical conditioning point of view, identify the possible CS, UCS and CR/UCR involved in the commercial.

    2. From an observational learning point of view, identify factors in the commercial that might make it effective for Sammy.

    3. Would Sammy be likely to ask his parents to buy him a Friendsie? Why or why not?

II. At the tender age of 37 years, Harold walked into a casino and, though he hadn't intended to, spent the rest of that day and night pulling the handle of a slot machine that struck his fancy. He played quarter after quarter, tirelessly. And, as it happened, he kept playing well past the point that a small weight in one of the spinning reels accidently shifted and reduced his changes of a good pay-off to nearly zero. Yet Harold played on and on, and hardly seemed to notice any difference.

    1. What schedule of reinforcement was Harold on? Would he have been as enthralled on one of the other schedules? Why or why not?

    2. Why didn't Harold quit playing when the machine broke?

    3. How might children's "tantrums" resemble Harold's behavior?

operant conditioning — reinforcement

III. Marla was an institutionalized child, having been orphaned soon after birth. The orphanage, although designed with humanitarian principles in mind, was hopelessly under-funded and understaffed. Thus, for the first year or so of her life, Marla's cries and bids for attention often went unanswered. After that year, the orphanage's situation im-proved and a good many more caregivers were hired. But they all noticed that Marla was very quiet and cried very rarely, even when in need of food or a diaper change. And as time went by they noticed that she had very little to say.

  1. Give an operant conditioning explanation of Marla's minimal communication.

  2. Discuss possible attitudes on Marla's part in terms of learned helplessness.

  3. Speculate as to long-range effects of this first year's experience upon Marla.

APPLICATIONS

Try each of the projects, noting answers to the questions as you go.

I. Suppose you encounter a child who is extremely afraid of stuffed toy animals, whatever the original reason, and you decide to devise a plan for eliminating this phobia.

  1. How might you go about it from a classical conditioning perspective?
  present fear stimulus in a less threatening method. Films, observance of others' behaviors
  2. How might you go about it from an operant conditioning perspective?
  Films, interaction w/ fear stimulus + have pos. outcomes
  3. How might you use observational learning?
  Films

II. From the textbook material on punishment, devise a procedure for training a puppy to "ask" to go outside instead of soiling the rug when needing to eliminate.

  1. What characteristics of delivery of punishment would be important?
  Consistency, Immediate
  2. How might you use reinforcement in conjunction with punishment?
  frighten when bad/reward when good.
  3. Are there any methods you might use that do not involve punishment?
  Take the dog outside frequently — it will learn why it's going.

III. For further clarification of the different types of reinforcement and punishment, develop definitions of "positive" and "negative" punishment that are consistent with the definitions of positive and negative reinforcement.

  1. What do positive and negative refer to?

  2. What happens to the stimulus in "positive" versus "negative" punishment? What kind of stimulus is necessary in each case?

  3. Which category do verbal reprimands, spankings, the response-cost technique, and the time-out technique fit into?

ANSWERS

Self-Test I

1. d	6. c	11. d
2. a	7. c	12. a
3. a	8. c	13. a
4. c	9. b	14. a
5. b	10. d	15. d

1. Papousek (1961, 1967): To assess age-related changes in susceptibility to conditioning of the rooting reflex, infants were first classically conditioned to turn their heads in response to a bell and then operantly conditioned to turn their heads at the sound of the bell to get milk; neonates took many more trials than older infants in learning the operant response.

2. Lepper, Greene, & Nisbett (1973): Children 3-5 years old experienced either a promised reward, no reward, or a surprise reward for engaging in an intrinsically satisfying activity; those who received the promised reward later engaged in the activity less, demonstrating that external rewards can undermine interest and are not always beneficial.

3. Homme, et al. (1963): As an application of the Premack Principle to control of children's behavior, a high-probability class of behaviors such as running around and yelling was made contingent upon a low-probability class of behaviors such as sitting quietly and paying attention; thus disruptive behaviors were brought under control.

4. Watson & Ramey (1972): One group of 8-week-olds were allowed to control the rotation of a mobile, whereas another group was not, and the no-control group became apathetic with regard to the mobiles and would not attempt to control them later when allowed to. This finding illustrated the potential effects of learned helplessness.

5. Perry & Parke (1975): Boys 8 years old were less likely to touch attractive toys if they were both punished for touching the attractive toys and reinforced for touching alternate unattractive toys, demonstrating that punishment beocmes more effective when reinforcement is used to shape alternative, incompatible behaviors.

6. Bandura (1965): Preschool children watched an adult model either be rewarded, be punished, or receive no consequences for aggressing against a Bobo doll; later, the punished-model children imitated the fewest of the model's behaviors, but it was found that they had learned just as much on how to aggress. This research demonstrated that children can learn by observation, independent of the operation of reinforcement and punishment.

7. Stoneman & Brody (1981): As a demonstration of how peer behavior affects whether children imitate TV commercials, 9-10-year-old boys were found to become either more or less likely to select advertised snacks as a direct function of what peers did.

8. Bandura & Menlove (1968): In developing a treatment for childhood fears, it was demonstrated that children who were afraid of dogs could reduce and in some cases eliminate their fears by watching films of child models interacting pleasantly with dogs.

9. Birch (1981): Preschoolers were reinforced for selecting a nonfavorite snack, and if they had also labeled and classified the various snacks into categories, they were later more likely to generalize their choices to a different snack in the same category. This research illustrated the role of verbal mediation in learning.

10. Gollin & Shirk (1966): Consistent with the "5 to 7" shift, older children did better on oddity problems presumably due to use of verbal mediators such as "odd." Younger children, who are presumed not to generate verbal mediators, found the oddity problems very difficult.

Self-Test II

1. d	6. d	11. c	16. d	21. d
2. d	7. b	12. d	17. b	22. b
3. c	8. c	13. b	18. d	23. a
4. a	9. d	14. d	19. d	24. c
5. a	10. b	15. b	20. c	25. d

Vignettes

I. (1) If we assume that positive attention from others elicits pleasure or satisfaction, the attention is the UCS, the pleasurable response is the UCR, and the pairing of the Friendsies CS with the UCS would condition a pleasurable CR with repeated viewings of the commercial. (2) Likely factors include the use of a somewhat older child who is also competent enough to go to the store and buy his own candy, probable use of stylish clothing and an attractive model, and use of a model who has lots of friends in the first place by implication. If the model were younger than Sammy or from a different social or ethnic group, the commercial might not be as effective. (3) Probably Sammy would want to buy the candy. One factor here is his age, since research suggests that younger children are less likely to question the purpose or intent of commercials.

II. (1) From Harold's viewpoint a variable-ratio (VR) schedule was in effect. In contrast, an FR schedule would be boring in its predictability and would seem more like work, unless Harold was winning money, which he wouldn't be, and it would be easy for him to figure this out. An FI schedule would induce Harold to simply "clock" the interval and then put his quarter in and win, which is not likely in a casino. Finally, a VI schedule would have much the same effect as a VR, except that his rate of responding would be slower and he probably wouldn't view the VI as "fair" because of the time delay. (2) Harold kept playing because the VR schedule made it harder for him to figure out that reinforcement had been cut back. VR schedules are more resistant to extinction because the subject doesn't perceive as readily that extinction has begun. (3) One view of tantrums is that they are maintained by partial reinforcement in the form of parents occasionally "giving in," in much the same sense as Harold's VR schedule. Whenever the parent gives in and does what the child wants, the child's behavior is strengthened. And if the parents decide to stop reinforcing tantrum behavior, it takes the child a while to figure out that this change has occurred.

III. (1) An operant conditioning interpretation is that Marla's communications were not reinforced, and so they were less likely to occur. Note that partial reinforcement might counteract this effect, although partial reinforcement requires a minimum number of occasions of occurrence if it is to maintain behavior. (2) Consistent with the research on learned helplessness, Marla might acquire an attitude that her communications have no effect and thus she might become apathetic about social interactions. (3) The effects might indeed be long-range, given firm establishment of an attitude of learned helplessness. However, the integral role of language in daily living, in conjunction with the many forms of reinforcement available through language use, would probably overcome her difficulties in this particular case.

Applications

I. (1) Positive counterconditioning could involve pairing a "pleasant" UCS with the previously acquired stuffed-toy CS for fear. The goal would be to eliminate the fear CR by substituting a "pleasurable" resonse, which in effect would alter the meaning of the CS to the child. (2) An operant conditioning approach could involve successive approximations to the stuffed toys, with other reinforcement such as praise and approval all along the way (also noting the need to help the child remain relaxed and confident during this process). The goal here is also to extinguish the fear response, though with an eye toward allowing intrinsic reinforcers in play to take over. (3) An observational learning approach could involve having the child watch other children "enjoy" playing with the stuffed toys, either live or on film, noting that the similarity of the models to the child would be an important consideration. Also note that this approach incorporates elements of the other two, in that the fear response gets extinguished and the child eventually plays with the stuffed toys and gains intrinsic reinforcement.

II. (1) Whatever punisher you use, catch the animal at the first signs of the behavior. Be consistent and punish the behavior every time it occurs. Be warm and friendly both before and after, and don't lose your temper or otherwise overreact and overpunish, no matter how expensive your rugs are. Overpunishment will also interfere with learning, especially where eliminatory behavior is concerned. Use scolding in addition to whatever physical punishment you employ, since dogs quickly learn the meaning of an angry voice. Note, however, that verbal rationales probably won't help with a dog. (2) The dog still needs to eliminate, of course, so carry the dog outside (or better, coax the dog outside if there's time). Allow the dog to eliminate, then use praise and affection as a reinforcer for the desired behavior. You might also give the dog a treat afterward, on an intermittent basis. (3) Verbal scolding might suffice, if you have already established this as a means of control (through classical conditioning). Otherwise, techniques such as response-cost and time-out probably won't work with a dog. The incompatible-response technique is actually what is described in #2, but if you don't use some kind of mild punishment in conjunction with reinforcement you may have to replace the rugs before the puppy figures things out. Finally, you will probably not get very far with the self-instructional approach with a dog. Each of these points should highlight the role of language in how children learn and develop, in contrast to how animals learn.

III. (1) "Positive" refers to the *presentation* of a stimulus as a consequence for behavior. "Negative" means that you take a stimulus away. What happens to the behavior thus depends upon whether that stimulus is pleasurable or aversive. (2) In "positive" punishment, you're going to present a stimulus. In turn, punishment means that the behavior is weakened or suppressed. Therefore, "positive" punishment would require an aversive stimulus. In "negative" punishment, you're going to take a stimulus away. Taking away a pleasurable stimulus whenever the behavior occurs will weaken the behavior, and so that's what you do. Note that whenever you use the word "negative," either in reinforcement or in punishment, the subject must *have* the stimulus in the first place or else you can't take it away. (3) Verbal reprimands and spankings are aversive, in most cases, and so they would represent "positive" punishment. In passing, however, note that "pleasurable" and "aversive" are in the eyes of the beholder. For example, a socially or interpersonally deprived child might actually view scoldings and spankings as desirable, on grounds that they might be better than no attention at all. Otherwise, the response-cost and the time-out techniques are both "negative" punishment, in that you take away something pleasurable each time the undesirable behavior occurs.

CHAPTER EIGHT

DEVELOPMENT OF LANGUAGE
AND COMMUNICATION SKILLS

OVERVIEW AND KEY TERMS

Read carefully. Recall examples and discussion as you go, and define each key term.

Although animals have limited forms of communication, the flexibility and productivity of human language sets us apart. An infinite number of messages can be produced from a small number of sounds, and language is also inventive. Language transmits ideas.

TWO BASIC QUESTIONS ABOUT LANGUAGE DEVELOPMENT

In the "what" of language, phonemes are the basic units of sound and phonology is the system by which sounds are combined to produce words. English uses 45 phonemes, although many more can be generated. Languages vary in the phonemes used. Morphemes are the basic units of meaning. Semantics involves how meaning is expressed in words and in sentences. Syntax refers to the structure of language, including how words are combined into sentences. Languages have rules for how words can and cannot be combined. Pragmatics concerns what to say and how to say it in particular situations. Language appropriate in one situation may not be in another, and the person addressed is an important consideration. All of these aspects of language are necessary for effective communication.

The "how" of language concerns children's acquisition of the many skills necessary for communication. Empiricist learning theorists stress language learning through imitation and selective reinforcement. Nativists such as Chomsky stress an inborn language acquisition device (LAD), with a view that imitation and reinforcement alone are not sufficient to explain how children acquire the many complexities of language. According to the nativists, the child actively creates a "theory" of language using the abilities of the LAD.

BEFORE LANGUAGE: THE PRELINGUISTIC STAGE

Prelinguistic stage infants are responsive to language but cannot combine sounds to produce meaningful words. Infants seem programmed to attend to human speech. Neonates synchronize their movements to speech, can recognize mother's voice, and will perform operant behaviors to hear recorded speech. They can also discriminate some phonemes.

Psycholinguists propose that prelinguistic vocal development is the same for all children. Crying is at first reflexive, although pain cries serve as distress signals. Fake cries are used to attract attention. Then come coos, indicators of contentment. At about 3-4 months of age babbles appear, beginning as single syllables and later involving repetitions as in echolalia. Younger infants babble sounds present in all languages. By 10-12 months of age, infant babbling has narrowed down to the phonemes of the language being spoken around the child. And then early vocables appear, soon followed by the child's first words.

Although babbling is based on maturation, 6-10-month-old infants adjust their babbling to match qualities of the language being used and situations the infant is in. During the first 6 months of life, infants coo and babble at the same time caregivers are speaking, as if to harmonize. By 7-8 months, infants instead vocalize during the pauses in others' speech, as if trying to communicate. Parents also shape this behavior by giving the infant a chance to respond. And parents use voice intonation to maintain the infant's attention and to elicit positive affect, as discussed in Box 8-1. Parents also tend to overestimate how well their infants understand them during the latter part of the first year. But throughout, from the 11th or 12th month on, children have better <u>receptive language</u> than <u>productive language</u>.

ONE WORD AT A TIME: THE HOLOPHRASTIC STAGE

The first meaningful <u>holophrase</u> marks entrance into the <u>holophrastic stage</u>, in which communication involves one-word utterances. Productive vocabulary begins with one or two words, eventually reaching about 50 words by age 18 months and an average of 186 words by age 24 months. This early vocabulary consists mainly of nominals. Objects that "do something" interest the infant most, and thus the infant learns the words for these objects first.

A majority of holophrastic infants use <u>referential communication</u>, but some infants prefer <u>expressive communication</u> that conveys feelings and regulates social interactions. First-borns tend to be referential, perhaps because mothers have more time to name objects for them. Later-borns tend to be expressive, perhaps because mothers with more than one child are interested more in attention and control.

Young children often <u>overextend</u> the meaning of a word to include more referents than it should, and at times they also <u>underextend</u> and overrestrict word meanings. These tend to occur in stages as the child gradually acquires the actual meaning of a word. The <u>semantic features hypothesis</u> holds that children infer meaning from perceptual features of objects, whereas the <u>functional similarity hypothesis</u> holds that children infer meaning for what objects "do," each hypothesis being a possible explanation for children's semantic errors. Overextensions may also occur because the child lacks an alternative and may be trying to elicit the correct word from another person.

Other points about the holophrastic stage are: (1) Children use intermediate levels of semantic generality when naming objects, probably because parents teach this level. (2) Children's first verbs tend to be "action" verbs that describe their own behavior or the behavior of their toys. (3) The first adjectives typically describe the current condition of objects, and later adjectives incorporate aspects such as color and size. And (4) holophrastic utterances convey more meaning than the word itself, as can be seen from the context in which words are emitted and also the gestures children use to augment one-word statements.

FROM HOLOPHRASES TO SIMPLE SENTENCES: THE TELEGRAPHIC STAGE

<u>Telegraphic speech</u> begins around 18-24 months of age, as children begin to produce two-word utterances that are similar in construction across different languages. Rate of language development varies from child to child, however, and so psycholinguists use <u>mean length of utterance (MLU)</u> as a measure. MLU is based on the number of morphemes incorporated in an utterance.

Function words are omitted in telegraphic speech, and it may be that the child simply doesn't know these words at this stage. It is also possible that telegraphic speech occurs because the child's memory is limited to producing only two or three meaningful words at a time.

Telegraphic speech seems to involve its own possibly universal grammar. Braine's <u>pivotal grammar</u> describes telegraphic speech in terms of pivot and open words. A <u>semantic (or functional) grammar</u> notes that this speech also contains open-open constructions.

Pivot-open constructions are called reference operations, and open-open constructions are called relational operations. In the latter, for example, agent-action relations place noun before verb, and action-object relations place verb before noun, which indicates that telegraphic speech conforms to certain rules. And three-word utterances are often overlapping combinations of two-word utterances.

The pragmatics of early speech begins in infancy, well before the first word. A 3-month-old may vocalize to attract an adult's attention. A 6-month-old may gesture to convey meaning. A 10-11-month-old can point, which often causes the adult to name what is being pointed at. The effectiveness of gestures is indicated in American Sign Language, as discussed in Box 8-2. And beyond gestures, toddlers are also aware of pragmatics such as standing close enough to the listener or raising one's voice, making adjustments when talking to another toddler, and so on.

LANGUAGE LEARNING DURING THE PRESCHOOL PERIOD

Preschool children produce longer sentences that are also more complex. Language development accelerates during this period as children insert function words, use some negations, and ask some well formed questions by the end of the third year of life.

Brown's research indicates that children acquire grammatical morphemes in an order based on complexity of meaning. Children also learn suffixes more easily than prefixes. Having learned a grammatical morpheme, they tend to overregularize and apply the rule to irregular nouns and verbs as well. Having previously been using the correct irregulars, they now begin saying things such as "tooths" and "foots." Such errors are taken as evidence that children actively acquire linguistic rules.

Transformational grammar describes how simple declarative statements are transformed into questions, negations, imperatives, relative clauses, and compound sentences. As MLU passes 2.5, children begin to produce transformations which develop in orderly stages. The stages for asking questions include (1) rising intonation on telegraphic sentences and occasional use of "Wh-" words, (2) consistent use of "Wh-" words but the rest of the sentence not reordered, and (3) syntactically correct questions. Within this sequence, concrete-referent "Wh-" questions appear before abstract-referent questions. A comparable sequence for learning to make negations has also been described. And when MLU reaches 3.5-4.0, complex and compound sentences begin to appear. By age 5-6 years, the child's language is very similar to that of an adult.

An understanding of relational contrasts such as big/little, before/after, and I/you also develops during the preschool years. The I/you contrast is among the first. Acquisition of spatial contrasts follows a sequence based on the frequency with which adults use the words and the degree of semantic complexity involved. And during the preschool period children attend mainly to the order of words in sentences as the cue for meaning, which produces many semantic errors and causes misinterpretation of passive constructions until near the end of the preschool period.

Use of pragmatics continues to improve during the preschool period, as children learn polite ways to phrase requests and how to tailor speech for younger and older listeners.

REFINEMENT OF LANGUAGE SKILLS

During middle childhood, children return to using correct irregular forms and also acquire correct personal pronouns. Other improvements include use of tag questions and understanding of passive sentence constructions. Children also seem to apply the minimum distance principle (MDP) in understanding subject-verb relationships, although children younger than 9 or so often overextend the rule and misunderstand statements involving verbs such as "promise" and "ask."

By age 6, children have a receptive vocabulary of 8,000-14,000 words and they are

118

beginning to be aware of hierarchical semantic relations. The ability to infer meaning not directly expressed in statements (as in semantic integration problems) also improves, enabling an understanding of sarcasm. Linguistic inference is based on metalinguistic awareness of the properties of language, and this awareness enables the child to appreciate semantic riddles, phonological ambiguities, and absurdity riddles as described in Box 8-3. By age 10-11, children can understand some metaphors and proverbs.

Development of effective communication skills includes the ability to evaluate the effectiveness of messages one transmits and receives, and grade-school children become much better on tasks assessing effective communication.

THEORIES OF LANGUAGE DEVELOPMENT

Learning theories based on operant conditioning stress reinforcement by adults as the primary way children learn to talk. Skinner stressed shaping and selective reinforcement of babbling into words, then words into grammatical sentences, and so on. Another way reinforcement might operate is the communication pressure hypothesis, noting that language improvement progressively serves the child's needs better. But research indicates that parents reinforce children for semantic truth value rather than grammatical correctiveness, and parents are just as likely to respond to the child's needs after an ungrammatical request as after a grammatical one.

Social learning theorists have argued that children learn language by imitation of others' speech. However, children's telegraphic statements omit rather than imitate many parts of speech, and children also general novel statements that do not appear in adult speech. Adults do not normally say things such as "allgone cookie." And children have difficulty imitating grammatically correct statements before they have acquired the rule.

Clues to language learning are provided by how adults talk to children. When parents talk to their children a lot, children develop larger productive vocabularies and longer utterances sooner. Parents and older siblings often shorten and repeat statements to a young child, as in motherese, and adults' use of longer and more complex sentences tend to stay just ahead of the child's skills. Expansions of the child's telegraphic utterances does not necessarily help, but recasting and adding information apparently does. In general, child-adult conversation is necessary to language development. Passive exposure to language, as in watching TV, will not suffice.

The nativist perspective, such as that of Chomsky, posits that humans inherit an LAD specialized for language learning. Overregularization is cited a evidence that children actively extract and formulate rules on their own. The characteristics of adult speech as noted above provide an ideal environment for the operation of an LAD. Other evidence is that language is uniquely human and therefore apparently biological. Although chimpanzees such as Washoe, Sarah, and others have been able to learn the rudiments of language, as described in Box 8-4, their carefully tutored skills do not surpass those of a 2-3-year-old human who has received no formal instruction. Other evidence for the nativist position includes specialization of language functions in the left cerebral hemisphere, noting in passing that damage usually produces aphasia. Finally, there is the critical period hypothesis: Evidence on the learning of a second language, the degree of recovery from traumatic damage to cerebral structures, and other sources indicates a critical period for language learning spanning birth to puberty. And the apparent existence of language universals such as stages of babbling and first words, orderly development of consonant and vowel phonemes, sequencing of holophrastic then telegraphic then more complex sentences, and other aspects of syntax all imply a biological basis for language development. Contradicting evidence includes the fact that adults can learn second languages to proficiency, plus the case of Genie as described in Box 8-5. In general, the LAD hypothesis has received little direct support and is more a description of how language is acquired than an explanation.

Interactionist theory, such as the approach taken by Piaget, stresses common experiences and underlying biologically based cognitive development as the source of language universals. The reciprocal nature of language use between child and companions is also noted. And Piaget's theory of cognitive development parallels certain aspects of early language acquisition, such as children's first words incorporating their own actions or the actions of objects they manipulate. Similarly, use of hypothetical statements seems to depend on having formed concepts rather than having acquired grammar. But interactionist theory is also primarily descriptive rather than explanatory.

SELF-REVIEW

Fill in the blanks for each item. Check the answers for each item as you go.

1. Humans are capable of generating thousands of auditory patterns that can be used to produce an infinite number of messages, through _language_; in contrast, animals can only employ a very limited array of messages in _communicating_ with each other.

language
communicating

TWO BASIC QUESTIONS ABOUT LANGUAGE DEVELOPMENT

The "What" Question

2. What children acquire in language includes: (1) the basic sounds, called _phonemes_, (2) the basic units of meaning, called _morphemes_, (3) the structure of language, called _syntax_, and (4) the rules of context and situation, called _pragmatics_.

phonemes
morphemes
syntax
pragmatics

The "How" Question

3. Two basic theories of language development are learning theory, which includes emphases on how parents _reinforce_ language behavior and how children _imitate_ adult models, versus psycholinguistic theory, which emphasizes built-in biological mechanisms such as the _LAD_.

reinforce
imitate

LAD

BEFORE LANGUAGE: THE PRELINGUISTIC STAGE

The Infant's Reactions to Language

4. The neonate's apparent "preprogramming" to respond to language includes (1) looking in the direction of a _speaker_, (2) synchronizing body movements to _breaks_ and _pauses_ in others' speech, (3) recognizing mother's voice by about _3_ days of age, and (4) early abilities in the discrimination of basic speech _sounds_.

speaker
breaks, pauses
3

sounds or phonemes

Producing Sounds: The Infant's Prelinguistic Vocalizations

5. Early, universal forms of vocalization include (1) hunger, anger, pain, and fake _cries_, (2) _cooing_ as a sign of contentment, and (3) _babbling_ of sounds present throughout all human languages.

cries, cooing
babbling

6. Babbling begins at about _3 - 4_ months of age, and by 10-12 months of age it has narrowed down to the sounds present in the language the child is _hearing_; then the initial approximations to words, called _vocables_, appear around the end of the first year, and the first meaningful _word_ appears at about 10-13 months of age.

3 - 4

hearing
vocables
word

120

Are Prelinguistic Vocalizations Related to Meaningful Speech?

7. Phonological development depends in large part upon biological _maturation_ , but the infant also matches babbling to his or her linguistic environment, which indicates _learning_ .

          maturation
          learning

What Do Prelinguistic Infants Know about Language?

8. During the first 6 months infants coo and babble while their caregivers are speaking, as if trying to _harmonize_ ; but by 7-8 months babbling seems to reflect communication attempts because it occurs more in _response_ to others' speech.

          harmonize

          response

9. Caregivers communicate with prelinguistic infants to some extent by varying their voice _intonations_, and by employing _gestures_ to indicate meanings of words; however, infants apparently do not understand words as such until about _12 - 13_ months of age.

          intonations
          gestures
          12 - 13

ONE WORD AT A TIME: THE HOLOPHRASTIC STAGE

10. The infant's first meaningful utterances are one-word _holophrases_ that convey meaning mainly through context.

          holophrases

The Infant's Choice of Words

11. A majority of the infant's first 50 words are names for objects, both general and specific; these are called _nominals_ and are likely to involve objects that move or that can be manipulated.

          nominals

Individual Differences in Language Production

12. In the one-word stage, a majority of infants learn and use primarily nominals first, and these children are _referential_ communicators; however, many infants have a more diverse vocabulary that includes words for feelings and for regulating social interactions, and these children are called _expressive_ communicators.

          referential

          expressive

Early Semantics: The Development of Word Meanings

13. Using words too generally is called _overextention_ , and using words too specifically is called _underextention_; in explaining these types of errors, as well as how children infer the meanings of words as language use develops, the semantic _features_ hypothesis holds that children attend to the perceptual aspects of referents whereas the _functional_ similarities hypothesis states that children attend more to what the referents "do."

          overextention
          underextention

          features
          functional

FROM HOLOPHRASES TO SIMPLE SENTENCES: THE TELEGRAPHIC STAGE

14. Children begin to use telegraphic utterances that contain _two_ words at about _18 - 24_ months of age, and the variability of language development from here onward is such that progress is best measured by the average number of _morphemes_ per utterances as in the MLU.

          two, 18 - 24

          morphemes

Characteristics of Telegraphic Speech

15. Telegraphic speech omits the _function_ words such as articles and prepositions, perhaps because child doesn't know these words or because the child's _memory_ is very limited and cannot process more than two or three words at a time.

          function

          memory

Grammatical Analyses of Early Speech

16. Grammars for young children's telegraphic speech indicate the presence of word "classes," which include _pivot_ constructions and _open_ constructions; these occur in specific orders and combinations, indicating that telegraphic speech is based on _rules_ children consistently employ.

pivot
open

rules

The Pragmatics of Early Speech

17. A developmental sequence in children's use of pragmatics includes (1) vocalizing to attract adult _attention_ by about 3 months of age, (2) using _gestures_ as an aid to communication by about 6 months, (3) _looking_ in the direction pointed to by an adult at about 10-11 months, (4) using a _finger_ to point by about 12 months, and (5) using gestures in conjunction with speech from about _14_ months onward.

attention
gestures
looking
finger

14

18. Toddlers also vary their speech to compensate for _distance_ between them and a listener, to monitor the reactions of another person to see if communications are being _understood_, and to tailor their speech according to the age of the _listener_.

distance

understood
listener

LANGUAGE LEARNING DURING THE PRESCHOOL PERIOD

Acquiring Grammatical Morphemes

19. Research indicates that grammatical morphemes are acquired in a specific order that reflects their _semantic_ complexity; as children begin to acquire these morphemes, they tend to apply them to irregular verbs and nouns as well, which is referred to as _overregularization_.

semantic

overregularization

Mastering Transformational Rules

20. During the preschool period children learn how to transform statements in order to ask _questions_, to negate, and to form complex and compound _sentences_; each of these aspects of syntax develops in orderly _stages_ through which the child eventually acquires correct forms.

questions
sentences
stages

Semantic Development

21. One of the first relational contrasts acquired by preschool children is the _I / you_ contrast; relational contrasts involving _spatial_ adjectives such as big/little and tall/short appear next, and spatial contrasts also develop in an orderly sequence.

I / you
spatial

Pragmatics and Communications Skills

22. Preschool children continue to improve in their ability to alter their language usage to fit the _situation_ and to allow for whether the listener is an adult or another _child_.

situation
child

REFINEMENT OF LANGUAGE SKILLS

Later Syntactic Development

23. General progress in language development during the grade-school years includes (1) a return to using correct _irregular_ forms of verbs and nouns, (2) improved understanding of active as well as _passive_ sentence constructions, and (3) generally correct use of _personal_ pronouns; however, they continue to make errors in interpreting subject-verb relationships due to an

irregular

passive
personal

overreliance on the minimum _distance_ principle.   distance

Semantics and Metalinguistic Awareness

24. Middle childhood is also marked by (1) an increasingly large _receptive_ vocabulary of perhaps 8,000 to 14,000 words, (2) improved proficiency in making semantic _integrations_ in order to draw conclusions, and (3) a beginning ability to detect hidden, perhaps _sarcastic_ meanings of statements; many such language skills depend upon an understanding of language itself, which is called _metalinguistic_ awareness.

receptive
integrations

sarcastic

metalinguistic

Growth of Communication Skills

25. As indicated by research on how children communicate when they do not have face-to-face contact with a listener, grade-school children become more proficient at _evaluating_ the messages they send and receive in order to clarify.

evaluating

THEORIES OF LANGUAGE DEVELOPMENT

Learning Theories

26. Skinner's theory of how children learn to talk is that parents _reinforce_ children for correct language use, through a process of _shaping_ sounds into words, words into sentences, and so on; but major problems with this explanation are that parents reinforce children more in accord with "_truth_ value" of utterances and that parents tend to satisfy their children's needs independent of whether the utterances are _grammatically_ correct.

reinforce
shaping

truth

grammatically

27. Social learning theorists offer explanations of language learning based on observation and _imitation_ of adult speech, but problems here are that children often produce _novel_ utterances that could not result from imitation and that even when parents try to get children to _imitate_ correct speech the attempts are often unsuccessful.

imitation
novel

imitate

28. Parents attempt various ways of enhancing children's language development, including _expansions_ of telegraphic utterances by filling in function words and _recasts_ of utterances by rearranging them into more complex forms; but perhaps the most important role of parents is to provide day-to-day _conversation_ with the child.

expansions
recasts

conversation

The Nativist Perspective

29. Chomsky proposes that children have a biologically programmed language _acquisition_ device through which they extract the _regularities_ of language and thus learn rules.

acquisition
regularities

30. Evidence for the nativist perspective includes (1) that only humans have true _language_, (2) that the left cerebral hemisphere _specializes_ for language functioning, (3) that there is to some extent a _critical_ period for language learning, and (4) that there are language _universals_ in the early timing and order of many aspects of language development.

language
specializes
critical
universals

The Interactionist Perspective

31. An interactionist perspective notes that models are necessary and thus _imitation_ plays a role, encouragement of speech aids children and thus _reinforcement_ plays a role,

imitation
reinforcement

and many of the processes seem built-in and thus biological
Maturation plays a role as well.   maturation

32. Piaget takes an _interactionist_ perspective, noting   interactionist
that language universals might exist because all children share
certain early _experiences_ and also that _cognitive_ devel-   experiences, cognitive
opment is reflected in language development.

SELF-TEST I

Consider each alternative carefully. Then choose the best one.

1. Throughout the first few years language development generally follows a sequence from
simple to complex, i.e., from
   a. phonology to morphology to syntax
   b. morphology to phonology to syntax
   c. phonology to syntax to morphology
   d. morphology to syntax to phonology

2. The correct order of infant vocalizations over the first year of life is
   a. crying, babbling, cooing, first word
   b. babbling, crying, cooing, first word
   c. cooing, crying, first word, babbling
   d. crying, cooing, babbling, first word

3. As the infant approaches the point of uttering the first meaningful word,
   a. babbling narrows down to the language sounds the child is hearing
   b. meaningful vocables begin to appear in the child's vocalizations
   c. both of the above
   d. none of the above

4. Which of the following is a 19-20-month-old child in the telegraphic stage <u>least</u> likely to utter?
   a. nominals
   b. action words
   c. modifiers
   d. function words

5. During the holophrastic stage, a child might use the word "car" to apply only to the
family car and no others; this would be an example of
   a. overextension
   b. underextension
   c. overregularization
   d. expansion

6. During the telegraphic stage, children use
   a. pivot-open constructions
   b. open-open constructions
   c. word order as an indicator of meaning
   d. all of the above

7. With regard to grammatical morphemes, children typically
   a. learn irregular words early and continue to use them throughout development
   b. use overregularized word forms until about 9-10 years of age
   c. start with irregular word forms, then overregularize, then return to irregulars
   d. overregularize nouns but not verbs.

124

8. Transformational grammar refers primarily to
   a. pragmatics
   b. syntax
   c. morphology
   d. phonology

9. A 4-5-year-old child is likely to misinterpret
   a. negations
   b. passive constructions
   c. both of the above
   d. none of the above

10. By the first or second grade, children 6-8-years old are generally capable of
    a. using tag questions
    b. making semantic integrations
    c. understanding simple puns
    d. all of the above

11. For the grade-school child, metalinguistic awareness in involved in
    a. thinking about messages
    b. evaluating messages
    c. clarifying messages
    d. all of the above

12. Evidence in favor of learning-theory explanations of language development includes
    a. observations that parents reinforce correct usage of grammar by children
    b. observations that children learn syntax through direct imitation
    c. observations that children learn semantics through direct imitation
    d. all of the above

13. Evidence against learning-theory explanations of language development includes
    a. children's use of original sentences that could not be learned by imitation
    b. parent's tendencies to reinforce truth value rather than correct grammar
    c. parents' abilities to satisfy children's needs whether grammar is correct or not
    d. all of the above

14. Evidence in favor of nativist explanations of language development includes
    a. the existence of language universals
    b. the preschool child's tendency to overregularize nouns and verbs
    c. .the left-hemisphere specialization of language function
    d. all of the above

15. Piaget's view that language development depends upon underlying cognitive structures is basically
    a. a learning-theory position
    b. a nativist position
    c. an interactionist position
    d. none of the above

RESEARCH SUMMARY AND REVIEW

Using the textbook, review the research efforts indicated and write a summary of the important findings. Note the general purpose or context of the research.

1. Stern, Spieker, & Mackain (1982), page 292: _____

_____

_____

2. Thomas, Campos, Shucard, Ramsay, & Shucard (1981), page 293: _____

_____

_____

_____

_____

3. Nelson (1973, 1981), page 294: _____

_____

_____

_____

4. Brown (1973), page 304: _____

_____

_____

_____

_____

5. Shatz & Gelman (1973), page 309: _____

_____

_____

_____

_____

6. Krauss & Glucksberg (1977), page 313: _____

_____

_____

_____

7. Gardner & Gardner (1969, 1974): _____

_____

_____

_____

_____

8. Premack & Premack (1972), Premack (1976), page 320: _____

_____

_____

_____

Consider each alternative carefully.   Then choose the best one.

1. Morphology refers to
    a. how phonemes are combined into meaningful units
    b. how grammatical markers modify nouns and verbs
    c. both of the above
    d. none of the above

2. Modification of language to make it appropriate in differing contexts and situations is
    a. phonology
    b. morphology
    c. syntax
    d. pragmatics

3. The nativists' "language acquisition device" (LAD) is viewed as
    a. located in a specific area of the left hemisphere
    b. a teaching device for aphasic children
    c. a set of cognitive and perceptual abilities
    d. none of the above

4. With regard to language development, neonates in the first few days of life can
    a. synchronize body movements to breaks and pauses in others' speech
    b. recognize mother's voice, given adequate exposure
    c. learn operants that will produce recorded speech
    d. all of the above

5. Which of the following cries appears last?
    a. the hunger cry
    b. the pain cry
    c. the anger cry
    d. the fake cry

6. A 7-month-old infant's babbling is characterized by
    a. production of sounds present in all languages
    b. echolalia
    c. production while others are speaking, as if harmonizing
    d. all of the above

7. A 10-month-old infant's babbling is characterized by
    a. production of sounds present in all languages
    b. production while others are speaking, as if harmonizing
    c. pragmatic adjustments to the situation, such as changes in intonation
    d. all of the above

8. In Stern, Spieker, and Mackain's (1982) study, mothers varied their voice intonations in attempting to communicate with their infants, and the implication was that the infants responded differently as a result; this would favor
    a. learning-theory explanations of language development
    b. nativist explanations of language development
    c. interactionist explanations of language development
    d. none of the above

9. In the study by Thomas, et al. (1981), younger infants (11 months old) did not gaze at "known" referents any more than at "nonsense" referents, even though their mothers told them what to look at; this indicates that
    a. 11-month-old infants are less inclined to obey their mothers
    (b.) the infants did not know the meanings of the "known" words
    c. the infants did not understand their mother's gestures
    d. all of the above

10. If your 15-month-old looks out the window of the house and says "car!", this means
    a. the infant has recognized a car passing outside
    b. the infant is practicing with using the word to describe your car
    c. the infant wants to go for a ride in your car
    (d.) any of the above, depending upon the context

11. In accord with research, the odds are that your infant's first word will be
    (a.) a noun
    b. a verb
    c. an adjective
    d. an article

12. Nelson's (1973, 1981) research efforts indicated that "expressive" communicators
    a. tend to be later-born children
    b. tend to come from less educated families
    c. have more diverse vocabularies
    (d.) all of the above

13. Eve Clark's semantic features hypothesis states that children tend to infer the meaning of words on the basis of
    (a.) perceptual characteristics
    b. functional characteristics
    c. both of the above
    d. none of the above

14. The three telegraphic utterances "Cow jumped," Doggies barked," and "See horsie" have a mean length of utterance (MLU) of
    a. 2.0
    (b.) 3.0
    c. 3.3
    d. 4.1

15. Typically, mothers will name or describe things their infants point at; this favors explanations of language development based on
    (a.) learning theory
    b. biological maturation
    c. interactionist theory
    d. none of the above

16. If deaf infants are given adequate exposure and practice with sign language, they go through a sequence of babbling in sign, using holophrastic signs, then telegraphic signs, and so on; this favors explanations of language development based on
    a. overregularization
    (b.) biological maturation
    c. semantic features
    d. metalinguistic awareness

17. The consistent order in which children acquire English grammatical markers is
    (a.) "-ing," "'s," "-ed"
    b. "-ing," "-ed," "'s"
    c. "-ed," "-ing," "'s"
    d. "-ed," "'s," "-ing"

18. Learning to ask questions correctly involves
    a. using rising voice intonation appropriately
    b. inserting appropriate grammatical morphemes
    c. rearranging word order
    d. all of the above

19. Complex sentences begin to appear in the child's speech when
    a. the child turns about 24 months of age
    b. MLU reaches 3.5-4.0
    c. orregularization drops out
    d. all of the above

20. Typically, the first relational contrast mastered by the child is
    a. tall/short
    b. before/after
    c. I/you
    d. more/less

21. Generally, 4-year-olds do not laugh at puns, word riddles, or "knock, knock" jokes
    a. because they do not yet have a sense of humor
    b. because they lack metalinguistic awareness
    c. both of the above
    d. none of the above

22. In the Krauss & Glucksberg (1977) study, preschool children could not communicate well across an opaque screen in describing and copying a block-stacking task, because of
    a. their poor psychomotor coordination
    b. lack of metalinguistic awareness about clarifying
    c. their inability to speak in grammatically correct sentences
    d. all of the above

23. Research indicates tha a child's language development can be aided if the parents
    a. ask the child questions
    b. make requests of the child
    c. issue commands to the child that invite verbal responses
    d. all of the above

24. Expansions of a child's telegraphic utterances are often ineffective in aiding language development, but recasts often help; this is probably because
    a. recasts are novel and maintain the child's attention
    b. recasts do not contain additional ideas or information
    c. expansions are usually too complex
    d. expansions do not parallel the child's utterances

25. The accomplishments of Washoe in learning American Sign Language and Sarah in learning to use symbolic plastic tokens clearly illustrate that
    a. human language in its adult form depends upon a language acquisition device
    b. chimpanzees can be taught to use language at the level of a 2½-3-year-old child
    c. limited intellectual capacities of the chimpanzee prevent language usage
    d. all of the above

VIGNETTES

Consider the story, then answer each question using material from the textbook.

I. Susan and her father were playing outside one afternoon. Suddenly, a thought seemed to flicker through her mind, taking priority over their game of hide-and-seek. She said, "Cookie." Then she went inside and soon returned, protesting, "Cookies gone. Cookies all goed! Where cookies goed?" When Susan's father accompanied her inside again to the kitchen, they found two different bags of cookies on the counter. But Susan kept insisting that the cookies she wanted were all gone.

1. Identify the errors of syntax in Susan's speech.

2. Identify the semantic error in Susan's use of "cookie," and discuss this in terms of the semantic features hypothesis.

3. About how old would you guess Susan is? Why?

II. One day Jimmy's mother accompanied him to his room for some lessons in picking up his toys. The lessons mainly involved sorting out the many small parts and putting them in the sets they came in, so he could play with them. And, of course, part of the idea was to clear a path through the debris to make it possible to walk through Jimmy's room. The strategy his mother chose was to sit near the corner of the room and give instructions on what to do. At one point in the clean-up she said, "Now pick up all the parts to your space shuttle. Pick them up *after* you find the box, of course." In response, Jimmy immediately started scouting around and picking up the parts, with no attempt to find the box, but his mother didn't correct him because she was happy enough that he was doing the work without grumbling. Then having picked up all the parts he could see, Jimmy noticed something missing and said, "Where's the astronaut? Who lost my astronaut?" And his mother replied, "The astronaut was lost by *you*. And you know it." Then Jimmy said, "*I'm* not lost! The *astronaut* is lost, silly!"

1. Identify the sources of Jimmy's confusion in each of the two instances.

2. Restate Jimmy's mother's instructions to avoid the confusion.

3. Predict how old Jimmy will probably be before he understands such constructions.

III. Anna and Mark were next-door neighbors. Each was 5 years old, and each had a plastic toy builder's set that included hammer, screwdrivers, nuts and bolts and washers, wrenches, and other interesting things. One afternoon Anna was playing with her builder's set and she decided she could make something even more interesting if she had more nuts and bolts. So, having recently learned to use the telephone, she called Mark and asked him to bring over his nuts and bolts to combine with hers. Although she didn't exactly know their correct names, she described them in great detail in terms of their color, general shape, and mostly what you do with them. Shortly, Mark showed up with his plastic nails and a wrench. And so, they quickly decided to go back to his house to find the items Anna wanted.

1. Whose "fault" was Mark's error? Why?

2. What sort of underlying cognitive skill do the children lack?

3. About how old will they be when they can communicate effectively on such a task?

APPLICATIONS

Try each of the projects, noting answers to the questions as you go.

I. One of the more interesting milestones an infant reaches is the "first word," which typically comes around the end of the first year. However, children vary, and it is more accurate to consider the changes taking place prior to the first word if you're trying to anticipate when this event might occur. For this project:

1. Summarize vocal changes that take place just prior to the first word.

2. Summarize changes in pragmatics that take place just prior to the end of the prelinguistic period.

3. Using Table 8-1, predict what type of word it's likely to be, assuming that the infant turns out to be a referential communicator. Similarly, predict the most likely type of first word for an expressive communicator.

II. Assume you're interacting with a child about 20 months of age, a child who is fairly typical in using two- and three-word utterances. Also assume that you're interested in doing whatever you can to improve the child's language development as the two of you talk and interact, with emphasis on syntax.

1. What types of restatements of the child's utterances might be helpful?

2. What about corrections regarding grammatical markers? Would this be likely to help? Why or why not?

3. How might "baby talk" and motherese help or hinder language development at this age?

III. As an adult, when you attempt to learn a foreign language, you use somewhat different tactics than a child does when first learning a language. For one thing, you learn alternate words for things you already know and understand, and for another you take advantage of metalinguistic awareness in looking for the structure of the new language and having it explained to you in a language you already know. For this project, however, assume that you are magically and instantly transported to a strange, faraway land where no one speaks English, and the language you must now learn in order to survive is quite alien from your own. Thus, in many respects, your quest might be very similar to that of a child first learning to communicate.

1. Where would you start? What would you need to learn first, and how might you go about it?

2. In particular, how would you go about learning syntax?

3. Could you expect to eventually speak the language like a native? Why or why not?

ANSWERS

Self-Test I

1. a	6. d	11. d
2. d	7. c	12. c
3. c	8. b	13. d
4. d	9. b	14. d
5. b	10. d	15. c

Research Summary and Review

1. Stern, Spieker, & Mackain (1982): In assessing how infants come to understand the meaning of changes in voice intonation, 2-6-month-olds and their mothers were videotaped and it was found that mother exaggerate intonations and vary them to get the infant's attention, to keep the infant in a good mood, and to elicit positive affect.

2. Thomas, et al. (1981): As an exploration of whether infants actually understand words their parents think they do, mothers tried to instruct their infants under conditions where pointing and gesturing were prevented by a screen; 13-month-olds understood the words reasonably well, but 11-month-olds apparently did not.

3. Nelson (1973, 1981): Infants' first 50 words were classified according to type, and

a majority of the words were nominals, at least for children who were referential communicators, and these children tended to be first-borns; the vocabulary of the expressive communicators contained more personal/social and action words, and these children tended to be later-borns. The research was basically exploratory in nature.

4. Brown (1973): Assessment of children's acquisition of grammatical morphemes yielded an invariant sequence in which these are acquired in English as a function of the degree of semantic and syntactical complexity.

5. Shatz & Gelman (1973): Children 4 years old were observed to adjust their statements in explaining a toy either to a 2-year-old or to an adult, by using shorter sentences versus more complex ones and by employing attention-getting devices with the younger child, thus indicating that children in this age range have a beginning understanding of pragmatics.

6. Krauss and Glucksberg (1977): To explore age-related changes in communication skills, pairs of children were separated by a screen and asked to communicate information about how to stack blocks with unfamiliar designs on them; younger children did poorly, and improvement was systematic up through about age 10 years.

7. Gardner & Gardner (1969, 1974): Washoe the chimpanzee was taught American Sign Language, and in addition to acquiring the vocabulary of about a 2-2½-year-old, she also learned rudimentary communication with humans, such as asking questions and describing objects and events. Many aspects of her language development paralleled that of a child, thus shedding light indirectly on human language development.

8. Premack & Premack (1972), Premack (1976): Sarah the chimpanzee was taught to use symbolic plastic tokens, and she acquired language usage at the level of a 2½-3-year-old both in terms of vocabulary and syntax, including using language skills to learn new vocabulary. This study also shed light on human language development.

Self-Test II

1. c	6. d	11. a	16. b	21. b
2. d	7. c	12. d	17. a	22. b
3. c	8. a	13. a	18. d	23. d
4. d	9. b	14. b	19. b	24. a
5. d	10. d	15. a	20. c	25. b

Vignettes

I. (1) "Cookies gone" leaves out function words "The" and "are"; "Cookies all goed" refers to something like "The cookies all went away," thus leaving out function words and also overregularizing the past tense of "to go"; "Where cookies goed" probably should be "Where did the cookies go," thus leaving out function words and markers and also the rearrangement necessary to ask a question. (2) Implicitly, Susan is using "cookie" in an undergeneralized sense, as if it applies to only one type of cookie which she prefers. In accord with the semantic features hypothesis, she would do this because of its particular size, shape, color, taste, or other perceptual features that are meaningful for her. Later, of course, she'll learn the brand name. (3) A good guess puts Susan around 2½ years of age. Telegraphic speech characterizes the 18-36-month-old. Overregularization characterizes the 2½-6-year-old. And transitional questions occur in the age range of 2½-4 years.

II. (1) In the first case, Jimmy attends to sentence order rather than the meaning of "after," although he probably does understand this word. Hence he looks for the space shuttle parts before searching for the box. In the second case he attends to the sentence as if it were active, such as "The astronaut lost you." In addition, the statements were probably too long for his memory span and also too complex. (2) Simply say, "Find the box, then pick up the parts..." and "You lost the astronaut...." (3) Jimmy is probably about 4 years old, and on average will understand his mother's constructions by about 6.

III. (1) Anna lacks skills in thinking about, evaluating, and clarifying messages. Mark does also. Both lack the metalinguistic awareness that would enable them to narrow down the specific intent of the message. (2) Metalinguistic awareness with regard to the effectiveness of communication is necessary to realize that there is a communication problem in the first place. (3) In accord with the Krauss and Glucksberg (1977) study, the children will probably be 9 or 10 years old-before they can communicate effectively in such a situation, at least in those situations where either of them is unfamiliar with the names of the ojects.

Applications

I. (1) Babbling narrows down to the sounds of the language the infant is hearing. Multisyllabic echolalia appears. Vocables appear. Pitch variations in babbling in response to mother and father are present. And the infant has been engaging in conversational turn-taking when babbling to companions. (2) In terms of pragmatics, the infant can respond to gestures and pointing by others even when not knowing the word used, which necessarily includes understanding that meaning is being conveyed in the first place. But the infant doesn't point until the very end of the first year. (3) Logically, the first word will probably be a nominal, and in turn most likely a general nominal that refers to some familiar and interesting object. In addition, semantic development is based largely on imitation, since the child must learn the arbitrary ways sounds are combined to represent objects and the like. Thus the first word is likely to be one the infant has heard a number of times, which might be a specific nominal such as "mama" or "dada" if the parents have been deliberately using these words around the infant. Otherwise, if the child is an expressive communicator, the chances improve that a word such as "'top" (for stop) or "hi" might be first, but a nominal is still more likely.

II. (1) Expanding telegraphic utterances to include function words might or might not help, although changes in voice intonation, plus gesturing, might make these expansions more effective through maintaining the child's attention. Recasting the utterances into questions or into more complex statements would be more likely to maintain the child's attention in the first place and the trigger the child's processing of new information by adding linguistic novelty (moreso than simple expansions). Note that recasts also add or ask for new information and are thus more conversational and interesting. (2) Adding grammatical marker morphemes probably would not be any more effective than adding function words in general. Also, Brown's research indicates that these are learned in order of complexity, which implies a maturational basis that limits the amount of acceleration possible. (3) On the positive side, toddlers might find baby talk more interesting and entertaining and at times easier to understand because of its simplicity. On the negative side, since children acquire language by extracting rules from what they hear, baby talk both models incorrect rules and prevents vocabulary building as well, at least if it is used very often.

III. (1) You would start with words that represent relatively tangible objects and situations, by pointing and gesturing to induce the natives to provide the word. You would probably also have some new sounds to learn, in the context of specific words. Thus you would begin with semantics, one word at a time, probably with emphasis on foods. (2) Given some vocabulary, you would then try to listen and extract rules for how to combine the words into simple and then more complex utterances, such as "Want food now!" But here you would learn much faster than a child, because of your metalinguistic awareness and more or less knowing what you are looking for. (3) Nativists would say you are beyond the critical period and thus would never speak the language like a native. Certain phonemes would probably always be difficult for you, at the very least. Empiricists would more likely predict a high level of acquisition, with time, since you would no longer be using English to interfere with your learning. Thus any remaining differences between your language and that of a native would be inconsequential.

CHAPTER NINE

COGNITIVE DEVELOPMENT

OVERVIEW AND KEY TERMS

Read carefully. Recall examples and discussion as you go, and define each key term.

WHAT ARE COGNITION AND COGNITIVE DEVELOPMENT?

Cognition refers to mental processes by which we acquire knowledge, and cognitive development refers to changes that occur in mental skills and abilities between birth and early adulthood. Two important perspectives on cognition are Piaget's structural-functional approach and information-processing theory.

PIAGET'S BASIC IDEAS ABOUT COGNITION

Piaget's interest in children's wrong answers on standardized tests led him to study age-related differences in how children think. He kept detailed notes on his own three children, using the clinical method described in Box 9-1: The investigator asks questions or poses problems, and then follows up on the child's responses to clarify them and assess the child's reasoning.

To Piaget, intelligence is a basic life function through which the organism adapts to its environment. The child is a constructivist who acts on the environment and comes to understand it, and the child's mental constructions of reality depend on her or his cognitive maturity.

A schema is a pattern of though or action, i.e., a cognitive structure. Behavioral schemata are organized patterns of behavior by which the child represents and responds to the environment. These begin as reflexes, then are modified as the child explores objects and events. Symbolic schemata arise during the second year of life, and involve mental representations of events that the child uses to guide behavior. Operational schemata involve more purely cognitive operations performed on objects of thinking and are characteristics of children about age 7 years and older. The concept of reversibility of events, as a way of understanding the environment, is a cognitive operation.

All cognitive structures arise through two inborn intellectual functions: Organization refers to the combining of schemata into more complex ones, and the basic goal of organization is to further adaptation to the demands of the environment. In turn, adaptation occurs through the complementary processes of assimilation, in which new experiences are interpreted in terms of schemata the child has already acquired, and accommodation, in which previously acquired schemata are modified to incorporate new experiences. All cognitive functioning includes both processes, in varying degree, depending upon the situation and past experience.

PIAGET'S STAGES OF COGNITIVE DEVELOPMENT

Children progress through cognitive stages in an invariant developmental sequence, because each stage is built upon what went before.

During the sensorimotor stage (birth to 2 years), behavioral schemata are dominant. Children develop from reflexive to reflective organisms, in six substages. The first reflexive activity includes assimilation of novel objects to reflexive schemata and some accommodation to the objects. Primary circular reactions, such as voluntary thumbsucking, are repetitious behavioral schemata centered around the infant's own body. Secondary circular reactions are also repetitious, pleasurable behaviors, but they center on objects and events in the external environment, by chance and not intentionally. Coordination of secondary schemata involves the intentional combining of previously unrelated schemata to produce interesting events or to solve problems, and imitating the behavior of others first appears duirng this substage. Tertiary circular reactions are exploratory schemata based on trial and error, in which the infant experiments and invents new methods of producing interesting events or solving problems, and imitation becomes much faster in this substage. During the final sensorimotor substage, invention of new means through mental combinations, infants begin creating symbolic schemata by internalizing behavioral schemata. This includes inner experimentation, i.e., solving problems at a mental level without trial-and-error experimentation. Deferred imitation becomes possible in this substage. All infants complete these substages in the same order.

The object concept, according to Piaget, first appears during coordination of secondary schemata, although infants still confuse their own activity with the existence of objects. Object permanence improves during tertiary circular reactions, and the infant will search for an object where it was last seen. But infants still cannot solve invisible displacements. Object permanence is complete during invention of new means through mental combinations. However, as discussed in Box 9-2, Bower believes that infants understand object permanence earlier, during primary circular reactions, even though they will not search for objects during this substage. Object permanence in this research is indicated by the infant's surprise or anticipation of where an object should be. Bower proposes that errors in spatial reasoning, instead of lack of an object concept, account for younger infants' failure to search in Piaget's tasks.

In the preoperational stage (2 to 7 years), symbolic schemata predominate. Children have not yet acquired the operational schemata necessary to logical thinking, according to Piaget's theory, which emphasizes limitations and deficiencies of preoperational thought. The first of the two substages is the preconceptual period, in which the symbolic function appears. Pretend play also emerges, and as discussed in Box 9-3, children create rich fantasy worlds, invent imaginary playmates, use play as a means of coping with emotional crises, and play at role-taking. Although children continue to develop an understanding of the world around them, their thinking is limited by animism, transductive reasoning, and egocentrism. These limitations continue in the second substage, the intuitive period, although use of symbols improves. Perceptually based logic appears in class inclusion problems such as the "wooden beads," in which the child focuses only on one feature at this substage. In attempting conservation problems the child also focuses on only one feature, as in the liquid/beaker problem and the other tests of conservation. Thus the preoperational child's thinking is characterized by centration, which is overcome later as the child acquires operational schemata such as compensation. The cognitive skill of reversibility is also necessary in solving conservation problems.

Recent research indicates that preoperational children are less egocentric than Piaget supposed, and they sometimes can take others' points of view, although not always. Piaget may also have underestimated the preoperational child's causal reasoning. And various researchers have found that conservation problems can be taught to preoperational children by methods such as identity training. Apparently, reversibility and compensation are not absolutely necessary for conservation, in contrast to Piaget's view.

In the concrete operations stage (7 to 11 years), children are rapidly acquiring operational schemata and applying them to real or at least imaginable objects, situations, and events, but they cannot deal with hypothetical or abstract problems. In this stage children can construct mental representations such as a map (although researchers have

135

found that younger children can also). Concrete operations include <u>seriation</u> and <u>transitivity</u>, at least with real objects. Concrete operations such as classification and reversibility may also underlie appreciation of linguistic humor. In the concrete operations stage, children often display <u>horizontal decalage</u> and can solve some conservation problems but not others. Piaget attributes this to differing complexity of the problems, noting that operational skills evolve gradually as simpler skills lead to more complex ones. And the onset of education in most societies coincides with onset of concrete operations. A major contribution by Piaget is his emphasis that elementary-school children learn best by doing and by discovering important principles for themselves.

The formal operations stage (11-12 years and beyond) is characterized by the ability to reason abstractly and hypothetically. As illustrated in Box 9-4, concrete operators had difficulty with the three-eye assignment and gave much less creative answers. Formal operations thinking is hypothetical-deductive in solving problems, as in Piaget's "four-beaker" problem: Formal operators pursue a systematic plan in testing all combinations of the beakers and use many "if-then" propositions along the way. Systematic, abstract thinking also sets the stage for considering morality, justice, beliefs, and values as the child enters adolescence, although the transition to formal operations takes place very gradually over several years. Other researchers besides Piaget have found that many adults do not reason at the formal operations level, perhaps due to limited education or intellectual capacity.

Formal operations may be described as a <u>problem-solving</u> stage, and it has been suggested by other researchers that the great thinkers may function at an even higher level. Or there may be two levels beyond formal operations: <u>systematic reasoning</u>, and beyond that, <u>metasystematic reasoning</u>.

AN EVALUATION OF PIAGET'S THEORY

A major contribution of Piaget's theory is his view of children as naturally curious beings who actively explore and try to understand. His theory is the most detailed and integrated version of cognitive development. But one difficulty is the timing of the different stages. Another problem is the implication that development occurs abruptly, in stages, rather than continuously. Finally, Piaget's theory has been criticized as being merely a description of cognitive development rather than an explanation. But current researchers are working to address these criticisms and fill in the gaps.

THE INFORMATION-PROCESSING APPROACH

By analogy to computers, the human mind has hardware and mental software that enable thinking and reasoning. And just as computers have become increasingly sophisticated, the mind follows a developmental sequence of hardware and software improvements as the child develops. But computers process sequentially and are limited to their programs, whereas humans process simultaneously and create new information.

Attention is necessary to getting information into the human system. Young children have limited attention and persistence at tasks, and their curiosity interferes with systematic problem solving. Although younger children may know to look first at relevant stimuli and label them, older children are better at selectively attending without special training.

Given attention, <u>memory</u> processes come into play. Information to be stored passes through a <u>sensory register</u> to <u>short-term memory (STM)</u> and finally to <u>long-term memory (LTM)</u>. Conscious intellectual activity takes place in STM, which is limited both in time and in the amount of information it can hold. Changes in the capacity of STM are minimal throughout childhood. LTM is relatively permanent and has extremely large capacity. <u>Rehearsal</u> is one means of transferring information from STM to LTM. Repetition, naming, and symbolic doing are strategies in rehearsal. <u>Organization</u> of information in STM is another general strategy, and this can involve creating categories or chunking. A third strategy is _elaboration_ by adding sentences or images to information.

Development of memory is different for <u>recognition memory</u> versus <u>recall memory</u>. In general, recognition tasks are easier, and some capacity for recognition memory is inborn. By 2-3 months of age, infants store information in LTM and can recognize familiar activities; by 5-7 months, infants remember familiar faces. Preschool children have good recognition memory but limited recall, in part because they tend not to spontaneously rehearse. And training greatly improves children's use of rehearsal. Thus younger children have a <u>production deficiency</u> but not a <u>mediation deficiency</u>. Skills in rehearsal also tend to improve during middle childhood and beyond. Organization skills improve later, beginning around 9-10 years of age, although 6-8-year-olds can be taught to use categories and clusters. Elaborative skills generally do not appear before adolescence, which may relate to the younger child's more limited STM, lack of formal operations, or lesser knowledge about the world to be used in elaboration. From a different perspective, retrieval processes also show a developmental sequence. Instructing younger children to use categorical cues and elaboration aids recall, and thus poor recall may also involve retrieval deficiencies. <u>Metamemory</u> increases dramatically between ages 5 and 10. Younger children overestimate how much they can remember and underestimate how much study will be required to remember. Younger children also generally know less about how they remember things. But good metamemory is neither required for good recall nor a guarantee.

Siegler's research on developmental changes in problem-solving illustrates a rule-assessment approach to studying how children process relevant information. In the "balance scale" problem, situations and possible rules are determined in advance, to reveal how the children go about solving the problems. Older subjects progressively use more sophisticated rules.

INDIVIDUAL DIFFERENCES IN COGNITIVE STYLE

Children with an <u>impulsive</u> style of problem solving tend to go with the first idea that occurs to them, whereas children with a <u>reflective</u> style have a slower conceptual tempo and consider many alternatives before responding. The "matching familiar figures" test assesses time the child takes and number of errors the child makes, yielding an impulsivity-reflectivity score. Children become more reflective as they mature, but tend to maintain their relative standing on this dimension.

Reflective children are more attentive in the classroom and they may acquire skills such as reading, memorizing, and conserving more easily than impulsives, in spite of equivalent intelligence. Impulsives tend to initiate more social interactions with peers but may also be more physically aggressive and more prone to acting out. Impulsives can be reinforced for reflectivity or can learn reflectivity by observing models. Conceptual tempo can also be modified by teaching impulsives how to consider alternatives and how to verbalize as they go, which is more effective.

SELF-REVIEW

Fill in the blanks for each item. Check the answers for each item as you go.

WHAT ARE COGNITION AND COGNITIVE DEVELOPMENT?

1. The activity of knowing and the processes by which knowledge is acquired is called _cognition_ ; in turn, the changes that occur as the child matures and learns are referred to as cognitive _development_ .

    cognition

    development

PIAGET'S BASIC IDEAS ABOUT COGNITION

2. Piaget's early work in _intelligence_ testing led him to

    intelligence

believe that we should study _____ children think rather than
_____ children think.

| | how |
| | what |

3. Piaget's interview technique starts with asking the child
standard _____, but from there the interviewer follows
up according to how the child responds; this is basically the
_____ method.

questions or probes

clinical

What Is Intelligence?

4. Piaget's theory starts from the viewpoint that cognition is
how we _____ to our environment; in turn, children are active
explorers who _____ their understanding of reality.

adapt
construct

Cognitive Schemata: The Structural Aspects of Language

5. Cognitive structures through which we represent, organize,
and interpret experience are called _____.

schemata

How Is Knowledge Gained? The Functional Basis of Intelligence

6. Schemata are formed through the inborn cognitive functions
of (1) _____, in which simple schemata give rise to
more complex ones, and (2)_____, a related function
through knowledge is adjusted to fit the real world.

organization
adaptation

7. In turn, adaptation consists of (1) _____, in
which new experiences are interpreted in accord with existing
schemata, and (2) _____, in which existing schemata are modified to fit new experiences.

assimilation

accommodation

PIAGET'S STAGES OF COGNITIVE DEVELOPMENT

The Sensorimotor Stage (Birth to 2 years)

8. The sensorimotor stage is characterized by _____
schemata and a progression through six substages: (1) the infant
extends reflexes to objects in the environment in the substage
of _____ activity; (2) more complex habits centered on
the child's own body appear in the substage of _____ circular reactions; (3) pleasurable responses are extended to objects in the environment in the substage of _____ circular reactions; (4) deliberate and intentional behavior appears
in the substage of _____ of secondary schemata;
(5) the child begins to invent novel ways of interacting with
the environment in the substage of _____ circular reactions; and (6) behavioral schemata begin to be mentally internalized in the substage of _____ of new means through mental combinations.

behavioral

reflexive
primary

secondary

coordination

tertiary

invention

9. Learning new behaviors through imitating a _____ appears
during the coordination of _____ schemata, and accurate
imitation is present during _____ circular reactions.

model
secondary
tertiary

10. Piaget's work indicated that object _____ appears
during _____ of secondary schemata and is complete
during _____ of new means through mental combinations;
Bower's work indicates that object permanence begins during
_____ circular reactions.

permanence
coordination
invention

secondary

The Preoperational Stage (2 to 7 years)

11. Pretend play, in simple form, appears in the _____
period; complex, _____ pretend play appears early in the
preoperational period, and the child can pretend to play with

sensorimotor
symbolic

_____ playmates and also use play in practicing event-   imaginary
ual _____ roles.   adult

12. The list of deficits Piaget proposed as characteristic of
preoperational children's thinking includes: (1) attributing of
life to inanimate objects, called _____; (2) a tendency to   animism
view the world entirely from one's own perspective, called
_____; (3) a tendency to focus one's attention on   egocentricity
only one aspect of a problem, called _____; and (4)   centration
the lack of an ability to "mentally undo" an action in order to
solve a problem, i.e., a lack of _____ in thinking.   reversibility

13. Because of these deficits, according to Piaget, preoperational children cannot solve the "wooden beads," "liquid/beaker,"
and other _____ problems; however, recent research-   conservation
ers have discovered that preoperational children can solve these
problems after being provided with _____ training.   identity

The Concrete-Operational Stage (7 to 11 years)

14. Concrete operators can solve _____ problems,   conservation
although they can solve some before they can solve others, as in
horizontal _____; concrete operators also learn to solve   decalage
arrangements of objects according to a dimension such as length
or height, as in _____ problems, as well as problems of   seriation
"greater than" and "less than" which involve _____.   transitivity

The Formal-Operational Stage (Age 11-12 and Beyond)

15. Formal operators extend their problem-solving abilities to
abstract, _____ situations, and their thinking be-   hypothetical
comes much more systematic as in the "_____ _____" problem;   "four beaker"
in effect, formal operational thinking is much like that of a
_____.   scientist

AN EVALUATION OF PIAGET'S THEORY

The Issue of Timing

16. Piaget's test problems often deal with unfamiliar objects
presented in ways that may confuse the child, and thus his theory tends to _____ preoperational children's abili-   underestimate
ties in particular; but his overall _____ sequence of   invariant
cognitive development has been verified.

Does Cognitive Development Occur in Stages?

17. Other critics suggest that horizontal decalage really implies that cognitive abilities develop _____ rather   gradually
than in discrete stages, noting wide variation in the ages at
which children can solve different _____ problems.   conservation

Does Piaget's Theory "Explain" Cognitive Development?

18. Some argue that Piaget's theory _____ rather than   describes
explains cognitive development, a major point being that the
role played by biological _____ is not well specified.   maturation

Present and Future Directions

19. Current researchers are attempting to fill in the gaps in
Piaget's theory, in part by looking for relationships between
cognitive development and _____ maturation.   biological or
                                                                neurological

20. One distinction between computers and humans is that computers use _____ processing and humans are capable of
_____ processing.   sequential
                                                simultaneous

Attentional Processes: Getting Information into the System

21. Very young children are easily distracted and often fail to
solve problems because they are either unable or unwilling to
sustain _____ to the task at hand.   attention

Memory Processes: Retaining What One Has Experienced

22. The basic information-processing model of memory includes
mechanisms for (1) holding sensory input in the _____ reg-   sensory
ister, (2) interpreting and categorizing information in _____,   STM
and (3) storing the processed information more or less permanently in _____.   LTM

23. Strategies for transferring information from STM to LTM include (1) simply repeating the information, as in _____, rehearsal
(2) categorizing and grouping the information, through a process
of _____, and (3) adding to or expanding the in-   organization
formation, as in _____.   elaboration

24. Young children have less difficulty with _____   recognition
memory than with _____ memory, and the latter improves more   recall
slowly with age.

25. Middle childhood is marked by improvements in information-
storage strategies such as (1) rehearsal based on _____ med- verbal
iation, (2) categorizing information into meaningful _____,   clusters
and (3) adding information in the form of elaborative mental
_____ as in mnemonic devices; similarly, information-re-   images
trieval strategies _____ in middle childhood.   improve

26. The ability to think about memory itself, which is called
_____ , also improves in middle childhood; however,   metamemory
knowing about memory does not guarantee good _____.   recall

Hypothesis Testing and Problem Solving: Using Information One Has Retained

27. Siegler's research on problem solving emphasizes the _____   rules
children use at different ages and levels, which in turn reflect
what the child _____ to on problems such as the "balance   attends
scales."

The Current Status of Information-Processing Theory

28. Information-processing theory is still developing, and is
best viewed as a _____ to Piaget's theory rather than   complement
a replacement.

INDIVIDUAL DIFFERENCES IN COGNITIVE STYLE

29. Children who tend to proceed with the first hypothesis they
think of in solving a problem are called _____, wheareas impulsives
children who evaluate various hypotheses before proceeding are
called _____.   reflectives

Implications of Reflective and Impulsive Styles

30. Reflective children tend to be better at solving problems
because they are more attentive and less _____,   distractible
and yet differences are usually not obtained between reflectives

and impulsives on _____ tests, which implies   intelligence
that impulsives are simply more careless.

Can Conceptual Tempo Be Modified?

31. One of the more effective methods of teaching impulsives to
be reflective is the self-_____ approach, in which   -instructional
the child self-instructs comments to be careful and to slow down
while solving problems.

SELF-TEST I

Consider each answer carefully. Then choose the best one.

1. Piaget's approach to studying cognitive development emphasizes
    a. the clinical method
    b. the child's active role in learning
    c. limitations on understanding at different ages
    d. all of the above

2. Children use and acquire the three basic types of schemata in the order
    a. behavioral, operational, symbolic
    b. behavioral, symbolic, operational
    c. symbolic, behavioral, operational
    d. symbolic, operational, behavioral

3. Piaget's four general stages of cognitive development occur in the order
    a. sensorimotor, preoperational, formal operational, concrete operational
    b. sensorimotor, concrete operational, preoperational, formal operational
    c. sensorimotor, preoperational, concrete operational, formal operational
    d. any of the above, depending upon the individual child

4. By the beginning of the preoperational stage, the child
    a. is capable of deferred imitation
    b. has acquired the object concept
    c. has begun to use symbols in problem solving
    d. all of the above

5. According to Piaget, the preoperational child's understanding and knowledge of the
world is characterized by
    a. egocentrism
    b. reversibility
    c. compensation
    d. all of the above

6. Cognitive operations acquired <u>during</u> the concrete-operational stage, according to Piaget, include
    a. class inclusion
    b. relational logic
    c. conservation
    d. all of the above

7. Research evidence indicates the <u>least valid</u> criticism of Piaget's theory is that
    a. younger children may have skills that are underestimated due to lack of exper-
       ience with Piaget's tasks
    b. children may go through the stages in an entirely different sequence than that
       proposed by Piaget
    c. cognitive development does not occur in anything resembling discrete stages
    d. Piaget's theory describes rather than explains cognitive development

8. Strengths of Piaget's theory of cognitive development include
    a. an emphasis on the child as an active explorer and learner
    b. generation of considerable research on cognitive development
    c. applicability to children across differing cultures
    (d.) all of the above

9. Information-processing theories of cognitive development have generally
    a. been completely incompatible with Piaget's theory
    (b.) looked at different aspects of cognition than Piaget
    c. disproven most of Piaget's theory
    d. all of the above

10. The correct order in which input is processed is
    (a.) sensory register, STM, LTM
    b. sensory register, LTM, STM
    c. STM, sensory register, LTM
    d. STM, LTM, sensory register

11. In information-processing theory, "attention" generally refers to the transfer of information from
    a. STM to LTM
    b. sensory register to LTM
    (c.) sensory register to STM
    d. LTM to STM

12. In information-processing theory, "rehearsal" generally refers to the transfer of information from
    (a.) STM to LTM
    b. sensory register to LTM
    c. sensory register to STM
    d. LTM to STM

13. In information-processing theory, "retrieval" generally refers to the transfer of information from
    a. STM to LTM
    b. sensory register to LTM
    c. sensory register to STM
    (d.) LTM to STM

14. Metamory
    a. is necessary for good recall
    b. guarantees good recall
    c. both of the above
    (d.) none of the above

15. Children with an "impulsive" conceptual tempo are
    a. less attentive and less persistent on tasks
    b. prone to go with the first hypothesis they think of
    c. equivalent to "reflectives" on IQ tests
    (d.) all of the above

RESEARCH SUMMARY AND REVIEW

Using the textbook, review the research efforts indicated and write a summary of the important findings. Note the general purpose or context of the research.

1. Bower (1982), page 342: _____

_____

_____

_____

2. Mossler, Marvin, & Greenberg (1976), page 350: _____

_____

_____

_____

3. Field (1981), page 351: _____

_____

_____

_____

4. Inhelder & Piaget (1958), page 354: _____

_____

_____

_____

5. Miller & Weiss (1981, 1982), page 362: _____

_____

_____

_____

6. Kee & Bell (1981), page 368: _____

_____

_____

_____

7. Pressley & Levin (1981), page 368: _____

_____

_____

_____

8. Siegler (1978, 1981), page 371: _____

_____

_____

Consider each alternative carefully. Then choose the best one.

1. Piaget's theory of cognitive development is based on
    a. how children process information from input to storage
    b. development of structures and functions in intelligence
    c. conceptual tempos and cognitive styles
    d. all of the above

2. Piaget's intellectual function of "adaptation" is based on the child's
    a. assimilation of new experiences to existing schemata
    b. accommodation of schemata to fit new experiences
    c. both of the above
    d. none of the above

3. Circular reactions, whether primary, secondary, or tertiary, are best described as
    a. reflexive actions that are not involved in cognition
    b. basically pleasurable actions that are repeated for their own sake
    c. intuitive actions that incorporate symbols
    d. imitative actions that are eventually deferred

4. According to Piaget, the object concept appears during the substage _____; however, Bower's research indicates that the object concept appears during _____.
    a. coordination of secondary schemata, tertiary circular reactions
    b. tertiary circular reactions, reflex activity
    c. coordination of secondary schemata, primary circular reactions
    d. tertiary circular reactions, secondary circular reactions

5. A 4-year-old child who believes that automobiles are "alive" because they move is
    a. displaying animism
    b. experiencing horizontal decalage
    c. still egocentric
    d. capable of the symbolic function

6. According to Piaget, a preoperational child who invents imaginary playmates is
    a. on the verge of entering concrete operations
    b. practicing conceptual skills relevant to social and intellectual growth
    c. fixated in the sensorimotor stage
    d. seriously disturbed and in need of psychotherapy

7. In Piaget's view, preoperational children cannot solve conservation tasks such as the "liquid/beaker" problem because the children
    a. center on a single perceptual feature or dimension
    b. do not realize that the process is reversible
    c. do not understand that changes in one dimension compensate for another
    d. all of the above

8. Research by Mossler, Marvin, and Greenberg (1976) on preoperational egocentrism and by Field (1981) on identity training and conservation problems indicates that Piaget
    a. accurately described the abilities of preoperational children
    b. overestimated the abilities of preoperational children
    c. underestimated the abilities of preoperational children
    d. accurately described Swiss children but not American children

9. Generally, a child who is in the concrete-operational stage can
   a. solve the "wooden beads" problem
   b. solve the "liquid/beaker" problem
   c. sketch a map of a familiar route from one place to another
   (d.) all of the above

10. According to Piaget, the role of the elementary school teacher is to
    a. provide learning environments that allow the child to inquire and explore
    b. use real objects rather than the blackboard, thus allowing learning by doing
    c. create a setting that encourages discovery rather than memorization of facts
    (d.) all of the above

11. The purpose of the "four beaker" problem employed by Inhelder and Piaget (1958) is
    (a.) to assess the child's ability to employ a systematic plan
    b. to assess the child's ability to imitate what the experimenter has done
    c. to test for the skills involved in trial-and-error reasoning
    d. all of the above

12. Formal operations has been called a "problem-solving" stage; there may also be
    a. a "problem-finding" stage
    b. a stage of systematic reasoning
    c. a stage of metasystematic reasoning
    (d.) all of the above

13. Piaget's theory incorporates
    a. stages of cognitive development
    b. an invariant sequence of cognitive development
    c. cognitive development that is universal
    (d.) all of the above

14. In the analogy between humans and computers, the brain is like _____ and the strategies employed in thinking are like _____.
    (a.) hardware, software
    b. a sequential processor, a simultaneous processor
    c. software, hardware
    d. a simultaneous processor, a sequential processor

15. In the research efforts by Miller and Weiss (1981, 1982), younger children were more distracted by irrelevant stimuli and thus could not remember the relevant stimuli as well as older children; this was because
    a. the younger children had limited memory and could not process as much information
    b. the younger children were more distractible and could not attend as well
    (c.) the younger children attended to all of the stimuli, not just the relevant ones
    d. the older children did not use verbal mediation

16. Suppose you ask yourself whose work came first, Freud's or Piaget's; this would require you to retrieve information from _____ and compare it in _____.
    (a.) LTM, STM
    b. LTM, LTM
    c. STM, LTM
    d. STM, STM

17. Clustering and chunking are examples of
    a. rehearsal
    (b.) organization
    c. elaboration
    d. none of the above

18. The infant's habituation to a stimulus provides evidence that
    a. recognition memory is inborn
    b. recall memory is inborn
    c. both of the above
    d. none of the above

19. With regard to the use of verbal mediators as an aid to storage and retrieval of information, research generally indicates that younger children (age 5 years or so) have
    a. only a production deficiency
    b. only a mediation deficiency
    c. both a production and a mediation deficiency
    d. neither a production nor a mediation deficiency

20. Kee and Bell's (1981) research on the effects of having "categorical pictures" as
cues for children's and adult's recall of stimulus items indicated that
    a. cues are important for storage but not for retrieval
    b. cues are important for retrieval but not for storage
    c. cues are important both for storage and for retrieval
    d. cues are important neither for storage nor for retrieval

21. Pressley and Levin (1981) prompted children to elaborate while memorizing stimuli;
later, during recall, the younger children in the study who were reminded to use these
elaborations benefited greatly. This indicates the operation of
    a. a production deficiency
    b. a storage deficiency
    c. a retrieval deficiency
    d. none of the above

22. In Siegler's (1978, 1981) research on children's strategies in solving the "balance
scale" problems, it is possible to assess
    a. developmental age trends in problem solving
    b. specific rules employed in problem solving
    c. both of the above
    d. none of the above

23. There are three possible outcomes in Siegler's "balance scale" problems: left-side
down, right-side down, or balance. If you present six of these problems to a child who
uses no rules whatsoever in making predictions, the child should get, by chance,
    a. 5/6 correct
    b. 3/6 correct
    c. 2/6 correct
    d. 0 correct

24. With regard to cognitive style, "reflective" children
    a. consider various hypotheses before attempting to solve a problem
    b. have a slower conceptual tempo
    c. tend to do better of Piagetian tasks
    d. all of the above

25. In contrast to reflective children, "impulsives" are
    a. less intelligent
    b. less socially aggressive
    c. less likely to be rebellious
    d. none of the above

VIGNETTES

Consider the story, then answer each question using material from the textbook.

I. When baby Harry was about 8 months of age, his parents began encouraging him to sit at

146

the table in his high chair and eat his baby food with a spoon. They figured they were being a bit ambitious, given Harry's age, but they figured they had to start somewhere. Harry's mother figured that if she guided his hand with the spoon a few times, he might start learning to get a spoonful of food from the bowl to his mouth. And so she tried. But Harry had other ideas. Instead of trying to eat, he chose the joys of scooping up awkward, dripping spoonfuls and slinging them haphazardly into the air to watch them fly and splatter here and there.

1. Identify the probably secondary circular reactions Harry is employing.

2. Comment on any evidence that Harry is coordinating these to produce interesting outcomes.

3. Comment on whether Harry is capable of "imitating" the basics of how his parents eat a meal.

II. During much of her early childhood, Anita was locked in a closet for as much as an hour at a time whenever she misbehaved, and sometimes even when she didn't. Her parents often wished she weren't around, and, especially on these occasions, they could be very cold and rejecting. They were not at all the kind of parents Anita would have wanted. And so, during her many trips to the closet, she invented imaginary parents who were very warm and caring and loving to her all of the time. And she played and talked with them often, even when she wasn't in the closet.

1. What would Piaget say about the purpose of Anita's imaginary parents?

2. Where and how would Anita learn what "good" parents are like?

3. Would Anita's use of imaginary parents be healthy or unhealthy? Why?

III. Although Aaron was not a hyperactive child, he was quite "impulsive" and he very much preferred to be up and around and doing something rather than sitting still in his first-grade class. If he had to sit, he usually passed the time by pestering whoever was near him rather than doing classwork. What work he did do was careless and usually wrong, and by the middle of the schoolyear Aaron was in danger of being held back. Yet everyone agreed that Aaron was too smart to repeat a grade, if only he would "try."

1. How would you predict that Aaron would respond on conservation problems? Why?

2. What approach would you take in teaching Aaron to conserve, such as on the liquid/beaker problem?

3. Would you expect the training to generalize to other conservation problems? Why?

APPLICATIONS

Try each of the projects, noting answers to the questions as you go.

I. As an illustration of Piaget's idea of "adaptation," consider the following: Suppose you are an experienced driver of large automobiles with automatic transmissions, but you have driven little else. One day you find yourself behind the wheel of a friend's small "sporty" car, 5-speed transmission and all, faced with the challenge of driving it.

1. Identify assimilable aspects of the situation.

2. Identify aspects to which you would have to accommodate.

3. Throughout, note the interplay between assimilation and accommodation.

II. Suppose you find yourself with the materials necessary to do the liquid/beaker conservation task, and further suppose you have access to fairly typical children at 2, 5, and 8 years of age. For each age child, make predictions about their behavior when faced when faced with the task.

1. How might attention span limitations affect each child?

2. How might limitations on memory span affect each child?

3. Which child (or children) might solve the problem, and why, according to Piaget?

III. Let's suppose (quite possibly) that you are faced with the task of memorizing the six substages of the sensorimotor stage for an exam, and you must also note the basic age ranges and characteristics of the child's thinking during each substage.

1. Devise a method based on rehearsal.

2. Devise a method based on organization.

3. Devise a method based on elaboration.

ANSWERS

Self-Test I

1. d	6. d	11. c
2. b	7. b	12. a
3. c	8. d	13. d
4. d	9. b	14. d
5. a	10. a	15. d

Research Summary and Review

1. Bower (1982): Infants in the primary circular reactions substage were quite surprised when a toy previously hidden behind a screen wasn't there when the screen was removed, which indicated that the object concept may be present earlier than Piaget thought.

2. Mossler, Marvin, & Greenberg (1976): Children 2-3 years old were egocentric in thinking that their mothers could know about the content of a film just because the children did, but 4-6-year-olds did not respond egocentrically, in contrast to what Piagetian theory would predict.

3. Field (1981): Using identity training, it was demonstrated that preoperational children could learn to conserve liquids and could also generalize their understanding to other conservation problems prior to acquiring reversibility and compensation; this indicated that Piaget may have underestimated preoperational children's abilities.

4. Inhelder & Piaget (1958): On the "four beaker" task, concrete operators tended to give up or resort to trial-and-error when simple solutions (e.g., 1 + g, 2 + g, etc.) failed; formal operators continued to try more complex combinations and in a systematic fashion, thus demonstrating their different approach to problem solving as in Piaget's theory.

5. Miller & Weiss (1981, 1982): In the presence of distracting stimuli, older children showed better selective attention to relevant objects, but younger children remembered the irrelevant objects better; indications were that younger children may know how to remember such stimuli, but they are easily led astray by curiosity.

6. Kee & Bell (1981): On a memory task based on organization, children and adult subjects alike performed better when categorical cues were present both during storage and retrieval, indicating that organizational devices are important to both aspects of memory.

7. Pressley & Levin (1981): Children 6 and 11 years old were taught to use elaboration in learning stimulus pairs, and the younger children who were reminded to use elaboration during retrieval performed better than younger children who were not reminded. The implication was that younger children may have a retrieval rather than a storage deficiency in using memory.

8. Siegler (1978, 1981): Using tasks such as the "balance scale" problem, it was found that children and adults consistently used certain rules in solving problems and that the rules became more complex with higher cognitive development. In contrast to Piagetian procedures, this method allowed direct assessment of the rules employed.

Self-Test II

1. b	6. b	11. a	16. a	21. c
2. c	7. d	12. d	17. b	22. c
3. b	8. c	13. d	18. a	23. c
4. c	9. d	14. a	19. a	24. d
5. a	10. d	15. c	20. c	25. d

Vignettes

I. (1) Secondary circular reactions include scooping with a spoon and swinging the arm upward, in each case behaviors we assume Harry has practiced previously in different contexts and with different objects. (2) Coordinating these reactions (or schemata) is evident when Harry puts scooping and swinging together to get an interesting effect with his food. Later we might predict that Harry will acquire schemata associated with aiming, too, and then things will really get interesting. (3) Although it will take time and many repeated trials, Harry should at this age have a beginning capability of imitating more acceptable mealtime behavior, although his motor control is still very limited at this age.

II. We would of course predict many sad and difficult effects on Anita's personality and adjustment, going well beyond the imaginary parents she invented to (1) take the place of her real parents in order to cope with the conflicts engendered by their treatment of her. Piaget would further say that she compensates for unsatisfied needs in this fashion. (2) We could guess that she knows what parents could be like from watching TV or from other family members such as grandparents. Her role-playing would incorporate behaviors in the form of deferred imitation. (3) By implication, given the difficult circumstances, Anita's imaginary parents would provide a basically healthy and creative way of adapting, allowing at least a minimal satisfaction of needs in the absence of an alternative.

III. (1) As noted, "impulsives" tend to go with the first notion rather than reflect on alternatives. Aaron would be very likely to attend to the first dimension he notices on a conservation problem, and he would not pause to consider other aspects of the problem such as identity, reversibility, and compensation. (2) Field's identity training would at least make it more likely Aaron would attend to this aspect of the problem first. This might be coupled with Messer's direct training - self-instructional technique. (3) In accord with Field's research, we could reasonably expect generalization from this to other conservation problems, primarily through directing Aaron's attention to the "sameness" rule that applies throughout conservation problems.

Applications

I. First, note the overwhelming complexity involved in trying to specify the schemata operative in such a situation. This holds true even for the relatively simple behavioral schemata of infants. But some examples are: (1) You should assimilate things such as sitting behind a steering wheel, with an orientation forward, looking through a windshield, grasping a steering wheel, using your right foot for the gas pedal, operating the turn indicator with your left hand, and so on. (2) Accommodation would be evident in operating the gear shift differently, using the clutch with your left foot, coordinating clutch and gas and brake pedal movements, steering and turning the car differently because of its smaller size and handling, and so on. (3) As Piaget pointed out, all actions involve both assimilation and accomodation. Thus, although you sit in the same part of the car, the seat isn't the same, so you also accommodate; neither are the steering wheel, gas pedal, or turn indicator either completely the same or completely different. The gear shift is different, but it is still a gear shift, and assimilation is evident in your knowing what it's for in the first place. And although it's a different size car, it's still a car.

II. (1) The 2-year-old's attention would predictably wander. The 5-year-old would be more persistent and responsive to the fact of a problem in the first place, but attempts at problem-solving are still relatively unsystematic at this age. The 8-year-old should show reasonable consideration and persistence, including more systematic attempts to figure out the problem. Note that these factors operate independently of Piaget's theory of children's reasoning and cognition. (2) The 2-year-old might have difficulty even recalling what the poured liquid looked like at the beginning of the problem, which would rule out use of "sameness" or reversibility. The 5-year-old probably wouldn't have difficulty here, but might on more complex conservation problems. Memory should be no problem for the 8-year-old. (3) From Piaget's point of view, the 8-year-old should solve the problem through compensation or reversibility, concepts not yet acquired by the younger children, at least in terms of typical age ranges.

III. In each case, start with a list of the six substages nicely and neatly arranged with the ages and characteristics included. (1) A rehearsal strategy might be saying the substages and other info to yourself over and over until you more or less "drill" it in. This is the least efficient strategy, because it doesn't take advantage of the higher level abilities you are capable of using. (2) By itself, an organization approach would be the most efficient. First, perhaps, you might learn the substages by themselves (as analogous to clustering of "like" things), perhaps also employing an acronym to help you remember them all and in order (e.g., use RPSCTI). Having memorized this, next go back and fill in the ages: R, 0-1; P, 1-4; S, 4-8; C, 8-12; T 12-18; I, 18-24. Then set this aside and refresh yourself on meanings of words such as "circular," "primary versus secondary versus tertiary." As a final step, go back and put the meanings with the acronym letters and ages, which in effect creates a series of chunks, one for each substage.
(3) Elaboration could take various forms, and might be best used as an adjunct to organization. For example, in attaching the age ranges, you might elaborate by noting that there is a progression from smaller to larger units: R has a 1-month interval, P a 3-month interval, and from there the intervals are 4, 4, 6, and 6. Thus you might superimpose the series 13446 separately, noting that "a bigger child gets bigger intervals." You could also elaborate the acronym RPSCTI into something like "RiPS CiTIes," with an association such as "the infant that destroyed New York." Finally, you might consider a "meaningful" elaboration such as "R is first and the infant responds; P is next and the infant 'looks' inward; then S and the infant looks outward; then C and the infant puts it all together; then T and the infant looks for new actions; and I when the infant goes to symbols." These parallel the "Methods" portion of Table 9-1. And you can probably do better. The basic idea is to use visual images that more or less correspond to the key aspects of each substage.

CHAPTER TEN

INTELLIGENCE: MEASURING MENTAL PERFORMANCE

OVERVIEW AND KEY TERMS

Read carefully. Recall examples and discussion and you go, and define each key term.

   People typically think of intelligence as a "quantity" that reflects learning and
problem-solving ability, and people are likely to view an "intelligent" person as having
broad knowledge, logical thinking, common sense, wit, and creativity.

WHAT IS INTELLIGENCE?

   As it turns out, theorists often disagree on what intelligence is and what the origins of intelligence may be. Nativists such as Darwin view intelligence as being genetically determined. Galton extended this view, overlooking the possibility that the
child's environment and experiences contribute to intelligence. Current theorists such
as Eysenck and Jensen view intelligence as 70-80% heritable. Even so, we would still
know little about the development of an individual person. And other theorists view this
estimate as too high, stressing instead the interplay between heredity and environment.

   Definitions of intelligence often imply that it involves a single underlying attribute, but some definitions stress intelligence as a number of distinctly separate abilities. This issue has often been address by factor analysis, in which cluster of highly
correlated test items are interpreted as factors representing abilities. Spearman found
moderate correlations between many of the items on his test, and thus proposed a g factor
of general mental ability. In turn, he proposed that inconsistencies in a person's performance across tests were due to an s factor involving specific mental abilities. Thurstone used factor analysis to derive seven primary mental abilities, but these were also
intercorrelated and thus implied an common underlying ability. Cattell and Horn have recently argued that g and the primary mental abilities reflect two kinds of intelligence:
fluid intelligence, which is not learned and is based on biological maturation and funct-
tioning, and crystallized intelligence, which is based on learning and acquired knowledge
and thus increases throughout the life span. Guilford's "structure of intellect" model
yields 120 primary mental abilities based on the interaction between three cognitive di-
mentions: content, operations, and products. But scores on tests of Guilford's mental
abilities also tend to be intercorrelated. Throughout these various approaches to defining intelligence, problems are that investigators use different measures and that the way
in which factors are determined is basically subjective. Perhaps the best model to date
is that of a general intellectual factor plus a small number of yet-to-be-determined
specific abilities.

HOW IS INTELLIGENCE MEASURED?

   Intelligence testing essentially began with Binet and Simon, whose goal was to identify schoolchildren in need of remediation. Test items were developed by trying them out
on children known to be normal versus dull or retarded. On the assumption that intelli-

gence develops with age, items were later age-graded to produce mental age (MA) estimates. Eventually, Stern developed the idea of the intelligence quotient (IQ) based on the ratio of mental age to chronological age: IQ = MA/CA x 100. Thus the average IQ is 100. Terman then developed the Stanford-Bient by standardizing Binet's test on 1000 American schoolchildren and incorporating the idea of IQ. The Stanford-Binet has been revised and restandardized and is currently a popular test. IQ scores are now based on norms, however, rather than MA. Norms are derived by standardization, based on the assumption that IQ is normally distributed. Thus an IQ score provides information about the percentage of people in the population at a specified age who will score at or below that score.

The Wechsler intelligence scales (WPPSI and WISC-R) attempt to separate the measurement of "verbal" and "performance" IQ. A full-scale IQ is based on these in combination. The Stanford-Binet is often preferred for preschool children, whereas the WISC-R is more often used when children are between 6 and 16 years of age. The WISC-R is also more sensitive to possible brain damage or learning disorders, although it is only a starting point in such diagnoses.

Group tests of mental ability are less expensive and less time-consuming for the examiner. Group testing in the U.S. began in World War I with the Army Alpha Intelligence test. Currently popular group tests include the Lorge-Thorndike, the SAT, the ACT, and the GRE. Achievement tests are oriented more toward crystallized intelligence. Disadvantages include minimal contact between examiner and examinee.

Infant intelligence testing in the U.S. essentially began with the Gesell Developmental Schedules, which assess developmental milestones in motor development, adaptive behavior, language development, and personal/social behavior, yielding a developmental quotient (DQ) based on an average of 100. The Bayley Scales of Infant Development are currently popular and include a Motor scale, a Mental scale, and an Infant Behavioral Record, all of which assess the child's rate of development. Unfortunately, such instruments are poor in predicting an infant's later IQ, largely because different kinds of abilities are measured. However, instruments such as the Bayley scales are useful in detecting early neurological deficits and severe mental retardation.

A central question is whether IQ is a stable attribute. Except for infant tests, IQ scores do show stability for many individuals, although researchers have found that a substantial minority show wide fluctuations in IQ over time. Thus IQ is apparently not a good measure of potential intellectual ability. Instead, it provides an estimate of intellectual performance at a given point in time. Stability of IQ relates to the reliability of an IQ test. This and other principles of test construction such as item selection, validity, standardization, representative sampling, and use of standard test procedures are discussed in Box 10-1.

WHAT DO INTELLIGENCE TESTS PREDICT?

IQ tests correlate reasonably well with current school grades and also predict future school performance - at least for groups of children. Prediction of an individual's success in grade school, high school, or college, however, involves much more than an IQ or aptitude test score. The best predictor of future grades is previous grades considered in conjunction with factors such as study habits and motivation.

People with higher IQs tend to wind up in more prestigious occupations, but there is much variability. The relationship between IQ and job performance depends upon the nature of the work. In high-status professions where high IQ scores are often a condition of employment or training, no clear relationship between IQ and job performance exists.

As a predictor of health, adjustment, and life satisfaction, IQ scores seem to work reasonably well. However, as in Terman's classic longitudinal study of people who displayed high IQs as children, IQ does not necessarily "cause" better health, happiness, or adjustment. Only a small percentage of the high-IQ subjects showed maladjustments, and a large percentage were high achievers. But the more successful subjects came from better home environments.

FACTORS THAT INFLUENCE IQ SCORES

Evidence for heritability of intelligence comes from studies of selective breeding in animals (such as that of Tryon), studies of intellectual resemblance between family members, and studies of the effects of adoption. Jensen and Eysenck have both argued that IQ is about 80% heritable, whereas others have argued that an interplay between heredity and environment determines intelligence. Box 10-2 presents an extreme environmental position that factors in adoption and childrearing can account for all of the results of family and adoption studies regarding heritability, but the point remains that monozygotic children reared apart resemble each other more closely in IQ than dizygotic twins who are reared together.

The apparent effects on an impoverished home environment are that children perform lower on IQ tests. This leads to the cumulative deficit hypothesis that such children's IQs decrease with age, which has received research support. In turn, environmental enrichment improves IQ scores, also as verified by research.

SOCIOCULTURAL CORRELATES OF INTELLECTUAL PERFORMANCE

The HOME Inventory assesses quality of intellectual stimulation in six areas: (1) emotional and verbal responsivity of the mother, (2) avoidance of restriction and punishment, (3) organization of physical and temporal environment, (4) provision of appropriate play materials, (5) maternal involvement with the child, and (6) opportunities for variety in daily stimulation. Such measures have been found to be directly related to IQ, and, for a child 6-12 months of age, are better predictors of later IQ than performance on infant tests. Referential communication accuracy is also an important factor in the child's home environment. "Enriched" home settings include parents who are warm, responsive, and eager to be involved with the child, especially in learning activities. Studies of home environment, however, are often confounded with genetic effects.

Research on Dutch males indicates that brighter children come from smaller families and tend to be earlier in the birth order. These findings may reflect better intellectual stimulation when fewer children are present in the home, in that parents use more complex explanations, put more emphasis on achievement, and are more concerned about performance. It has also been argued that the average family intellectual level is important, noting that larger families have more children and thus a lower average level. Also of note is that single-parent households tend to yield lower IQ scores in children, although this may be confounded with socioeconomic status.

Excepting infants, children from lower- or working-class homes average 10-20 points lower on IQ tests than do middle-class children. But such differences are associated mainly with academic performance. Similarly, depending also on metropolitan versus rural residence, people of Black, Native American, or Hispanic ancestry score about 10-20 points lower than Whites. Group differences, of course, say nothing about individual IQ or skills. For example, some 15-25% of the Black population score higher than half of the White population.

One explanation of group differences in IQ is the "test bias" hypothesis: There is an apparent White middle-class bias in IQ tests which favors people familiar with mainstream English. Content is also based more on concepts and experiences likely to be familiar to middle-class Whites, a point which is underscored by Dove's Chitling Test. But relatively culture-free tests such as the Raven Progressive Matrices Test still yield group differences. Changes in test dialect have also not been found to eliminate group differences. And academic performance differences apparently correspond to IQ test differences. Zigler's motivational hypothesis holds that lower-class and minority children score lower due to wariness of examiners, lesser interest in the tests, and so on, but attempts to increase motivation during tests affect disadvantaged and middle-class children equivalently.

The genetic hypothesis controversially attributes group differences in IQ to heredity, in that the social, ethnic, and racial groups who score lower on IQ tests marry most often within their own population and thus set the stage for a restricted range of IQ-determining genes. Jensen, proposing that that intellect consists of Level I abilities involved in simpler kinds of learning and Level II abilities involved in more abstract reasoning and problem-solving, has argued that group differences arise in Level II abilities. This he attributes to heredity. But as illustrated in Box 10-3, within-group heritability says nothing about differences between groups, in that such differences can easily be due to the effects of environments. Another point is that studies of mixed-race children do not yield differences consistent with Jensen's view.

The environmental hypothesis holds that poor people and member of various ethnic or racial groups grow up in intellectually impoverished environments that include poor nutrition, less-educated parents, fewer resources to invest in children, and often the effects of prejudice in producing negative self-image and less motivation to do well on any kinds of tests. Studies of improved environments have demonstrated IQ increases with minority groups. And it is also noteworthy that IQ is not the only human characteristic necessary for good personal and social adjustment.

IMPROVING INTELLECTUAL PERFORMANCE THROUGH COMPENSATORY EDUCATION

Compensatory education projects such as Head Start are designed to provide disadvantaged children with skills and experiences that put them on an equal footing with middle-class children by the first grade. Early reports indicated success, as measured by IQ increases, but the differences tended to wash out after a year or two of grade school. However, long-term follow-up studies now indicate that the children maintain improvement on achievement tests in reading, language, and math, are less likely to drop out of high school, have more positive attitudes about achievement, and have mothers who are more satisfied with the children's performance in school. Thus the programs work. Similarly, home-based interventions such as the toy demonstration program yield IQ gains, and if mothers acquire better skills in stimulating intellectual development, the effects can generalize to younger siblings. Discussion groups involving disadvantaged parents have also been effective. But none of the various types of intervention have yet succeeded in transforming disadvantaged children into above-average achievers overall. Bronfenbrenner's prescription for intervention starts before the children are born and emphasizes the parents' overall involvement with their children throughout middle childhood.

SOME COMMON USES (AND ABUSES) OF IQ TESTS

IQ tests are often used to classify and sort schoolchildren into classrooms according to their tested mental abilities. But this often implies an assumption that IQ measures a "fixed" intellectual capacity, rather than simply performance at a given point in time. A low IQ score is not sufficient for labeling a child as retarded, since factors other than intellectual capacity may be involved. And even if we assume that IQ tests are accurate indicators of potential, sorting children into ability groups can create negative self-attitudes among low-scoring children and hinder their achievement. IQ tests are clearly not a panacea. By themselves, IQ scores have little to say about an individual's potential for future achievement.

SELF-REVIEW

Fill in the blanks for each item. Check the answers for each item as you go.

1. The person on the street often thinks of intelligence as a

single _quantity_ that reflects an individual's ability to learn and solve problems, but there are many different definitions of intelligence.

WHAT IS INTELLIGENCE?

2. The early nativist view of intelligence, such as that of _Darwin_ was that intelligence is _genetically_ determined at birth; Galton's early research on successes and accomplishments within _families_ tended to support this view, and modern-day theorists such as Jensen and Eysenck have estimated that intelligence is _70 - 80_ % heritable.

Darwin, genetically

families

70 - 80%

Is Intelligence a Single Attribute or Many Attributes?

3. Definitions of intelligence as a single attribute include an early one by Wechsler, in which intelligence is the capacity to _act_ purposefully, _think_ rationally, and _deal_ effectively with the environment.

act, think, deal

4. Spearman applied factor _analysis_ to a variety of measures of intellectual functioning and derived two basic factors: the _g_ factor of general mental ability and the _s_ factor of special, specific abilities.

analysis

g, s

5. Thurstone derived _seven_ primary mental abilities, but these were not completely independent and thus also implied the operation of a single _g_ factor.

seven

g or general

6. Cattell and Horn divided intelligence into two basic dimensions: abilities relatively free of environmental influences, called _fluid_ intelligence, and abilities that come from schooling and experiences, called _crystallized_ intelligence.

fluid
crystallized

7. Guilford's structure-of-intellect model is the most complex, proposing 4 types of things the person can think about, called _contents_, 5 types of actions or processes, which are called _operations_, and 6 types of results of thinking, which are called _products_; in combination, these yield _120_ primary mental abilities.

contents
operations
products, 120

HOW IS INTELLIGENCE MEASURED?

8. Modern intelligence tests trace to Alfred _Binet_ and Theophile Simon, who developed the concept of mental _age_ through their work on assessing schoolchildren; this eventually gave rise to the notion of IQ, which was defined as _MA/CA_ x 100.

Binet
age

MA/CA

Modern IQ Tests

9. In 1916 Terman revised and standardized the Binet test on _American_ children, thus creating the _Stanford_-Binet, which is called the first true IQ test.

American, Stanford-

10. Interpreting an IQ score involves use of the _normal_ distribution to determine the percentage of people falling at or below the score; in general, an IQ of 100 is average, and thus _50_ % of the population should score at or below 100.

normal

50%

11. Besides the Stanford-Binet, Wechsler's _WISC-R_ is a popular test with schoolchildren, and it is based on separate scores for _Verbal_ IQ and _Performance_ IQ which are combined to yield an overall _Full_-scale IQ score.

WISC-R

Verbal, Performance
Full-

12. Infant intelligence tests necessarily rely much less on

_____ skills; for example, the Gesell Developmental Sched-   verbal or language
ules and the Bayley scales are based on _____ for sensory,   norms
motor, adaptive, and social _____, yielding an overall   behavior
score for ___ instead of IQ.   DQ

13. An important question is whether IQ is a _____ attribute   stable
across time and development; except for infant tests, research
indicates that there are _____ correlations between early and   high
later IQ scores, at least where _____ averages are considered,   group
but some _____ show wide fluctuations in IQ over time.   individuals

14. In addition to being based on meaningful items, an IQ test
should yield the same score for an individual tested on different occasions, which is called _____, should measure   reliability
what it claims to measure, which is called _____, and   validity
should be based on a representative normative sample, which is
part of the process called _____.   standardization

WHAT DO INTELLIGENCE TESTS PREDICT?

IQ as a Predictor of Scholastic Achievement

15. Children who score higher on IQ tests also tend to do better
in school, and thus IQ is _____ correlated with aca-   positively
demic achievement; however, such findings are based on group
averages and do not imply that predictions about a particular
_____ can be based on IQ test results alone.   individual

IQ as a Predictor of Occupational Status

16. People with more prestigious jobs tend to score _____   higher
on IQ tests; however, the relationship between IQ and job performance is complex and depends upon the _____ of job.   type

IQ as a Predictor of Health, Adjustment, and Life Satisfaction

17. Terman's classic study of people who were intellectually
_____ as children indicated _____ correlation between   gifted, positive
IQ and measures of success and adjustment; however, many of the
people came from better home environments, and we do not know
from this research that high IQ _____ better adjustment.   causes

FACTORS THAT INFLUENCE IQ SCORES

The Evidence for Heredity

18. Three lines of evidence that imply the heritability of intelligence are (1) studies of _____ breeding in animals,   selective
(2) various types of _____ studies that indicate higher cor-   family
relations in IQ as a function of closer kinship, and (3) studies
of _____ children who turn out to resemble their biologi-   adopted
cal parents more than their adoptive parents.

19. But environmentalists argue that twin studies still include
an environmental component, in that (1) separated twins are often placed in very _____ homes, (2) monozygotic twins in   similar
particular tend to be treated _____ when reared in the   similarly
same home, and (3) adopted children are often placed in homes
very similar to those of their _____ parents.   natural or biological

Environmental Influences

20. Lines of evidence favoring environmental effects on intelligence include (1) fluctuations in children's IQ scores as a re-

sult of _____ home environments, and (2) moderate but sig-   unstable
nificant resemblance in IQ between children who are not related
_____ but who live in the same home due to adoption   genetically
and the like.

21. The "cumulative _____" hypothesis holds that children   deficit
who live in impoverished _____ display a progres-   environments
sively greater deficit in IQ with the passage of time; studies
that support this view include (1) those of communities in which
economic improvement was associated with improvements in children's _____, and (2) those in which disadvantaged children who   IQs
were _____ into middle-class homes displayed improvements   adopted
in IQ.

SOCIOCULTURAL CORRELATES OF INTELLECTUAL PERFORMANCE

The Home Environment as a Determinant of Intellectual Growth

22. Caldwell and Bradley's *HOME* inventory is based on direct   HOME
observation of the social and physical environment the   observation
child experiences, and early scores on the inventory are good
predictors of later *IQ* of the children.   IQ

23. Other important factors in the home environment include (1)
quality of the parents' language, as in "*referential* com-   referential
munication accuracy," (2) involvement of *parents* in children's   parents
learning activities, and (3) encouragement of the child toward
asking *questions* and attempting to *solve* problems.   asking, solve

Effects of Birth Order and the Family Configuration

24. Other things equal, children tend to be more intelligent if
they grow up in *small* size homes and if they are *first*-   smaller, first-
borns, perhaps because in each case they receive more parental
attention.

Social-Class, Racial, and Ethnic Differences in IQ

25. On the basis of group averages, children from lower- and
working-class homes score about *10-20* IQ points lower than mid-   10 - 20
dle-class children; similar differences have been obtained for
child of Black, Native American, or Hispanic ancestry as compared
to *White* middle-class children.   White

Why do Groups Differ in Intellectual Performance?

26. One explanation for ethnic and racial differences in IQ is
the "test *bias*" hypothesis, which argues that people who speak   bias
a somewhat different English dialect or who have differing cultural backgrounds would score *lower* because IQ tests are typ-   lower
ically *standardized* on middle-class Whites.   standardized

27. Zigler's _____ hypothesis holds that minority   motivational
children and lower-class children tend to be wary of _____   examiners
and less motivated to do well on IQ tests.

28. The genetic hypothesis attempts to explain IQ differences on
the basis of different _____ pools for ethnic and racial groups,   gene
at least where the more abstract Level ___ abilities are con-   II
cerned; but the evidence here is not compelling, and even so,
within-group _____ says nothing about (1) differ-   heritability
ences between groups or (2) what level of IQ an _____   individual
will display.

29. The environmental hypothesis notes that children of ethnic and racial minorities and lower-income families often grow up in homes that are less _____ stimulating and that include poor diet and frequent _____; this argument is supported by research in which children adopted into better home environments displayed _____ in IQ.

intellectually
undernourishment

increases

IMPROVING INTELLECTUAL PERFORMANCE THROUGH COMPENSATORY EDUCATION

30. A leading example of compensatory education is Project _____ _____, which is oriented toward helping disadvantaged children catch up with their middle-class counterparts by the time they enter the _____ grade.

Head
Start

first

31. Early reports on Head Start indicated significant _____ in IQ, but the projects were criticized because these differences tended to _____ _____ soon after the children entered grade school.

increases

wash out

Long-Term Follow-ups

32. Later research has re-established the success of Head-Start-type programs, indicating long-term improvements in achievement and attitudes toward school as assessed by scholastic _____ and by _____ with parents in addition to the children's IQ scores.

records
interviews

Home-Based Interventions

33. The more successful interventions involve the _____ as well as the children; one particularly effective approach to working with parents has been the _____ demonstration program.

parents

toy

Limitations of Compensatory Education

34. Although intervention programs have not succeeded in eliminating all differences between disadvantaged children and middle-class children, they have served a critically important function in preventing the intellectual _____ so often observed, and such programs appear to be most effective when they begin _____ in childhood and continue through _____ childhood.

decline

early, middle

SOME COMMON USES (AND ABUSES) OF IQ TESTS

35. IQ tests are most often used in schools to identify children who are not doing well, which is the _____ function and to sort children into different _____ groups; however, such use of IQ scores sets the stage for error because IQ scores are influenced by _____ factors and by _____ problems, in addition to being an estimate of intellectual ability at only a single point in time.

diagnostic
ability

motivational, emotional

SELF-TEST I

Consider each alternative carefully. Then choose the best one.

1. Intelligence is
   a. the ability to carry on abstract thinking
   b. the capacity to act purposefully and think rationally
   c. adaptive thinking or action
   d. any or all of the above, depending upon whom you ask

2. Which of the following views of intelligence focuses the most directly on development-al change throughout the lifespan?
    a. Spearman's g and s factor theory
    b. Thurstone's primary mental abilities theory
    c. Cattell and Horn's theory of fluid and crystallized intelligence
    d. Guilford's structure-of-intellect model

3. The original defining formala for IQ was
    a. IQ = CA/MA x 100
    b. IQ = CA/MA ÷ 100
    c. IQ = MA/CA x 100
    d. IQ = MA/CA ÷ 100

4. The order in which children's intelligence tests would be appropriate, from infancy through adolescence, is
    a. Bayley, Stanford-Binet, WISC-R
    b. Bayley, WISC-R, Stanford-Binet
    c. Stanford-Binet, Bayley, WISC-R
    d. Stanford-Binet, WISC-R, Bayley

5. IQ appears to be stable through development if
    a. it is defined as crystallized intelligence
    b. large groups of scores are averaged through test-retest correlation
    c. individual test-retest scores are compared directly
    d. all of the above

6. Of the following, IQ scores bets predict
    a. scholastic achievement
    b. occupational status
    c. job performance
    d. personal adjustment

7. Which of the following provide evidence that favors the environmentalists' views of intelligence?
    a. selective breeding studies with animals
    b. studies of monozygotic versus dizygotic twins
    c. adoption studies comparing children to biological parents
    d. adoption studies of disadvantaged children in middle-class families

8. The HOME inventory measures
    a. g versus s factors in children's IQ test scores
    b. children's academic performance
    c. parental influences on children's intelligence
    d. heritability percentages in IQ

9. Studies of family configuration in relation to IQ indicate that brighter children
    a. tend to come from smaller families
    b. tend to be born earlier in the birth order
    c. both of the above
    d. none of the above

10. The general finding the Blacks, Native Americans, and Hispanic Americans score 10-20 IQ points lower on average that Whites indicates that
    a. these peoples are genetically inferior in intelligence
    b. child-rearing practices among these peoples are inferior
    c. both of the above
    d. none of the above

11. Group differences in IQ
    a. can predict individual differences in every case
    b. can often predict individual differences, though there are exceptions
    c. can sometimes predict individual differences, especially along with other evidence
    d. cannot predict individual differences

12. The most likely explanation of ethnic, racial, and socioeconomic IQ differences is
    a. the test-bias hypothesis
    b. the genetic hypothesis
    c. the motivational hypothesis
    d. the environmental hypothesis

13. Generally, compensatory education such as Head Start has
    a. failed miserably with all children
    b. improved academic performance but not attitudes toward achievement
    c. improved attitudes toward achievement but not academic performance
    d. improved both academic performance and attitudes toward achievement

14. The ultimate goal of compensatory education is to
    a. boost disadvantaged children's IQ scores
    b. improve disadvantaged children's academic performance
    c. alter the ethnic lifestyles of disadvantaged children
    d. demonstrate the superiority of White middle-class values

RESEARCH SUMMARY AND REVIEW

Using the textbook, review the research efforts indicated and write a summary of the important findings. Note the general purpose or context of the research.

1. McCall, Applebaum, & Hogarty (1973), page 392: _____
_____
_____
_____
_____

2. Fincher (1973), Terman (1954), Terman & Oden (1959), page 396: _____
_____
_____
_____
_____

3. Wheeler (1932, 1942), page 399: _____
_____
_____
_____
_____

4. Dickson, Hess, Miyake, & Azuma (1979), page 402: _____
_____
_____

5. Yeates, MacPhee, Campbell, & Ramsey (1983): _____

_____

_____

_____

6. Rothbart (1971), page 405: _____

_____

_____

_____

7. Lazar & Darlington (1982), Collins (1983), page 413: _____

_____

_____

_____

_____

8. Levenstein (1970), page 414: _____

_____

_____

_____

_____

SELF-TEST II

Consider each alternative carefully. Then choose the best one.

1. Spearman's g intelligence factor is similar to Cattell and Horn's
   a. fluid intelligence
   b. crystallized intelligence
   c. both of the above
   d. none of the above
2. Guilford's structure-of-intellect model of intelligence yields
   a. three primary mental abilities
   b. seven primary mental abilities
   c. 100 primary mental abilities
   d. 120 primary mental abilities
3. In accord with the normal distribution, a majority of people should score
   a. in the IQ range 85-115
   b. at the lower end, below an IQ of 70
   c. at the upper end, above an IQ of 130
   d. at the lower and upper ends combined, below 70 and above 130

4. Wechsler IQ, as on the WISC-R and the WPPSI, is based on
   a. "verbal" intelligence
   b. "performance" intelligence
   c. both of the above
   d. none of the above

5. In accord with the types of material and items involved on the tests, the highest stability between tests in terms of correlation should occur between
   a. the Bayley and the Stanford-Binet
   b. the Bayley and the WISC-R Verbal Scale
   c. the Stanford-Binet and the WISC-R Verbal Scale
   d. the Stanford-Binet and the WISC-R Performance Scale

6. McCall, Applebaum, and Hogarty (1973) found wide fluctuations in IQ between test-retest occasions for some children, which suggested that
   a. these children's absolute intellectual capacity improved or declined
   b. changes occurred in the home environment of these children
   c. both of the above
   d. none of the above

7. The ability of an IQ test to measure what it is supposed to measure is an index of its
   a. reliability
   b. validity
   c. standardization
   d. all of the above

8. Terman's longitudinal study of gifted children indicated that
   a. child prodigies are frail and poorly adjusted
   b. child prodigies later tend to have disrupted marital relationships
   c. high IQ guarantees good health and adjustment
   d. none of the above

9. According to Kamin's extreme environmentalist view of studies of heritability and IQ, the previous family studies were
   a. flawed because separated monozygotic twins are often placed in similar homes
   b. flawed because adopted children's homes are often similar to the homes of the children's biological parents
   c. both of the above
   d. none of the above

10. According to the cumulative deficit hypothesis, disadvantaged children display
   a. MA that increases slower than CA
   b. CA that increases slower than MA
   c. MA and CA that increase at about the same rate
   d. changes that cannot be predicted in terms of MA and CA

11. The principle findings of the Wheeler (1932, 1942) longitudinal study of rural Tennessee children were, as the communities entered the social and economic mainstream, that
   a. the average IQ of the children increased
   b. the average IQ of the children decreased
   c. the average IQ of the children remained the same
   d. average IQ but not individual IQs remained the same

12. Evidence to the effect that environment has significant effects upon children's intellectual development includes
   a. Caldwell and Bradley's research on quality of the home environment
   b. Dickson, et al.'s research on referential communication
   c. Yeates, et al.'s research on quality of the home environment
   d. all of the above

13. Which of the following is __not__ assessed by the HOME inventory?
   a. parental involvement with the child
   b. provision of appropriate play materials
   c. socioeconomic status of the family
   d. emotional and verbal responsivity of the mother

14. As in Rothbart's (1971) study of birth order and children's intellectual development, it appears that
   a. mothers spend more time interacting with first-borns than with later-borns
   b. mothers spend more time interacting with later-borns than with first-borns
   c. mothers are more anxious about the performance of first-borns
   d. mothers are more anxious about the performance of later-borns

15. According to Zajonc's hypothesis as to how birth order and family size affect children's intellectual development, the main point is that
   a. people who decide to have small families are more intelligent
   b. people who decide to have large families are more intelligent
   c. the average intellectual level a first-born experiences is higher
   d. the average intellectual level a later-born experiences is higher

16. Children from single-parent homes probably score lower in IQ , on average, because
   a. the average intellectual level is lower
   b. a single parent cannot provide the stimulation two parents can
   c. single-parent homes also tend to be lower in socioeconomic status
   d. all of the above

17. As compared to urban-based ethnic groups, rural ethnic groups tend to
   a. score lower on IQ tests
   b. score higher on IQ tests
   c. score about the same on IQ tests
   d. be basically less intelligent

18. Dove's Chitling test
   a. illustrates the problem with culturally biased IQ tests
   b. illustrates the problem with culture-free IQ tests
   c. is a valid IQ test for Blacks
   d. favors the genetic hypothesis regarding IQ differences

19. According to the test-bias hypothesis, some racial and ethnic groups score lower on average IQ because
   a. they speak a different variant of English than middle-class Whites
   b. they have different conceptual experiences than middle-class Whites
   c. both of the above
   d. none of the above

20. Of the tests noted, the __least__ culturally biased would be the
   a. Raven Progressive Matrices
   b. WISC-R Verbal Scale
   c. Dove Counterbalance General Intelligence Test
   d. Scholastic Aptitude Test

21. Generally, as a __rebuttal__ of Jensen's genetic hypothesis,
   a. within-group variability explains between-group variability
   b. within-group variability predicts between-group variability
   c. within-group variability bears no relationship to between-group variability
   d. within-group variability and between-group variability are essentially the same

22. Research on middle-class White adoptions of disadvantaged Black children suggests
   a. such adoptions are the solution to racial differences in intellectual development
   b. racial differences in IQ are primarily genetic in nature
   c. racial differences in IQ are primarily environmental in nature
   d. none of the above

23. Long-term follow-up studies of the effects of Head Start programs, such as the studies by Lazar and Darlington (1982) and Collins (1983) indicate
   a. improvements on tests of basic academic skills
   b. improvements regarding attitudes toward academic achievement
   c. beneficial effects on maternal attitudes toward achievement
   d. all of the above

24. Slaughter's group discussion technique is an intervention aimed primarily at
   a. children
   b. mothers
   c. fathers
   d. schoolteachers

25. IQ testing, by itself, should not be used as the basis for
   a. sorting children into homogeneous classrooms based on ability
   b. assessing individual differences in basic intellectual capacity
   c. predicting specific academic achievement
   d. all of the above

VIGNETTES

Consider the story, then answer each question using material from the textbook.

I. A large coporation is considering using IQ testing to select employees and assign them
to various jobs (e.g., assembly-line versus clerical, intermediate-level management versus higher-level management). As the local "ace" psychological consultant, you've been
called in for advice and recommendations regarding this use of IQ tests. And so, they
have lots of questions for you.

   1. What basic problems and errors might they have in using IQ scores as a means
      of predicting individual ability?

   2. Individual issues aside, what types of jobs might IQ predict best, in terms of
      job performance? Why?

   3. Drawing from the research by Terman and colleagues, what could you tell the cor-
      poration about whether higher IQ "causes" prestige and success?

II. In the early 18th century, the Brightly family was well established and included many
cousins and distant relations who generally got along well with each other. But, one year
at the Brightly family reunion, a squabble developed over some very small thing that no
one remembers clearly. Thus the reunion turned into a brawl, with family members taking
sides, and the result was a split in the family that persists to this day. The split was
aided by a natural feature of the environment: Brightly Mountain. Thus the "east"
Brightly family aligned against the "west" Brightly family, and the east family members
changed their name to "Brightley" to accentuate the difference.

   1. If a modern-day researcher came along and found that the Brightleys were, on aver-
      age, brighter than their West Brightly counterparts, would this mean that the
      Brightleys were genetically superior? Why or why not?

   2. If the Brightleys were brighter, what environmental differences might be assessed
      in trying to account for such a finding?

   3. If instead the researcher gave no IQ tests, and simply noted that the Brightleys
      were more prosperous and more organized in their businesses and industries and
      such, would this mean that the Brightleys were brighter? Why or why not?

III. Julio was 6 years old and entering the first grade. His parents had immigrated from

164

Puerto Rico before he was born, and, although their English was limited, they tried to use English around the house as much as possible. As it happened, Julio's father knew only unskilled labor, and he worked very hard at maintaining the family's relatively low level of income. Julio's mother took care of Julio and his two sisters, and she hoped that she too would be able to find employment when the children were all in school. And the family was very close, even though there were times that there wasn't much money for "extras" for the children.

    1. What predictions might you make about Julio's IQ compared to his middle-class counterparts at school?

    2. What predictions might you make about Julio's IQ compared to his younger sisters?

    3. What predictions might you make about Julio's eventual academic achievement?

APPLICATIONS

Try each of the projects, noting answers to the questions as you go.

I. As an aid to understanding what intelligence might be, devise your own definition. List the basic abilities *you* think should be included.

    1. What abilities as described by Thurstone would you include? What would you add?

    2. What abilities as described by Cattell and Horn would you include? What would you add?

    3. Throughout, note any tendencies on your part to include things *you* do well.

II. Using the areas of the HOME inventory in conjunction with the textbook material on disadvantaged home environments, devise a list of characteristics you might expect to find in Julio's home (*Vignette III,* above).

    1. What might you expect to find with regard to HOME Subscale 1, Emotional and Verbal Responsivity of the Mother?

    2. What might you expect to find with regard to Subscale 4, Provision of Appropriate Play Materials?

    3. What might you expect to find with regard to Subscale 6, Opportunities for Variety in Daily Stimulation?

III. In anticipation of your someday becoming a parent, devise a basic list of things to to in promoting or augmenting good intellectual development during infancy and the pre-school years in particular.

    1. What conclusions can you draw from the HOME inventory?

    2. What implications are there in the discussions of disadvantaged environments?

    3. What information can you gain from the discussion of compensatory education?

ANSWERS

Self-Test I

1. d	6. a	11. d
2. c	7. d	12. d
3. c	8. c	13. d
4. a	9. c	14. b
5. b	10. d	15. d

Research Summary and Review

1. McCall, Applebaum, & Hogarty (1973): Within a sample of 140 children who had repeatedly taken IQ tests during childhood and adolescence, large fluctuations were found for some children. The implication was that IQ tests measure performance at a particular point in time rather that an absolute intellectual capacity or ability to learn.

2. Fincher (1973), Terman (1954), Terman & Oden (1959): A long-term study of 1500 gifted children (as measured by IQ) revealed high percentages of prefessional success and good social adjustment in the context of what intelligence may mean. However, a relationship between success and the quality of the child's home environment was also found, indicating that IQ was not the only factor involved in success.

3. Wheeler (1932, 1942): The children of an isolated mountain community displayed an 11-point average IQ increase over a 10-year period during which the community begin entering the social and economic mainstream, indicating possible effects of environment upon intelligence.

4. Dickson, et al. (1979): Clarity and accuracy of mothers' use of language with their children was found to be positively correlated with the children's IQs, thus indicating possible effects of "referential communication accuracy" upon intelligence.

5. Yeates, et al. (1983): In a study of developmental changes in IQ, the best predictor at child's age 2 years turned out to be mother's IQ, but by about age 4 years the best predictor was quality of the home environment (via the HOME inventory); thus environmental effects on IQ seemed to accumulate over time during the early years.

6. Rothbart (1971): In studying how family size and birth order affect IQ, it was found that mothers spent equivalent amounts of time interacting with the different children in their families but that the quality of interactions was more achievement oriented with first-borns than with later-borns.

7. Lazar & Darlington (1982), Collins (1983): Long-term follow-ups of compensatory program participants found that, although IQ gains were temporary, the children displayed stable gains in academic skills and attitudes toward academic achievement, and also that the mothers' attitudes toward achievement improved, in each case indicating the effectiveness of early intervention.

8. Levenstein (1970): A "toy demonstration" program based on intervention with disadvantaged 2-year-old and their mothers yielded mean IQ increase for the children over a 7-month period, as an example of the potential effects of such interventions.

Self-Test II

1. a	6. d	11. a	16. c	21. c
2. d	7. b	12. d	17. a	22. c
3. a	8. d	13. c	18. a	23. d
4. c	9. c	14. c	19. c	24. b
5. c	10. a	15. b	20. a	25. d

Vignettes

I. (1) Perhaps the main problem is that IQ is better viewed as a measure of current intellectual performance than as a measure of overall intellectualy ability. Another problem is that minority-group applicants might be penalized, as compared to White middle-class applicants. And the standardized tests might not reflect the many types of "ability" the corporation would be interested in. In each case, the potential error in mishiring or misassigning individuals is quite large. (2) From the research by Brody and Brody (1976) in the context of occupational success, perhaps the best predictive power would involve the middle levels of skills. This relates to the wider range of abilities people display at this level, as compared to the narrower ranges at either extreme. (3) Basically, you might point out that the gifted children in Terman's project may have been "gifted" in the first place because of family background. Such factors also influence IQ scores, as discussed at other points in the chapter. But, whatever the origins of high intelligence, occupational success also depends in part upon education and social opportunities. The children of the better families in Terman's studies did better, which de-emphasizes the role of IQ per se. Thus the corporation should be wary of overusing IQ tests for classication and hiring.

II. (1) One group being brighter than the other implies nothing about genetics, as in the discussion of corn planted on soils of differing growth potential. However, it might look quite different to a modern-day researcher who knew nothing about the family history. (2) Possibilities are that the Brightleys entered the modern social and cultural mainstream sooner, as a result of terrain. Much of the verbal content of IQ tests, presumably used here to determine who is "brighter," is based on mainstream experiences you can only acquire if you are exposed to them. Other possibilities would be that the Brightleys are economically better off, perhaps due to natural resources or the like, with differences ranging from basic nutrition all the way to quality of education. The Brightleys might also employ more effective childrearing practices, but note that you can't automatically assume this just because the children are brighter. (3) Cultural differences do not imply that one group is brighter than another, regardless of industrial and social systems and their efficiency. Stated differently, the achievements of American industry, for example, do not indicate that Americans are "smarter" than the peoples of less industrialized cultures. The same reasoning applies to subgroups within a culture, as in the case of the Brightleys and the Brightlys. Many other factors could be involved.

III. (1) No predictions about Julio's IQ are possible. You can say that Julio's language background may penalize him on standardized tests, but this won't necessarily occur. You can say that a *group* of children whose parents recently immigrated will probably, on average, score lower due to possible cultural or language differences in the home. But you still don't know how Julio will do. (2) No predictions about Julio versus his younger sisters are possible either. As with other group differences, being a first-born says nothing about the individual person. (3) And, of course, you can't make any reasonable predictions about how Julio will fare at school. In addition to reasons noted earlier, also note that IQ is only moderately correlated with academic achievement. Factors such as his motivation will also be involved in how well he does.

Applications

I. Since you are a college student, changes are you'll emphasize skills necessary to college work, such as (1) Thurstone's numerical reasoning, verbal meaning, word fluency, memory, and inductive reasoning. To these you might add more specific skills such as being able to do such things quickly (e.g., the night before an exam) and other skills such as speaking competently before groups and being able to chat glibly at social gatherings. (2) Similarly, in accord with Cattell and Horn, you would probably emphasize the acquired "crystallized" intelligence necessary for competence in college subjects as well as the "fluid" intelligence necessary to acquiring the knowledge and skills in the first place. (3) In addition to the mental set you might have as a college student, you might also find yourself emphasizing particular things you as an individual do well. These could include visual/motor skills involved in sports, driving a car, and whatever else you find it enjoyable or necessary to do from day to day. Or you might emphasize reasoning of a more philosophical sort and de-emphasize math if you aren't good at math. Without deliberate intent, it is still difficult to define intelligence without bringing your own frame of reference into play. Otherwise, note that a farmer might define basic intelligence in ways related to making crops grow, a mechanic might emphasize skills in building or repairing machinery, and a salesperson would predictably emphasize social and interactional and persuasive skills, in each case in terms of what is important in adapting to one's environment.

II. (1) From the limited description of Julio's home environment, we can guess that emotional and verbal responsivity is probably good. We can't tell about subtler characteristics such as referential communication accuracy, expect to note that Julio's parents' limited use of English would affect his ability to use English as well, at least prior to schooling. Perhaps the main point here is that living in a "disadvantaged" environment says nothing about the quality of interactions between parents and child, which can be good or bad at any socioeconomic level. (2) Given the limited income of the family, it might be that Julio's access to toys would be limited compared to that of a middle-class child. However, many beneficial toys can be provided with very little money. And many of the more expensive toys have little effect on intellectual skills. Thus we really can't make much of a prediction here either. (3) Except for how many books Julio may have (noting the possibility of using public libraries in spite of having limited income), no predictions are possible here either.

III. (1) Themes that occur throughout the HOME inventory are that you should be responsive, you should expose the child to situations and activities that foster intellectual development, and you should emphasize the transmission of basic language skills. Note the parallels that run throughout Chapters 6, 7, 8, and 9. (2) We can also learn from what is "missing" in disadvantaged environments, which are characterized in many cases (though not in all cases) by malnutrition, large family size with limits on the amount of interaction parents can provide, lower educational level which limits skills and knowledge parents can pass along, and neighborhoods that provide fewer opportunities for learning outside the home. Note also that you can improve your child's skills by improving your own skills and by making the best of whatever materials you have. (3) Regardless of your educational level, skills, and the like, you can still help your child by taking advantage of community resources such as nurseries and preschool educational settings. Similarly, as indicated by the toy demonstration program, you can acquire special skills in working with your child. All socioeconomic levels of children can potentially benefit from one or another aspect of compensatory education.

CHAPTER ELEVEN

ATTACHMENT: THE DEVELOPMENT OF
INTIMATE RELATIONSHIPS

OVERVIEW AND KEY TERMS

Read carefully. Recall examples and discussion as you go, and define each key term.

Hall viewed adolescence as the most crucial stage for forming a personal and interpersonal identity, but Freud's emphasis on social and emotional development during the
first five or six years of life is closer to the modern-day view.

A DEFINITION OF ATTACHMENT

Bowlby defines social attachment as a reciprocal affectional tie between two persons,
as measured by a tendency of both persons to maintain proximity to each other. Children
selectively form emotional relationships with attachment objects including parents, other
adults, and other children, beginning in infancy.

THE CAREGIVER'S ATTACHMENT TO THE INFANT

Klaus and Kennell's view is that mothers develop enduring attitudes toward their
children as a result of interactions with the child during the first few days of life.
Those who experience extended early contact with their infants may later be more involved
and nurturant, which leads to the sensitive period hypothesis concerning contact during
the first 6-12 hours. One possible explanation of these "early contact" effects is that
hormones present in the mother at the time of delivery enable emotional bonding, but this
does not explain why fathers also become engrossed with their infants as a function of
early contact. Another explanation is that the parents' intense emotional arousal after
delivery is reinterpreted in a positive way when the parents have contact with a responsive infant. Whatever the process, the sensitive period hypothesis views early contact as
essential to the formation of an optimal attachment. Other researchers disagree, at
least with the "permanent" effects of early bonding. Studies of attachment in which infants were adopted or premature, in each case ruling out early contact, argue against its
necessity in secure emotional bonding. Thus, while early contact may help, secure attachment builds on long-term social interactions between parents and their children.

As noted by Bowlby, the infant's reflexes, smiles, and babbles may have a positive
effect on parents and foster attachment. Smiling, as discussed in Box 11-1, may be a
biologically programmed response which promotes positive parent-infant interactions.
Early smiling is reflexive, but true social smiling begins as early as 3 weeks of age,
and a maturational role is suggested by the observation that all infants display social
similing at a "conceptual age" of 46 weeks - even if they are premature. A later mile-
stone is the discriminated smiling response at about 6 months of age, and both social
and cognitive-developmental factors influence when and how smiling occurs. The reflexive "distress" cry can also promote attachment, especially if the parent's responses are
effective in soothing the baby.

Lorenz and others have emphasized the baby's kewpie-doll appearance as a factor in eliciting attention. And caregivers and infants alike enjoy the synchronized routines that develop between them. But babies who are irritable and unresponsive, whether due to having been abused as children, having inappropriate expectations about the infant, or basically having not wanted the child in the first place, might not become closely attached. Family environments that include many other children or an unhappy marriage may also interfere with parent-to-infant attachments.

THE INFANT'S ATTACHMENT TO CAREGIVERS

Using children's responses when separated from caregivers as a measure, Schaffer and Emerson propose four stages of social attachment: (1) the asocial stage, in which social and nonsocial stimuli alike produce favorable reactions and a few unfavorable ones, (2) the stage of indiscriminate attachment, in which the infant prefers human company but is not selective about whom, (3) the stage of specific attachments, in which the mother or other primary caregiver is the child's one attachment object, and (4) the stage of multiple attachments, in which other family members or regular caregivers also become attachment objects. Once multiple attachments have been formed, the infant's preferences for various attachment objects may vary according to the situation. Fathers typically become objects of attachment, as discussed in Box 11-2, although the "quality" of attachment may be different with mother versus father.

Various explanations for attachment have been offered. Freud emphasized feeding and the oral gratification involved. Erikson emphasized feeding in the sense of fostering basic trust. Learning theorists have emphasized feeding as well as other forms of reinforcement, so that the mother becomes a secondary reinforcer. However, classic research by Harlow and Harlow and associates indicates that feeding is not the primary mechanism through which attachments are formed. Monkeys reared in isolation preferred a "terry-cloth" mother in spite of being fed from a "wire" mother, which leads to the idea of contact comfort as being more important in attachment, which is consistent with findings by Schaffer and Emerson that infants are attracted by the responsiveness and the total stimulation provided by caregivers. Cognitive-developmental theorists also note that object permanence is necessary for forming specific attachments, and research bears this out.

Ethological theorists emphasize inborn behavioral tendencies that may foster attachment, as in the work of Bowlby and Lorenz. Imprinting in fowl occurs during a critical period soon after birth. In mammals, "clinging" to a caregiver may be a pre-adapted characteristic related to survival and attachment. In human infants, executive responses such as sucking, grasping, and following, plus signaling responses such as smiling and crying, serve to maintain contact with the caregiver and foster attachment. In turn, adults may also be programmed to respond to the infant's signals. But this does not imply that attachment is "automatic."

DEVELOPMENT OF FEARFUL REACTIONS

Stranger anxiety, in most infants, appears around 6-7 months of age, peaks at 8-10 months, and usually subsides over the 2nd year of life. Some children remain fearful of intrusive strangers for several years. In general, stranger anxiety is more pronounced if familiar caregivers are not present, if the setting is not familiar to the baby, and if the stranger approaches too rapidly and "forces" himself or herself upon the baby. Babies are much less likely to show stranger anxiety to another child, at least during the 1st year of life.

The "fear of separation" hypothesis is that stranger anxiety actually represents the child's fear of losing the person(s) to whom she or he is attached. However, this notion does not explain why infants sometimes react positively to strangers even when mother is not present. The ethological perspective suggests that infants are preprogrammed to respond to danger signals, such as unfamiliar faces. During the second year of life infants use their attachment objects as secure bases from which to explore, and they show less stranger anxiety as they learn that novel stimuli (such as strangers) can be interesting rather than threatening. The cognitive-developmental view notes that 6-8-month-olds have stable schemata for familiar faces, and that what initially looks like "freezing" in response to strangers is actually a period of examining the discrepant stimulus and trying to understand it. Fear comes about when the infant can't explain who or what the stranger is. Presumably, other children do not evoke anxiety during the first year because the infant simply doesn't have schemata for children as such and thus does not feel threatened by them until later.

Separation anxiety appears in most children during the 7-12-month age range, peaks at 14-16 months, and very gradually becomes less frequent and intense over the next several years. However, these age periods vary somewhat across cultures. The "conditioned anxiety" hypothesis proposes that infants learn to fear separation because of prior pains and discomforts when the caregiver was not present, but this does not explain why separation anxiety is more pronounced away from home. The ethologists propose that inborn fear reactions to strange situations are responsible, in that the mother's absence produces much uncertainty. This also explains why infants show more separation anxiety in settings away from home. During the second year, infants use their caregivers as secure bases from which to explore, often retreating to the caregiver if confronted by something unusual. The cognitive viewpoint is that infants develop schemata for "familiar faces in familiar places," so that when mother leaves the room at home, the infant still "knows" where she is, unless she leaves the house, in which case the infant protests. Uncertainty, then, is what elicits separation protests.

Separation from time to time is inevitable. Separation anxiety can be eased by using "short" instructions to the child upon leaving and by avoiding lengthy explanations that may alert the child to a discrepancy and thus induce fearfulness. Photographs left with the younger child may also help. Preparing the child in advance helps mainly with older, preschool-age children.

LONG-TERM EFFECTS OF EARLY SOCIAL AND EMOTIONAL DEVELOPMENT

Most theorists agree with the early experience hypothesis that infancy is influential in determining later social and personality development. Research on the issue takes the form of looking at what happens to infants who do not develop secure attachments or who have minimal contact with a mother figure and develop no attachments.

Ainsworth and associates measure quality of attachment with the "strange-situations" test, which yields three general types of attachment: (1) secure attachment, indicated by active exploration with mother present, some distress when mother leaves and positive greetings upon her return, and minimal stranger anxiety with mother present; (2) anxious and resistant attachment, indicated by minimal exploration with mother present, great distress when mother leaves and a tendency to resist close contact when she returns, and marked stranger anxiety even when mother is present; and (3) anxious and avoidant attachment, indicated by minimal exploration with mother present, minimal distress when she leaves and an ambivalence about her return, and reactions to strangers more like ignoring them than being afraid. Secure attachment, the most common and preferable type, comes about through caregiver reponsiveness to the infant's needs. Anxious resistant attachment may involve ineffectual though well intentioned care. Anxious avoidant attachment is more a lack of attachment or a sense of detachment, and mothers of these infants are often rigid or self-centered persons who have rejected their babies. Research indicates that securely attached infants later are more curious and exploring, more involved with peers, and generally more popular, in accord with Erikson's theory. Insecurely attached infants later seem withdrawn and less self-directing. But the quality of attachment can change over time. Maternal employment does not necessarily lead to insecure attachment or other detrimental effects, as discussed in Box 11-3.

Minimal contacts with adults during infancy may produce children who are relatively unattached socially. Research by the Harlows on early social deprivation in infant monkeys provides clues. After social deprivation over the first 3 months of life, in-

171

fant monkeys were terrified when exposed to other monkeys and they displayed self-destructive behaviors. With continued exposure to others, however, these monkeys recovered. Monkeys isolated 6 months or longer showed only minimal recovery and preferred to be alone or with other isolate monkeys. Monkeys isolated 12 months or longer were extremely withdrawn, apathetic, and passive to the extent of being injured or killed by normal monkeys in play. Long-range follow-ups of monkeys isolated 6 months or longer also indicated bizarre patterns of sexual behavior. But research using younger-peer therapy with the isolates indicated that the effects of early deprivation can be overcome.

Research on early deprivation in humans has focused on children reared in the impoverished social environments of some institutions, where infants and caregivers have only minimal contact due to understaffing. Such infants often become developmentally retarded and apathetic toward humans, and these tendencies may persist into adolescence if deprivation continues over the first few years of life. The maternal-deprivation hypothesis attributes these effects to the lack of warmth and attention from a primary mother figure and hence the child's lack of attachment. However, studies in adequately staffed institutions reveal that children need not be mothered by a single mother figure in order to develop normally. The stimulus deprivation hypothesis focuses on lack of sensory stimulation in general, which is also a characteristic of deprived institutional environments. But research indicates that social stimulation is also necessary. The social stimulation hypothesis emphasizes the need for sustained, responsive interactions with companions as a basis for secure attachment, noting the learned helplessness effect as an explanation of why deprived infants frequently become passive and apathetic.

Recovery from early deprivation can be accomplished by placing the children in homes where they receive individual attention from responsive caregivers. An "enriched" environment is also necessary. Recovery depends in part on how long the child was in the deprived environment, and children deprived for the first 3 years have difficulties that are hard to overcome. This does not imply, however, that the first 3 years qualifies as a "critical period." Recent research suggests that younger-peer therapy may work well with such children.

SELF-REVIEW

Fill in the blanks for each item. Check the answers for each item as you go.

1. Hall said that the most critical stage in personality development is _____, but Freud claimed that the foundations of adult personality are laid down during the first ___ to ___ years of life; today's view is moderate, although the first few years are still viewed as important.

adolescence

5

6

A DEFINITION OF ATTACHMENT

2. Attachment involves a close _____ relationship between caregiver and child, and it is a relationship which works both ways in the sense of being _____; people who are attached will _____ often, and will attempt to maintain close physical _____ to each other.

emotional

reciprocal
interact
proximity

THE CAREGIVER'S ATTACHMENT TO THE INFANT

Early Emotional Bonding

3. Klaus and Kennell have proposed that a mother's attitude toward her infant depends upon a _____ period for bonding during the first ___-___ hours after the child is born, and they have also proposed that this bonding occurs because of the level of certain _____ in the mother's body; however,

sensitive
10 - 12

hormones

this does not explain how _____ become attached to their   fathers
infants, and a better explanation for both parents emphasizes
the pairing of emotional arousal with the fact of being handed
an _____, affectionate infant at the time of birth.   attentive

5. The balance of the research indicates that the effects of
early contact with the infant are relatively _____ and may   small
not last very long, which means that parents who do not have extensive early contact can still become _____ to infants.   attached

Infant Characteristics That Promote Caregiver-to-Infant Attachments

6. Infant reflexes such as rooting, grasping, and smiling can
_____ the caregivers, as can the baby's "_____ doll"   reinforce, kewpie
appearance; a related factor in attachment is the infant's matching of movements and behaviors with those of the parents, which
yields _____ routines that entertain infants and   synchronized
parents alike.

Problems in Establishing Caregiver-to-Infant Attachments

7. Babies who are hard to love, and thus at risk for alienating
their caregivers, can be identified early through the _____   Brazelton
_____ _____ Assessment Scale.   Neonatal Behavioral

8. Characteristics of caregivers that may interfere with attachments include (1) if the caregivers are emotionally _____,   insecure
(2) if the caregivers have erroneous preconceived _____   notions or ideas
about how the child should behave, (3) if the caregivers didn't
really _____ the child in the first place, and (4) if the fami-   want
ly is large and the caregivers are _____ have too
many small children to take care of.

THE INFANT'S ATTACHMENT TO CAREGIVERS

Development of Primary Social Attachments

9. Schaffer and Emerson's stages of social attachment include
(1) from birth to 6 weeks, the _____ stage, (2) from 6   asocial
weeks to 6-7 months, the stage of _____attachments,   indiscriminate
(3) from about 7 months on, the stage of _____ attach-   specific
ments, and (4) from about 8-9 months on, the stage of _____   multiple
attachments.

10. Freud based early attachments on _____ gratification, later,   oral
Erickson stressed the role of developing a basic sense of _____   trust
through the parents' being reliable in their _____ practices   feeding
with the child and also avoiding _____ the child from bottle   weaning
or breast too early.

12. Learning theorists have often emphasized how associations are
formed on the basis of pleasurable sensations, and thus they have
shared the psychoanalysts' view that _____ is very import-   feeding
ant to attachment; however, classic research by Harlow and Zimmerman on monkeys reared with "wire" versus "terrycloth" mothers
indicates that "_____ _____" is more important.   contact comfort

13. In cognitive-developmental theory, the infant must first acquire the concept of _____ _____ before forming   object permanence
attachments specific to the mother or another caregiver.

14. Ethological theorists have noted the presence of _____   critical
periods in fowl, which lead to chicks _____ on their   imprinting
mother or another moving object; in turn, human infants are said

to have inborn responses that aid in attachment, which include sucking and grasping and others that serve an _____ function, plus smiling and vocalizing and others that serve a _____ function in maintaining contact with caregivers.

executive

signaling

15. The prevailing view based on research with humans is that attachment depends upon (1) the caregiver's _____ toward the infant and (2) the total amount of _____ the caregiver provides for the infant.

responsiveness
stimulation

DEVELOPMENT OF FEARFUL REACTIONS

Stranger Anxiety

16. Wary, fearful reactions toward strangers appear when the infant is about ___ - ___ months of age and then decline during the second year; some infants rarely experience this _____ anxiety, yet for others it may not decline until the _____ years, at least in some situations.

6 - 7
stranger
preschool

17. If a familiar companion is present, stranger anxiety tends to _____; if the child is in a familiar setting when the stranger appears, the anxiety tends to _____; if the stranger approaches quickly and picks the child up, stranger anxiety tends to _____.

decrease
decrease

increase

18. Psychoanalysts have proposed that stranger anxiety stems from fear of being _____ from the attachment object; ethologists view stranger anxiety as biologically programmed _____ of an unusual object, which declines during the second year in accord with the secure _____ phenomenon; and the cognitive-developmentalists emphasize that the stranger's face is a highly _____ stimulus with respect to the now-formed schemata for familiar faces.

separated

avoidance
base

discrepant

Separation Anxiety

19. Separation anxiety appears about ___-___ months of age and often continues into the _____ period, in our culture.

7 - 12
preschool

20. Psychoanalysts and some learning theorists have proposed that separation anxiety represents a conditioned _____ tracing to discomforts that aren't attended to if the caregiver is absent from time to time; but this does not explain why separation anxiety is less likely when the child is at _____ or why it appears very early in cultures where infants are rarely _____ from their caregivers.

anxiety

home

separated

21. Ethologists propose that children are programmed to fear a wide variety of _____ situations, which includes being separated from caregivers; later, the child's explorations with the caregiver as a _____ base make separations seem less strange and unusual.

strange

secure

22. Cognitive-developmentalists add that the child develops schemata for familiar _____ in familiar _____; when the mother is not in the same room with the child, separation anxiety occurs only when the child is uncertain as to where she is.

faces, places

LONG-TERM EFFECTS OF EARLY SOCIAL AND EMOTIONAL DEVELOPMENT

23. One point upon which most theorists agree is the _____ _____ hypothesis, which emphasizes the importance of

early
experience

174

early emotional events upon the development of _____.   personality

Individual Differences in the Quality of Attachments

24. Ainsworth proposes three categories of attachments between
mother and child: (1) the preferable _____ attachment,   secure
marked by exploration and _____ stranger anxiety while the   little
mother is present and _____ when she leaves; (2) anxious   distress
and _____ attachment, marked by lack of exploration and   resistant
_____ stranger anxiety while the mother is present and _____   much, distress
when she leaves; and (3) anxious and _____ attachment,   avoidant
marked by _____ exploration or stranger anxiety when the mo-   little
ther is present and _____ if any distress when she leaves.   little

25. According to Erikson, secure attachment leads to a basic
sense of _____, whereas insecure attachment leads to a basic   trust
sense of _____.   mistrust

The Unattached Infant: Effects of Restricted Social Contacts during Infancy

26. After 3 months of social deprivation, Harlow and Harlow's
isolated infant monkeys tended to _____ other monkeys but   avoid
soon recovered if allowed to play with a normal monkey; after 6
months of such deprivation, social isolates avoided other monkeys and also were very _____ even when attacked, and such   passive
monkeys required extensive _____-_____ therapy to recover.   younger-peer

27. Studies of human children reared from birth in understaffed,
impoverished institutional _____ yield findings sim-   environments
ilar to the Harlows' research: after a year of such rearing,
infants display signs of developmental _____, and if   retardation
the deprivation lasts as long as ___ years the effects are very   3
difficult to overcome.

28. A stable mother figure is not present in many settings where
children develop normally, and thus the _____ _____   maternal deprivation
hypothesis cannot explain the effects of impoverished institutional environments.

29. Sensory stimulation alone has not been found to be effective
in counteracting the effects of social isolation in monkeys, and
thus the _____ _____ hypothesis cannot explain   stimulus deprivation
the effects of impoverished institutional environments.

30. The idea that sustained interactions with responsive companions is the necessary ingredient for normal development is called
the _____ _____ hypothesis; for example, a sus-   social stimulation
tained lack of responsiveness of caregiver to infant can lead to
the apathy, withdrawal, and _____ _____ that   learned helplessness
characterizes infants in impoverished institutional environments.

SELF-TEST I

Consider each alternative carefully. Then choose the best one.

1. Given the necessary conditions, infants are likely to become attached to
    a. mothers
    b. fathers
    c. other children
    (d.) all of the above

2. The balance of research on the long-range effects of early emotional bonding generally indicates that
    a. extended contact during the first few days is necessary for secure attachment
    b. physical contact during the first few hours is necessary for secure attachment
    (c.) early contact effects are not large and are often temporary
    d. none of the above

3. The idea that the infant's reflexive smiling and "kewpie doll" appearance contributes to caregiver attachment is basically
    a. a psychoanalytic perspective
    (b.) an ethological perspective
    c. a cognitive-developmental perspective
    d. a social-learning perspective

4. Caregiver-to-infant attachment is more difficult when
    a. the infant is irritable and unresponsive
    b. the caregiver is emotionally insecure
    c. many other children are present in the home
    (d.) all of the above

5. Early feeding experiences have been assumed to form the basis for infant attachment in
    a. psychoanalytic theory
    b. traditional learning theory
    (c.) both of the above
    d. none of the above

6. Stranger anxiety is likely when
    a. the infant is in a familiar place
    (b.) the infant's mother is not present
    c. both of the above
    d. none of the above

7. The secure-base phenomenon as an explanation for why stranger anxiety declines during the second year of life is a product of the
    a. psychoanalytic perspective
    (b.) ethological perspective
    c. cognitive-developmental perspective
    d. social-learning perspective

8. The "strange circumstances" explanation for separation anxiety from an ethological perspective is most similar to the
    a. psychoanalytic hypothesis of oral gratification
    b. learning theory "conditioned anxiety" hypothesis
    (c.) cognitive-developmental discrepant schemata explanation
    d. none of the above

9. Cognitive-developmentalists generally explain stranger and separation anxiety through
    (a.) the operation and interpretation of schemata
    b. innate biological programming
    c. learned avoidance and anxiety
    d. emotional bonds between caregiver and child

10. Separation anxiety and stranger anxiety are both likely when
    (a.) the child is in an unfamiliar setting
    b. the child has an anxious/avoidant attachment with caregivers
    c. the child is about 2 years of age
    d. the child has acquired an attitude of learned helplessness

11. Psychoanalytic theorists and social-learning theorists generally agree upon
    a. the conditioned anxiety hypothesis
    b. the early experience hypothesis
    (c.) both of the above
    d. none of the above

12. On a long-term basis,
    a. early secure attachment is permanent even if conditions change
    b. early insecure attachment is permanent even if conditions change
    c. both of the above
    (d.) none of the above

13. Early social deprivation produces emotional and interpersonal disturbances
    a. in monkeys but not in humans
    b. in humans but not in monkeys
    (c.) both in humans and in monkeys
    d. neither in humans nor in monkeys

14. The effects of early social deprivation in monkeys
    (a.) are best overcome through interaction with younger monkeys
    b. are best overcome through interaction with older monkeys
    c. are best overcome through interaction with human caregivers
    d. cannot be overcome if deprivation lasts more than 6 months

15. Research indicates that the central factor in explaining the effects of impoverished and understaffed institutional environments on children is
    a. maternal deprivation
    b. stimulus deprivation
    (c.) social deprivation
    d. all of the above

RESEARCH SUMMARY AND REVIEW

Using the textbook, review the research efforts indicated and write a summary of the important findings. Note the general purpose or context of the research.

1. Stern (1977), page 431: _____

_____

_____

_____

_____

2. Schaffer & Emerson (1964), page 434: _____

_____

_____

_____

_____

3. Harlow & Zimmerman (1959), page 436: _____

_____

_____

_____

_____

4. Lester, Kotelchuck, Spelke, Sellers, & Klein (1974), page 438: _____

_____

_____

_____

_____

5. Main & Weston (1981), page 438: _____

_____

_____

_____

_____

6. Levitt (1980), page 441: _____

_____

_____

_____

7. Lewis & Brooks (1974), Brooks & Lewis (1976), page 442: _____

_____

_____

_____

8. Corter, Zucker, & Galligan (1980), page 446: _____

_____

_____

_____

9. Ainsworth, Blehar, Waters, & Wall (1978), page 448: _____

_____

_____

_____

10. Harlow (1962), Harlow & Harlow (1977), page 453: _____

_____

_____

_____

11. Suomi & Harlow (1972), Cummins & Suomi (1976), page 455: _____

_____

_____

12. Goldfarb (1943, 1947), page 457: _____

_____

_____

_____

_____

13. Clark & Hanisee (1982), page 459: _____

_____

_____

_____

_____

SELF-TEST II

Consider each alternative carefully. Then choose the best one.

1. The first theorist to emphasize the events of early childhood as a major contributor to personality development was
   a. Hall
   b. Freud
   c. Lorenz
   d. Piaget

2. Klaus and Kennell's view of early emotional bonding places <u>primary</u> emphasis upon
   a. how much contact the father has with the infant soon after birth
   b. the timing of the contact between father and infant soon after birth
   c. how much contact the mother has with the infant soon after birth
   d. the timing of the contact between mother and infant soon after birth

3. In full-term infants, true social smiling in response to a human face begins at about ____ weeks of age, which corresponds to a conceptional age of ____ weeks.
   a. 3, 40
   b. 6, 40
   c. 3, 46
   d. 6, 46

4. The cognitive-developmentalists propose that the discriminated smiling response is
   a. conditioned by reinforcement of smiling by caregivers
   b. a result of the development of schemata for familiar faces
   c. learned through imitation of parents' smiling
   d. all of the above

5. The idea that infants have inborn capacities for synchronized routines, such as proposed by Stern (1977), is basically
   a. a learning theory perspective
   b. an ethological perspective
   c. a cognitive-developmental perspective
   d. a psychoanalytic perspective

6. Early detection of infants who may be hard to love is best accomplished by
   a. the Brazelton Neonatal Behavioral Assessment Scale
   b. the "strange situations" test
   c. infant intelligence tests
   d. the younger-peer test

7. According to Schaffer and Emerson (1964), the order in which infants pass through stages of attachment during the first months of life is
   a. asocial, specific, indiscriminate
   b. asocial, indiscriminate, specific
   c. specific, asocial, indiscriminate
   d. specific, indiscriminate, asocial

8. As in Harlow and Zimmerman's (1959) research, if an infant monkey is fed from the "wire" mother and never from the "terrycloth" mother, the infant will when frightened
   a. run to the wire mother
   b. run to the terrycloth mother
   c. run to the experimenter
   d. freeze motionless

9. Taken together, the research by Schaffer and Emerson (1964) and by Harlow and Zimmerman (1959) indicates that the infant's attachment to the mother depends primarily upon
   a. warmth and social stimulation provided by the mother
   b. feeding practices employed by the mother
   c. oral gratification provided by the mother
   d. early emotional bonding between infant and mother

10. In accord with the findings of Lester, et al. (1974), the role of overall intellectual development in the forming of attachment is that
   a. object permanence must be present prior to the forming of specific attachments
   b. specific attachments must form before the development of stable schemata
   c. stable schemata must develop before object permanence
   d. all of the above

11. In Main and Weston's (1981) experiment with infants exposed to a "friendly clown," it was found that securely attached infants showed the least distress; this was a test of
   a. separation anxiety
   b. stranger anxiety
   c. both of the above
   d. none of the above

12. In Levitt's (1980) experiment, infants who could control a stranger's appearance during a peek-a-boo game later responded more favorably to the stranger; this indicates that
   a. stranger anxiety depends upon the availability of familiar companions
   b. stranger anxiety depends upon the setting
   c. stranger anxiety depends upon the stranger's behavior
   d. all of the above

13. Brooks and Lewis (1976) found that infants reacted less negatively to a strange child than to either a midget or an adult; thus stranger anxiety depends in part upon
   a. the size of the stranger
   b. adult-like characteristics of the stranger
   c. both of the above
   d. none of the above

14. In terms of the typical age ranges that are involved,
   a. separation anxiety appears earlier than stranger anxiety, and declines sooner
   b. stranger anxiety appears earlier than separation anxiety, and declines sooner
   c. separation anxiety appears earlier than stranger anxiety, and declines later
   d. stranger anxiety appears earlier than separation anxiety, and declines later

15. Cross-cultural research, such as that of Ainsworth (1967), indicates that
    a. children in some cultures do not show separation anxiety
    b. the age at which separation anxiety appears is universal
    c. the age at which separation anxiety appears depends in part on childrearing
    d. no relationship exists between age and the appearance of separation anxiety

16. Corter, Zucker, and Galligan (1980) found that infants generally did not protest separation until their mothers went into an area that violated their schemata for her whereabouts; this is consistent with the cognitive-developmental viewpoint that
    a. separation anxiety depends upon formation of schemata for familiar faces
    b. separation anxiety depends upon formation of schemata for familiar places
    c. both of the above
    d. none of the above

17. The least likely technique for easing separation anxiety for a toddler who must be left in an unfamiliar setting would be to
    a. have the alternative caregiver immediately pick up the child
    b. have the mother briefly explain to the child that she will soon return
    c. give the child a photograph of the mother to look at from time to time
    d. have the mother give the child instructions to play until she returns

18. Ainsworth's "strange-situations" test assesses the quality of infant attachment to the mother as a function of
    a. exploration while the mother is present
    b. stranger anxiety while the mother is present
    c. emotionality when the mother leaves and when she returns
    d. all of the above

19. Research indicates that secure attachment produces toddlers who
    a. are extremely upset when separated from their caregivers
    b. are extremely anxious when confronted by strangers
    c. both of the above
    d. none of the above

20. After 3 months of social deprivation, the Harlows' monkeys were typically
    a. eager to interact with adult monkeys
    b. eager to interact with normal peer monkeys
    c. eager to interact with other isolate monkeys
    d. avoidant of other monkeys in general

21. Research by Suomi and Harlow (1972) and by Cummins and Suomi (1976) on overcoming the effects of early social isolation in monkeys indicates that
    a. regular exposure to younger monkeys is effective
    b. regular exposure to same-age monkeys is effective
    c. regular exposure to adult monkeys is effective
    d. the effects cannot be overcome by exposure to other monkeys

22. Goldfarb (1943, 1947) studied children placed in foster homes after a year in a deprived institutional environment, by comparing them to children who remained in the institution for the first 3 years; results indicated that long-term deprivation of this type
    a. interferes with intellectual development
    b. interferes with social development
    c. both of the above
    d. none of the above

23. Apparently, the most important aspect of understaffed, deprived institutional environments in their effects on infants is
    a. maternal deprivation
    b. stimulus deprivation
    c. social deprivation
    d. none of the above

24. Clark and Hanisee's (1982) study of Asian war orphans indicated that
    a. children cannot recover from the emotional and social effects of disrupted early attachments
    b. children cannot recover from the intellectual effects of disrupted early attachments
    c. both of the above
    (d) none of the above

25. At this point in time, research on the possibility of recovery in children who experience early social and sensory deprivation indicates that
    a. the effects are completely reversible
    b. the effects are completely irreversible
    c. the effects are insignificant in the first place
    (d) none of the above

VIGNETTES

Consider the story, then answer each question using material from the textbook.

I. Mona was a product of prepared childbirth, in which her mother did not use anesthesia and her father was present throughout delivery. Mona spent most of the next few hours in the birthing room with her parents, and from the beginning they adored almost everything she did. She was a beautiful baby. She had round little cheeks and a pudgy little nose and bright, sparkling eyes that seemed full of enthusiasm for everything, and she often smiled in her own special way. Her parents soon became fond of telling everyone how happy Mona made them, and how thrilled they were that she was happy with them as well.

   1. What might Klaus and Kennell say as to why Mona's parents started out with such good attachment?

   2. What might Lorenz and Bowlby say about why attachment started out so well?

   3. What might Bowlby in particular say about Mona's smiling?

II. As Walter approached one year of age, his parents began to notice that he was often apathetic and uninterested in much of anything, including them. He often seemed not to care whether they were around or not, and nothing seemed to make him either happy or upset, even though he was physically healthy. And so they began to wonder what was wrong, and they wondered if it had something to do with their busy schedules and their use of day care from the time that Walter was about 4 months old. Or, they thought, maybe it had something to do with how they interacted with him.

   1. How might you classify Walter's attachment in Ainsworth's system? Why?

   2. What factors in day care would you take a look at in trying to understand Walter's behavior?

   3. What factors in Walter's interactions with his parents might you consider?

III. When Freddy was about 8 months old he met his Aunt Matilda for the first time. She lived in another city, and although she had been yearning to see him for months, this was the first time she had been able to get time off to make the trip. Matilda has "talked" to Freddy several times on the telephone and had enjoyed listening to him chuckle and laugh, and so she figured he would recognize her. Thus when Freddy's mother greeted her at the door, Aunt Matilda flew past her and went straightaway for Freddy with a big, eager smile on her face. But when she picked him up, he started screaming at the top of his lungs and wouldn't stop no matter what Aunt Matilda did in trying to soothe him. Freddy's mother soon had to intervene, first soothing Freddy and then soothing Matilda.

1. Was Freddy's reaction normal? How would you explain it?

2. Why would having heard Aunt Matilda's voice on the phone not help?

3. What might Aunt Matilda do differently to minimize Freddy's distress?

APPLICATIONS

Try each of the projects, noting answers to the questions as you go.

I. Suppose you are a researcher and you set up a situation similar to that described in the research by Harlow and Zimmerman (1959), in which an infant monkey is fed from one of two surrogate "mothers." However, in your experiment, one major aspect is different: The two mothers are both made of terrycloth and are identical in all respects, except that the infant monkey is fed from only one of them. After several months of this rearing, you tally up the amount of time the infant has spent with each surrogate mother and you also use Harlow and Zimmerman's test for attachment by turning a wind-up toy loose in the monkey's chamber.

  1. Which monkey should the infant spend more time with? Which monkey should the infant run to when frightened? Why?

  2. Could you, in a different sense, study this monkey's behavior in terms of the effects of early social deprivation, as in Harlow and Harlow's (1977) research? Why or why not? Are there any key differences in the procedure?

  3. How would you go about overcoming the effects of isolation upon this monkey?

II. Imagine the following situation, which might well happen to you sometime (if it hasn't already). You've just come home from visiting a friend, and with you came a perfectly adorable little kitten about 7-8 weeks old. You aren't exactly clear on how it happened. But, setting aside a vague notion of deliberateness in how your friend just had to show you the "babies," you now settle down to ponder why you had that sudden impulse to adopt one. And, of course, you begin to contemplate what you can do to ensure that the little critter become thoroughly attached to you.

  1. By analogy, what might Bowlby, Lorenz, and Stern say about your impulse to adopt?

  2. What general rules might you formulate toward creating secure attachment?

  3. If your pet becomes securely attached to you, and vice versa, what later behavior toward other humans might the kitten display?

III. Devise a checklist of the kinds of things you might look for in visiting a children's home or orphanage, with regard to the children's development of attachment. Note in particular the positive aspects you think should be present in this type of institution.

  1. What personal characteristics of the caregivers would be desirable?

  2. What childcare considerations would be most important with infants?

  3. In particular, what effects might the presence of multiple caregivers have?

Self-Test I

1. d	6. b	11. c
2. c	7. b	12. d
3. b	8. c	13. c
4. d	9. a	14. a
5. c	10. a	15. c

Research Summary and Review

1. Stern (1977): Interactional synchrony between infant and mother was observed in detail, with the interpretation that synchronized routines of this type set the stage for reciprocal social attachment.

2. Schaffer & Emerson (1964): In an 18-month longitudinal study of Scottish infants, infant-to-caregiver attachment was found to develop through stages; additional findings were that the feeding schedule and the age at weaning were not primary determinants of attachment, which led to the theory that responsiveness and the total stimulation provided by the caregiver are the most important factors in attachment.

3. Harlow & Zimmerman (1959): In assessing the effects of feeding on infant-to-caregiver attachment, infant monkeys were fed either from a "terrycloth" surrogate mother or from a "wire" surrogate mother. Regardless of feeding, the monkeys became attached to the terrycloth mother, with the implication that warmth and contact-comfort are more important than feeding in the formation of primary social attachments.

4. Lester, et al. (1974): In verifying Schaffer's hypothesis that object permanence is necessary before infants can form specific attachments, it was found that 9-month-old infants who scored high in object permanence showed stronger separation protests than 9-month-old who scored low; in addition, 12-month-olds high in object permanence displayed more separation protest following the departure of either the father or the mother.

5. Main & Weston (1981): A study of 43 infants who were classified as securely attached to mother, father, or both parents indicated (1) quality of attachment to one parent did not predict quality of attachment to the other, and (2) stranger anxiety was least pronounced with infants securely attached to both parents, and also offset to some extent with infants securely attached to one parent, either mother or father.

6. Levitt (1980): Infants who could "control" a peek-a-boo game with a stranger were later more likely to interact positively with the stranger; thus, in the context of understanding stranger anxiety and how to minimize it, the factor of allowing the infant to regulate initial interactions with a stranger appears important.

7. Lewis & Brooks (1974), Brooks & Lewis (1976): In two related research efforts designed to shed light on stranger anxiety, it was found that infants react less negatively to another child than to an adult, even if the adult is a midget; thus characteristics other than "size" of the stranger are involved.

8. Corter, Zucker, & Galligan (1980): Infants were first exposed to a situation in which they should develop schemata for their mothers' whereabouts, and the infants did not cry or fuss; later, when their mothers went to a different place outside the room, the infants became upset, demonstrating that violating an infant's schemata for where mother is leads to separation anxiety.

9. Ainsworth, et al. (1981): In developing a multidimensional approach to understanding attachment, it was found that the "strange situations" test reliably sorted infants into

securely attached, insecurely attached (anxious and resistant), and insecurely attached (anxious and avoidant) categories, on the basis of exploration, stranger anxiety, and separation anxiety.

10. Harlow (1962), Harlow & Harlow (1977): Isolating infant monkeys from birth produced emotional and social disturbance that was progressively more severe and harder to overcome according to the length of isolation; this classic line of research underscored the importance of attachment to personality development.

11. Suomi & Harlow (1972), Cummins & Suomi (1976): As a demonstration that the effects of early social deprivation in monkeys can be overcome, with implications that extend to humans, isolated monkeys received younger-peer therapy and developed into normal adults.

12. Goldfarb (1943, 1947): In assessing how permanent the long-term effects of early institutional deprivation are for human infants, a group of infants that left for foster homes during the first year of life were compared to infants who stayed in the institution for 3 years; longitudinal data indicated that the infants who left fared much better in intellectual, social, and emotional development, which implied that the effects of social deprivation during the first 3 years of life are very difficult to overcome.

13. Clark & Hanisee (1982): Asian war orphans who were adopted into middle- and upper-SES American homes later score significantly above average on intelligence tests and assessments of social maturity, in spite of the malnutrition and social/interpersonal disruptions they had previously experienced; the implication was that early deprivation of various types can be overcome.

Self-Test II

1. b	6. a	11. b	16. c	21. a
2. d	7. b	12. c	17. a	22. c
3. c	8. b	13. b	18. c	23. c
4. b	9. a	14. b	19. d	24. d
5. b	10. a	15. c	20. d	25. d

Vignettes

I. (1) Klaus and Kennell, in accord with their research, would emphasize the presumed cuddling and skin-to-skin contact during the "sensitive period" of 6-12 hours after birth, in accord with emotional bonding. (2) An ethological emphasis might be on innate behaviors and characteristics of the infant that promote caregiver-to-infant attachment, here including Mona's smiling, her bright eyes, and her attractive "kewpie doll" appearance. (3) But Mona's parents are pleasantly mislead in believing that her smiling shows either that she is happy with them or that she feels good. Early smiling is reflexive, although it could aid in fostering attachment anyway.

II. (1) In Ainsworth's system, Walter would probably be classified as insecurely attached (anxious and avoidant), depending upon results of the "strange situations" test. By implication, he would explore little, would show little response to strangers either way, and would protest little when separated from parents. (2) As in Box 11-3, you might consider whether there are enough caregivers to go around, whether they are warm and responsive, and how much time is allocated to attending quickly to infants' needs and signals - including simply holding and cuddling the infants. Also note that the day care might be very good for other infants but not Walter, if he alienated the caregivers by being "hard to love." (3) Considerations would include the amount of time each parent spends with Walter during off hours, whether they respond warmly and consistently to his needs, whether they provide him other forms of stimulation, and so on. Also note that the case is similar to that of learned helplessness, with implications there as well.

III. (3) Freddy's behavior is consistent with that of an 8-month-old's stranger anxiety in the particular case where a stranger comes on too strong. Notes on explaining the behavior are that he might need a few moments to figure "what" Aunt Matilda is, before he can get around to figuring out "who" she might be. In such a situation, his fear seems adaptive. Also note that he had no opportunity to regulate the sequence of events. (2) Research indicates that infants form "recognition" schemata more on the basis of visual cues, such as faces. It is also unlikely that an 8-month-old would associate a telephone voice with a voice in person. (3) Slowing things down would have helped the most in minimizing Freddy's anxiety. Aunt Matilda might also have smiled and "coaxed" while maintaining her distance and waiting for Freddy to indicate that he wanted her to come closer, thus allowing him a degree of control. Another possibility would have been to have Freddy's mother help, by handing him to Aunt Matilda slowly and staying within reach, to allow him something of a base for exploration.

Applications

I. (1) Feeding is apparently not the most important factor in attachment, but it is still a factor, as indicated. Thus in this situation your infant monkey might well spend more time with and run to the mother from which the monkey is fed. (2) Results might or might not be the same with this monkey. The terrycloth mother would afford a degree of contact comfort the fully isolated monkeys did not have. However, research suggests that the caregiver's "responsiveness" is necessary for normal attachment, and the surrogate mother would hardly be responsive. Thus the disruptive effects of isolation should still occur. (3) As in the description of younger-peer therapy, you would use gradually increasing exposure to a younger monkey to counteract the effects of isolation. How long your monkey was isolated would determine how difficult the effects are to overcome.

II. The answers for this *Application* depend upon generalizing from humans back to animals, which is probably no riskier than generalizing from animals to humans, as long as we are careful not to anthropomorphize. (1) An ethological view might stress behaviors and characteristics that make a kitten "easy to love," and a 7-8-week-old kitten can be irrestible (even if you don't especially care for full-grown cats). There are also analogs to the "kewpie doll" appearance, and the possibility of interactional synchrony between you and the kitten. And you might ponder a natural-selection process in cats, by virtue of their having been human pets for many, many generations, in which the "cuter" ones are more likely to be adopted and given a chance to reproduce. (2) Spend a lot of time cuddling your kitten. Be warm and responsive. Play with it. Be patient about "housetraining." When outside, stay close and provide a secure base for exploration. And of course feed it regularly, respond quickly to its needs (within reason), and love it. (3) If it becomes securely attached, it should be more sociable and confident around other humans. It should be curious in strange situations, rather than terrified.

III. (1) Notes are that the caregivers should be warm and responsive, and disposed to their work with kindness and a basic enjoyment of children. Trained caregivers should be especially alert to "difficult" children and how to work with them. Caregivers should not be the kind of people who are hard to reach. They should also be willing to form attachments with the children, plus knowledgeable about children's development and needs as discussed throughout the textbook. (2) Social responsiveness is indicated very strongly with infants, which includes interacting on a "needs" basis in addition to daily routine. This means responding to crying and distress of all kinds, to foster the basic sense of trust necessary to secure attachment. Above all, given that different caregivers will be present at different times, responsiveness includes spending enough time with each infant to allow specific and multiple attachments to develop. (3) Research indicates that multiple caregiving does not necessarily have negative effects, and may have some positive ones additional to other parenting approaches. A specific mother figure is apparently not necessary. And as discussed throughout the chapter, the quality of interactions is the most important consideration. Infants are quite capable of forming multiple attachments to a number of responsive caregivers.

CHAPTER TWELVE

THE SELF AND SOCIAL DEVELOPMENT

OVERVIEW AND KEY TERMS

Read carefully. Recall examples and discussion as you go, and define each key term.

The unique combination of attributes tha characterizes each individual person is called the <u>self</u>. An early hypothesis about the development of self was the notion of the <u>looking-glass self</u>, wherein one's personal identity was said to be a reflection of how others react to him or her. Many theorists believe that infants have no concept of self until they realize that they exist independent of the world around them. Thus, according to this view, self-concepts emerge as a result of experience.

DEVELOPMENT OF THE SELF-CONCEPT

"Self" as separate from others begins to appear in the first few months of life, as ego begins to form, and as schemata shift from primary circular reactions to secondary circular reactions and infants are acting on objects external to their bodies. Piaget suggested that infants think of themselves in terms of what they can do to the environment, so that the actions they can perform represent the origins of the <u>self-concept</u>.

The ability to "recognize" oneself in mirrors and photographs develops in the second year of life, and 18-24-month-olds indicate a sense of self in this fashion. This corresponds with maturation of the object concept and the forming of initial mental images. By the end of the second year, children are also using words such as "I," "me," and "mine," versus "you." The <u>categorical self</u>, which involves describing oneself as having a certain age, size, gender, and so on, becomes refined during the preschool period. Children 3-5 years old can easily classify "boys" versus "girls" of different ages into discrete age categories. By the time children enter grade school they know that they will always be male or female, thus forming a stable gender self-concept. During preschool children dwell on physical characteristics, possessions, and actions they can perform to define themselves. This is consistent with Erikson's stage of <u>autonomy versus shame and doubt</u> with its emphasis on acquiring competence and taking pride in accomplishments during the early preschool years, followed by the stage of <u>initiative versus guilt</u> in later preschool years. The beginnings of a distinction between <u>public self</u> and <u>private self</u> also appear during the preschool period.

In middle childhood and adolescence, self-descriptions gradually become less concrete and more abstract, so that by the early teens, traits, beliefs, motivations, and interpersonal affiliations are more important. The aspect of private self that allows us to think one thing but do another also develops in later childhood and early adolescence, as does a beginning awareness of being able to "control" what we think and feel.

<u>Self-esteem</u>, which involves what we think of ourselves in terms of cognitive, social, and physical competence as well as self-worth, seems well established by middle childhood. These feelings about the self also seem to involve the looking-glass self, because children's impressions of their own competencies are corroborated by teachers and peers. Some

competencies are more important to children than others, as grade-school children undergo Erikson's stage of industry versus inferiority and measure their competencies against those of peers. Research indicates that self-esteem declines somewhat as the child enters puberty, perhaps due to (1) self-dissatisfaction with one's changing body image, (2) a loss of status in moving from grade school to junior high school, or (3) acquisition of formal operations and a resulting tendency to view one's "real self" less favorably than one's "ideal self." Erikson attributes this decline in self-esteem to the adolescent identity crisis. Box 12-1 describes four stages or "statuses" in the process of identity formations: (1) identity diffusion, with no commitments to attitudes or values, (2) identity foreclosure, with preliminary commitments typically as a result of others' suggesttions, (3) moratorium, which constitutes the identity crisis as such and includes active exploration of attitudes and values, and (4) identity achievement, in which the identity crisis is resolved and long-term commitments to a personal and interpersonal identity are made. Recent research suggests that American youth may experience the identity crisis later than Erikson had assumed, with college serving as an extended moratorium for many of those who attend.

KNOWING ABOUT OTHERS

Milestones in children's understanding of others often precede understanding of self. Knowledge about others, as well as about oneself, is called social cognition.

Preschool children's impressions of other people are based on the same concrete sources of information that they use to describe themselves, including shared activities, physical appearance, and possessions. During middle childhood children's impressions of others become increasingly abstract. Barenboim proposes a three-step sequence in impression formation during grade school: (1) the behavioral comparisons phase, (2) the psychological constructs phase, and (3) the psychological comparisons phase. These changes in impression formation seem to be related to cognitive-developmental changes proposed by Piaget.

Selman proposes the development of role-taking skills as an important aspect of social-cognitive development. Presumably, the ability to understand another person and form an accurate impression requires being able to take that person's perspective and understand internal factors that account for her or his behavior. Selman's stages of social perspective-taking include (0) the egocentric perspective, (1) social-informational role-taking, (2) self-reflective role-taking, (3) mutual role-taking, and (4) social and conventional system role-taking. These five role-taking stages closely parallel Piaget's overall stages of cognitive development. Over the course of middle childhood, children become more selective in forming friends as they become better at assessing other people's values and motives. Those who are better at role-taking enjoy higher social status among peers, perhaps because they are better at inferring others' needs. Equal-status contacts with peers seem to foster development of role-taking skills, as when play or other activities require children to integrate their points of view with those of other children. Research on cooperative study groups also bears this out. Social cognition and social development are thoroughly intertwined.

SOCIABILITY: DEVELOPMENT OF THE SOCIAL SELF

Sociability refers to one's willingness to interact with others and to seek their attention or approval. Although sociable relations and attachments differ in several respects, both of these aspects of social development begin with parent-child interactions during infancy.

By 6 weeks of age many infants have come to prefer human company to nonsocial interactions, and another baby will often elicit a sociable response. Touching, smiling, vocalizing, and gesturing to another baby develop during the first year of life, and children become progressively more sociable to adult strangers during the second and third years. But individual differences in sociability are observable early. The genetic hypothesis, with research evidence based on twin studies, suggests that genotype influences responsiveness to other people. The "security of attachment" hypothesis notes that environmental effects are also important, in that more securely attached infants are more sociable. The "ordinal position" hypothesis notes that first-borns often are more sociable than later-borns, perhaps because they receive more parental attention. However, it may also be that later-borns learn to be wary of others from being dominated by siblings.

During the preschool period, sociability undergoes a transformation in which children direct their bids for attention less to adults and more to other children. Nurseries and preschool probably contribute to this effect; however, shy and otherwise unsociable children may become even more withdrawn without special help. Box 12-2 describes techniques in helping such children, which include reinforcing appropriate social behaviors, modeling social skills, and cognitive approaches such as coaching and role-playing that help children think about how to deal with other children. Parents who are warm and supportive and require their children to follow "rules" of social etiquette tend to foster sociability, whereas permissive parents often foster aggressive behavior and overprotective parents often foster sociability toward adults but avoidance of other children.

ALTRUISM: DEVELOPMENT OF THE PROSOCIAL SELF

Prosocial behaviors such as helping, sharing, and cooperating are often reflections of altruism. Such behaviors are present by the end of the first year of life, in simple form, and expressions of sympathy or compassion are not unusual during the second year, although there are large individual differences in infants and toddlers. During the preschool period children exhibit altruism more during pretend play early and then later perform more acts of actual helping. In grade school, altruism continues to develop, and boys and girls alike show increases in their willingness to share with and to help others. Helping is more likely among same-sex peers in preschool and grade school, but more in accord with need of the recipients as children get older.

Culture influences altruistic, prosocial behavior. Competitiveness as a cultural value may interfere with sharing and cooperating. Most societies, however, endorse the norm of social responsibility. Reinforcement of altruistic behavior can be effective, if the adult also models the behavior and is respected by the child. In addition, specially designed cooperative activities such as the "bridges" game, which requires children to work together, can foster prosocial behavior as discussed in Box 12-3. Verbal altruistic exhortations are beneficial if the model also practices what he or she preaches. And aiding children in developing an altruistic self-concept by using labels such as "nice" or "helpful" as they share with other children is effective.

Another factor that affects altruism is the child's level of moral reasoning. Mature moral reasoners are generally more altruistic and may even help someone they don't like. Empathic arousal is also important as a mediator of altruistic behavior, at least with older children who have the capacity to assume the perspective of others, appreciate their needs for assistance, and then follow through with the appropriate response.

Parents who have warm and affectionate relationships with their children and who both practice and preach altruism tend to foster such behavior. Power-assertive discipline and love-oriented discipline, as proposed by Hoffman, interfere with development of altruism and tend to make the child more self-centered. Inductive (victim-centered) discipline, which informs the child of the harm caused to another, is more likely to promote altruism by encouraging role-taking, performance of helpful acts, and an altruistic self-concept.

THE DEVELOPMENT OF AGGRESSION

Aggression refers to acts intended to cause harm to another who is motivated to avoid such treatment. Hostile aggression is an end in itself, whereas instrumental aggression is a means to some nonaggressive end.

Age-related changes in aggression during the preschool period include: (1) a decrease in temper tantrums, (2) an increase in aggressive behavior, which peaks at about age 4, (3) an increase in aggressive responses to frustration from about age 3 on, (4) a change in precipitating events, in that younger children aggress more as a result of being thwarted by parents, and older children aggress more as a result of conflicts with peers, and (5) a change from more physical and instrumental aggression to more verbal and hostile aggression. Overall, however, 5-year-olds are less aggressive than 4-year-olds, perhaps as a result of preschool socialization. The slight increase in hostile aggression seen among older children may involve improvement of role-taking skills. And in grade school, aggression continues to decline except as a response to children "known" to be aggressive.

Individual differences in aggression are relatively stable on into adolescence, although more so for males than for females. Girls show a greater decline in aggression and are also less aggressive in the first place, a difference that appears in many cultures and perhaps has a biological basis. Some societies are more aggressive that others, and children's aggression reflects such values.

Familial influences are important. Cold and rejecting parents who use erratic physical punishment and who condone aggression are likely to raise hostile and aggressive children. But the child's temperament in turn can push the parents to condoning aggression. Another factor is the coercive home environment, in which family members constantly struggle with one another and use negative reinforcement. Aggression in these homes is met with counteraggression, and children eventually become resistant to punishment as a means of control. Box 12-4 describes ways to modify such a family system through teaching parents to control unruly children with noncoercive methods such as time-out, positive reinforcement, and warmth and affection.

Many approaches to controlling aggression in children have been proposed. The catharsis hypothesis emphasizes allowing children to express aggressive urges from time to time, to "drain" them away. But the cathartic technique does not work, and it may backfire through teaching children that aggressive outbursts and attacks are acceptable. The incompatible response technique focuses upon ignoring aggressive acts and reinforcing incompatible, prosocial acts. This also has the effect of not reinforcing aggressive acts that are designed to gain attention and not providing an aggressive model who employs physical punishment. Another method involves creating nonaggressive environments, such as play areas that minimize interpersonal conflicts and also toys that do not suggest aggressive themes. Empathy training with regard to victims can also help.

ACHIEVEMENT: DEVELOPMENT OF THE COMPETENT SELF

Definitions of achievement motivation take various forms, including pursuing goals, taking pride in accomplishments, and being independent, responsible, and willing to work. White's effectance motivation concept proposes an inborn drive to master the environment, a concept similar to that of Piaget. Social learning theorists emphasize that achievement motivation is learned. McClelland's need for achievement (n Ach) is a learned motive to compete and strive for success, with the goal of self-fulfillment. Harter proposes two motives involved in achievement: an intrinsic orientation to satisfy one's needs for oneself, and an extrinsic orientation for external incentives.

Influences from the home environment, such as quality of attachment, affect the child's achievement motivation. An intellectually stimulating environment also helps, through challenging the child's orientation toward mastery. As discussed in Box 12-5, parents can foster n Ach by encouraging independence and a desire to do well, especially if the parents take an approach of rewarding successes and responding neutrally to failures during the child's attempts to solve problems.

Children also differ in their expectations about being able to achieve, and those who expect to achieve usually do. To some extent, girls outperform boys during grade school, and yet girls tend to underestimate their ability to achieve. However, boys tend to overestimate their ability to achieve. Such effects may reflect modeling of different sex-roles in the home. And parents traditionally expect more from boys academically. Daughters' successes are attributed more to hard work, and sons' successes more to ability, and these parental attributions are then reflected in children's achievement expectancies.

Locus of control is another factor in achievement. <u>Internalizers</u> take personal responsibility for successes and failures and thus try harder, with a tendency to achieve at high levels. <u>Externalizers</u> do not try as hard, as a result of believing that luck, fate, or others' actions determine what happens anyway. Parents who set performance standards and encourage self-reliance are more likely to rear internalizers, because the child learns that her or his own efforts are instrumental in producing outcomes. And, as noted earlier in the context of fostering achievement motivation, parents who reward successes and respond neutrally to failures are also more likely to produce internalizers.

SELF-REVIEW

Fill in the blanks for each item. Check the answers for each item as you go.

1. An individual's unique combination of attributes, motives, and behaviors is called the _____; in turn, much of what we are or will become may depend upon how others see us, which is called our _____-_____ self.

self

looking-glass

DEVELOPMENT OF THE SELF-CONCEPT

The Self as Separate from Others

2. Many developmentalists, including Piaget, believe that infants are born without a self-_____, and that the infant does not differentiate self from the surrounding _____.

concept

environment

When Do Children Recognize Themselves?

3. An infant may have a subjective sense of self and nonself by about age ___-___ months, but the ability to recognize oneself (as by the rouge test) apparently does not appear until the latter part of the _____ year of life.

5 - 6

second

The Preschooler's Conceptions of Self

4. Another indication of self-concept is that by the end of the second year toddlers are using _____ pronouns, and they also begin to notice how people differ and to classify themselves along lines of the _____ self; in particular, preschool children's self-concepts center around their physical characteristics, their possessions, and the _____ they can perform well.

personal

categorical

actions

5. During the preschool years, children begin to distinguish between what other people can see of them, called the _____ self, versus what is not observable, called the _____ self; but we do not know at what age children realize that the products of their thinking are also private.

public

private

Conceptions of Self in Middle Childhood and Adolescence

6. In middle childhood, categorical self is expressed more in terms of concrete, _____ attributes; by adolescence, categorial self depends more on abstract _____ attributes such as traits, beliefs, and interpersonal affiliations.

physical

psychological

7. Throughout middle childhood and into adolescence, awareness

191

of private _____ becomes more complex and more _____ .   self, abstract

Self-Esteem: The Affective Component of Self

8. Harter's self-concept scale evaluates child self-concept in
the areas of _____ , _____ , and physical competence,   cognitive, social
as well as overall self-_____ ; clear-cut feelings about   -esteem, -worth
oneself are present by _____ childhood, and these seem to   middle
depend upon how other people perceive and react, in accord with
the classic idea of the _____ - _____ self.   looking-glass

9. Self-esteem tends to decline as children enter adolescence,
because of the _____ crisis; Erikson thought that the   identity
identity crisis is resolved by age 15-16, but research indicates
that the onset of the crisis occurs more in _____ adolescence   late
and its resolution may extend into _____ adulthood.   early or young

KNOWING ABOUT OTHERS

Age Trends in Impression Formation

10. Impression formation is included within the area of study
called social _____ ; Barenboim proposes a three-phase   cognition
developmental sequence to describe changes in children's impressions of others: (1) the behavioral _____ phase, (2)   comparisons
the psychological _____ phase, and (3) the psychological   constructs
_____ phase.   comparisons

Role-Taking as a Determinant of Social Cognition

11. Selman emphasizes that knowing about others depends upon being able to take others' _____ , which refers to the   perspectives
development of _____-_____ skills; in turn, this ability is   role-taking
related to overall _____ development and progresses   cognitive
through five _____ from birth through adolescence.   stages

12. Acquiring role-taking skills results in children becoming
more selective about whom they call _____ ; mature role-tak-   friends
ers also tend to be more _____ with other children, and   popular
the reverse also seems true, in that social experiences with
peers lead to better _____-_____ skills.   role-taking

SOCIABILITY: DEVELOPMENT OF THE SOCIAL SELF

13. Just as early interactions with caregivers lead to attachment, early experiences also affect how _____ the child   sociable
with a wider array of people than are involved in attachment.

Sociability during the First Three Years

14. By 6 weeks of age infants prefer to be with someone rather
than to be _____ , and the infant will often make _____   alone, sociable
responses to other infants from about age 3-4 months onward; in
general, sociability tends to _____ over the first few   increase
months and years of life.

Individual Differences in Sociability

15. The genetic hypothesis holds that sociability is to some extent a _____ attribute; the "security of attachment" hy-   heritable
pothesis notes that _____ toward others varies direct-   sociability
ly with the quality of attachment to _____ ; and the   caregivers or parents
"ordinal position" hypothesis notes that _____ -borns tend to   first-
be more sociable than _____ -borns.   later-

Sociability during the Preschool Period

16. Given that the child can adapt to the new setting, the most common effect of nursery school is to help children become more _____ toward other children; "therapies" for helping shy children adapt include (1) _____ appropriate social behaviors, (2) _____ social skills, and (3) cognitive approaches such as _____ and _____-_____ techniques.

sociable
reinforcing
modeling
coaching, role-playing

Is Sociability a Stable Attribute?

17. Longitudinal data indicate that sociability is a reasonably _____ attribute, and that socially rejected children are at risk for later _____ disturbances that may need therapy.

stable
emotional

ALTRUISM: DEVELOPMENT OF THE PROSOCIAL SELF

Developmental Trends in Altruism

18. Prosocial behavior is present by the end of the _____ year of life, and many children also disply very early signs of trying to _____ other children who are in distress; research indicates that compassionate behavior in young children is more likely when the mother uses _____ explanations that draw attention to what other people feel when they are hurt.

first

comfort

affective

19. Sharing, helping, and other forms of altruism generally tend to _____ throughout the preschool period and middle childhood, beginning with the child's tendency to help others who are of the same _____, and, as this bias wanes, children come to base their decisions to help more on actual _____ for assistance.

increase

sex
need

Training Altruism: Cultural and Social Influences

20. Apparently, a cultural emphasis on competition tends to interfere with _____ in some situations; however, altruistic behavior can be taught through _____ of the behavior directly, through "practicing what you preach" and other forms of _____, and through having children play games that require _____ toward a group goal.

altruism
reinforcement

modeling
cooperation

Cognitive and Affective Contributors to Altruism

21. In addition to role-taking ability, contributors to altruism include _____ reasoning and especially the ability to experience others' emotions through _____, both of which become more more closely related to altruistic behavior as age increases.

moral
empathy

Who Raises Altruistic Children?

22. One important factor in parenting which tends to foster altruism is _____ what you preach with regard to helping others; another factor is the use of _____ discipline, which encourages the child to consider the _____ that inappropriate behavior causes others.

practicing
inductive
harm

THE DEVELOPMENT OF AGGRESSION

What Is Aggression?

23. Aggression is an act in which the actor _____ to inflict harm, either as an end in itself as in _____ aggression or as a means to a nonaggressive end as in _____ aggression.

intends
hostile
instrumental

Origins of Aggression

24. A young infant's quarrelsome behavior is more likely to be an _____ means to an end, without deliberate aggressive _____; acts that we interpret as attempts to harm or intimidate an adversary do not appear until about the latter part of the _____ year of life.

instrumental
intent

second

Age-Related Changes in the Nature of Aggression

25. During the preschool period, unfocused temper tantrums tend to _____, whereas the overall amount of aggression tends to _____; younger preschool children are more likely to be aggressive after conflicts with _____, whereas older ones are more aggressive after conflicts with _____.

decrease
increase
parents
peers

26. Beyond preschool, overall aggression tends to_____, although hostile aggression increases somewhat perhaps as children become better at inferring hostile intent as they develop better _____-_____ skills.

decrease

role-taking

Is Aggression a Stable Attribute?

27. Although the quality of aggression changes with age, aggression itself is a reasonably stable attribute at least through _____; from there, aggression tends to decline markedly, at least for the _____ sex, as a probable result of sex-_____.

adolescence
female
typing

Sex Differences in Aggression

28. Females are also _____ aggressive than males from early childhood on, and they are less likely to be the _____ of aggression by peers.

less
targets

Cultural Influences

29. Overall tendencies to commit aggressive acts vary widely across _____, although within any given culture large _____ differences are present.

cultures
individual

Familial Influences

30. Hostile, aggressive children tend to come from homes in which parents are _____ and rejecting, use physical punishment in an _____ fashion, permit the child to freely express aggressive_____, and generally allow a highly _____ to exist within the home.

cold
erratic
impulses, coercive

Methods of Controlling Aggression

31. Perhaps the least effective way to reduce or eliminate children's aggression is to encourage the "draining away" of anger and frustration through _____; more likely approaches include (1) reinforcing acts that are _____ with aggression, (2) reducing the likelihood of aggression in the first place by providing nonaggressive _____, and (3) modeling or otherwise teaching children to _____ with others.

catharsis
incompatible

environments
empathize

ACHIEVEMENT: DEVELOPMENT OF THE COMPETENT SELF

32. Children may have an intrinsic _____ motivation to master the environment, but individual differences in achievement _____ suggest that learning and the child's environment are also important factors.

effectance

motivation

What Is Achievement Motivation?

33. McClelland views "*n* Ach" as a _____ motive to compete   learned
and strive for success; Harter expresses a similar point of view
in the concept of _____ orientation as one reason why   intrinsic
children attempt to achieve, and she adds that children also work
hard to please others or to earn rewards due to an _____   extrinsic
orientation.

Home and Family Influences on Achievement

34. Achievement motivation in the form of willingness to explore
and attempts at control of the environment shows individual variability as early as the _____ year of life; factors related   first
to achievement motivation include _____ of attachment and   security
whether the home environment provides stimulating _____   challenges
which foster the child's discovery and problem-solving, plus whether parents encourage achievement by _____ the child's   reinforcing
successes and responding _____ to failures.   neutrally

Can I Achieve? The Role of Expectancies in Children's Achievement Behavior

35. Whether children will attempt to achieve also depends upon
whether they _____ to succeed, which is affected in part by   expect
the sex-role _____ conveyed by parents and others.   stereotypes

Why Do I Succeed (or Fail)? Locus of Control and Children's Achievement Behavior

36. In turn, a child's achievement expectancies depend in part
on _____ of control; higher achievement motivation is likely   locus
with an _____ locus of control, which arises in part as   internal
a result of parents' encouragement of self-_____ and par-   reliance
ents' setting of clear-cut performance _____.   standards

SELF-TEST I

Consider each alternative carefully. Then choose the best one.

1. Many developmentalists, such as Mead, Mahler, and Piaget believe the infant is born
   a. without a sense of self
   b. with a sense of self only in conjunction with others
   c. with a public self but not a private self
   d. with a primitive but relatively complete sense of self

2. The child's early development of a sense of self occurs in the sequence
   a. self-recognition, public versus private self, categorical self
   b. self-recognition, categorical self, public versus private self
   c. categorical self, self-recognition, public versus private self
   d. categorical self, public versus private self, self-recognition

3. How a person feels about her or his qualities and characteristics is called
   a. self-concept
   b. looking-glass self
   c. categorical self
   d. self-esteem

4. The correct order of Erikson's second, third, and fourth psychosocial stages is
   a. autonomy vs. shame and doubt, initiative vs. guilt, industry vs. inferiority
   b. initiative vs. guilt, autonomy vs. shame and doubt, industry vs. inferiority
   c. industry vs. inferiority, initiative vs. guilt, autonomy vs. shame and doubt
   d. initiative vs. guilt, industry vs. inferiority, autonomy vs. shame and doubt

5. As children approach and enter adolescence, their use of concrete, categorical descriptions general _____ and their basic self-esteem generally _____.
   a. increases, decreases
   b. increases, increases
   c. decreases, increases
   d. decreases, decreases

6. Children who form their impressions of other children on the basis of "helpfulness" are in the
   a. behavioral comparisons phase
   b. psychological constructs phase
   c. psychological comparisons phase
   d. reciprocal role-taking phase

7. Children who are more sociable with peers generally
   a. are securely attached
   b. have good role-taking skills
   c. are later-borns
   d. all of the above

8. Throughout childhood, sociable behavior tends to be
   a. directed toward fewer and fewer persons
   b. directed toward more and more persons
   c. increasingly directed toward significant adults such as teachers
   d. none of the above

9. Research indicates that altruism
   a. tends to decrease as children grow older
   b. is an inborn characteristic that is difficult to modify
   c. is more characteristic of girls than of boys
   d. none of the above

10. Altruism is improved when
   a. parents practice empathy training
   b. parents use inductive discipline
   c. parents practice what they preach
   d. all of the above

11. Over the preschool period, typically,
   a. instrumental aggression decreases and hostile aggression increases
   b. instrumental aggression increases and hostile aggression decreases
   c. both instrumental and hostile aggression increase
   d. both instrumental and hostile aggression decrease

12. Children who are highly empathic tend to be
   a. more altruistic and less aggressive
   b. less altruistic and more aggressive
   c. more altruistic and more aggressive
   d. less altruistic and less aggressive

13. The incidence of children's aggression can be reduced through
   a. the cathartic technique
   b. the incompatible response technique
   c. both of the above
   d. none of the above

14. Children's striving for achievement may result from
   a. effectance motivation
   b. a learned achievement motive (n Ach)
   c. external incentives
   d. all of the above

15. Achievement motivation in children is enhanced by
    a. insecure attachment
    (b.) positive achievement expectancies
    c. external locus of control
    d. all of the above

RESEARCH SUMMARY AND REVIEW

Using the textbook, review the research efforts indicated and write a summary of the important findings. Note the general purpose or context of the research.

1. Lewis & Brooks-Gunn (1979), page 469: _____

_____

_____

_____

_____

2. Harter (1982), page 473: _____

_____

_____

_____

_____

3. Barenboim (1981), page 477: _____

_____

_____

_____

4. Selman (1976, 1980), Gurucharri & Selman (1982), page 479: _____

_____

_____

_____

5. Bridgeman (1981), page 481: _____

_____

_____

_____

_____

6. Orlick (1981), Orlick & Foley (1979), Orlick, McNally, & O'Hara (1978), page 490: ____

_____

_____

7. Barnett, Howard, Melton, & Dino (1982), page 493: _____

_____

_____

_____

8. Grusec & Redler (1980), page 492: _____

_____

_____

_____

9. Hartup (1974), page 495: _____

_____

_____

_____

10. Patterson (1976, 1980), page 498: _____

_____

_____

_____

11. Van Doorninck, Caldwell, Wright, & Frankenberg (1981), page 503: _____

_____

_____

_____

SELF-TEST II

Consider each alternative carefully. Then choose the best one.

1. The term "looking glass self" refers to
   a. being able to recognize oneself in a mirror
   b. formation of self on the basis of how other people react to you
   c. the ability to take another person's perspective
   d. all of the above

2. Research on visual self-recognition suggests that the ability to recognize oneself
    a. is present during the first year of life
    b. is not observed among mentally retarded children
    c. characterizes normally reared but not socially isolated adolescent chimpanzees
    d. none of the above

3. A sense of private self appears
    a. after a sense of public self
    b. prior to a sense of public self
    c. at the same time as a sense of public self
    d. at the same time as object permanence

4. The developmental progression in the categorical self through middle childhood and adolescence, in terms of referents children use, is
    a. from concrete to abstract
    b. from physical to psychological
    c. both of the above
    d. none of the above

5. In her research on children's self-esteem, Harter (1982) found that
    a. self-esteem depends upon the situation the child is in
    b. self-esteem is well established by middle childhood
    c. children's evaluations of self correspond to others' evaluations
    d. all of the above

6. Research on the adolescent identity crisis in America indicates that the probable effect of attending college is to
    a. extend the moratorium period
    b. accelerate the progression to identity achievement
    c. bypass the identity foreclosure period
    d. all of the above

7. Barenboim's (1981) psychological comparisons phase in impression formation corresponds to Piaget's
    a. sensorimotor period
    b. preoperational period
    c. concrete operational period
    d. formal operational period

8. Selman's interpersonal dilemmas are designed to assess
    a. role-taking skills
    b. self-esteem
    c. sociability
    d. aggression

9. According to Selman, preschool children
    a. are egocentric and incapable of social role taking
    b. are capable of social-informational role taking
    c. are capable of self-reflective role taking
    d. are capable of mutual role taking

10. Children with good role-taking skills tend to be
    a. more popular
    b. more sensitive to the needs of others
    c. more likely to form intimate relationships
    d. all of the above

11. A primary distinction between sociability and emotional attachment is that
    a. attachment is temporary, whereas sociability is enduring
    b. sociability is directed toward peers but not adults
    c. attachment is directed toward fewer targets and is more intense
    d. sociability does not originate with early caregiver interactions

12. With regard to development of sociability, perhaps the major implication of studies of monozygotic versus dizygotic twins is that
   a. quality of attachment is the primary determinant of sociability
   b. ordinal birth position is insignificant to differences in sociability
   c. both of the above
   d. none of the above

13. Which of the following would be the least preferable way to improve the social skills of withdrawn, unpopular children entering preschool?
   a. reinforce socially appropriate behaviors
   b. punish socially inappropriate behaviors
   c. model social interaction skills
   d. coach the child on the hows and whys of social skills

14. Other things equal, altruistic behaviors during preschool and middle childhood
   a. tend to increase, where girls are concerned
   b. tend to increase, where boys are concerned
   c. both of the above
   d. none of the above

15. As compared to U.S. children, Mexican children tend to be
   a. more cooperative
   b. less altruistic
   c. more aggressive
   d. none of the above

16. Cooperative activities and games such as those of Orlick and associates tend to
   a. increase altruism
   b. decrease altruism
   c. have little effect of altruism
   d. have only temporary effects on altruism

17. Grusec and Redler's (1980) self-concept training had more effect on 8-year-olds than on 5-year-olds most likely because
   a. 8-year-olds are just beginning to use psychological descriptors of self
   b. 8-year-olds are beginning to see traits as stable aspects of their character
   c. both of the above
   d. none of the above

18. According to Barnett, et al.'s (1982) research, a likely order of events involved in deciding to assist a needy other is
   a. empathy, role taking, altruism
   b. empathy, altruism, role taking
   c. role taking, empathy, altruism
   d. role taking, altruism, empathy

19. Inductive discipline has the effect of fostering altruism in children because
   a. it encourages social role taking
   b. it models altruistic behavior
   c. it enhances the child's altruistic looking-glass self
   d. all of the above

20. According to Hartup's (1974) observational study of children's aggression,
   a. the amount of aggression children display varies with age
   b. the factors that elicit aggression vary with age
   c. the form of aggression varies with age
   d. all of the above

21. With regard to sex differences in aggression,
   a. girls are less aggressive than boys in the first place
   b. girls are less likely than boys to remain aggressive beyond puberty
   c. both of the above
   d. none of the above

22. According to Patterson's (1976, 1980) research, aggressive children are likely to live in coercive home environments characterized by
   a. love-oriented parental discipline
   b. positive reinforcement of coercive tactics by all family members
   c. ongoing hostility
   d. all of the above

23. McClelland's *n* Ach applies to situations in which
   a. external incentives are the primary determinant of achievement
   b. one's behavior can be evaluated against a standard of excellance
   c. the primary determinant of achievement is innate effectance motivation
   d. none of the above

24. Research by van Doorninck, et al. (1981) on environments conducive to the development of children's scholastic achievement indicates that
   a. lower-class families foster poor achievement
   b. emotionally responsive caregivers foster high achievement
   c. physically unstimulating environments are unrelated to achievement
   d. none of the above

25. Research on child-rearing practices that foster good achievement indicates that
   a. independence training is beneficial
   b. direct achievement training is beneficial
   c. rewarding successes and responding neutrally to failures is beneficial
   d. all of the above

VIGNETTES

Consider the story, then answer each question using material from the textbook.

I. In the seventh grade, Jerry's self-esteem began to take a downward turn and he began to realize that he didn't feel very good about himself. He began wondering just exactly who he was, and it seemed to him that there was nothing he could really do well. Jerry also found himself pulling away from friends he had known since he first began going to school, and it seemed that there was no one who really understood him.

   1. What might Erikson have to say about about Jerry's plight?

   2. What might Harter predict is important to Jerry's decline in self-esteem?

   3. What other social and developmental factors might be responsible?

II. Phil, at age 9, had consistent problems in getting along with his schoolmates, and he often felt that he didn't understand them and they didn't understand him either. He typically didn't know how they would react when he asked them for something, and so he rarely bothered to ask. Instead, he mostly did what he wanted and took the consequences. At recess Phil usually watched rather than joining in, And, mostly, he was unhappy.

   1. How would you evaluate Phil's role-taking skills in Selman's system?

   2. What could you predict about Phil with regard to altruism, and why?

   3. What could you predict about Phil with regard to aggression, and why?

III. Linda, now comfortably into the beginnings of adolescence in terms of its physical changes, at least, had decided to become a nurse. Everyone agreed that this was the best plan for her, and also that her high grades and hard work at school would see her through. Everyone agreed that Linda was well suited to be a nurse. She cared about people, and she seemed to get a lot out of helping and comforting her classmates in distress. So, Linda took it for granted that she would be a nurse.

1. Where would you classify Linda in Erikson's (and Marcia's) identity statuses?

2. How would you rank Linda on altruism, and why?

3. How would you rank Linda on achievement motivation, and why?

APPLICATIONS

Try each of the projects, noting answers to the questions as you go.

I. Suppose you're working with preschool children, and you begin to notice that two or three relatively "likable" kids are somehow not getting along with the rest and don't participate much in games and other group activities. Thus, being a caring and responsive caregiver, you set out to do what you can to help them.

1. With regard to building self-esteem appropriate to their level of self-concepts, what kinds of things about each child might you emphasize in talking to them?

2. What techniques might work in helping them become more sociable with the others?

3. What effects might your helping them acquire prosocial behaviors have?

II. Again, suppose you're working with preschool children, and you notice that several of the kids are consistently aggressive and hostile in dealing with the rest, especially with regard to taking away toys and getting a few kicks and slaps in the process. As a starting point, you begin to wonder where such behavior comes from.

1. What would you guess about basic styles and characteristics of discipline the parents of the children employ?

2. What overall type of home environment would be mostly likely?

3. How normal is this behavior, in light of research by Goodenough and by Hartup?

III. Having wondered about the aggressive children in *Application II*, now suppose you set out to do something about their behavior and help them, both for their own sakes and to help the other children in the preschool who are the recipients of the aggressive acts. Assume that you have the cooperation of the parents as well as the other caregivers at the school.

1. List effective ways adults could deal directly with aggressive acts.

2. List effective ways other children could be included in your "therapy."

3. Describe procedures you would definitely avoid using with these children.

ANSWERS

Self-Test I

1. a	6. c	11. a
2. b	7. d	12. a
3. d	8. b	13. b
4. a	9. d	14. d
5. d	10. d	15. b

1. Lewis & Brooks-Gunn (1979): In assessing early origins of self-concept, it was found that 18-24-month-olds typically touched their own noses rather than the mirror images in response to the "rouge" test, which indicated they recognized the images as themselves.

2. Harter (1982): Using a self-concept scale, it was found that by middle childhood children have well established feelings of self-esteem, that self-esteem depends upon the particular situation, and that children's self-evaluations correspond to evaluations by other children. This research effort was primarily normative and exploratory.

3. Barenboim (1981): Children's descriptive statements about friends were analyzed, with indications of a three-phase developmental sequence involving behavioral comparisons, psychological constructs, and psychological comparisons as how children form impressions over the middle childhood years; these phases corresponded to overall cognitive development.

4. Selman (1976, 1980), Gurucharri & Selman (1982): Children's responses to interpersonal dilemmas were analyzed, yielding a five-stage developmental sequence in role-taking abilities: egocentric, social-informational, self-reflective, mutual, and social and conventional system role taking. These are thought to represent an invariant sequence.

5. Bridgeman (1981): Fifth-grade students were assigned either to cooperative interdependence or control (traditional classroom) conditions in studying and learning; those who had to cooperate later showed improvement in role-taking skills, indicating the effects of social experiences upon role taking.

6. Orlick (1981), Orlick & Foley (1979), Orlick, et al. (1978): A series of experiments in which preschool children who participated in cooperative activities with common goals indicated inprovements in cooperation and in altruistic behaviors, which implies that one way to foster altruism is to help children discover the benefits of working together.

7. Barnett, et al. (1982): Children who were high in empathy were more helpful than low empathizers after focusing on the plight of others (i.e., role taking) but not after focusing on personal concerns, thus shedding light on the interplay between role taking, empathy, and altruism.

8. Grusec & Redler (1980): Verbal self-concept training promoted altruism in 8-year-olds but not in 5-year-olds, presumably because psychological descriptors have more impact on the former than on the latter in conjunction with age-related trends in how children define self and the extent to which they understand traits as stable aspects of self.

9. Hartup (1974): Normative research on age-related changes in aggression by preschool and by early grade-school children (in conjunction with Goodenough, 1931) indicated that the overal incidence of aggresion declines with age and yet the incidence of hostile aggression shows a slight increase perhaps related to abilities in inferring anothers' intent; situational and other factors in aggression were also assessed.

10. Patterson (1976, 1980): In studying origins of aggression in children, it was found that highly aggressive children tend to come from coercive home environments characterized by hostility and negative reinforcement, which promotes countercoercion by the child and a general resistance to punishment.

11. Van Doorninck, et al. (1981): A long-term study of children's achievement as a function of home environment (as assessed by the HOME inventory) indicated that the more stimulating home environments foster higher achievement, thus providing clues to the origins of achievement behavior in children.

1. b	6. a	11. c	16. a	21. c
2. c	7. d	12. d	17. c	22. c
3. a	8. a	13. b	18. c	23. b
4. c	9. a	14. c	19. d	24. b
5. d	10. d	15. a	20. d	25. d

Vignettes

I. (1) Erikson might say that Jerry is in the midst of the industry versus inferiority crisis, perhaps as a result of measuring himself against peers in terms of personal and interpersonal competence, or it is possible that Jerry is in the status of identity diffusion; in either case, Erikson might note to those concerned that Jerry is going through a normal phase of development. (2) Harter's system, as well as Erikson's, would emphasize the role of cognitive and social competencies in self-esteem, also noting that other children may be responding to Jerry in ways similar to how he views himself. (3) Other factors would include his beginning entrance into puberty and the corresponding physical changes, possibly his recent transition from elementary to junior high school (if applicable), and his possible entrance into the more abstract realm of formal operational thinking, whereby Jerry might become concerned because his "real self" does not measure up to his "ideal self."

II. (1) Phil is apparently in the egocentric or the social-informational stage, as evidenced by his lack of insight and anticipation as to what others will think and do. Normatively, this makes him a bit behind at age 9 in development of role-taking skills, which also means that his classmates might be critical of his inability to see their points of view. (2) Role-taking skills appear to be a major contributor to altruism, and thus Phil might be less inclined to help, share, and cooperate as compared to his classmates. (3) Good role-taking skills also decrease the probability of aggression, in that the child is more aware of the impact of aggression upon others. Thus Phil might well be more aggressive at times as a direct result of caring less about the harm he causes or because he is likely to assume that others' negative behaviors toward him have an aggressive intent.

III. (1) Marcia's interpretation of Erikson places Linda in the identity foreclosure status, in that she apparently accepts being a nurse on the basis of others' opinions, without much in the way of self-evaluation. (2) Linda's tendency to empathize with others and to enjoy helping when necessary would probably rank her high in altruism, which might be well suited to a variety of helping professions including nursing. (3) Pride and a sense of self-fulfillment indicate a high ranking on *n* Ach, especially in view of her good grades and hard work. She also seems to be operating both from an intrinsic orientation (similar to *n* Ach and from an extrinsic orientation (grades, also approval from others), which would be a powerful combination. And note that her looking-glass self also includes an emphasis on achievement.

Applications

I. (1) Research indicates that preschool children form self-concepts on the basis of concrete descriptors, and thus for each child you might attend to and emphasize special characteristics such as being able to run fast, play certain games well, climb well, or whatever you've noticed each child can "do." Also note how Harter's area of "physical competence" figures in with self-esteem. (2) Basically, you want to set social interactions in motion in ways that will lead to positive experiences. As described in Box 12-2, you might employ reinforcement of socially appropriate behaviors, modeling of social skills, and cognitive techniques such as coaching and role-playing. Note that your goal is to get the children to a point that natural processes of interaction with peers will take over, thus minimizing the need for you and other adults as "agents." (3) Prosocial behaviors such as sharing, helping, and cooperating tend to elicit the kinds of positive responses from other children that might set a natural process of socialization in motion, in turn leading to more sharing, helping, and so on, including participation in the group.

II. (1) Aggression is more likely in children when parent-child interactions are characterized by coldness, hostility, and rejection, and also when parents use either power-assertive or love-oriented discipline. Also note that parents who apply physical punishment in an erratic fashion and who permit their child to express such impulses foster aggression. (2) Patterson's coercive home environment is likely, in terms of interactions both with parents and with siblings. Factors include aversive interactions characterized by self-interest, negative reinforcement as a means of control between family members, and a general atmosphere of emotional disruption and frustration. (3) Normatively, these children seem to be displaying instrumental aggression more than hostile aggression, and thus, if they are at the lower end of the preschool range, are within normal limits.

III. (1) Adult techniques might include standing firm in the face of aggression and not giving in to countercoercion, using control procedures such as time-out, setting behavioral contracts based on rewards for cooperation, sharing, and so on, and emphasizing looking for occasions of appropriate behavior to respond to with warmth and praise. The incompatible response technique might include ignoring aggressive behavior as much as possible, but note that ignoring "instrumental" aggression might not be effective in that this type of aggression is not usually oriented toward attracting adult attention in the first place, and ignoring it means that the child is still reinforced by getting the toy, etc. Other techniques might include structuring of the environment to minimize the occasions for instrumental aggression in particular, plus incorporating direct empathy training similar to what takes place in inductive discipline. (2) As noted in *Application I*, prosocial behavior by one child tends to elicit prosocial behavior from another, setting a reciprocal process in motion. And other children could also be used as models for non-aggressive ways to obtain what one wants. Empathy training might be most effective if other children expressed their feelings to the aggressive children directly, in terms of how it feels to be a victim. (3) You would avoid overreacting and becoming coercive yourself, and you would avoid use of physical punishment, in each case to keep from serving as a model for aggression. Also note the types of aggression you could and could not ignore. And in particular, you would not employ the cathartic technique, because it does not reduce aggression and may in fact serve to instigate aggression.

CHAPTER THIRTEEN

SEX DIFFERENCES AND SEX-ROLE DEVELOPMENT

OVERVIEW AND KEY TERMS

Read carefully. Recall examples and discussion as you go, and define each key term.

Although biological heritage is a factor contributing to differences between the sexes, social sex typing begins in the hospital nursery or delivery room as parents begin to respond differently to boys and to girls.

CATEGORIZING MALES AND FEMALES: SEX-ROLE STANDARDS

Societies impose sex-role standards on the individual, which dictate how males versus females are expected to behave. The female's childbearing role is responsible for many female sex-role standards within the expressive role, including being nurturant, warm, and sensitive to the needs of others. Males are encouraged toward an instrumental role, with a "provider" orientation that dictates being dominant, assertive, and competitive. Thus we have distinct stereotypes about what a "real" boy and a "real" girl are like, and in spite of advances in women's rights, such stereotypes are slow in changing. Many cultures have similar expectations and sex-role standards for females and males.

SOME FACTS AND FICTIONS ABOUT SEX DIFFERENCES

Although group averages tell us little about the individual, Maccoby and Jacklin's review of research indicates that some sex-role standards may be accurate. Verbal skills develop earlier in females than in males, and females display clear superiority in such abilities by adolescence. Males do better on tests of visual/spatial and arithmetic reasoning, with the differences between the sexes also increasing in adolescence. Males also tend to be more physically and verbally aggressive. Other researchers have found males to be more active, more willing to take risks, and more likely to engage in rough play. Females seem more interested in infants and are generally less demanding.

Other attributes that may differentiate the sexes include females being likely to report feeling timid or fearful, even where no differences in fearful behavior are found. Males tend to be more competitive, where differences are found. And although girls tend to be more nurturant and perhaps more empathic, they are not necessarily more altruistic.

Maccoby and Jacklin propose that many myths about sex differences persist because people remember the "confirming" instances and ignore the "disconfirming" ones. Research indicates that sex-standard schemata influence impressions about males and females. Contrary to myth, girls are not more "social," more "suggestible, or less "analytic" than boys, and the sexes do not differ in self-esteem or achievement motivation.

People tend to undervalue the accomplishments of females and overvalue those of males. Female success is more likely to be attributed to luck or to hard work, male success more to ability. Parents and teachers may reinforce these attitudes by reacting differently to boys than to girls. And people tend to rate professions in which females are making progress as being lower in prestige.

DEVELOPMENTAL TRENDS IN SEX TYPING

In understanding gender and developing gender identity, toddlers initially focus on clothing and hairstyles rather than gross body characteristics. But by age 2 years or so, some children can readily label people as male or female even if such cues are ambiguous. By age 2½-3, most children have a sense of basic gender identity but do not yet have a sense of gender constancy. Conserving gender appears at about the same time as Piaget's conservation skills. Sex-role stereotypes appear along with basic gender identity. And research indicates that 2½-3½-year-olds already have many sex stereotypes. By middle childhood, children are stereotyping males and females along psychological dimensions.

Sex-typed behavior appears early, often before basic gender identity. A preference for sex-typed toys may appear during the second year of life. Three-year-olds already prefer same-sex playmates. In Western cultures, boys face stronger sex-role pressures than do girls, and boys are quicker to adopt sex-typed preferences. Between ages 4 and 10, girls are more likely to retain an interest in cross-sex toys. Many of these effects seem attributable to the traditionally higher status afforded the masculine role. Lower-class children show earlier and stronger sex-role preferences than middle-class children, perhaps because lower-class parents are more likely to accept traditional sex roles and to emphasize sex-typing. Behaviors that are consistent with "masculine" sex-role standards are stable over time for males but not for females, whereas behaviors consistent with "feminine" sex-role standards are more stable for females than for males.

THEORIES OF SEX TYPING AND SEX-ROLE DEVELOPMENT

The biological explanation of sex differences notes that the sexes differ in (1) chromosomal makeup, (2) hormonal balance, (3) gonads, (4) internal reproductive system, and (5) external genitalia, any of which might relate to psychological differences. Girls could be biologically predisposed to being expressive, and boys to being instrumental. But parental expectations and other social factors appear to interact with biological predispositions in determining the roles children adopt.

Hutt's hypothesis is that males, by virtue of having only one X chromosome, are more susceptible to X-linked recessive traits and disorders. And by virtue of having a Y chromosome, males would potentially inherit a wider array of attributes genetically.

Money and associates have studied hormonal contributions to sex differences. The testicular feminization syndrome is a genetic anomaly in which males develop female genitalia. Similarly, as a result of drugs given the mother to prevent miscarriage, some females have become androgenized females. Money and associates followed some of these cases into childhood to assess other effects as a result of exposure to androgen, finding that these females were often tomboys and were generally more aggressive than nonandrogenized females.

Another line of biological research involves the "timing of puberty" effect, which may help to explain sex differences in visual/spatial abilities. But biology is not destiny. Early corrective surgery with androgenized females minimizes adjustment problems. And Box 13-1 describes a genetic male who adjusted well to the female role. Thus, sex-role socialization is a primary factor. Mead's studies of New Guinea tribes indicates that males and females can easily adjust to sex-role socialization essentially opposite to that of Western societies. And research on the timing-of-puberty effect indicates that biological predispositions and socially transmitted values both contribute to children's visual/spatial abilities. Sex-linked predispositions can be modified and even reversed by social and cultural influences.

Money and Erhardt's biosocial theory emphasizes critical episodes in the formation of sex-role preferences. Prenatal choice points are (1) conception and the inheritance of XX or XY chromosomes, (2) development of male or female internal reproductive system, in

207

accord with presence or absence of male hormones, and (3) development of male or female external genitalia, also in accord with homones; postnatal choice points are (4) labeling and sex-typing of the child during the first 3 years, leading to the establishment of a basic gender identity, and (5) hormonal and social influences at puberty, which contribute to one's adult gender identity.

Freud's psychoanalytic theory is both social and biological. Social sex-typing occurs through identification, during the preschool years. Boys emulate their fathers as a way of reducing castration anxiety and resolving the Oedipus complex. However, masculine sex-typing can be disrupted through absence of a masculine model, insufficient castration anxiety, or a biologically "feminine" constitution. Girls identify with their mothers and resolve the Electra complex, for reasons such as the mother's former attractiveness and benevolence and the father's tendency to reinforce feminine behavior. But feminine sex-typing can be disrupted if the mother is a poor feminine role model, if the girl over-identifies with her father, or if she has a biologically "masculine" constitution. Critics of Freud point to research indicating that preschool children are relatively ignorant about gential anatomy, and thus would not experience the kinds of conflicts Freud viewed as essential. In addition, warm and nurturant fathers foster good sex-role identification, in contrast to Freud's view that a hostile, threatening father is necessary here.

Social learning theorists emphasize (1) direct tuition of sex-appropriate behaviors through reinforcement and punishment by adults, and (2) observational learning of sex-role attributes from same-sex models. Direct tuition includes buying children sex-typed toys, dressing them differently, and reinforcing them for acting like "girls" or "boys." Research indicates that this process increases in intensity during the preschool years, and peers also play a role by ridiculing play with cross-sex toys. Observational learning, according to Bandura, comes about through reinforcement of same-sex imitation and through children's percpetions of themselves as similar to same-sex models. However, research indicates that gender identity is already well established before children actually attend more to same-sex models, which poses a problem for this theory. A similar issue is that school-age chidlren and adolescents are not markedly similar to same-sex parents in basic personality traits, which means that identification with the same-sex parents is not the only factor involved. And, viewing the family as a social system, it seems that children often develop sex-role attributes more in accord with establishing a "niche" in the family than by imitating same-sex models. Observational learning is likely, however, with regard to the child's exposure to thousands of "male" versus "female" characters in storybooks, in TV dramas, and even in TV commercials.

Kohlberg's cognitive-developmental theory of sex-typing reverses the other theories' emphasis on modeling, with a view that children first make a cognitive judgment about gender and then seek models and become sex-typed. Kohlberg's stages are (1) basic gender identity, (2) gender stability, and finally (3) gender consistency. If effect, Kohlberg argues that children are self-motivated to acquire attributes consistent with their gender, and the theory finds support in its correspondence with other aspects of cognitive development as well as the observed sequence in which gender identity develops. Box 13-2 describes further support in terms of predictions about children's evaluations of sex-role stereotypes. But Kohlberg's theory is contradicted in that children have begun to acquire sex-role stereotypes and patterns of sex-typed behavior prior to basic gender identity.

Table 13-5 outlines an integrative approach to understanding sex-typing. During the prenatal period, biological developments are prominent. From birth to 3 years of age, in accord with social-learning theory, parents label the child as male or female and reinforce behaviors considered appropriate, which fosters basic gender identity. From about 3-6 years of age the child attends to models of both sexes but focuses more on the gender appropriateness of a model's actions. From age 6 on, the child attends selectively to same-sex models as a result of acquiring gender consistency, and the motivation to do so is now intrinsic, with a goal of making behavior consistent with self-concepts.

SEX TYPING IN THE NONTRADITIONAL FAMILY

Since nearly 50% of U.S. marriages end in divorce, another focus of research is upon single-parent and other nontraditional families in which the father is absent. Maternal absence from the home due to employment is also an issue.

Research on the effects of maternal dominance in intact families, as with Hetherington's It scale, indicates that sons may adopt fewer masculine characteristics and will often imitate their mothers more than their fathers. Maternal dominance does not seem to affect sex-typing in daughters, except in encouraging the daughters to attempt the more traditionally masculine professions.

When the father is absent, sons tend to be more dependent, less aggressive, and less achievement-oriented, especially if the father leaves the home prior to the son's fourth birthday; few such effects occur if the departure is after the son is 6 years old. Whether the disruptive effects of early father absence persist depends upon various factors, including whether other male models are present. Some boys develop compensatory masculinity, especially in lower-class homes. Father absence also has indirect effects such as changes in the mother's childrearing techniques toward overprotectiveness and reliance on power-assertive discipline. Father absence apparently has little effect on daughters' sex-typing. However, father-absent girls may later relate differently to males. Daughters of widows have been found to be more uncomfortable with males, to the point of being shy and retiring. Daughters of divorce tend to be overly assertive with males and perhaps more manipulative and promiscuous. In each case these behaviors may reflect the mother's attitudes toward men. For example, daughters of divorce often view their mothers as unhappy without a mate and may adopt an attitude of doing whatever is necessary to attract a male. Such problems can arise in the absence of the daughter's opportunity to relate to a father figure, although not all girls from father-absent homes are affected.

The daily absences of employed mothers do not appear to disrupt the sex-typing of either boys or girls. However, research indicates that both sons and daughters of working mothers tend to have more egalitarian attitudes toward sex roles than do children of homemakers. Daughters of working mothers also tend to be more independent, more competitive, and less oriented toward traditional feminine interests.

PSYCHOLOGICAL ANDROGYNY: A NEW LOOK AT SEX ROLES

"Sex-appropriate" refers to traditional views of sex roels, and many psychologists view these standards as restrictive and potentially harmful. Bem has proposed that masculinity and femininity are better viewed as two separate dimensions than as opposites on a single dimension. An androgynous person would be high both on masculinity and femininity. Research indicates that a bit less than one-third of the population correspond to Bem's description of the androgynous individual.

Bem argues that androgyny is a desirable characteristic because such people are not constrained by sex-role stereotypes and thus can adapt to a wider variety of situations. Research provides some support for this hypothesis while also indicating that androgynous persons are higher in self-esteem.

Androgynous children tend to come from families in which parents are androgynous themselves, and where both parents are nurturant and highly involved with the children. But being androgynous or having androgynous parents does not necessarily mean that the children will be more competent, which is a question for future research. Also of note is that androgyny may affect children more during adolescence than during childhood. And being androgynous does not mean that men will be less "masculine" or women less "feminine" because the emphasis is upon taking the best of each of the traditional roles.

SELF-REVIEW

Fill in the blanks for each item. Check the answers for each item as you go.

1. Gender indoctrination begins in early _____, as parents and other react differently to males and females and thus initiate the process of the child's _____-_____.

infancy

sex-typing

CATEGORIZING MALES AND FEMALES: SEX-ROLE STANDARDS

2. Values, motives, and behaviors considered more appropriate for one sex than for the other are called sex-_____ _____; traditionally, in Western cultures, females have been encouraged to adopt a nurturant, _____ role, and males have been encouraged to adopt an assertive, _____ role.

-role standards

expressive
instrumental

3. Masculine stereotypes include characteristics such as being aggressive, independent, competitive, and dominant, which project a sense of _____; feminine stereotypes include characteristics such as tacftulness, tenderness, awareness of others' feelings, and so on, which project a sense of _____.

competency

warmth

SOME FACTS AND FICTIONS ABOUT SEX DIFFERENCES

Sex Differences That Appear to Be Real

4. Maccoby and Jacklin's review indicates that four sex-role _____ are reasonably accurate: (1) females seem to have greater _____ abilities, (2) males display greater _____/_____ abilities, (3) males score higher on tests of _____ reasoning, and (4) males are more physically and verbally _____, in each case where group averages are compared.

stereotypes
verbal
visual/spatial
arithmetic
aggressive

Attributes That May Differentiate the Sexes

5. Differences that are sometimes found are that females are more likely to _____ feeling fearful, that males are more competitive and more _____, and that females are more nurturant and empathic but not more _____ than males.

report
dominant
altruistic

Cultural Myths

6. Stereotypes not supported by research are that (1) girls are more interested in _____ activities, (2) girls are more conforming and _____, (3) girls have lower self-_____, (4) boys excel at higher-level _____ tasks, (5) boys are more logical and _____, and (6) girls generally lack _____ motivation.

social
suggestible, esteem
cognitive
analytical
achievement

Evaluating the Accomplishments of Males and Females

7. Female success is more likely to be attributed either to hard _____ or sheer _____, whereas male success is more likely to be attributed to basic _____; in turn, parents and teachers often contribute to such attitudes by what they _____ females versus males to be capable of.

work, luck
ability
expect

DEVELOPMENTAL TRENDS IN SEX-TYPING

Development of the Gender Concept

8. Child learn discrimination between the sexes early and can label themselves as boys or girls by age ___-___; the ability to conserve gender, called gender _____, appears about the same age as other forms of conservation, about age ___-___, and children learn that their own gender is constant before they learn that other people's gender is _____.

$2\frac{1}{2}$ - 3
constancy
5 - 7

constant

Acquiring Sex-Role Stereotypes

9. Stereotypes appear along with awareness of basic _____
_____, during the toddler period; sex-role stereotypes   gender
are fairly concrete, but later become more focused on the more   identity
abstract _____ attributes of sex roles.   psychological

Development of Sex-Typed Behavior

10. Sex-typed behavior first appears during _____, and a   infancy
preference for _____-_____ playmates is present during the tod-   same-sex
dler period; throughout development, boys face stronger pressures
to conform to appropriate _____-_____ behavior and are quicker   sex-role
to adopt sex-role _____.   standards

11. Longitudinal research indicates that behaviors such as
achievement and general sex-typed activity are _____ from   stable
early childhood into adulthood, whereas other behaviors that conflict with prescribed sex-role _____ are not stable.   standards

THEORIES OF SEX-TYPING AND SEX-ROLE DEVELOPMENT

The Biological Approach

12. Biological theorists believe that _____ and _____   genetic, hormonal
differences between the sexes predispose males and females to
adopt the traditional sex roles; other theorists believe that
biological predispositions _____ with environmental ef-   interact
fects to produce sex-typed patterns of behavior.

13. One point about males' ___ genetic makeup is that a _____   XY, wider
range of genetic information is present, which might explain why
boys more often display developmental _____.   disabilities

14. Hormones influence physical and psychological characteristics, as evidenced by the testicular _____ syndrome   feminization
in which males develop female genitalia, and by cases in which
females, due to their mothers receiving hormones to prevent
_____, developed male genitalia and otherwise became   miscarriage
_____; with these females, later sex-role behaviors   androgenized
were more like those of _____.   males

15. But biology is not destiny, which is underscored by the research on the cases of sexual reassignment as well as by Mead's
observations of other _____ in which females and males   cultures
adopt sex roles _____ to those of Western cultures.   opposite

16. Money and Erhardt's biosocial theory outlines a number of
critical events that combine to determine eventual sex-role preferences: the first is at _____, when the child inherits   conception
either ___ or ___ genetic makeup; the next is about 6 weeks lat-   XX, XY
er, when the first sex _____ are secreted; then at about   hormones
3-4 months after conception the external _____ form; the   genitalia
fourth event spans the first ___ years after birth, involving   3
social experiences that lead to basic gender _____; and   identity
the final critical event occurs with the onset of _____,   puberty
as the finishing touches in response to physical and psychological changes yield _____ gender identity.   adult

Freud's Psychoanalytic Theory

17. To Freud, sex-typing occurs through the process called
_____ with the same-sex parent, with the child's   indentification
motivation arising from either the Oedipus or Electra _____;   complex

however, this process assumes that the _____ child is   preschool
aware of differences between male and female _____,   genitalia
which is apparently not the case.

Social-Learning Theory

18. According to social-learning theorists, gender identity and
sex-role preferences are acquired in two basic ways: through
parents' direct _____, with reinforcement, and through the   tuition
child's observation of same-sex _____; research indicates   models
that both processes do occur, although there is a problem for
this theory in that attending to _____-_____ models comes well   same-sex
after the development of basic gender _____.   identity

Kohlberg's Cognitive-Developmental Theory

19. Kohlberg reverses the emphasis of the other theories, arguing
that a cognitive decision about one's gender identity occurs
_____ rather than _____ selective attention to same-sex   before, after
models; gender development is based on cognitive development and
occurs in three stages, which are (1) basic gender _____,   identity
(2) gender _____, and (3) gender _____, but   stability, consistency
research indicates a problem in that sex-_____ is already   -typing
well underway before basic gender identity is present.

An Attempt at Integration

20. Money and Erhardt's theory emphasizes the early _____   biological
developments important to sex-typing, while social-learning theory describes how children learn to prefer or perform sex-typed
_____ and acquire a _____ gender identity; Kohlberg's   behaviors, basic
theory describes the cognitive changes that occur in 3-6-year-
olds' gender identities, culminating in gender _____,   consistency
at which point children will attend _____ to same-sex   selectively
models; thus all of the theories contribute.

SEX-TYPING IN THE NONTRADITIONAL FAMILY

21. Since nearly ___% of U.S. marriages end in divorce, nearly   50%
___% of all children born in the 1970s will spend several years   40%
in a single-parent home; a related issue that might also affect
sex-typing is that more than ___% of mothers with school-age   50
children are employed outside the home.

Effects of Maternal Dominance

22. Hetherington's ___ scale assesses children's sex-role pref-   It
erences; research indicates that, in mother-dominant homes, sex-
typing of _____ is affected more than sex-typing of _____,   boys, girls
except that girls are more likely to aspire to traditionally
_____ occupations.   masculine

Effects of Father Absence

23. In fatherless homes, boys tend to adopt somewhat less traditionally _____ sex-role preferences, at least if the   masculine
father departs before the boy is about ___ years old; some re-   4
searchers have found, however, that when such boys get older they
may display an exaggerated _____ masculinity, par-   compensatory
ticularly if they come from _____-class backgrounds.   lower-

24. Effects of father absence on girls depend in part on whether
the father's absence is due to _____, in which case girls   divorce
may later tend to be more assertive and uninhibited in their re-

lations with _____, or whether father absence is due to the
father's _____, in which case girls may later tend to be somewhat _____ and retiring; these differences presumably reflect
the mother's _____ about men.

males
death
shy
attitudes

Effects of Maternal Employment

25. When the mother works outside the home, effects are that the
children tend to be less _____ in their sex-role attitudes and tend to endorse fewer sex-role _____.

traditional
stereotypes

PSYCHOLOGICAL ANDROGYNY: A NEW LOOK AT SEX ROLES

26. The traditional view of masculinity and femininity is that
they lie at opposite ends of a single _____, but Bem's
view is that _____ separate dimensions are involved and that a
person could be high or low on both; thus a person who scores
high on both dimensions is _____, and these individuals can be detected as early as _____.

dimension
two

androgynous
middle childhood

Is Androgyny a Stable Attribute?

27. Research indicates that androgynous individuals can display
desirable attributes of either sex-role, such as instrumental
masculine _____ and warm and expressive feminine
_____; in addition, although the research is not con-
clusive, androgynous individuals have been found to be more self-
confident and more _____ among peers.

independence
nurturance

popular

Who Raises Androgynous Offspring?

28. Androgynous chidlren are more likely when the parents are
themselves _____, and also if the parents are both
highly involved and _____ toward their children; in addition, daughters of mothers who _____ are more androgynous
than those of mothers who are not employed.

androgynous
nurturant
work

Implications and Prescriptions for the Future

29. A major implication of the androgyny concept is that the notion of masculine superiority is a _____; good and adaptive adjustment tends to be associated with _____.

myth
androgyny

SELF-TEST I

Consider each alternative carefully. Then choose the best one.

1. The basic process by which children acquire gender identity and also the motives, values, and behaviors considered appropriate for their sex is called
    a. stereotyping
    b. sex-typing
    c. sex-role standardization
    d. androgenization

2. In our society as in many others, girls are often encouraged to assume a warm and nurturant _____ role and boys are often encouraged to assume a competitive, assertive _____ role.
    a. instrumental, expressive
    b. expressive, instrumental
    c. instrumental, instrumental
    d. expressive, expressive

3. Cross-cultural data indicate that intense socialization of children into rigidly defined sex roles is likely where
    a. the people live in large, cooperative family units with division of labor
    b. the people depend primarily on strength and physical prowess for survival
    c. both of the above
    d. none of the above

4. Research generally indicates that male-female sex-role differences are
    a. determined entirely by genetics
    b. determined entirely by learning and environment
    c. determined by genetics and environment in interaction
    d. nonexistent and entirely mythical in nature

5. Male-female differences in areas such as dominance, competition, and fearfulness
    a. are well established by research
    b. are sometimes found by research and sometimes not
    c. reflect clear-cut genetic differences
    d. are entirely mythical

6. Male-female differences such as females being more suggestible and compliant
    a. are well established by research
    b. are sometimes found by research and sometimes not
    c. reflect clear-cut genetic differences
    d. are entirely mythical

7. Typically, female success is more likely to be explained in terms of _____,
whereas male success is more likely to be explained in tersm of _____.
    a. luck and effort, effort and luck
    b. luck and effort, ability
    c. ability, luck and effort
    d. none of the above

8. As compared to preschool children, 6-7-year-olds
    a. tend to become more flexible in their beliefs about sex-role stereotypes
    b. tend to become less flexible in their beliefs about sex-role stereotypes
    c. do not differ in their beliefs about sex-role stereotypes
    d. none of the above

9. As compared to middle-class parents, working-class parents are less likely to
    a. model sex-typed behaviors for their children
    b. encourage and reinforce sex-typed behaviors for their children
    c. both of the above
    d. none of the above

10. A major problem with Freud's theory of sex-typing is that
    a. children do not identify with same-sex parents
    b. preschool children are not sufficiently clear on genital anatomy
    c. warm and nurturant parents do not foster good identification
    d. children do not identify with cross-sex parents

11. In social-learning theory, parents begin shaping and reinforcing sex-typed behavior
    a. during infancy and the toddler period
    b. during the preschool period
    c. during the middle childhood period
    d. none of the above

12. Within the family social system, effects are such that a child's sex-typing is
    a. determined primarily by the same-sex parent
    b. determined primarily by the cross-sex parent
    c. more stereotyped if only same-sex siblings are present
    d. more stereotyped if only cross-sex siblings are present

13. Research indicates that possible effects of father absence on daughters are that
    a. daughters become more androgynous
    b. daughters become more feminine
    c. daughters later relate to males somewhat atypically
    d. all of the above

14. Daughters of working mothers tend to be
    a. more androgynous
    b. more independent
    c. more inclined to aspire to traditionally male professions
    d. all of the above

15. Generally, androgynous persons
    a. are more flexible and adaptive
    b. score higher on IQ tests
    c. are extremely rare
    d. all of the above

RESEARCH SUMMARY AND REVIEW

Using the textbook, review the research efforts indicated and write a summary of the important findings. Note the general purpose or context of the research.

1. Kuhn, Nash, & Brucken (1978), page 523: _____

_____

_____

_____

_____

2. Jacklin & Maccoby (1978), page 523: _____

_____

_____

_____

_____

3. Fagot (1978), page 534: _____

_____

_____

_____

_____

4. Damon (1977), page 538: _____

_____

_____

_____

_____

5. Hetherington (1965), page 540: _____

215

6. Hetherington (1972, 1977), page 543: _____

_____

_____

_____

_____

SELF-TEST II

Consider each alternative carefully. Then choose the best one.

1. Values, motives, and classes of behavior considered more appropriate due to one's sex, male or female, are called
    a. gender concepts
    ⓑ sex-role standards
    c. sex types
    d. sex dimensions

2. Adjectives typically used to describe males reflect *Competency* and adjectives typically used to describe females reflect *warmth?* .
    a. warmth, competency
    b. competency, warmth
    c. warmth, warmth
    ⓓ competency, competency

The answer in the back says "d".

3. Cross-cultural research generally indicates that the sex-role stereotypes common in Western societies
    a. are quite different from those of other societies
    ⓑ. are quite similar to those of many other societies
    c. are preferable to those of most other societies
    d. display no relationship with respect to those of other societies

4. An accepted idea about boys <u>not</u> supported by Maccoby and Jacklin's review is that boys
    a. do better on arithmetic reasoning than girls do
    b. are more aggressive than girls
    ⓒ are more analytical than girls
    d. are better at visual/spatial tasks than girls

5. Gender constancy refers to the child's ability to
    a. label himself or herself as a boy or as a girl
    b. label others as male or female
    ⓒ understand that biological sex is unchanging
    d. none of the above

6. Children typically learn to conserve gender by about age
    a. 2-3 years
    b. 3-5 years
    ⓒ 5-7 years
    d. 7-9 years

7. Kuhn, Nash, and Brucken's (1978) research indicated that sex-role stereotypes are first
   a. present during infancy
   b. present during toddlerhood
   c. present by age 4-5
   d. present by age 6-7

8. Jacklin and Maccoby's (1978) research on toddler playing in dyads indicated that
   a. boys prefer to play with boys
   b. girls prefer to play with girls
   c. both of the above
   d. none of the above

9. A male-oriented society such as that of the U.S. creates social pressures such that
   a. boys develop sex-role preferences sooner than girls
   b. girls do not develop stable sex-role preferences
   c. both of the above
   d. none of the above

10. Compared to working-class children, middle-class children are
    a. more likely to accept traditional sex-role standards
    b. less likely to accept traditional sex-role standards
    c. no more or no less likely to accept traditional sex-role standards
    d. unlikely to accept any sex-role standards, traditional or otherwise

11. Hutt's biogenetic explanation of sex differences on the basis of XX versus XY chromo-some composition notes that
    a. girls have a wider range of variability and are more adaptive
    b. girls are more likely to inherit defective recessive genes
    c. both of the above
    d. none of the above

12. In the testicular feminization syndrome,
    a. males are injected with female hormones
    b. females are injected with male hormones
    c. males have a genetic anomaly that makes them insensitive to male hormones
    d. females have a genetic anomaly that makes them insensitive to female hormones

13. Gender reassignment of androgenized females tends to cause serious adjustment prob-lems if it occurs after age
    a. 1 year
    b. 3 years
    c. 5 years
    d. 7 years

14. In Money and associates' research on androgenized females,
    a. the females behaved a lot like males
    b. the females behaved a lot like super-females
    c. the females displayed no interest in having children
    d. no differences between these females and normal females were found

15. Freud's notion of identification is most similar to the social-learning notion of
    a. direct tuition
    b. androgyny
    c. imitation
    d. social reinforcement

16. Fagot's (1978) study of parental responses to sex-typed behavior in their children verified that parents strongly influence sex-typing through
    a. direct tuition of sex-typed behaviors
    b. modeling of sex-typed behaviors
    c. both of the above
    d. none of the above

17. In Kohlberg's theory of sex-typing, children go through three stages in the order
    a. basic gender identity, gender consistency, gender stability
    b. basic gender identity, gender stability, gender consistency
    c. gender consistency, basic gender identity, gender stability
    d. gender stability, basic gender identity, gender consistency

18. Damon's (1977) research on Kohlberg's theory indicated that children are least flexible in their interpretations of sex-role stereotypes around age
    a. 2-3 years
    b. 4-5 years
    c. 6-7 years
    d. 8-9 years

19. Hetherington's "It" scale assessment of the effects of parental dominance on children's sex-typing indicated that
    a. boys from mother-dominant homes tend to be less masculine
    b. girls from mother-dominant homes tend to be less feminine
    c. both of the above
    d. none of the above

20. Hetherington's "It" scale assessment of the effects of parental dominance on children's sex-typing indicated that
    a. boys identify with the dominant parent, mother or father
    b. boys identify with the mother, regardless of dominance
    c. boys identify with the father, regardless of dominance
    d. none of the above

21. Young boys who are separated from their fathers early in life tend to be
    a. relatively unaffected in sex-role development
    b. more emotionally dependent and less aggressive
    c. less emotionally dependent and more aggressive
    d. more emotionally dependent and more aggressive

22. Boys in father-absent homes tend to be most affected in sex-role development if the father's absence occurs
    a. after the age of 8 years
    b. after the age of 6 years
    c. between the age of 4 and 6 years
    d. between birth and 4 years of age

23. Girls in father-absent homes tend to be affected in their sex-role development
    a. only if the father is absent due to death
    b. only if the father is absent due to divorce
    c. only if the mother is employed
    d. very little by father absence

24. According to Bem's views on psychological androgyny, masculine and feminine are
    a. opposite ends of a single dimension
    b. opposite ends of two separate dimensions
    c. two separate dimensions
    d. terms that should be dispensed with in favor of unisexuality

25. Research on androgynous individuals suggests that
    a. androgynous males are less masculine than traditionally sex-typed males
    b. androgynous females are less feminine than traditionally sex-typed females
    c. androgynous persons enjoy higher self-esteem than traditionally sex-typed persons
    d. all of the above

Consider the story, then answer each question using material from the textbook.

I. Bobbi was 5 years old and thoroughly aware of being a girl, since everyone had agreed with her about this as far back as she could remember. To Bobbi, this meant doing "girl" things, including playing mostly with other girls. Some "girl" things she liked and some she didn't, and so she often wondered whether she wanted to be a girl or a boy. In particular, she wondered about being a mommy or a daddy when she grew up, because she didn't like the kinds of chores her mommy did around the house, the way things were.

    1. Where does Bobbi stand with regard to development of gender identity?

    2. What social-learning processes in sex-typing are probably operating in her home?

    3. What might Freud have to say about Bobbi and identification?

II. At about age 4 Carl developed a preference for getting into his mother's make-up and clothing whenever possible. He liked to wear his mother's shoes and hats in particular, and sitting in front of a mirror experimenting with her make-up would occupy him like no other activity. His parents were concerned, but they decided to wait patiently to see if this was simply some kind of phase he was going through.

    1. What sorts of parent and sibling interactions might relate to Carl's behavior?

    2. Does Carl's behavior reveal anything about his sex-typing? Why or why not?

    3. What might Freud have to say about Carl's behavior?

III. At about age 4 Rita developed a preference for getting into her father's toiletries and clothing whenever possible. She like to wear her father's shoes and hats in particular, and sitting in front of the mirror experimenting with his electric razor would occupy her like no other activity. Her parents were concerned, but they decided to wait patiently to see if this was simply some kind of phase she was going through.

    1. Did you react any differently to this story than to Carl's? Why might you have?

    2. What sorts of parent and sibling interactions might relate to Rita's behavior?

    3. Does Rita's behavior reveal anything about her sex-typing? Why or why not?

APPLICATIONS

Try each of the projects, noting answers to the questions as you go.

I. The next time you go to a shopping mall or to the grocery store, take a small notebook and something to write with. Look for parents with infants. Make notes on (a) whether the parent is male or female, and (b) whether the infant is dressed as a "boy" or as a "girl." Also include a "can't tell" category.

    1. Will you see more mother-infant pairs or father-infant pairs? Why?

    2. What can you predict about how many of the children will be dressed in accord with sex-typing?

    3. Would a number of infants in the "can't tell" category tell you anything about the current status of androgyny? Why or why not?

II. Here's an introspective project that deals directly with *your* sex-role attitudes. Using Table 13-1, rate yourself on the characteristics as follows: Use a scale from 1 to

5, where a 1 = "descriptor on the left" and a 5 = "descriptor on the right." "In the middle"gets a 3; and use 2 or 4 when you simply lean one way or the other without strong feelings. Then, having done this, average your ratings separately for the competency and the warmth-expressive clusters.

　　1. What averages might be obtained for traditionally sex-typed persons? Why?

　　2. What average might be obtained for an androgynous person? Why?

　　3. Do *your* averages say anything about your own sex-typing? Why or why not?

III. Suppose you were to replicate Kuhn, Nash, and Brucken's research effort (page 523), using a male doll named Michael and a female doll named Lisa, but with children (a) about 6-7 years old and (b) about 11-12 years old. All other procedures are the same.

　　1. Which group of children might use the descriptors in Table 13-1? Why?

　　2. Which group might display the strongest beliefs in stereotypes? Why?

　　3. If you were to switch the dolls' names, calling the male doll Lisa and the female doll Michael, what kinds of reactions might you expect from each group?

ANSWERS

Self-Test I

1. b	6. d	11. a
2. b	7. b	12. d
3. c	8. b	13. c
4. c	9. d	14. d
5. b	10. b	15. a

Research Summary and Review

1. Kuhn, Nash, & Brucken (1978): Children 2½-3 years old displayed knowledge of sex-role stereotypes in thier responses to a male and a female doll, and those who knew the most had begun to view gender as a stable attribute. Major implications involved the very early age at which sex-typing apparently begins.

2. Jacklin & Maccoby (1978): Toddlers 33 months old displayed preferences for same-sex rather than cross-sex play, with implications that sex-typing begins very early and has specific kinds of effects on social behavior.

3. Fagot (1978): In assessing whether and how much parents contribute to children's sex-typing, it was found that parents clearly reinforced "sex-appropriate" behaviors while discouraging "sex-inappropriate" acts during interactions with their 20-24-month-old toddlers. The data demonstrated that direct tuition of sex-roles begins very early.

4. Damon (1977): Verification of Kohlberg's theory of sex-typing was obtained, with a particular note that 6-7-year-olds are more intolerant of sex-inappropriate behavior than are either younger or older children, possibly because they are beginning to conserve gender.

5. Hetherington (1965): Using the It scale, it was found that boys tend to imitate the dominant parent, becoming more masculine or less masculine accordingly, whereas girls were not strongly affected one way or the other. These findings illustrate possible differential sex-typing effects upon boys and girls in response to familial influences.

6. Hetherington (1972, 1977): Girls in fatherless homes did not differ from girls in in-

tact homes with regard to sex-typing, but it was found that daughters of widows tended to be shy and retiring in later interactions with males, in contrast to daughters of divorce tending to be assertive and uninhibited. Corresponding effects were observed in the girls' marriages and choice of mates. Explanations involving mothers' attitudes toward fathers were offered to account for these differential effects of father absence.

Self-Test II

1. b	6. c	11. d	16. a	21. b
2. d	7. b	12. c	17. b	22. d
3. b	8. c	13. b	18. c	23. d
4. c	9. c	14. a	19. a	24. c
5. c	10. b	15. c	20. a	25. c

Vignettes

I. (1) She has not yet developed a sense of gender constancy, even for herself, and in Kohlberg's system she has acquired basic gender identity but has not yet reached gender stability. (2) The implication is that Bobbi's parents are employing direct tuition and reinforcement for "girl" behavior, as well as modeling in the form of her mother's traditional housewife role, whether deliberately or otherwise. (3) Classical psychoanalytic theory might argue that sex-typing is more difficult for girls, which might be a source of conflict about being male or being female. Otherwise, Bobbi would be placed in the Phallic stage, experiencing the Electra complex but not yet identifying with the mother.

II. (1) Possibilities include Carl's mother being the dominant parent and thus the preferred model for sex-typing or other non-sex-related behavior, plus Carl having all male siblings and thus reacting differently to establish a niche, plus Carl's parents being relatively androgynous and egalitarian about sex-typing in general. (2) Actually, however, such behavior might not reflect sex-typing at all, and might instead be only a reflection of a child's basic curiosity. Other characteristics such as playmate preferences, toy preferences, and the many aspects of the instrumental and expressive roles might be considered in determining how Carl stands on sex-typing. (3) If the mother were the dominant parent, and if other, more female sex-role preferences were also present, Freud might argue that identification has gone awry through the father not being sufficiently threatening to force resolution of the Oedipus complex. Freud might also say that Carl has inherited a feminine constitution.

III. (1) You might automatically have responded with somewhat more alarm to Carl's behavior than to Rita's, in view of the pervasive pressures in our society toward males in particular. As discussed, the traditional male role is more clearly defined and in many respects more "competent" and desirable than the role traditionally ascribed to females. If you did not react this way, you probably have fewer stereotypes about males and females lurking in your unconscious. (2) Possibilities here are much the same as in *Vignette II*, although Hetherington's research indicates that parental dominance, mother versus father, is less of a factor. (3) As in the discussion about Carl, more information would be necessary to rule out general curiosity on Rita's part. However, it is also noteworthy that girls tend to adopt sex-role preferences later than boys, at least in Western societies, and also that "tomboy" behavior is more likely to be tolerated by parents and others.

Applications

I. (1) Odds are that most of the parents you see alone with an infant will be female, although you will probably find more fathers out alone with their infants nowadays that you would have a few years ago. Sex roles are changing. But they still have a long way to go if they are to become egalitarian. In passing, note that if you do the project in a grocery store, you will probably see many more females than males, with or without infants. Grocery shopping is another of those traditional female roles. (2) A good guess is that most of the infants will be easily identifiable. Parents' efforts at sex-typing their children begin early and tend to persist. Also note that it is unlikely that many infants will be dressed in "cross-sex" fashion, even when not noticeably sex-typed. (3) A lot of "can't tells" might imply that times are changing and that more parents are seek- a neutral approach to this aspect of childrearing. Note, however, that less masculine boys and less feminine girls would not be a necessary byproduct of reducing stereotypes and promoting an androgynous outlook on life.

II. (1) Relatively low averages in each cluster would be traditionally feminine, and rel- atively high averages in each cluster would be traditionally masculine. In other words, each role contains both desirable and undesirable characteristics as traditionally de- fined. (2) In accord with Bem's conceptualization, it is possible to score highly both on traditional masculine and feminine characteristics. Thus a high average on the com- petency cluster and a low average on the warmth-expressive cluster would be androgynous (note that "low" is the desirable direction for warmth-expressiveness as the Table is constructed). (3) With caution, of course, this exercise probably does say something about your sex-typing, if you were reasonably objective in your ratings. Note one basic problem, however: You might be aggressive in one situation and not in another, at times competitive and at other times not, appropriately gentle in one situation but not so gen- tle in another. Would such variations then mean that you fluctuate between masculine and feminine? Perhaps not, but traits such as these can be hard to assess.

III. (1) Table 13-1 descriptors are primarily psychological, which means that they would be likely only with the older children. Younger children's descriptors would be much more concrete and based on observable characteristics. (2) The 6-7-year-olds should display stronger stereotypes, in accord with Damon's research. This is consistent with concrete operators' view that rules carry the force of natural laws and that children in this age range are actively seeking and exaggerating sex-role standards as a normal developmental phase. (3) In turn, the 6-7-year-olds should protest the loudest about the "misnaming," with utter conviction that something is amiss. They might even try to correct you on the names. In contrast, the older children might seek explanations for the naming and work through reasons why it might have occurred, in view of their emerging abilities to think more abstractly.

CHAPTER FOURTEEN

MORAL DEVELOPMENT AND SELF-CONTROL

OVERVIEW AND KEY TERMS

Read carefully. Recall examples and discussion as you go, and define each key term.

Moral development refers to acquiring a sense of right and wrong with respect to the society's code of ethics. McDougall suggested that moralization begins with the influence of reward and punishments on the "amoral" infant, proceeds through control by praise and blame, and eventually reaches a stage akin to internalization of moral principles. Society also makes demands of children that do not involve right or wrong, but which also require "will power" and self-control.

A DEFINITION OF MORALITY

Definitions of morality vary, but most people would agree that morality implies an ability to distinguish right from wrong and to act accordingly. Psychological research has focused on moral affect (the emotional component), moral reasoning (the cognitive component) and moral behavior (the observable actions).

PSYCHOANALYTIC EXPLANATIONS OF MORAL DEVELOPMENT

Freud's emphasis was on moral affect. The superego determines the acceptability of the means selected by the ego to gratify impulses from the id. Very young children are amoral because they are dominated by their ids, and thus parental rewards and punishments are necessary. As the superego develops, it eventually represents internal control.

Freud's theory of oedipal morality is that during the phallic stage boys begin to internalize their fathers' moral standards as they resolve the Oedipal conflict. Girls undergo a similar process in resolving the Electra conflict, but girls develop weaker superegos than boys do. A major problem with Freud's theory is that highly punitive parents tend to rear remorseless and shameless children rather than children who are morally mature. Another problem is the lack of evidence that girls have weaker superegos than boys. Erikson rejected oedipal morality, arguing that children internalize moral standards of both parents and that moral self-controls involve both ego and superego.

COGNITIVE-DEVELOPMENTAL THEORY: THE CHILD AS MORAL PHILOSOPHER

Cognitive-developmentalists have emphasized moral reasoning and a progression through an invariant sequence of stages, each of which arises from the preceding stage. Piaget saw moral maturity in terms of respect for rules and a sense of social justice, and he used "moral dilemmas" to identify stages in development of moral reasoning. The premoral period involves little concern or awareness of rules. The stage of heteronomous morality involves moral realism, and the child focuses more on the consequences of behavior than on its intent, within a belief that moral rules are absolutes. Heteronomous children favor expiatory punishment and believe in immanent justice. The stage of autonomous morality

223

involves focusing on the intent of behavior rather than its consequences, plus an understanding of rules as relative rather than absolute. The autonomous child favors reciprocal punishment and knows that immoral acts often go unpunished. Piaget believed that heteronomous morality results from the cognitive deficits of egocentrism and realism. Parents reward or punish the child in accord with rules, and the child focuses on the results. Egocentrism leads the child to believe that his or her rules apply to everyone, and thus such deficits must decline before the child can move to autonomous morality. And Piaget claimed that "equal-status" contact with peers is necessary (1) to lessen a child's overemphasis on adult authority, (2) to increase respect for self and peers, and (3) in leading to an understanding that rules are cooperative agreements rather than absolutes.

Many of Piaget's observations are supported by research, but it seems that younger children do have some understanding of an actor's intentions, when moral decision-making situations are such that intentions can be inferred by the child. Otherwise, in Piaget's original dilemmas, children rely mainly on consequences. Another problem with Piaget's theory is that children distinguish between moral rules and social-conventional rules, and they tend to view violations of the latter as less "serious." And, although Piaget held that premoral children do not respect rules as such, 2½-5-year-olds have been found to display a strong respect for moral rules.

Kohlberg's theory refines Piaget's theory and extends it into adolescence and young adulthood. Kohlberg's moral dilemmas focus on the underlying reasoning children use in making a decision about morality. While agreeing with Piaget as to an invariant sequence, Kohlberg notes that younger children focus more on fear of punishment than on respect for authority. With emphasis on "method of thinking" in solving moral dilemmas, Kohlberg proposed three levels and six stages of moral development. In preconventional morality, Stage 1, the child focuses on "bad" in terms of whether punishment accompanies an action: an act is bad if it gets punished, and anything else is acceptable. In preconventional Stage 2, the emphasis reverses to "good" applied to acts which are hedonistically self-serving: an act is good if it is rewarded. In conventional morality, Stage 3, a "good-boy/good-girl" attitude prevails, with an orientation toward pleasing people and being "nice." In conventional Stage 4, the emphasis expands to conforming to authorities and maintaining the social order as "good," with deviation from established norms and laws as "bad." In postconventional morality, Stage 5, an internalized sense of democratic principles and moral justice has developed. Rules and laws are now considered unjust if they do not express majority opinion and maximize social welfare. In postconventional Stage 6, internalized principles of universal justice have developed, and these self-chosen points of conscience take precedence over conflicting rules and laws regardless of origin.

Kohlberg's original research indicated consistent patterns of reasoning corresponding to the six stages, which in turn followed age trends and thus suggested an invariant sequence. Replications across other cultures tend to verify this sequence as universal. However, Kohlberg believes that few people ever reach postconventional morality, because they are not exposed to situations and experiences that are necessary if such an abstract level of reasoning is to emerge. Otherwise, both experimental attempts to modify children's moral reasoning and longitudinal studies of individual children suggest that the stages do develop sequentially. Children clearly prefer moral reasoning slightly more advanced than their own and tend to reject less sophisticated reasoning, and moral reasoning two stages higher is too difficult to comprehend. Nor do subjects "skip" stages, although they may at times regress back to earlier ones. Research also indicates relatively good correspondence between growth of moral reasoning and cognitive skills. Role-taking abilities are necessary (though not sufficient) for conventional morality, and formal operations are necessary for postconventional morality. Moral development thus occurs in conjunction with cognitive development and with relevant social experiences.

Criticisms of Kohlberg's theory are as follows. Moral reasoning might or might not represent the actual behavior a person might engage in. Another problem is that people display much less "stage consistency" when the dilemmas are more closely related to real-life situations, especially where negative consequences for oneself are involved. Varying the severity of consequences in the Heinz dilemma affects judgments of what is right and wrong, as well as the maturity of the moral reasoning employed. And there is a question of sex differences, in that females may exhibit a different pattern of moral development than males as a result of sex-role differences in childrearing. Box 14-2 presents Gilligan's theory that the expressive, nurturant, empathic female role leads to a more interpersonal emphasis in morality. Adult moral development, in the context of pregnant women deciding whether to have an abortion, is proposed as involving three levels alternated with two transitions. Level I is a self-focused, individual survival orientation that largely ignores the needs of others. The first transition occurs as a result of conflict between selfishness and a sense of "doing the right thing." Level II reverses the emphasis to others instead of oneself, and "good" becomes self-sacrifice within the idea of not hurting others. The second transition occurs from conflict between neither hurting others nor oneself, with responsibility to others being defined as "good" and responsibility to oneself being defined as "truth." Level III incorporates a more abstract orientation toward nonviolence and not hurting anyone, or at least minimizing the harm to all concerned. Gilligan argues that Level III may look like Kohlberg's Stage 3, in its emphasis on personal and interpersonal obligations, but that Level III is actually as abstract and postconventional as Kohlberg's higher stages.

MORALITY AS A PRODUCT OF SOCIAL LEARNING

Social-learning theorists favor a doctrine of specificity: Moral behavior depends upon the situation, and morality is more a question of one's moral habits than one's underlying attributes such as conscience. Early, large-scale research on moral conduct indicated that children's moral behavior was inconsistent from situation to situation. In particular, children who cheated on some tasks might not cheat on others, and those who cheated were just as likely to say that cheating was wrong. Other researchers have found more consistency in moral behavior, however, thus leading back to the idea that an underlying trait of morality may exist. But the setting is still a major factor in morality.

An important society standard for morality is the extent to which an individual resists temptation to commit forbidden acts when detection or punishment are unlikely. Research has often employed the "forbidden toy" paradigm and has indicated that children can acquire inhibitory controls through reinforcement as well as punishment. Severely punitive agents tend to rear antisocial children, and the effects of punishment may be to suppress a behavior only while the punitive agent is present. Yet, reasonable punishment that attaches a negative emotional response to a prohibited act can be effective. Punishment is most effective when it occurs during the early stages of a transgression, when it is moderately intense, when it is consistently administered, and when the punitive agent is otherwise warm and friendly. Punishment is more effective when accompanied by cognitive rationales, and the resulting resistance to temptation is more stable. Aronfreed argues that cognitive rationales may become conditioned to the anxiety from punishment, and that they also provide the child with good reasons for not performing the undesired behavior. Rationales can vary from concrete to abstract, and they are most effective when tailored to the child's cognitive level. Social models can serve to teach the child to resist temptation, if the child is clearly aware of what the model is doing and if the model also provides a rationale. In addition, serving as a model of moral restraint may, in itself, further moral development in children. And being reminded to be "honest," in the sense of fostering an honest self-image, can also be effective.

Cognitive-developmentalists, along with psychoanalytic theorists, favor the idea of unitary morality: Moral character is reasonably consistent and is largely an interplay between moral affect, reasoning, and behavior. Social-learning theorists note inconsistency across situations and view moral affect, reasoning, and behavior as separate modalities that are integrated to some extent as the individual matures.

WHO RAISES CHILDREN WHO ARE MORALLY MATURE?

Some parents use love-oriented discipline and withhold affection and approval, and other parents use power-assertive discipline relying on their superior power to control the child's conduct. Neither of these techniques is as effective in promoting moral development as is induction, which includes cognitive rationales, pointing out of harmful consequences, and appealing to the child's pride and desire to be "grown up." Also important is stressing the needs and emotions of victims. Hoffman suggests that induction fosters cognitive standards, draws attention to affective components of morality such as guilt and shame, and usually involves an emphasis on what the child "should" do in terms of moral behavior. Box 14-3 describes an experiment which underscores inductive discipline as effective, noting the other-oriented emphasis on harmful effects of misbehavior.

THE DEVELOPMENT OF SELF-CONTROL

Basically, self-control involves the ability to defer immediate gratification and to regulate one's behavior in the pursuit of future outcomes that are more valuable or desirable. Toddlers and preschool children are often impulsive and uninhibited, and thus the ability to delay immediate gratification must develop.

Verbal commands to a preschool child to inhibit motor behavior often have an opposite effect, perhaps because the wording of commands such as "Don't hit...." includes a positive instructional component of "hit" that seems to stimulate the ongoing action. In contrast, 5-6-year-olds are more likely to respond appropriately to verbal commands. And younger children seem to attend more to the "physical energy" of a command than to its semantic content, so that when parents command louder, the preschool child is likely to do exactly the opposite. Reflective children are better than impulsives at inhibiting motor behavior.

Delay of gratification involves postponing being rewarded, in favor of larger incentives, and this ability depends both on the characteristics of the person and the context in which delay choice is made. Patience is also an important factor. Delay-choice increases with age, with children showing a clearer preference for the more valuable delayed incentives by about age 10 years. Children who tend to choose delayed rewards score higher on IQ tests, perform better at school, have stronger achievement motivation, are rated as more responsible and socially mature, and are more likely to resist temptations to violate rules. Mischel proposes three variables that affect delay choice: (1) confidence that the delayed incentive will be given, (2) relative value of the immediate and deferred incentives, and (3) length of the delay. Another consideration is the self-restraint displayed by models and companions: Children exposed to impulsive models become more impulsive, and those exposed to nonimpulsive models become less impulsive. Moreover, an adult's well reasoned verbal persuasion to delay is more effective than a power-assertive technique. Box 14-4 illustrates another consideration, which is that young children will sometimes delay their own gratification to earn rewards for friends.

A preference of larger, delayed incentives is adaptive in some cultures and not in others, and children show corresponding development of delay choice. In a nomadic culture or in one where promises about deferred incentives are unlikely to be kept, immediate gratification is more adaptive.

Patience depends on finding something to do while waiting for a valuable, delayed incentive. Freud emphasized fantasizing about the incentive as one means of maintaining one's resolve. Social-learning theorists proposed an attentional hypothesis stating that focusing the child's attention on the desirable qualities of the deferred incentive would foster patience, but the reverse can occur when incentives are physically present and can produce frustration and an inability to wait. Thus the distraction hypothesis was proposed: Children who have a "fun" way to think about something else instead of the later incentive tend to be more patient. Another method is the self-instructional technique, in which children instruct themselves to ignore the delayed incentive or to think about how it is a "good idea" to wait. Children also respond to the labeling technique, in which they are labeled as "patient" persons, thus fostering a self-concept that waiting is indeed within their capabilities. Grade-school children are better than preschool children at devising their own strategies for being patient.

Self-control even in young, preschool children does seem to be possible, if the child is helped to recognize the benefits of waiting and is aided in developing strategies to bridge the delay interval. In each case, it helps to enlist the child as an "ally" by stressing that he or she is a "patient" person who can successfully wait.

SELF-REVIEW

Fill in the blanks for each item. Check the answers for each item as you go.

1. Every society has codes of ethics or _____ rules which maintain the _____ order and make it possible for the individual to _____ appropriately within the society.

moral
social
function or behave

2. McDougall suggested three stages of moral development: (1) a stage in which conduct is determined by use of _____ and _____, (2) a stage in which conduct depends more on social _____ and _____, and (3) a highest stage based on what are now called _____ moral principles.

rewards
punishments
praise, blame
internalized

A DEFINITION OF MORALITY

3. Most definitions of morality include an ability to tell _____ from _____, and an ability to _____ on this distinction; psychological research on moral development has focused on (1) the emotional or _____ component, (2) the thinking or _____ component, and (3) the observable _____ component.

right
wrong, act

affective
cognitive, behavioral

PSYCHOANALYTIC EXPLANATIONS OF MORAL DEVELOPMENT

4. Freud believed that infants are basically _____, thus requiring an emphasis on rewards and punishments because the child's _____ has not yet formed.

amoral

superego

Freud's Theory of Oedipal Morality

5. According to Freud, the superego develops during the _____ stage as a result of identification with the _____-_____ parent, as each child resolves either the _____ or the _____ conflict.

phallic
same-sex
Oedipal, Electra

Erikson's Views on Moral Development

6. Erikson argues that children _____ the moral principles of both parents, and also that moral development is determined jointly by the superego and the _____.

internalize

ego

COGNITIVE-DEVELOPMENTAL THEORY: THE CHILD AS MORAL PHILOSOPHER

7. As in other aspects of cognitive-developmental theory, moral development is said to occur in an _____ sequence in which each _____ evolves from the _____ stage.

invariant
stage, previous

Piaget's Theory of Moral Development

8. Piaget's theory consists of three stages in moral development: (1) the essentially rule-less _____ period, (2) the stage of _____ morality in which judgments reflect mainly the consequences of an act, and (3) the stage of moral relativism in which judgments are based on intentions underlying an act.

premoral
heteronomous

autonomous

227

9. Heteronomous children, in their belief in absolute morality, favor _____ punishment and accept the idea of _____ justice; autonomous children, in their belief in moral relativism, usually favor _____ punishment and also know that many rule violations go _____.

expiatory
immanent
reciprocal
unpunished

10. The heteronomous child's morality is governed by (1) the inability to take others' perspectives, called _____, and (2) the tendency to confuse one's thoughts with external reality, called _____.

egocentrism

realism

Tests of Piaget's Theory

11. Piaget's dilemmas tend to underestimate the abilities of the _____ child, who it seems is capable of using others' intentions in making moral judgments; another problem is that heteronomous children make distinctions between moral rules and _____-_____ rules and are less likely to view the latter as _____.

heteronomous

social-conventional
absolute

Kohlberg's Theory of Moral Development

12. Kohlberg's earliest level of _____ morality consists of Stage 1, the _____ and obedience orientation, and Stage 2, the naive hedonism orientation in which acts that are _____-_____ are viewed as acceptable; next comes the level of _____ morality, consisting of Stage 3, the "good-boy/good-girl" orientation with emphasis on _____ others and doing what is "_____," and Stage 4, with its social-order orientation emphasizing _____ to societal rules.

preconventional
punishment

self-serving
conventional
pleasing
nice
conformity

13. Kohlberg's highest level consists of Stage 5, with its morality-by-contract orientation emphasizing one's own _____ moral principles based on _____ procedures, and Stage 6, with its individual-conscience orientation and an emphasis on abstract, self-chosen_____; these comprise the level of _____ morality.

internalized
democratic

ethics
postconventional

Tests of Kohlberg's Theory

14. Research efforts by Kohlberg and others indicate clear age _____ in the moral reasoning levels and stages, verified by research across many _____: but many persons do not reach the _____ level of moral reasoning .

trends
cultures
postconventional

15. Kohlberg's _____ sequence of moral development finds research support, at least for the first ___ stages; his theory also parallels overall _____ development, in that conventional morality requires _____-_____ ability and postconventional morality requires _____ operational thought.

invariant
4
cognitive
role-taking
formal

16. Problems with Kohlberg's theory are that moral reasoning does not necessarily predict moral _____, and that females are sometimes found to be functioning at _____ stages than males; females may develop a different type of moral reasoning based less on _____ and other social conventions that on the _____ orientation they acquire through sex-role socialization.

behavior
lower

laws
interpersonal

MORALITY AS A PRODUCT OF SOCIAL LEARNING

17. In contrast to psychoanalytic and cognitive-developmental viewpoints, social-learning theorists emphasize that morality

depends more on the _____ the person is in, in accord   situation
with the doctrine of _____, and not as much on the   specificity
person's _____ moral principles.   internalized

How Consistent is Moral Behavior?

18. Indications are that children do show some consistency in
moral behavior, but that situational variables, such as the importance of the _____ involved, the probability of being   goal
_____ and _____ after the act, and the encour-   detected, punished
agement given by _____ also affect a child's willingness to   peers
lie, cheat, steal, or break other rules.

Determinants of Children's Resistance to Temptation

19. Reinforcement can aid in the development of moral controls,
especially when rewards are provided for alternative behaviors
that are _____ with prohibited acts; in practice,   incompatible
however, it is often hard to recognize that a child has actually
_____ temptation and thus deserves to be _____.   resisted, reinforced

20. Fear of punishment does not appear to lead to effective self-
_____, but punishment can be effective if it attaches neg-   -control
ative _____ to the prohibited act, which in turn depends on   affect
factors such as the _____ of punishment and whether the act   timing
is punished _____ each time it occurs.   consistently

21. Punishment is also more effective if accompanied by appropriate cognitive _____ which provide the child with   rationales
reasons for inhibiting unacceptable behaviors; these rationales
work best if they suit the child's level of _____ reasoning.   moral

Is Morality a Stable and Unitary Attribute?

22. Research indicates that the consistency of moral behavior
across situations _____ with age, as does the correspond-   improves
ence between moral reasoning and moral _____; thus, while   behavior
there is some consistency to our moral _____, morality   character
cannot be described as a _____ attribute.   unitary

WHO RAISES CHILDREN WHO ARE MORALLY MATURE?

23. The most effective parenting style in promoting moral development appears to be _____ discipline; in contrast, pow-   inductive
er-assertive discipline tends to produce children who are morally _____, and love-oriented discipline has _____   immature, limited
effects on moral development if any.

THE DEVELOPMENT OF SELF-CONTROL

24. Self-control typically refers to the ability to defer immediate _____ in favor of more desirable or valuable   gratification
_____-_____ goals, and this ability develops _____.   long-term, gradually

Motor Inhibition

25. Toddlers and preschool children, when loudly commanded to
stop doing something, may actually respond more to the physical
_____ of the command than to its _____ content, with   energy, semantic
the effect that they continue the activity.

Delay of Gratification

26. The choice to delay gratification in favor of a more valuable
long-term goal depends upon factors such as (1) the child's ____,   age

(2) the child's sense of _____ about whether the delayed   confidence
incentive will actually occur, (3) the relative _____ of each   value
incentive, immediate versus deferred, (4) the _____ of the   length
delay interval, (5) what kinds of choices are _____ by   modeled
adults and peers, and (6) what kinds of cognitive _____   rationales
the child has been given to justify delaying gratification.

27. Children are more likely to be patient and wait if they
have something else to think about other than the deferred incentive, in accord with the _____ hypothesis; preschool   distraction
children can be more patient if they are instructed to tell themselves to wait, as in the _____-_____ technique,   self-instructional
and telling children they are "patient" persons can also help as
in the _____ technique.   labeling

A Final Note on Self-Control

28. Younger children have been found to be less likely both to
_____ to pursue a delayed incentive and to be successful in   choose
_____ for it, but this does not mean that they lack the   waiting
_____ to delay gratification; younger children can learn   ability
to use effective delay _____.   strategies

SELF-TEST I

Consider each alternative carefully. Then choose the best one.

1. Psychoanalytic theorists emphasize the _____ component of morality, cognitive-
developmentalists the _____ component, and social-learning theorists the _____
component.
    a. reasoning, behavioral, affective
    (b) affective, reasoning, behavioral
    c. reasoning, behavioral, affective
    d. affective, behavioral, reasoning

2. Psychoanalytic theorists and cognitive-developmentalists agree that
    a. moral maturity implies an internalization of moral principles
    b. internalized morality stems from threat and fear of punishment
    (c) moral development is the same for boys and for girls
    d. none of the above

3. Cognitive developmentalists and contemporary social-learning theorists agree that
    a. the child is a moral philosopher
    b. moral principles are internalized
    c. morality is a stable trait across situations
    (d) none of the above

4. Piaget's theory and Kohlberg's theory share an emphasis on
    a. moral development in an invariant sequence
    b. moral development as a function of cognitive development
    c. stages in moral development
    (d) all of the above

5. Piaget's theory assigns moral absolutism to the stage of _____ morality and
moral relativism to the stage of _____ morality.
    (a) heteronomous, autonomous
    b. heteronomous, premoral
    c. autonomous, heteronomous
    d. autonomous, premoral

6. Research indicates that Piaget underestimated the moral development of _____ and that Kohlberg may have underestimated the moral development of _____.
   a. females, younger children
   b. females, females
   c. younger children, females
   d. younger children, younger children

7. Kohlberg's research on moral development is based on
   a. whether children respond correctly to moral dilemmas
   b. the underlying thought structures implied by responses to moral dilemmas
   c. both of the above
   d. none of the above

8. McDougall, Piaget, and Kohlberg share an emphasis on
   a. internalized moral principles
   b. young children as being essentially amoral
   c. both of the above
   d. none of the above

9. The social-learning theorists' doctrine of specificity states that
   a. moral reasoning depends upon the situation
   b. moral behavior depends upon the situation
   c. behavior may or may not reflect internalized moral principles
   d. all of the above

10. The "forbidden toy" paradigm can be used to assess
    a. the doctrine of specificity
    b. resistance to temptation
    c. self-control
    d. all of the above

11. The main problem with use of reinforcement in establishing moral controls is that
    a. it is not nearly as effective as punishment
    b. reinforceable moral acts often go unnoticed by adults
    c. it is incompatible with inductive discipline
    d. unacceptable acts are also reinforced if others fail to detect them

12. Research generally indicates that preschool children
    a. are incapable of motor inhibition
    b. cannot delay gratification
    c. cannot resist temptation
    d. none of the above

13. Delay-of-gratification choices are least likely with
    a. adolescents
    b. grade-school children
    c. preschool children
    d. toddlers

14. Children generally have more difficulty waiting for a deferred incentive when
    a. they think about the positive qualities of the incentive
    b. the delay interval is relatively short
    c. they are distracted from thinking about the incentive
    d. an adult tells them they are capable of waiting

15. Resistance to temptation
    a. is an aspect of moral development
    b. is an aspect of self-control
    c. both of the above
    d. none of the above

Using the textbook, review the research efforts indicated and write a summary of the important findings. Note the general purpose or context of the research.

1. Nelson (1980), page 562: _____

_____

_____

_____

_____

2. Nucci & Nucci (1982), page 563: _____

_____

_____

_____

_____

3. Kuczynski (1983), page 582: _____

_____

_____

_____

_____

4. Bandura & Mischel (1965), page 584: _____

_____

_____

_____

_____

5. Toner & Smith (1977), page 588: _____

_____

_____

_____

_____

SELF-TEST II

Consider each alternative carefully. Then choose the best one.

1. A definition of morality that reflects most adults' viewpoints includes
    a. the ability to distinguish right from wrong
    b. the ability to act on the distinction between right and wrong
    c. both of the above
    d. none of the above

2. Freud's psychoanalytic theory of moral development stresses identification due to
   a. love of the same-sex parent
   b. love of the opposite-sex parent
   c. fear of the same-sex parent
   d. fear of the opposite-sex parent

3. Erikson's theory of moral development differs from Freud's in that
   a. identification with both parents is emphasized
   b. the role of the Oedipus and Electra complexes is deemphasized
   c. the role of the ego is emphasized
   d. all of the above

4. Piaget's basic means of studying moral development was to assess
   a. awareness of moral rules
   b. abilities in self-control
   c. forbidden-toy dilemmas
   d. all of the above

5. In Piaget's stage of heteronomous morality, the child believes in
   a. reciprocal punishment and immanent justice
   b. reciprocal punishment and the absence of immanent justice
   c. expiatory punishment and immanent justice
   d. expiatory punishment and the absence of immanent justice

6. In Piaget's stage of autonomous morality, the child believes in
   a. reciprocal punishment and immanent justice
   b. reciprocal punishment and the absence of immanent justice
   c. expiatory punishment and immanent justice
   d. expiatory punishment and the absence of immanent justice

7. Piaget may have underestimated the morality of the heteronomous child because
   a. moral actions do not always reflect moral beliefs
   b. information about intentions was not clear in Piaget's dilemmas
   c. information about consequences was not clear in Piaget's dilemmas
   d. moral actions do generally reflect moral beliefs

8. Another problem with Piaget's theory is that preschool children tend to believe in
   a. moral rules as absolute but social-conventional rules as relative
   b. moral rules as relative and social-conventional rules as relative
   c. moral rules as absolute and social-conventional rules as absolute
   d. moral rules as relative but social-conventional rules as absolute

9. In Kohlberg's system, the shift from external consequences to internalized principles
as the determinants of morality occurs between
   a. Stage 2 hedonism and Stage 3 good-boy/good-girl morality
   b. Stage 3 good-boy/good-girl morality and Stage 4 law-and-order morality
   c. Stage 4 law-and-order morality and Stage 5 democratic morality
   d. Stage 5 democratic morality and Stage 6 individual-conscience morality

10. Most adults function most of the time at Kohlberg's level of
    a. preconventional morality
    b. conventional morality
    c. postconventional morality
    d. none of the above

11. Longitudinal data on American males with respect to Kohlberg's invariant sequence and
other aspects of the proposed stages in moral development indicate that
    a. subjects progressed through the moral stages in the order specified
    b. some subjects occasionally skipped a stage
    c. both of the above
    d. none of the above

12. Gilligan's research involving abortion dilemmas with pregnant women suggests that sex differences in moral reasoning reflect
    a. delayed cognitive development on the part of females
    b. delayed moral development of the part of females
    c. female cognitive development based on the expressive, empathic role
    d. female moral development based on the expressive, empathic role

13. Punishment is effective as a means of enhancing moral development if
    a. it occurs early in the sequencing of unacceptable behavior
    b. it is administered consistently with regard to unacceptable behavior
    c. it is administered by a warm and friendly agent
    d. all of the above

14. Cognitive rationales on why a forbidden act should be inhibited do not work when
    a. they are not accompanied by punishment
    b. delayed punishment is employed
    c. the punishing agent is aloof and impersonal
    d. none of the above

15. Research indicates that _____ discipline tends to inhibit moral development, whereas _____ discipline tends to promote moral development.
    a. power-assertive, love-oriented
    b. inductive, power-assertive
    c. power-assertive, inductive
    d. love-oriented, inductive

16. In Kuczynski's (1983) research on Hoffman's discipline types, "other-oriented" discipline was effective in suppressing a forbidden act
    a. while the experimenter was present
    b. while the experimenter was absent, before disinhibition of the act
    c. while the experimenter was absent, after disinhibition of the act
    d. all of the above

17. In the study by Bandura and Mischel (1965), impulsive children watched an adult model choose delayed incentives, and nonimpulsive children watched an adult model choose immediate incentives; the results indicated that
    a. modeling is effective in fostering delay choices
    b. modeling is effective in fostering immediate choices
    c. both of the above
    d. none of the above

18. Children are likely to choose to delay gratification if
    a. they believe they can be patient
    b. the delayed incentive has a subjectively greater value than the immediate one
    c. they trust the person who will deliver the delayed incentive
    d. all of the above

19. The choice to delay gratification is least likely with
    a. older children
    b. delinquent children
    c. more intelligent children
    d. children high in achievement motivation

20. Research by Kanfer, Stifter, and Morris on preschool children's willingness to delay gratification to produce a desirable outcome for another child indicated that
    a. preschool children simply will not delay gratification to help another child
    b. preschool children cannot delay gratification, regardless of the purpose
    c. preschool children will always delay gratification to help a personal friend
    d. preschool children will sometimes delay gratification to help a personal friend

234

21. Research on nomadic Aboriginal children indicates that
    a. the ability to delay gratification is genetically determined
    b. delay of gratification is universally more likely with older children
    c. delay of gratification is universally more likely with more intelligent children
    (d.) delay of gratification is strongly affected by cultural values

22. With regard to factors influencing patience, research clearly indicates that children are likely to be able to wait for a delayed incentive if they
    a. focus on the incentive's desirable qualities to know it is worth waiting for
    (b.) distract themselves from the incentive's desirable qualities to avoid temptation
    c. both of the above
    d. none of the above

23. In research by Toner and associates on the "waiting game," the self-instruction "It is good if I wait" was effective in improving the patience of
    a. none of the children
    b. preschool children but not grade-school children
    c. grade-school children but not preschool children
    (d.) both groups of children, but more so with preschool children

24. In the research by Toner and associates on the "waiting game," the labeling technique of telling children "I hear you are very patient...." was effective with
    a. none of the children
    b. preschool children but not grade-school children
    c. grade-school children but not preschool children
    (d) preschool and grade-school children

25. Research by Mischel and Mischel on children's own awareness of how to be patient while waiting for a deferred incentive indicated that
    a. older children are more aware of the need to focus on the deferred incentive
    b. older children are more likely to choose consummatory ideation while waiting
    (c.) younger children are more likely to choose consummatory ideation while waiting
    d. none of the above

VIGNETTES

Consider the story, then answer each question using material from the textbook.

I. In 1969, Frank found himself in a dilemma as a result of a letter that came in the mail one day. It seemed that he had two basic choices: He could submit to the draft and most certainly go to Viet Nam, which meant killing and also risking being killed. Or, he could refuse to be drafted, and most certainly go to prison. Frank was torn between a sense of duty to his country, a strong belief that he should not kill, and a basic desire for self-preservation that ruled out both risking being killed and suffering in prison. And so, he went to Canada.

    1. Should he have done that? Why or why not?

    2. In Kohlberg's system, what would you consider in assessing a person's responses to *Question 1*?

    3. In Gilligan's system, what would you consider in assessing a person's responses to *Question 1*?

II. Richard's parents were determined that he would "do right." Richard was 4 years old, and any deviations from the correct behavior specified by his parents were dealt with quickly and efficiently with spankings, taking away of TV privileges, and whatever else seemed appropriate at the time in the way of punishment. Richard's parents felt that discipline was the key, in and of itself, and that Richard didn't need to know why nearly as much as he needed to know that his misbehavior would be punished. Richard's father in particular believed that a stern, unyielding authority figure would provide the best model for moral development and character.

    1. Which of Hoffman's discipline types is being employed?

    2. What might Freud predict about Richard's moral development?

    3. What might social-learning theorists predict about Richard's moral development?

III. Martha's parents were determined that she would "do right." Martha was 4 years old, and any deviations from the correct behavior specified by her parents were dealt with quickly and efficiently with explanations as to why the behavior was wrong, what effects it had on others, and occasionally spankings of a relatively mild but embarrassing sort usually accompanied by comments that Martha should "act her age." Martha's mother in particular believed that a warm, basically empathic model would be best for Martha's moral development and character.

    1. Which of Hoffman's discipline types is being employed?

    2. What might Freud predict about Martha's moral development?

    3. What might social-learning theorists predict about Martha's moral development?

APPLICATIONS

Try each of the projects, noting answers to the questions as you go.

I. Design a Kohlberg-style dilemma for the following situation: The actor is taking a very important final exam in a college course, and the opportunity to copy another student's paper presents itself.

    1. What kind of background might be necessary in creating a situation likely to elicit moral reasoning?

    2. What might you have the actor do, and why?

    3. What sorts of adjustments and considerations might be necessary in providing a fair test of *young* children's moral reasoning?

II. Suppose it comes to your attention that your 7-8-year-old child (or someone else's) has developed a habit of shoplifting. Work out a plan for eliminating this behavior, based on the social-learning material on moral development.

    1. Would you use punishment? If so, how?

    2. What kinds of cognitive rationales might you employ?

    3. In particular, which of the above procedures might be most effective in eliminating the behavior when the child is not being watched?

III. Suppose your 4-5-year-old child (or someone else's) has a habit of taking toys away from other children, rather that waiting to "take turns." From the material on delay choices and self-control, work out a plan for altering this behavior.

    1. What considerations might be involved in helping the child learn to make a delay choice in the first place?

    2. What considerations are there in helping the child be "patient"?

    3. In particular, what cognitive strategies might you employ?

Self-Test I

1. b	6. c	11. b
2. c	7. b	12. d
3. d	8. c	13. d
4. d	9. d	14. a
5. a	10. d	15. c

Research Summary and Review

1. Nelson (1980): When making moral judgments on cartoons in which the actor's intentions were clear, 3-year-olds used these to evaluate the actor's behavior, in contrast to Piaget's findings regarding the premoral period; this illustrated that Piaget may have underestimated the moral reasoning abilities of preschool children.

2. Nucci & Nucci (1982): Children 7-14 years old were observed to react more strongly to moral rule violations than to social-conventional rule violations, indicating that the moral absolutism of Piaget's heteronomous stage may have been overstated because children do not necessarily view all rules in the same light.

3. Kuczynski (1983): Other-oriented discipline was more effective than self-oriented discipline or unelaborated prohibition in convincing 9-10-year-olds to work at a monotonous task without being distracted by toys; this analogue to Hoffman's inductive discipline was effective even when an adult was absent and a "disinhibiting" instruction was given.

4. Bandura & Mischel (1965): "Impulsive" 9-10-year-olds improved in self-restraint after watching an adult model select delayed incentives, and "nonimpulsives" became more impulsive after watching an adult model select immediate incentives; this indicated that willingness to delay gratification depends in part on the behavior of companions.

5. Toner & Smith (1977): Using the self-instruction "It is good if I wait," preschool girls displayed more patience than those who were told nothing or told to concentrate on the deferred incentive; similar results were obtained with grade-school girls, except that more of the girls apparently used spontaneous distraction strategies even when told nothing, indicating that they knew to distract themselves in order to be patient.

Self-Test II

1. c	6. b	11. a	16. d	21. d
2. c	7. b	12. d	17. c	22. b
3. d	8. a	13. d	18. d	23. d
4. a	9. c	14. d	19. b	24. d
5. c	10. b	15. c	20. d	25. c

Vignettes

I. (1) As with Kohlberg's "Heinz" dilemma, either a "yes" or a "no" response is reasonable. The point is that moral reasoning at any of the levels can lead to either conclusion. (2) Stage 1 reasoning might emphasize negative consequences of the actions rather than intentions. Stage 2 concentrates on intentions with a focus on hedonism and what is best for Frank. Stage 3 considers what others would or would not approve of. Stage 4 reasoning focuses on the law-and-order implications of Frank's behavior. Stage 5 might look at Frank's decision in terms of the fairness of the draft law. And Stage 6 decisions would be based on individual conscience and principles that transcend law. (3) Level 1 might emphasize individual survival; the first transition, a conflict between self-interest and

and the interests of others; Level II, self-sacrifice; the second transition, self-interest and the interests of others in terms of what is "right"; and Level III, a move to principles of nonviolence.

II. (1) This style is basically power-assertive, because of methods and also the implication of an arbitrary discipline "for its own sake." (2) Freud might predict good moral development; note the implications of a cold, threatening approach which should elicit fear and enhance the process of Richard's identification with his father. (3) Social-learning theory might predict anger and rebellion by Richard, with correspondingly immature moral development.

III. (1) This is Hoffman's inductive discipline, in its emphasis on explanations (cognitive rationales) as to why a behavior is wrong. (2) Freud might predict poor moral development on several counts: Martha is a girl, which means that she has less incentive for moral development in the first place, and to make things worse, the element of anxiety necessary to identification with the mother is nowhere in evidence. (3) Social-learning theory predicts mature development of a sense of guilt and shame, in part through empathy with "victims." Cognitive rationales provide standards Martha can internalize, and her behavior when an adult is not watching is more likely to be moral. Also note that occasional mild spankings, within reasonable guidelines, should not interfere.

Applications

I. A workable dilemma here could take many forms, the basic idea being to create a "balanced" situation that is difficult to resolve and thus will elicit the underlying moral reasoning of interest. (1) As an example: Give the actor a neutral name, such as John or Jane. Suppose Jane's graduation depends upon passing the course. Suppose she studied reasonably well all along, missing a few but not many classes, and she has a *C* going into the final exam. But the instructor assigned copious amounts of outside reading at the last minute, which is the instructor's prerogative, but which hardly seems fair. (2) Thus the stage is set as Jane starts to take the exam and hardly recognizes the first few questions, which are based on the extra material. When the instructor leaves the room on the "honor system," Jane cheats just enough to pass, just as Heinz stole the medicine. Having the actor commit an act is more likely to elicit moral reasoning than having the actor refrain from committing the act. (3) Although the process of taking tests without cheating begins early in grade school, this situation might be a bit abstract for young children. In accord with Nelson's research, it would be necessary to spell out the intentions of the actors more, and also the consequences. Note the possible use of cartoon illustrations as an adjunct to the story.

II. (1) Punishment could be employed without harmful effects, if punishment were within reasonable limits. With a 7-8-year-old, withholding of privileges might be preferable to physical punishment. Also note the need for internalized controls that function when no one is watching. The gap between when the child steals and when it is later detected could also be bridged by cognitive rationales. And you might use praise as reinforcement for the incompatible response of going in and buying something instead of stealing it. (2) Cognitive rationales might include simple instructions that it is wrong to steal, that people who steal are bad persons, and so on. Much more effective rationales would emphasize how stealing hurts others and makes them feel bad. And you might utilize the child's pride and desire to be "grown up," noting that it is immature to steal. (3) Cognitive rationales should be the most effective when no one is watching, through providing internalized standards for behavior.

III. Self-control overlaps with moral development where issues of aggressive behavior and resistance to temptation are involved. Thus the considerations in *Application II* apply here as well. Also note, from the material on self-control: (1) The child must be able to trust you as to the toy coming later, and the child must believe that she or he can wait. (2) A likely possibility is to distract the child with another toy or activity during the waiting interval. (3) In particular, consider self-instructional strategies such as "It is good if I wait my turn," and consider labeling the child as "patient."

CHAPTER FIFTEEN

THE FAMILY

OVERVIEW AND KEY TERMS

Read carefully. Recall examples and discussion as you go, and define each key term.

Socialization is the process by which children acquire the beliefs, values and behaviors deemed significant and appropriate by older members of their society. Although many institutions and agencies participate in the socialization of each succeeding generation, the primary agent of socialization is the family.

BASIC FEATURES AND FUNCTIONS OF THE FAMILY

The norm in contemporary Western society is the nuclear family, but many American children now spend time in a single-parent family. And in many cultures people live in extended families. The most widely recognized function of the family is parenting, which LeVine proposes has three basic goals: (1) the survival goal of ensuring that the children live, (2) the economic goal to promote the child's self-sufficiency, and (3) the self-actualization goal incorporating cultural values, morality, prestige, and personal satisfaction. In many cultures, promoting survival means maintaining close contact with children 24 hours a day, and infants are not named until it is clear that they will survive. And the economic goal is served in various ways according to resources and industries the culture provides. Self-actualization, finally, depends upon the fit between the individual's sense of self-fulfillment and values the culture endorses.

SOME CAUTIONARY COMMENTS ABOUT THE STUDY OF FAMILIES

There is no "best way" to study families. Box 15-1 describes three basic research strategies, each of which has advantages and shortcomings: (1) the interview or questionnaire technique, (2) observational methodologies, and (3) analogue experiments. The middle-class bias is another important consideration, in that much of the research on families has yielded results that may not generalize to other socio-economic levels. And the directionality issue is a problem in that interactions among parents and children are reciprocal in nature, whereas much of the research on families has assessed only how parents affect children and not vice-versa.

The family social system consists of both parents and their children, and the interactions are complex even in a family of three. Thus, how one parent interacts with the child may differ according to whether the other parent is present, and quarrels between parents affect each parent's behavior and the child's behavior as well. Families also exist in a larger social system that includes their religious communities, neighborhoods, and many other ecological factors. Childrearing practices and interactions may also differ in reconstituted families.

INTERACTIONS BETWEEN PARENTS AND THEIR INFANTS

The transition to parenthood affects both parents and may influence their relation-

ship. Mothers often become more "feminine," and fathers may show more interest in feminine activities. The presence of a baby alters daily routines and may also affect the
level of intimacy between parents. Infants who are temperamental or who require special
care often disrupt vulnerable marriages but improve marriages that are on firm ground.

Mothers who are warm, sensitive, and responsive tend to have many positive effects
on their infants. Teenage mothers, perhaps because many are often unmarried or have very
little social support, tend to have less favorable attitudes toward childrearing. In contrast, mothers over 30 tend to be very responsive to their infants. And research has recently focused on father-infant interactions. Fathers who were present in the delivery
room tend to be more responsive to their infants. Fathers in general tend to be more
boisterous than mothers in interactions with infants, often serving as special playmates.
And fathers can serve all important caregiving functions and even offset the negative effects of insecure mother-infant attachment.

Indirect parental effects occur when one parent influences the other, which in turn
affects the child. Marital strife produces indirect effects that contribute to poor interactions between parent and infant, whereas good marital relationships produce more positive effects.

PARENTAL EFFECTS ON PRESCHOOL AND SCHOOL-AGE CHILDREN

During the preschool years and beyond, permissiveness/restrictiveness is one major
dimension of parenting that influences the child. Permissive parents allow more freedom
in exploration, expression, and decision-making. Restrictive parents make many demands,
limit freedoms, and apply more rules and regulations. A second major dimension is warmth/
hostility. Warm parents are nurturant, affectionate, and approving, with a tendency to
limit signs of disapproval. Hostile parents are quicker to criticize and punish, and are
reluctant to show their children signs of approval.

Baumrind's research indicates three parental styles with distinct effects on children. Authoritarian parenting emphasizes adherence to absolute standards of behavior with
little give and take between parent and child. Daughters of authoritarian parents usually turn out average in cognitive and social skills; sons tend to turn out below average
in cognitive skills but average in social skills. Authoritative parenting emphasizes the
setting of standards that are more rational, with sharing of the reasons and much give and
take between parent and child. Both sons and daughters of authoritative parents display
high cognitive and social skills. Permissive parenting emphasizes few standards of behavior, with extreme give and take and little use of overt power. Sons and daughters of permissive parents often display low cognitive and social skills. The dimension of warmth/
hostility interacts with these styles. For example, an authoritarian/rejecting style may
produce children who are inhibited, masochistic, and perhaps even suicidal. And a per-
missive/rejecting style tends to make children hostile, rebellious, and delinquent.

Other things equal, warm and accepting parents produce children who are securely attached, relatively altruistic, generally obedient, high in self-esteem, satisfied with
their gender identities, and oriented toward internalized moral principles. In contrast,
cold and rejecting parents make children anxious, emotionally frustrated, irritable, and
poorly socialized, with an increased risk of serious mental and behavioral disorders. As
discussed in Box 15-2, hostile parenting is associated with an increased risk that the
child will later become clinically depressed, especially where parents are derisive.

Power-assertive and love-oriented forms of discipline lead children to comply with
rules mainly from fear of negative consequences. Inductive discipline fosters compliance
by employing rationales as to why transgressions are wrong. Power assertion also tends
to make children more self-centered, whereas induction yields a more altruistic outlook.

But the ways in which children respond to parenting styles affect whether the parents
can maintain the style. Child characteristics such as defiance and high activity level
lead parents toward more coercive forms of discipline. Parenting styles also change as

the child grows older, and previously power-assertive parents may become more inductive as the child begins to understand verbal and cognitive appeals. Another consideration is how the child views the parents' style of discipline, as discussed in Box 15-3. Younger children value autonomy and physical nurturance highly, whereas older children and adolescents better understand that parents who set reasonable limits are reflecting love and concern and other forms of psychological nurturance.

Belief in the "American dream" is more likely among middle- and upper SES families, and the problems faced by lower- and working-class families may lead them to adopt different outlooks on life. High-SES families focus on influence and power, with expectations that children will make good grades, attend college, and become professionals. Low-SES families focus more on their powerlessness and tend to encourage their children to prepare for steady work. Low income living is more stressful, which may in turn cause parents to become critical and restrictive toward their children.

Research indicates that middle-class mothers are similar to working-class mothers in the amount of close contact provided infants, but middle-class mothers are more likely to provide distal stimulation as well. As compared to lower-class mothers, middle-class mothers show more "involvement" with their children as time goes by and are more inclined to use verbal labeling and to include praise and approval when attempting to teach their children. These conclusions are based on group averages, however, and they say nothing about the parenting styles of an individual mother from a particular social class. And it is a mistake to label high-SES parenting as necessarily more competent than low-SES parenting, because "competent" parenting depends heavily on the culture or subculture in which a child is reared. Perhaps the closest thing to a general law of parenting is that warmth, sensitivity, and responsiveness to children's needs are associated with positive developmental outcomes in all cultures and subcultures. But beyond these basic ideas, we are being ethnocentric if we favor one style of childrearing for all settings.

EFFECTS OF SIBLINGS AND THE FAMILY CONFIGURATION

Generally, children are more positive in their interactions with parents than with siblings, and sibling interactions tend to include more instances of hitting, yelling, and acts of coercion. Sibling rivalry often begins early when older siblings object to the attention parents give an infant, and as the child grows older the intensity of these conflicts is likely to increase as the child becomes more capable of retaliation. Cross-sex sibling interactions tend to be more negative than same-sex interactions, perhaps because mothers pay more attention to cross-sex younger children. However, too much attention to the older sibling can also produce negative behavior by that child.

On the positive side, older children are often prominent caregivers for their younger siblings. Older siblings can serve as attachment objects, models, and teachers, and both the younger and older siblings benefit from these interactions.

Ordinal position has various associated effects. First-borns tend to be more oriented toward achievement and more sociable and outgoing, but they are often found to be less confident than later-borns in social situations. First-borns are also more likely to be affectionately obedient toward parents. Later-borns seem to establish better social relations with peers, and last-borns tend to be the most popular with peers. Parents contribute to ordinal position effects by treating children differently, as when mothers are more likely to stress achievement with first-borns. And the popularity of later-born children may be explained by their need to develop tolerance and powers of negotiation in dealing with older siblings.

THE IMPACT OF DIVORCE

The immediate effects of divorce upon the child are often stressful and likely to produce anger, fearfulness, and depression. Up to a year or more may be required before the child begins to readjust to life in a single-parent home.

Hetherington proposes that children of divorce go through a crisis phase of a year or more, followed by an adjustment phase. During the crisis phase the child may become more "difficult" and the custodial parent more punitive, thus developing a coercive relationship. Parent-child relations during the year prior to the divorce are a reliable predictor of children's reactions after the divorce. Children of divorce, however, often fare better than those who remain in conflict-ridden nuclear families. Children of divorce tend to adjust better if the noncustodial parent continues to provide the family with financial and emotional support, and a cordial relationship between ex-marital partners helps the child. Box 15-4 discusses what happens when the father instead of the mother becomes the custodial parent.

The typical reconstituted family include mother, her children, and stepfather. Boys in such homes often adjust quite well, but girls tend to be more anxious and to display more anger toward their mothers compared to girls in intact homes. These sex differences in reactions to a reconstituted family do not seem attributable to quality of the stepfathers' parenting as such. And, compared to children in single-parent homes, children of both sexes seem to fare better in reconstituted families.

EFFECTS OF MATERNAL EMPLOYMENT

If the mother provides for quality day care and is a responsive caregiver when she is at home, maternal employment does not seem to adversely affect a child's social and emotional development. Children of working mothers have been found to be at least as outgoing and socially adaptable, and they sometimes are more independent and better adjusted than children in families where the mother remains a homemaker. However, recent research suggests that the child's cognitive development and academic achievement may suffer somewhat if the mother works. This does not mean that all mothers should stay at home, because family interactions can be stressful when a mother wants or needs to work and yet stays at home for one reason or another.

WHEN PARENTING BREAKS DOWN: THE PROBLEM OF CHILD ABUSE

Child abuse is a major problem in the U.S., and the incidence of battered children seems to be increasing. One estimate is that between one and two million children are subjected to serious violence or neglect each year. Children who are unresponsive, defiant, hyperactive, irritable, or ill are at greater risk than children who are easier to care for. Some parents may be predisposed to abuse children. And although abusive parents come from all backgrounds, abusers often display a pattern of negative emotional reactions to the child's social signals. Parents who were themselves abused or unloved as children are more likely to become abusive to their own children.

Situational factors can trigger child abuse. Children in large families where caregivers are overburdened with childrearing responsibilities are more at risk. Child abuse is also more frequent in some "high risk" neighborhoods. And throughout our society, a very permissive attitude toward physical punishment and violence may be a contributing factor to child abuse.

Strategies in preventing child abuse and helping the parents overcome it take various forms. Crisis lines and crisis nurseries help during emergencies. And Parents Anonymous functions as a support group to help parents understand and overcome their abusive tendencies. In turn, babies at risk for child abuse can be identified through neonatal assessment, and hospital observation of how parents interact with their children can give warning signs of future abuse. While many abusive parents can be helped and will eventually stop abusing their children, other parents remain highly abusive, and in such cases the need arises to place the children in foster or adoptive homes.

Fill in the blanks for each item. Check the answers for each item as you go.

1. The process by which children acquire the beliefs, values, and behaviors deemed important in their society is _____,   socialization
which serves society in at least three ways: (1) regulating
children's _____, (2) promoting their personal _____,   behavior, growth
and (3) perpetuating the social _____, in each case through a   order
primary social institution called the _____.   family

BASIC FEATURES AND FUNCTIONS OF THE FAMILY

2. In the U.S., the traditional _____ family nowadays takes   nuclear
many different forms, including more recently the _____-par-   single
ent home which affects some ___-___% of American children.   40 - 50%

The Functions of a Family

3. Perhaps the most widely recognized functions of the family
are those that affect _____, in terms of caregiving, nur-   children
turing, and training.

The Goals of Parenting

4. LeVine's hierarchy of goals families have for their children
notes (1) physical health and the _____ goal, (2) devel-   survival
opment of self-sufficiency within the _____ goal, and   economic
(3) personal satisfaction and acquisition of cultural values
within the goal of _____-_____.   self-actualization

SOME CAUTIONARY COMMENTS ABOUT THE STUDY OF FAMILIES

5. Basic approaches to studying families include (1) _____   interview
or questionnaire studies, which generate enormous amounts of information but are highly subject to _____ _____ on the   response bias
part of the parents; (2) naturalistic _____ methodol-   observation
ogies, which can be extremely accurate except for problems such
as the effects of the _____'s presence, and (3) labora-   observer's
tory _____ experiments, which can directly indicate how   analogue
parenting techniques affect children's behavior but which may
not _____ the real family environment.   simulate

The Middle-Class Bias

6. Research based on middle-class White families may or may not
apply to other _____ groups, and we should not as-   sociocultural
sume that White middle-class patterns of childrearing are necessarily more _____ than other parenting techniques.   competent

The Directionality Issue

7. Parents affect children, but children also affect what childrearing strategies the parent use, in _____ fashion;   reciprocal
for example, parents' use of discipline depends in part upon how
children have previously _____ to that discipline.   responded or reacted

Reconceptualizing Family Effects: The Family as a Social System

8. How each parent behaves toward the child also depends upon
what the other parent does; in addition, factors such as the
_____ of the marriage affect the child, and at the same   quality
time the child's behavior can affect the quality of the parents'

marriage in _____ action.   reciprocal

The Changing American Family

9. Most family research has focused on the traditional nuclear
family consisting of _____, _____, and one or more   mother, father
_____; changes are now that more mothers are _____   children, working
outside the home and that more children are living in _____-   single-
parent homes or in _____ families.   reconstituted

INTERACTIONS BETWEEN PARENTS AND THEIR INFANTS

The Transition to Parenthood

10. Typically, the birth of a baby makes mothers more _____   feminine
and leads fathers to become somewhat less _____; more   masculine
general effects on the marriage depend upon whether the parents
are emotionally _____ and how difficult the child is in   mature
terms of _____.   temperament

The Effects of Parents on Their Infants

11. Mothers who are warm and responsive to their infants tend to
foster _____ attachments which facilitate child development;   secure
a key dimension in the mother's behavior is her _____   sensitivity
to the child's wants and needs.

12. Indirect parental effects on the infant occur when one parent's behavior influences the other _____'s behavior in   parent's
turn influencing the _____; such effects can either be nega-   child
tive or positive depending upon the _____ of the par-   quality
ents' marital relationship.

PARENTAL EFFECTS ON PRESCHOOL AND SCHOOL-AGE CHILDREN

Two Major Dimensions of Childrearing

13. Parents who allow their children little autonomy and who impose many rules and regulations are said to be _____,   restrictive
whereas parents who allow children freedom in exploring and in
expressing opinions are more _____; parents who use   permissive
encouragement and approval rather than criticism and punishment
are displaying _____, whereas parents who are highly critical   warmth
and rejecting are displaying _____.   hostility

Patterns of Parental Control

14. Baumrind characterizes parenting that is rigid and controlling
_____, parenting that is directive but flexible as   authoritarian
_____, and parenting that is nondirective and high-   authoritative
ly accepting as _____; research indicates that the   permissive
highest cognitive and social competencies are associated with
the _____ parenting style, and that either of the   authoritative
more restrictive parenting styles coupled with a hostile attitude by parents tends to produce children who are withdrawn, inhibited, and possibly _____.   masochistic

Parental Warmth/Hostility

15. Children who have warm, loving parents tend to be _____   securely
attached, have _____ inclinations if the parents also   altruistic
practice what they preach, have relatively high _____-esteem   self-
and good _____-taking skills, and _____ moral   role-, internalized
standards, among other characteristics.

244

Patterns of Parental Discipline

16. In contrast to power-assertive or love-withdrawal styles of disciplining children, _____ discipline is relatively non-_____, tends to be associated with parental _____ instead of hostility, and is most like the _____ style of discipline suggested by Baumrind.

inductive
-punitive, warmth
authoritative

17. But patterns of parental discipline depend, in part, on the capabilities of the child at different _____; during the first few years, for example, _____ appeals are not likely to be effective and discipline tends to be more _____-_____.

ages
cognitive
power-assertive

Social-Class Differences in Parenting

18. Expectations for the child vary according to socioeconomic status of the family: higher-SES parents are more likely to expect their child to "_____ _____," whereas lower-SES parents are more likely to expect their child to "_____ ____"; and the stresses associated with lower-SES living also affect parenting, in that the parents may become less _____ to children and may be less precise in the _____ instructions they use.

get ahead
get by

responsive
verbal

19. But although middle-class parenting might seem _____ in its positive effects on children, such a view would be highly _____ if applied to all cultures and subcultures; for example, individualism may need to be suppressed in cultures where respect for group authority is necessary to _____, and the only set of standards by which to evaluate the basic _____ of parenting are those of one's own culture.

better

ethnocentric

survival

competence

EFFECTS OF SIBLINGS AND THE FAMILY CONFIGURATION

The Nature of Sibling Interactions

20. Generally, sibling interactions are more _____ than parent-child interactions, and siblings are more likely to use annoying and coercive _____ with each other; yet, on an absolute basis, _____ sibling interactions are actually more common than negative ones.

negative

behaviors
positive

Origins and Determinants of Sibling Rivalry

21. The birth of a baby tends to result in older siblings receiving less _____ from parents and demanding attention in _____ ways; later sibling quarrels are more likely with _____-sex siblings, in part due to differential treatment by the mother.

attention
inappropriate
cross

Positive Effects of Sibling Interactions

22. However, older siblings often serve as caregivers and thus become _____ _____ for younger siblings; they also serve as social _____ and as _____, which is beneficial for the older siblings as well.

attachment objects
models, teachers

Characteristics of First-Born and Later-Born Children

23. First-borns tend to be oriented more toward success and _____, more interested in _____ interactions with peers although less self-_____ in social situations, and more _____ to authority; later-borns tend to be more _____ in relations with peers, perhaps from having to develop social skills in dealing with _____ _____.

achievement, social
-confident
obedient
popular
older siblings

THE IMPACT OF DIVORCE

The Immediate Effects

24. Divorce is typically a highly _____ event for children; generally, _____ children fare better through being able to _____ reasons why the divorce occurred and through being better equipped to _____ with problems to be faced.

stressful
older
understand
cope

The Crisis Phase

25. The crisis phase often lasts _____ _____ or more, during which time the child may become more "_____" and cranky and the custodial parent may become more _____ as a result.

one year
difficult
coercive

26. Factors that minimize the disruptive effects of divorce include whether the noncustodial parent continues to provide both _____ and _____ support for the family and whether the parents maintain a _____ working relationship with regard to childrearing.

financial, emotional
cordial

Long-Term Reactions to Divorce

27. Although children may harbor long-term negative feelings about their parents' divorce, research indicates that they eventually make _____ adjustments and also fare better than children who remain in _____-_____ nuclear families.

positive
conflict-ridden

Children in Reconstituted Families

28. Effects of remarriage depend upon sex of the child: Boys tend to be _____ toward stepfathers, whereas girls tend to show anger toward their _____.

warmer
mothers

EFFECTS OF MATERNAL EMPLOYMENT

29. Children of working mothers tend to hold _____ stereotyped views of sex roles, tend to be more _____-sufficient and independent, and are typically _____ sociable with peers; however, some research suggests that children of working mothers score _____ on standardized tests of cognitive development and academic achievement.

less
self-
more

lower

WHEN PARENTING BREAKS DOWN: THE PROBLEM OF CHILD ABUSE

Who Is Abused?

30. Any child could become a target of _____, but those children who defy and ignore adults are likely to elicit stronger forms of _____ which may escalate into abuse; even infants who are irritable and _____ may become targets of child abuse.

abuse

punishment
unresponsive

Who Are the Abusers?

31. Only about ____ out of 10 child abusers has a serious mental illness; one note is that parents who were themselves abused as _____ are later more likely to become child abusers.

1

children

Social-Situational Triggers: The Ecology of Child Abuse

32. Abused children often come from large _____ in which there are many small children to care for; the risk of child abuse also increases in deteriorating _____; and it is possible that our society's permissive attitudes toward _____ and the use of physical _____ are con-

families

neighborhoods

violence, punishment

tributing factors in child abuse.

How Can We Help Abusive Parents and Their Children?

33. Strategies helpful in controlling or preventing child abuse
include (1) 24-hour hotlines and crisis _____ , (2) support groups such as _____ Anonymous, (3) early detection
of high-risk _____ , and (4) a variety of media efforts such
as public service _____ ; in cases of repeated
abuse, it is also sometimes necessary to _____ the leg-
al custodial rights of the parents and place the child in a foster or adoptive home.

nurseries
Parents
infants
announcements
terminate

SELF-TEST I

Consider each alternative carefully. Then choose the best one.

1. Socialization is
    a. a means of regulating children's behavior
    b. a process by which children acquire adaptive knowledge and skills
    c. the means by which a social order perpetuates itself
    (d) all of the above

2. The contemporary norm in Western society is the
    (a) nuclear family
    b. single-parent home
    c. extended family
    d. reconstituted family

3. In some societies, children are not named until late in the first year after birth;
families in such societies are concerned primarily with the
    (a) survival goal of parenting
    b. economic goal of parenting
    c. self-actualization goal of parenting
    d. none of the above

4. Reliability of data on families is an issue of concern in
    a. interview studies
    b. questionnaire studies
    c. observational methodologies
    (d) all of the above

5. Analysis of cause-and-effect relationships within families is most likely with
    a. interview and questionnaire studies
    b. observational methodologies
    (c) analogue experiments
    d. none of the above

6. The authoritarian, authoritative, and permissive parenting styles reflect
    (a) the permissiveness/restrictiveness dimension
    b. the warmth/hostility dimension
    c. both of the above
    d. none of the above

7. Inductive discipline is most likely in Baumrind's
    a. authoritarian parenting style
    (b) authoritative parenting style
    c. permissive parenting style
    d. none of the above

8. After reviewing the literature on parenting, we can safely say that
    a. authoritarian, power-assertive parenting is best
    b. authoritative, inductive parenting is best
    c. permissive, love-withdrawal parenting is best
    d. what is best depends upon the culture

9. Sibling interactions that are predominantly negative are most likely in the context of
    a. siblings as attachment objects
    b. siblings as teachers
    c. sibling rivalry
    d. none of the above

10. Research on ordinal birth position indicates that later-borns are
    a. more achievement oriented
    b. more socially responsible
    c. more popular
    d. all of the above

11. Research on the impact of divorce generally indicates that
    a. parents should always stay together for the sake of the children
    b. children fare better if the noncustodial parent stays away after divorce
    c. children are much less affected by divorce if the mother is the custodial parent
    d. none of the above

12. Following divorce, the custodial parent often tends to become more
    a. authoritarian and power-assertive
    b. authoritative and inductive
    c. permissive and inclined toward love-withdrawal
    d. all of the above

13. Research clearly indicates that the effects of maternal employment upon the child
    a. are negative, with respect to cognitive development
    b. are neutral and have no effect on cognitive development
    c. are sufficiently ambiguous as to suggest that mothers quit work and stay at home
    d. none of the above

14. The likelihood of child abuse is increased when
    a. the mother works outside the home
    b. the parent was abused as a child
    c. the child's father figure is a stepparent
    d. all of the above

15. Research generally indicates that
    a. abusive parents are nearly always neurotic or psychotic
    b. abusive parents respond positively to a child's positive social gestures
    c. physical punishment is often the first step in the development of child abuse
    d. the only solution to child abuse is to remove the child from the home

RESEARCH SUMMARY AND REVIEW

Using the textbook, review the research efforts indicated and write a summary of the important findings. Note the general purpose or context of the research.

1. Buss (1981), page 607: _____

_____

_____

_____

2. Crook, Raskin, & Eliot (1981), page 617: _____

_____
_____
_____

3. Weisz (1980), page 619: _____

_____
_____
_____

4. Zussman (1980), page 620: _____

_____
_____
_____

5. Kendrick & Dunn (1980), Dunn & Kendrick (1981b), page 623: ____

_____
_____
_____

SELF-TEST II

Consider each alternative carefully. Then choose the best one.

1. LeVine's research on family goals for children indicates that
    a. economic goals are satisfied first
    b. survival goals are satisfied first
    c. self-actualization goals are satisfied first
    d. no particular hierarchy exists in the satisfying of goals

2. Research indicates that obedience, cooperation, and responsibility are emphasized in
    a. agricultural and pastoral societies
    b. hunting and foraging societies
    c. war-like societies
    d. none of the above

3. Data on severe forms of discipline such as spanking children, verbally abusing them, and the like can be collected in
    a. interview and questionnaire studies
    b. field experiments
    c. analogue experiments
    d. none of the above, due to research ethics

4. The middle-class bias in much of the published research on families is such that
    a. findings may not generalize to lower-SES families
    b. findings may not generalize to middle-SES families
    c. both of the above
    d. none of the above

5. Research by Buss (1981) and others on family reciprocal effects indicates that
    a. disciplinary style depends upon the particular act the child commits
    b. disciplinary style depends upon the child's history of responding to discipline
    c. the child's overall activity level influences disciplinary style
    d. all of the above

6. The "Cinderella" syndrome, if valid, would apply in
    a. intact nuclear families
    b. single-parent families
    c. extended families
    d. reconstituted families

7. Other things equal, the likelihood of mothers being psychologically satisfied and responsive to their children
    a. decreases with age of the mother
    b. remains the same with age of the mother
    c. increases with age of the mother
    d. displays no clear relationship to age of the mother

8. In Baumrind's research, permissive parenting typically led to
    a. low social and cognitive competencies in boys but not in girls
    b. low social and cognitive competencies in girls but not in boys
    c. low social and cognitive competencies in boys and in girls
    d. none of the above

9. When parents are typically cold and rejecting, their children tend to be
    a. securely attached
    b. altruistic
    c. high in self-esteem
    d. none of the above

10. Research by Crook, et al. (1981) demonstrated that later episodes of major depression when children reach adulthood are more likely if
    a. mothers are hostile and rejecting
    b. fathers are hostile and rejecting
    c. both of the above
    d. none of the above

11. Research by Weisz (1980) on children's views of parenting indicated that
    a. within limits, children prefer use of control by parents
    b. within limits, children and adolescents prefer use of control by parents
    c. no children prefer use of control by parents, regardless of its extent
    d. within limits, all children and adolescents prefer use of control by parents

12. In Zussman's (1980) research, parents performed a cognitive task while their children could simultaneously get into mischief; this was an example of
    a. the interview approach
    b. the questionnarie approach
    c. naturalistic observation
    d. an analogue experiment

13. Maccoby's review indicates that higher-SES parents, as compared to lower-SES parents,
    a. tend to stress neatness, cleanliness, and staying out of trouble
    b. tend to show more warmth and affection toward their children
    c. are more permissive
    d. none of the above

14. Research indicates that middle-class mothers, as compared to working-class mothers,
    a. are more likely to engage in physical contact with their children
    b. are more likely to provide distal stimulation for their children
    c. are less likely to engage in physical contact with their children
    d. are less likely to provide distal stimulation for their children

15. Research on sibling rivalry suggests that
    a. this type of conflict is most likely between boy-boy pairs
    b. this type of conflict is most likely between girl-girl pairs
    c. this type of conflict peaks during the preschool period and declines thereafter
    d. none of the above

16. Research by Dunn & Kendrick indicates that older siblings who receive lots of attention from mothers during a younger sibling's first few weeks of life are
    a. more likely to play with the younger sibling
    b. more likely to have a positive attitude toward the younger sibling
    c. more likely to form an attachment with the younger sibling
    d. none of the above

17. Parents may tend to be more affectionate and attentive toward their first-born children, which suggests that
    a. first-borns would be more popular with peers
    b. first-borns would feel closer to their parents
    c. later-borns would be more achievement oriented
    d. later-borns would feel closer to their parents

18. Hetherington's research indicates that, following divorce, the custodial parent
    a. is likely to become more punitive
    b. is likely to place a stronger emphasis on controlling the child
    c. both of the above
    d. none of the above

19. Fathers, as custodial parents,
    a. tend to have more problems in childrearing than mothers do
    b. are more likely to report that their children are well behaved
    c. perceive their relationships with their children as basically coercive
    d. all of the above

20. Living with a stepfather
    a. is more stressful for girls than for boys
    b. makes boys somewhat resentful and coercive toward their mothers
    c. increases a girl's affection for her mother
    d. all of the above

21. In families where the mother is employed outside the home, children tend to
    a. be less independent
    b. hold more stereotyped views of the sexes
    c. be more sociable and outgoing
    d. all of the above

22. Children are at minimal risk for abuse and neglect when
    a. they are infants
    b. they are physically ill and in need of careful monitoring
    c. they are emotionally responsive
    d. all of the above

23. Abusive parents
    a. tend to be mentally ill or emotionally disturbed
    b. almost always have a history of abuse by parents
    c. tend to be irritated by their children's social signals
    d. all of the above

24. Statistics generally indicate that child abuse in the U.S.
    a. is decreasing
    b. is not a widespread problem
    c. is largely confined to "high risk" neighborhoods
    d. none of the above

25. A major problem in attempting to eliminate or reduce child abuse is that
    a. most abusive parents have a serious mental illness that is difficult to treat
    b. parents who will abuse their infants cannot be identified
    c. authorities are reluctant to separate abused children from their parents
    d. it is the right of the parent to use whatever form of discipline seems warranted

VIGNETTES

Consider the story, then answer each question using material from the textbook.

I. Oscar's parents, as far back as he could remember, had always been very interested in him and how he was doing at school, both in class and with his schoolmates. He didn't always care for the rules they set for him, but he usually figured there was a reason, and his mother would explain the reason most of the time. He loved his parents very much and he often bragged on them a bit with his friends. And Oscar knew they loved him, too.

    1. Which of Baumrind's parenting types do Oscar's parents fit?

    2. What can you predict about how Oscar gets along at school?

    3. How might Oscar be affecting the behavior of his parents?

II. Peggy's parents, as far back as she could remember, had always been rather aloof and hard to talk to. They hoped she would do well in school and get along with her class-mates, or at least they said they did. But she wasn't really sure. Mostly, she was on her own where matters outside the home were concerned. And it was up to her when (and if) she did her homework, as well as when she came and went. If she stayed too late, her mo-ther would explain why that was a problem and would attempt a compromise. Peggy loved her parents. And she hoped they loved her, too, but sometimes she wondered.

    1. Which of Baumrind's parenting types do Peggy's parents fit?

    2. What can you predict about how Peggy gets along at school?

    3. Can you predict what SES Peggy's parents belong to?

III. Lynn was 5 months old and cried a lot, so much so that her neighbors in the apart-ment complex thought she might be an abused or neglected child. The apartment project was an inexpensive one, with walls that were very thin, and it seemed that Lynn often cried and protested without anyone coming to help. Sometimes, her crying would suddenly pick up in intensity, as if something had just happened. Finally, the neighbors decided to intervene, and they went next door to meet Lynn's parents for the first time and see what they could find out.

    1. If you were Lynn's neighbors what would you consider about Lynn herself, in terms of behaviors or characteristics that might increase her risk for child abuse?

    2. What would you consider about Lynn's parents, in trying to determine the likeli-hood that they are child abusers?

    3. If you decided that child abuse was occurring, what might you do next?

APPLICATIONS

Try each of the projects, noting answers to the questions as you go.

I. As part of planning a research effort, you must decide how to go about studying the phenomenon in question. For purposes of illustration, suppose you have targeted "sibling rivalry" for an exploratory study to assess its forms and the extent to which it occurs in variations of the nuclear family. What types of methodology might you employ?

    1. Discuss advantages and shortcomings of an interview approach.

    2. Discuss advantages and shortcomings of an observational approach.

    3. Discuss advantages and shortcomings of an analogue experiment.

II. Suppose you find yourself counseling a married couple who are contemplating divorce due to quarreling, fighting, and a basic desire not to live with each other. Among other things, they are very concerned about what will happen to their children and what effects the divorce might have.

    1. What could you tell them about possible effects on their children if they stay together in spite of not being able to get along with each other?

    2. What could you tell them about immediate and long-range effects of the divorce on their children, along with how to minimize such effects?

    3. What could you tell them about mother versus father custody of the children?

III. Suppose you find yourself working along with a branch of a local service agency that has become aware of an alarming rate of child abuse in one particular area of town, an area characterized by gradual deterioration, a high crime rate, and many low-income families in which the father is absent from the home.

    1. What is it about this kind of neighborhood that might contribute to child abuse?

    2. What might you do at the neighborhood and community level to combat child abuse?

    3. What kinds of changes might you attempt at a more individual level in working with families in which child abuse occurs?

ANSWERS

Self-Test I

1. d	6. a	11. d
2. a	7. b	12. a
3. a	8. d	13. d
4. d	9. c	14. b
5. c	10. c	15. c

Research Summary and Review

1. Buss (1981): Mothers and fathers of highly active 5½-year-old children were likely to get into power struggles while helping their children perform cognitive tasks, whereas parents of less active children had more peaceful and harmonious interactions; indications were that child temperament directly affects how parents relate to their children.

2. Crook, Raskin, & Eliot (1981): Hospitalized depressed patients were compared to non-

depressed adults with respect to their childhood relationships with their parents, and the ratings of the depressives indicated their parents to be more hostile, detached, and rejecting but not more restrictive or controlling; implications were that parental warmth/hostility has long-range effects on personality development.

3. Weisz (1980): Children 7-17 years old submitted contest entries on "Why Mom is the greatest," and analysis of the results indicated that younger children value physical nurturance and autonomy more, whereas older children value psychological nurturance and a bit more control by parents, indicating correspondence between children's views and those of developmental theories.

4. Zussman (1980): An analogue experiment in which parents tried to perform a cognitive task while keeping their young children out of mischief indicated clearly that stress causes a parent to be less responsive and more critical and punitive in interactions with with his or her child.

5. Kendrick & Dunn (1981), Dunn & Kendrick (1981b): Studies assessing the form and origins of sibling rivalry indicated that older children compete with infants for attention from parents, later harass the younger siblings, and increasingly initiate quarrels; behaviors were more positive between same-sex sibs and more negative between cross-sex sibs.

Self-Test II

1. b	6. d	11. b	16. d	21. c
2. a	7. c	12. d	17. b	22. c
3. a	8. c	13. a	18. c	23. c
4. a	9. d	14. b	19. b	24. d
5. d	10. c	15. d	20. a	25. c

Vignettes

I.(1) Authoritative parenting is indicated, through parents setting the rules but leaving room for explanations and for some variability in Oscar's behavior. Also note Oscar's love and respect for his parents, consistent with responses to Weisz' study on "Why mom is the greatest." (2) For boys, Baumrind's research indicates high cognitive and social competencies associated with authoritative parenting, including achievement motivation, cooperation with adults and peers, and leadership. (3) As Oscar responds favorably to limits set by his parents in this fashion, things run smoothly in the family and the parents' approach is reinforced. Thus processes that might result in more punitive parenting (such as resistance and defiance on Oscar's part) are not set in motion.

II. (1) Permissive parenting is indicated, through the relative absence of firm rules and the presence of a democratic atmosphere; the idea here is that children do need some limits and, in turn, respect reasonable rules. Note that Peggy's parents seem warm enough but are aloof and detached, which gives rise to doubts on her part about whether they really care about her. (2) For girls, Baumrind's research indicates low cognitive and social competencies in areas such as achievement motivation and interactions with adults and peers. (3) The most likly possibility is that Peggy's family is in the middle-to upper-SES range, wherein permissive parenting is more often found. Note, however, that all parenting styles occur at all levels, and, tempting though it may be, you really can't make a strong prediction about economic or educational level of the family here.

III. A word of caution is in order: The presence of characteristics associated with abused children and their parents does not necessarily mean that child abuse is taking place. Concrete evidence would be necessary, most likely involving observable signs of harm to the child or a direct witnessing of the abuse. However, the likelihood would increase as follows: (1) Lynn's parents might be more likely to abuse her if she were irritable, unresponsive to their attempts to soothe her, physically ill much of the time, or otherwise a source of stress to them. (2) With regard to Lynn's parents, you might consider the quality of their marriage (have you also heard fighting, etc.), whether they have an adequate source of income, whether they seem to know much about parenting, whether their expectations and demands regarding her behavior are reasonable, and perhaps whether they wanted her in the first place. And, as in Frodi and Lamb's research, you might assess their general emotional responses to her smiles and to her cries. Note also the implication of a "high risk" neighborhood. (3) In most states, if you were a mental health professional, you would have an obligation by law to report suspicion of child abuse to an appropriate public agency for investigation and possible intervention. Less drastic measures might include attempting to persuade the parents to seek various kinds of treatment such as marital or family therapy or participation in Parents Anonymous, as well as taking advantage of a child-abuse hotline or crisis nursery if available.

Applications

I. (1) You could interview the parents, the children themselves, or adults with regard to their own childhoods. Each of these approaches could generate much information, especially on an emotionally charged subject such as sibling rivalry, but each is subject to inaccuracy as a result of relying on people's memories and subjective appraisals of what took place. Also note the issue of social desirability, in that most people believe they "should" get along with siblings, more or less. (2) You could station yourself as unobtrusively as possible in a home and observe siblings directly, such as at mealtimes or during play. Given checks on observer reliability, this could yield detailed and accurate information except for the possibility that your presence might change things. And social desirability of certain behaviors might be a problem here as well; you might not see everything that normally goes on. (3) An analogue experiment might set up key situations and "load" the situations for competition and other likely precipitators of sibling rivalry. However, the somewhat artificial context in which the research occurs might cause the children to behave differently than normal, and even more importantly, research ethics involving possible harmful effects would come into play. You can't let children harm one another in the ways they might occasionally do in the normal environment. Thus each approach has its advantages and shortcomings.

II. (1) The arguments and conflicts of an unhappy marriage may have worse effects on the children than the divorce itself, at least in the long run. Also note the discussion of indirect parental effects on children as a function of marital strife. (2) They can probably expect a "crisis" phase lasting a year or more, during which the relationships between the children and the custodial parent might become more coercive as a result of stresses on each. These effects could be minimized, however, through continuing emotional support (and perhaps financial support) by the noncustodial parent, also noting the desirability of a cordial working relationship between them with regard to the children. (3) Research indicates that either parent can be effective as the custodial parents, although fathers approach the situation somewhat differently (see Box 15-4). Also note the preliminary research evidence that boys may fare somewhat better with fathers and girls may fare better with mothers.

III. (1) Potential contributors to child abuse include primarily those which yield stress on the parents, such as living in a physically unattractive and impoverished setting, being isolated from interpersonal and social support systems, having few opportunities for the children to play outside the home, and generally lacking pride in one's living circumstances. (2) Establish Scouting groups and other activities for the children to get them out of the home more and thus relieve some of the stress on parents. Try to get a community renovation project going, and look for financial help along these lines. Help establish safe playgrounds. And in general, target community pride for the major thrust of your efforts at this level. (3) At a more individual level, work with families on finding adequate sources of income and perhaps employment, to offset financial stressors. Perhaps establish a Parents Anonymous group if there isn't one nearby, or get parents together to establish a crisis nursery system.

255

CHAPTER SIXTEEN

BEYOND THE HOME SETTING:
EXTRAFAMILIAL INFLUENCES

OVERVIEW AND KEY TERMS

Read carefully. Recall examples and discussion as you go, and define each key term.

THE EARLY WINDOW: EFFECTS OF TELEVISION ON CHILDREN AND YOUTH

The average TV set runs more than 6 hours per day, and 70% of American families have more than one TV set. People alter their daily schedules to conform to TV schedules, and U.S. children between 3 and 11 years old watch an average of 3 to 4 hours of TV per day. By age 7-8 years many children are watching programs intended for adult about half of the time. Young children are attracted most by fast action, special effects, and rapid change of content, and, although they often watch violent programs, research indicates that they prefer situation comedies. TV causes less time to be spent on parent-child activities, which leads to Bronfenbrenner's warning that the primary danger of TV lies in what it prevents. Research on whether children become social isolates or suffer in academic achievement from watching TV, however, is not conclusive as yet.

About 80% of all prime-time TV programming contains at least one violent incident, and the average is 7.5 violent acts per hour. Children's Saturday morning programming averages about 25 violent acts per hour. Experimental data indicate that children become more aggressive from watching TV violence, in contrast to the beneficial effects of pro-social television. Correlational research also implies that violent programming leads to aggressive behavior, and, unfortunately, young children don't easily distinguish fantasy from reality with regard to violence as a means of dealing with conflicts. The densensi-tization hypothesis suggests that exposure to violence increases viewer's tolerance for aggression and may blunt normal emotional reactions. Aside from organized social action, parents can help by pointing out subtleties such as TV aggressor's motives and the unpleasant consequences that usually result for those who aggress, and can suggest more constructive alternatives the aggressor might have employed.

Children also learn social stereotypes from TV, including emphases on males as more powerful and competent than females and minorities as working in lower-status occupations and being more prone to antisocial behavior. In contrast, programs such as *Sesame Street* can be effective in countering minority stereotypes, and other programs such as *Freestyle* have been designed to counter sex-role stereotypes.

The average child watches about 20,000 TV commercials each year, and children often press their parents to buy the products. Commercials can also alter play preferences.

Prosocial programming for children is increasing, and commercial TV series such as *Fat Albert and the Cosby Kids* portray themes that can benefit children. *PBS* programming such as *Sesame Street* and *Mister Rogers' Neighborhood* often incorporates attention-getting devices and prosocial themes that have a positive influence on interpersonal behaviors.

The Children's Television Workshop (CTW) has joint public and private funding and is committed to programs that facilitate intellectual development. Evaluations of *Sesame*

Street indicate improvement in cognitive skills. Research indicates that *The Electric Company* is successful in teaching reading skills if an adult is present to help the child apply the material. But in spite of such benefits, TV is still a one-way medium in which the child is a passive recipient, and, because of the potential for abuse, developmentalists are not in agreement about the extent to which TV should be used to socialize children. Yet, TV is already communicating social values in this respect.

THE SCHOOL AS SOCIALIZATION AGENT

American children attend school about 5 hours per day, 180 days per year. Thus our schools exert a strong influence, through teaching basic knowledge and skills and also through the informal curriculum which transmits social values and responsibility.

With regard to cognitive development, one issue is whether schools foster cognitive abilities that might otherwise not emerge. Schoolchildren reach Piagetian milestones earlier than those who do not attend, and they are also more likely to use special strategies such as elaboration when categorizing and memorizing information, but another possibility is that schoolchildren are simply better at taking tests.

Rutter describes effective schools as those which promote achievement, social skills, attentiveness, positive attitudes toward learning, low absenteeism, continuation of education, and skills that lead to employment. Children in effective schools outperform their intellectual counterparts in ineffective schools. Monetary and physical characteristics are less important to school effectiveness than are factors such as getting students "involved," and, at the elementary level, having smaller classes.

Special classrooms, as in ability tracking, appear to be more effective at the secondary than at the primary level. But ability tracking can undermine the motivation and self-esteem of low-ability children, and effective ability tracking depends upon assigning children to special areas of study. Box 16-1 discusses "mainstreaming," the approach of integrating handicapped children into regular classrooms, which has both pros and cons.

Traditional classrooms are highly structured and lecture-oriented, typically including a "zone of activity" in which some students participate more than others. In contrast, open classrooms stress active involvement by all students, plus individual and small-group work. Research comparing the two basic approaches is mixed. And children who need more structure than others many benefit more from traditional classrooms.

Exposure to intellectually capable peers helps the individual student, although some of the most effective schools are those for disadvantaged children. Other general contributors to effectiveness in schools are academic emphasis on teaching and performance, efficient classroom management that does not detract from teaching, nonpunitive discipline, and good staff agreement and morale. Effective schools also emphasize success instead of failure and give praise and recognition for achievement.

The teacher's influence on the student depends in part on the teacher's evaluation of the student's capabilities, as in the Pygmalion effect, which can work either to the child's benefit or detriment as teachers treat high- and low-expectancy student differently in the classroom. Another issue is the teacher's style, as in Baumrind's authoritarian instruction, authoritative instruction, and laissez-faire instruction, which correspond largely to her parenting styles. Authoritative instruction seeks control through the use of reason, with emphases on give and take between teacher and students and on creativity and autonomy within established rules, and this approach fosters high quality work that takes place even when the teacher is not present in the classroom. Other notes are that teaching is more effective when tailored to the abilities of students: high-ability students perform better with fast-paced, challenging instruction, whereas low-ability students many need slower-paced instruction that includes much encouragement.

U.S. public schools are typically oriented toward the middle class, both in terms of textbooks used and the types of parents who become actively involved in school activities. Minority students may get stereotyped by teachers as being less capable, and disadvantaged students may receive social promotions even when their performance is substandard. But, as discussed in Box 16-2, grade retention has both positive and negative effects on those children who repeat a grade, depending in part on the child's self-concept and how extensive his or her deficiencies are.

Mandatory school desegregation was intended to foster more positive attitudes between racial and ethnic groups, and also to foster increases in self-esteem and overall academic achievement of minority groups. Mixed results have been obtained with regard to reducing racial prejudice, depending upon what happens in peer interactions after integration. Short-term research has indicated either no effect or negative effects on minority self-esteem. But consistent improvements in academic achievement of minorities have been associated with desegregation.

THE SECOND WORLD OF CHILDHOOD: PEERS AS SOCIALIZATION AGENTS

Much of the socialization of the child comes about through interactions with peers. Developmentalists focus on peers as "social equals" for the child. Peer contacts increase with age from infancy through middle childhood, peaking prior to adolescence, and contacts with adults correspondingly decrease. However, research indicates that children actually spend less time with age-mates than with older and younger children, preferring same-sex interactions throughout childhood.

The Harlows' research on "mother-only" monkeys versus "peer-only" monkeys indicates that parents provide a sense of security for children and that peers provide opportunity to develop competent adaptive social behavior. Thus each type of interaction is necessary to normal social and personality development. Children who are rejected by peers are later more likely to develop antisocial behavior and emotional disturbances, especially if insecure attachment and a poor home environment are also present. Box 16-3 describes factors that contribute to good peer relations. And an authoritative parenting style is helpful to peer relations, whereas the other styles may foster hostility, aggression,. shyness, and other attributes that interfere with peer relations. Later-borns tend to be more popular. Good role-taking skills help in peer relations. Attractive children are typically more popular and have higher self-esteem, and children who are perceived by peers as friendly, calm, cooperative, and supportive are more popular than children who are pushy, disruptive, critical, and self-serving.

Peers influence each other through reinforcement and punishment, and they also serve as social models who can be as effective in determining behavior as adult models. Peers are more likely to serve as models if they are the same age as the child or older, and if they are of the same sex. And the fact of being imitated is also reinforcing, at least if model and imitator are of equivalent status. When an older child teaches a younger child, both children are likely to benefit, as discussed in Box 16-4.

Peer groups share norms and work together with a sense of "belonging." Peer groups become more clearly established during middle childhood, especially in setting norms for behavior. Conformity to peer-group pressures peaks during middle childhood and subsides from adolescence on, especially where conformity to behaviors the child or the child's parents disapprove of is involved. Yet adolescents are more likely to conform in ambiguous situations, in situations where other peer-group members strongly endorse a behavior, and when peers are older and more competent than the child in question. Patterns of conformity are complex, and the stereotype of "blind" conformity among adolescents is a myth.

Cross-pressures between parents and peers provide one reason why adolescence is often described as a stormy period. Conformity in situations where any of several courses of action are possible increases with age, but the relative influence of parents versus peers depends in part on the situation. Peers are more likely to sway decisions about status norms, friendship choices, and group or personal identity, whereas parents tend to be more influential regarding academic decisions and future aspirations. Other points are that peer-group pressures are not necessarily deviant, and that it is important to view peer-group and parent pressures in terms of how they combine as well as how they may counteract each other. Parents also often have indirect effects on behavior of children, as when parents of other peer-group members influence the child in question.

   Peer-group influences vary considerably from society to society. Examples are that Oriental cultures teach more emphasis on respecting the advice of elders, and that some societies greatly restrict interactions wtih peers because of competing family responsibilities. Research indicates that Russian children are more likely to resist deviant peer pressures than are U.S., German, and English children. Russian children have been found to be more conforming to adult norms than American children when responses will be reviewed by peers, whereas American children tend to be more deviant under these circumstances. The difference apparently relates to Russian teachers' direct use of the peer-group as a means of socializing children, within an emphasis on teamwork rather than individual accomplishments. Russian peer groups are extensions of the adult sociopolitical viewpoint, whereas American peer groups are allowed to develop many of their norms on their own, which can thus sometimes conflict with adult norms.

SELF-REVIEW

Fill in the blanks for each item. Check the answers for each item as you go.

THE EARLY WINDOW: EFFECTS OF TELEVISION ON CHILDREN AND YOUTH

Children's Use of Television

1. In the U.S., children of preschool and middle-childhood ages watch an average of ___-___ hours of TV per day; by age 18, the a child born today will have spent more time watching TV than in any other activity expect _____.

3-4

sleeping

2. Children age 7-8 years prefer programs with fast-paced _____ and special _____; children often watch programs containing _____ for these reasons, but survey data indicate that children actually prefer _____ _____.

action
effects
violence
situation comedies

3. Bronfenbrenner notes that there is less danger in the behavior produced by TV that in the behavior it _____, because TV tends to limit family _____; but research indicates that TV watching does not affect how much time children spend doing _____ and neither does it affect their enthusiasm for _____ interactions.

prevents
interactions

homework
peer

Effects of Televised Violence

4. By age 16 the average child in the U.S. will have witnessed more than 13,000 _____ on TV; Saturday morning cartoon shows contain an average of ___ violent acts per hour, and research data of various kinds indicate that the general effect of TV violence is to increase _____ by children.

killings
25

aggression

5. Young children cannot easily distinguish _____ from reality with regard to TV, and thus they may become convinced that the world is a _____ place; and a steady diet of TV violence tends to desensitize children and increase their basic _____ for violence.

fantasy

violent

tolerance

Television as a Source of Social Stereotypes

8. TV _____-role stereotyping is common, as _____ are often portrayed as more dominant and intelligent; stereotyping of racial _____ is decreasing, but non-Whites are still more often portrayed as very _____ people who are more likely to be

sex-, males

minorities
poor

259

involved in _____ activities.   illegal

9. Research indicates that children, after watching programs
designed to eliminate stereotypes, (1) develop more favorable
_____ toward and are more likely to _____ with members   attitudes, play
of other ethnic or racial groups, and (2) become less prone to
believe in rigid sex-role _____.   stereotypes

Children's Reactions to Commercial Messages

10. In the U.S., the average child watches about _____ com-   20,000
merical messages each year, and children may become angry and
resentful toward _____ who will not buy them the products.   adults

Television as a Prosocial Instrument

11. Commerical programs that contain helping or altruistic acts
can foster _____ behavior in children; *PBS* programming   prosocial
often contains prosocial themes that have a positive influence
on children's _____ behavior even though the children's   social
_____ behavior may not decrease.   aggressive

Television as a Contributor to Cognitive Development

12. Evaluations of *Sesame Street* indicate that it is _____   highly
effective in improving basic academic skills with disadvantaged
children, as well as _____ their general interest in   improving
school activities; but programs such as *Sesame Street* have been
criticized in that the child is a _____ recipient rather   passive
than an active processor of information and that the child may
become too accustomed to the fast pace and thus be _____ by   bored
the slow pace of the classroom.

Should Television Be Used to Socialize Children?

13. Controversial issues in the use of TV include the possibility of its use for _____ indoctrination and its possi-   political
ble role as a subtle form of "_____"; but it can   brainwashing
also be argued that TV is _____ being used in this fash-   already
ion as a potent agent of _____.   socialization

THE SCHOOL AS A SOCIALIZATION AGENT

14. In addition to teaching academic skills, schools also have
a more social _____ _____ involving obedience   informal curriculum
to rules and authority and development of citizenship; thus
schools may have a pronounced effect on the child's social and
emotional _____.   development

Does Schooling Promote Cognitive Development?

15. In general, schoolchildren reach Piagetian _____   milestones
in cognitive development _____ than children who do not   earlier
attend school, and schoolchildren are more likely to acquire
specific cognitive rules such as learning to _____.   learn

Determinants of Effective and Ineffective Schooling

16. Schools are generally more effective when (1) they employ a
clearcut emphasis on _____ goals, (2) classrooms are man-   academic
aged so as not to waste _____, (3) discipline does not rely on   time
physical _____, and (4) there is a business-like at-   punishment
mosphere that _____ students to learn.   motivates

17. Problems with traditional classrooms are that they typically

260

contain a _____ of _____ so that not all students have the same access to the teacher; "open" classrooms counteract this problem, but students who are restless, distractible, and poorly _____ to work on their own may not benefit.

zone of activity

motivated

The Teacher's Influence

18. In the Pygmalion effect, teachers communicate either positive or negative _____ to particular students and also interact with them differently, which tends to lead to _____-fulfulling prophecies.

expectations
self-

19. Baumrind's teaching styles correspond to the styles by which she categorizes _____; in particular, high demands by the teacher coupled with give and take between teacher and student tend to foster good _____ and the ability to work in-dependently, as in the style of _____ instruction.

parents

productivity
authoritative

The School as a Middle-Class Institution: Effects on Disadvantaged Youth

20. Teachers who employ stereotypes may become negative toward disadvantaged children and have lower _____ about their abilities, while at the same time grading the children less rigorously and employing _____ _____ to avoid re-taining the child in a grade.

expectations

social promotions

21. School desegregation was designed to (1) _____ Whites' attitudes toward Blacks, (2) _____ Blacks' attitudes toward Whites, and (3) improve Blacks' self-_____ and academic _____; these goals have generally not yet been realized except for some _____ gains in Blacks' _____ achievement.

improve
improve
-esteem
achievement
small, academic

THE SECOND WORLD OF CHILDHOOD: PEERS AS SOCIALIZATION AGENTS

Who or What is a Peer?

22. Developmentalists generally view children's peers as social "_____" in terms of behavioral complexity or status; thus peer interactions help children understand _____.

equals
themselves

The Role of Peers in the Socialization Process

23. Drawing from research by Harlow and Harlow, absence of peer contact produces offspring who are social _____; in conjunc-tion with observations of the "concentration camp" children, the indications are that peer contacts are highly important in pro-moting the development of _____ and _____ pat-terns of social behavior.

misfits

competent, adaptive

24. Determinants of popularity among peers include (1) having parents who are _____ and responsive and who promote _____ attachment, (2) having an athletic, _____ body type, (3) being a _____-born sibling, (4) having good _____-taking skills, (5) being facially _____, and (6) being rel-atively friendly, cooperative, and _____.

warm, secure
mesomorphic
later-, role-
attractive
nonaggressive

25. Peers often employ reinforcement and punishment to _____ behavior and conduct, and they also serve as important social _____; in turn, children seem to benefit from and enjoy being models for other children, depending upon the _____ of the imitator.

shape

models
status

26. Although children become _____ responsive to peer pressures as they mature, there are some situations in which they

increasingly

respond to _____-_____ by siding with parents; peers   cross-pressures
are more influential that parents in conflicts involving norms
for _____, choice of _____, and questions of per-   status, friendships
sonal or group _____; parents are more influential than   identity
peers where scholastic _____ and decisions involving   achievement
future _____ are concerned.   aspirations

The Role of the Peer Group in Other Societies

27. Bronfenbrenner's cross-cultural research on English, German,
Russian, and American children indicates that (1) the greatest
willingness to take part in peer-group misconduct occurs with
_____ children and the least with _____ children;   English, Russian
(2) willingness to take part relates to how much _____ is spent   time
with peers; and (3) peer-group norms as such correspond more to
adult norms in _____ than in the _____, perhaps because   Russia, U.S.
teachers in Russia place more emphasis on the peer group as an
agent of socialization.

SELF-TEST I

Consider each alternative carefully. Then choose the best one.

1. Indications are that children spend more time _____ than in any other activity except sleeping.
  a. watching television
  b. socializing with peers
  c. at school
  d. in play activities

2. Verified negative effects of TV on children include
  a. development of tolerance for violence
  b. increased aggression
  c. learning of minority and sex-role stereotypes
  d. all of the above

3. Which of the following has been more or less eliminated from commercial TV?
  a. violence
  b. sex-role stereotyping
  c. social and racial stereotyping
  d. none of the above

4. Verified positive effects of TV include
  a. acquisition of prosocial skills
  b. acquisition of academic skills
  c. both of the above
  d. none of the above

5. If you were especially concerned with helping your child to read, you and the child
together might watch
  a. *Mister Rogers' Neighborhood*
  b. *Sesame Street*
  c. *The Electric Company*
  d none of the above

6. Research generally verifies that effective schools
  a. have more money and physical resources
  b. use ability tracking with younger students
  c. place younger students in open classrooms
  d. none of the above

7. Research indicates that effective schools
   a. have a clear focus on academic goals and standards
   b. actively encourage good work
   c. employ noncorporal discipline
   d. all of the above

8. Of Baumrind's instruction styles, the least likely to be found in effective schools is
   a. authoritarian instruction
   b. authoritative instruction
   c. laissez-faire instruction
   d. all of the above are equally likely

9. Grade retention is more likely with
   a. children who experience a negative Pygmalion effect
   b. lower-class children
   c. children of racial and ethnic minorities
   d. all of the above

10. Research generally indicates that school desegregation has led to
    a. major reductions in racial prejudice, especially that of Whites toward Blacks
    b. consistently positive effects on Blacks' self-esteem
    c. modest but significant gains in academic achievement for Blacks
    d. all of the above

11. In research on peers as socialization agents for children, "peer" typically means
    a. a child within 3-4 months of age
    b. a child within a year or so of the same age
    c. a child within 3 years of age
    d. a child at the same level of behavioral complexity

12. Research on the overall effects of peer interactions indicates that they are
    a. necessary but not sufficient for normal social development
    b. sufficient but not necessary for normal social development
    c. both necessary and sufficient for normal social development
    d. neither necessary nor sufficient for normal social development

13. Peer groups are best characterized as having
    a. basically positive effects on personality development
    b. basically negative effects on personality development
    c. both positive and negative effects on personality development
    d. niether positive nor negative effects on personality development

14. With regard to the normative function of peer groups, conformity to peers is likely
    a. among younger children in most cases
    b. among older children in virtually all cases
    c. when the child has a high status in the peer group
    d. none of the above

15. In resolving cross-pressures, adolescents are most likely to follow the peer group if
    a. friendship choices and issues of personal identity are involved
    b. issues of scholastic achievement and academic choices are involved
    c. the peer-group's norms directly oppose those of most adults
    d. the question of "Who am I to be?" is involved

RESEARCH SUMMARY AND REVIEW

Using the textbook, review the research efforts indicated and write a summary of the important findings. Note the general purpose or context of the research.

1. Stein & Friedrich (1972), page 649: _____

_____
_____
_____
_____

2. Drabman & Thomas (1974), Thomas, Horton, Lippincott, & Drabman (1977), page 649: _____
_____
_____
_____
_____

3. Rosenthal & Jacobson (1968), page 666: _____
_____
_____
_____

4. Lewin, Lippitt, & White (1939), page 667: _____
_____
_____
_____

5. Plummer (1982), page 670: _____
_____
_____
_____

6. Alexander & Harlow (1965), Suomi & Harlow (1975), page 675: _____
_____
_____
_____

SELF-TEST II

Consider each alternative carefully. Then choose the best one.

1. In Bronfenbrenner's view, the primary danger of TV viewing by children lies in
    a. violent programs
    b. situation comedies
    c. the social behavior it prevents
    d. its passive-recipient nature

2. The most violent programs, in accord with research by Gerbner and associates, are
   a. Children's Television Workshop programs
   b. prime-time adult programs
   c. situation comedies
   d. Saturday morning cartoon shows

3. Prime-time programming averages ____ violent acts per hour, and by age 16 an average child will have watched _____ of killings of TV.
   a. 7.5, thousands
   b. 25, thousands
   c. 7.5, hundreds
   d. 25, hundreds

4. Stein and Friedrich's (1972) experiment in which preschool children watched daily episodes of violent programming indicated the greatest increases in aggression for
   a. children initially above average in aggression
   b. children initially average in aggression
   c. children initially below average in aggression
   d. none of the children in the study

5. Research by Drabman, Thomas and associates on desensitization effects of watching violent programming indicated that children, with continuing exposure,
   a. become more aroused and more inclined to intervene in daily aggression
   b. become more aroused and less inclined to intervene in daily aggression
   c. become less aroused and more inclined to intervene in daily aggression
   d. become less aroused and less inclined to intervene in daily aggression

6. Research indicates that children who watch programs such as *Sesame Street* and *Freestyle*, respectively, display acceptance of
   a. fewer minority stereotypes and more sex-role stereotypes
   b. more minority stereotypes and fewer sex-role stereotypes
   c. more minority stereotypes and more sex-role stereotypes
   d. fewer minority stereotypes and fewer sex-role stereotypes

7. Research by the Educational Testing Service on *The Electric Company* and its effects on reading skills indicated that
   a. disadvantaged children benefitted but middle-class children did not
   b. middle-class children benefitted but disadvantaged children did not
   c. all types of children benefitted if they watched in the company of an adult
   d. no children benefitted to any appreciable extent

8. As an agent for socialization of children, prosocial TV
   a. is basically ineffective
   b. is uniformly beneficial
   c. has both benefits and liabilities
   d. tends to have a brainwashing effect

9. The "informal curriculum" of schools includes
   a. respect for rules and authority
   b. cooperation with classmates
   c. citizenship
   d. all of the above

10. Research by Rutter and associates on British schools indicated that
    a. schools differ in the effectiveness of formal but not informal curricula
    b. schools differ in the effectiveness of informal but not formal curricula
    c. schools differ both in the effectiveness of informal and formal curricula
    d. schools differ neither in the effectiveness of formal nor informal curricula

11. "Mainstreaming" is basically an extended version of
    a. ability tracking
    b. mixed-ability instruction
    c. traditional classroom instruction
    d. open-classroom instruction

12. Research on the effectiveness of mainstreaming is generally
    a. conclusive and in favor of this approach to education
    b. conclusive and against this approach to education
    c. inconclusive with regard to this approach to education
    d. biased in favor of the researchers' points of view

13. "Zone of activity," with respect to the child's perspective, refers to
    a. more effective places to sit in traditional classrooms
    b. less effective places to sit in traditional classrooms
    c. more effective places to sit in open classrooms
    d. less effective places to sit in open classrooms

14. Rosenthal and Jacobson's (1968) Pygmalion effect involves teachers'
    a. communication of different expectations to different students
    b. differential use of praise and other reinforcement with students
    c. differential use of criticism and punishment with students
    d. all of the above

15. Lewin, Lippitt, and White's (1939) research indicated that student productivity while the teacher is absent from the classroom is highest with
    a. authoritarian instruction
    b. authoritative instruction
    c. laissez-faire instruction
    d. none of the above

16. Plummer's (1982) research on grade retention indicated that retainees are likely to
    a. be less popular with peers and suffer loss of self-esteem
    b. neither be less popular with peers nor suffer loss of self-esteem
    c. be less popular with peers but not suffer loss of self-esteem
    d. suffer loss of self-esteem but not be less popular with peers

17. Apparently, school desegregation has been limited in reducing racial prejudice because
    a. desegregation has been involuntary and thus resented in most cases
    b. minority students have not displayed increases in academic achievement
    c. students of differing racial backgrounds stick together in integrated schools
    d. minority students have shown much less acceptance of Whites than vice versa

18. During the middle-childhood period children interact most often with
    a. cross-age companions
    b. near-age companions
    c. same-age companions
    d. adult companions

19. Harlow and associates' research on "mother only" and "peer only" monkeys indicated that normal social development necessarily requires interaction
    a. with adults, but not with peers
    b. with peers, but not with adults
    c. both with adults and with peers
    d. neither with adults nor with peers

20. The six concentration-camp children studied by Anna Freud and Sophie Dann
    a. were psychotic and could not form positive relationships outside their group
    b. were developmentally retarded and could not learn new language skills
    c. both of the above
    d. none of the above

266

21. Characteristics such as having an attractive name and a pretty face
    a. lead directly to higher popularity in the peer group
    b. lead directly to lower popularity in the peer group
    c. are positively correlated with popularity in the peer group
    d. are essentially unrelated to popularity in the peer group

22. Other factors aside, a child is _least_ like to imitate
    a. a younger peer
    b. a same-age peer
    c. an older peer
    d. an adult

23. Children who serve as tutors for other children tend to experience
    a. improved self-concepts
    b. improved attitudes toward school
    c. increases in levels of aspiration
    d. all of the above

24. Adolescents tend to resolve cross-pressures in favor of parental advice where
    a. friendships are involved
    b. questions of personal identity are involved
    c. academic and scholastic choices are involved
    d. none of the above

25. Cross-cultural research by Bronfenbrenner and associates on the role of peer groups indicated that
    a. peer-group standards are generally inconsistent with adult norms
    b. children regardless of culture are highly likely to conform to deviant group norms
    c. peer groups are not effective agents of socialization in most cultures
    d. none of the above

VIGNETTES

Consider the story, then answer each question using material from the textbook.

I. In the seventh grade, Dan was muscular, well coordinated, and past most of the changes of entering puberty. He spoke with a deeper voice than most of his friends and he usually had lots of input on what to do and when to do it. Yet, Dan was modest about himself and relatively unassuming, and he could go along with his friends as well as he could be the leader. People generally liked him. And he usually made good grades.

1. Discuss the possibility of a Pygmalion effect for Dan and his teachers.

2. Discuss the possibility of a *peer-group* "Pygmalion effect" between Dan and peers.

3. What can you say about the probability of Dan being imitated by peers?

II. In the seventh grade, Agnes was relatively pale and well behind the rest of her classmates with regard to entering puberty. She spoke with a timid, whiny sort of voice that often conveyed complaints about one thing or another, and most of the time she was unhappy or at least seemed so. Agnes was modest and unassuming about pretty much everything except her insect collection, which she regarded as one of the best anywhere. And this may have been true, because Agnes devoted most of her time to it. She wished she knew of other people who shared her interests, because she was very lonely. People generally didn't care much for Agnes. And except for biology, her grades weren't much to speak of.

1. Discuss the possibility of a Pygmalion effect for Agnes and her teachers.

2. Discuss the possibility of a *peer-group* "Pygmalion effect" between Agnes and peers.

3. What can you say about the probability of Agnes being imitated by peers?

III. Stewart's difficulty in keeping up with his classmates in arithmetic, reading, and spelling began to be apparent in the second grade. Indications were that he was mildly retarded. In class, his teacher often had difficulty getting him to sit still, and his attention quickly wandered away from whatever tasks he was assigned. Though likable and pleasant enough and fairly popular with his classmates, Stewart's distractibility often got him into trouble with his teacher. And so, his teacher pondered what to do.

1. Discuss the pros and cons of Stewart being in a traditional classroom with mixed-ability instruction.

2. Discuss the pros and cons of open-classroom instruction for Stewart.

3. Can you make any predictions about Stewart's popularity with his peers as he and they get older? Why or why not?

APPLICATIONS

Try each of the projects, noting answers to the questions as you go.

I. *Roadrunner* cartoons have been popular for many years, and if you've never seen one, you can still catch them on Saturday mornings and perhaps on weekday afternoons. For this project, do an informal analysis of *Roadrunner* (or similar) cartoons in light of the material on the effects of television.

1. What characteristics of the cartoons might capture children's attention?

2. Consider potential effects of these kind of cartoons on children's aggression and tolerance for violence.

3. Consider potential effects of cartoons such as this upon children's acquisition of prosocial behavior.

II. Imagine yourself as a scriptwriter for a TV commercial to advertise a new chocolate candy bar (such as "Friendsies," *Vignette I, page 111*). The commercial is to be oriented toward children of all ages and designed to convince them that having the candy bar is the most wonderful thing that could ever happen to them. As you sit down to start on the design for the commericial, consider the material from this chapter.

1. What production characteristics would best capture a child's attention?

2. How might peer-group social modeling be incorporated?

3. How might you interpret Bronfenbrenner's comment about the effects of television in the context of such commercials?

III. Suppose you move to a new city, and in the process of deciding where to live you also explore options as to what school your 8-year-old might attend. With this in mind, you visit classrooms at potential schools with an eye toward selecting the school that might be best for your child, who is a fairly typical third-grader.

1. What type of classroom discipline might you prefer, and why?

2. What would you prefer along the lines of academic emphasis and standards?

3. What would you probably *not* place much emphasis on?

Self-Test I

1. b	6. d	11. d
2. d	7. d	12. a
3. d	8. b	13. c
4. c	9. d	14. d
5. c	10. c	15. a

Research Summary and Review

1. Stein & Friedrich (1972): Preschool children who watched violent programming once a day become more aggressive, especially if they were initially above average in aggressive behaviors toward other children; those who watched prosocial or neutral programming displayed no increases in aggression, demonstrating the differential effects of TV.

2. Drabman & Thomas (1974), Thomas, et al. (1977): Children 8-10 years old displayed an increased tolerance for violence after watching violent TV programming, as indicated by slower reactions in reporting aggressive misbehavior by younger children and also by lowered physiological emotional reactions to violent programming, thus demonstrating potentially harmful effects of TV violence.

3. Rosenthal & Jacobson (1968): Arbitrary labeling of some students as "rapid bloomers" led to these students showing greater gains in IQ and reading skills over an 8-month period; implications were that teacher expectations can create a "Pygmalion" effect.

4. Lewin, Lippitt, & White (1939): A classic study on styles of classroom instruction indicated that authoritarian methods yield high productivity but little independent initiative, laissez-fair methods yield low productivity overall, and democratic "authoritative" methods yield both high productivity and high independent initiative.

5. Plummer (1982): Second- and fifth-grade students responded mostly favorably to classmates retained in a grade, in terms of potentially liking the person, believing that the person would be of more assistance in school work, and preferring the person as a playmate, in each case indicating that grade retention is not necessarily detrimental.

6. Alexander & Harlow (1965), Suomi & Harlow (1975): "Mother only" monkeys displayed persistent abnormal social behavior with peers, and "peer only" monkeys displayed abnormal social behaviors toward monkeys other than those in their peer group; implications were that both peer and adult interactions are necessary for normal social development.

Self-Test II

1. c	6. d	11. b	16. b	21. c
2. d	7. c	12. c	17. c	22. a
3. a	8. c	13. a	18. a	23. d
4. a	9. d	14. d	19. c	24. c
5. d	10. c	15. b	20. d	25. d

Vignettes

I. (1) Indications are that Dan is highly sociable and popular, which sets the stage for a Pygmalion effect with his teachers. He might well be regarded as a "rapid bloomer," especially in light of his being comfortably into puberty at this age. Thus he might get extra attention and so on from his teachers, as part of how he makes good grades. But, of course, he might be very capable independent of such an effect. (2) Dan's popularity might trace to his apparently mesomorphic body type, his early entrance into puberty, and his seemingly good role-taking skills. Thus his peers "expect" much of him, which might have effects very similar to those of the Pygmalion effect in enhancing his sociability and popularity. (3) Chances are that Dan provides an "example" for peers and is imitated by them in many subtle ways. Note that he apparently enjoys high status in his peer group.

II. (1) Pygmalion effects work both ways. Agnes, in many ways, is an "opposite" to Dan as described, and thus her teachers might get into a pattern of expecting less from her and perhaps being more critical and punitive. This might in turn affect her achievement efforts and thus her grades. (2) Insect collecting is probably not one of those pastimes that would endear a seventh-grader to her peers, especially given the rest of the description. Thus negative expectations and self-fulfilling prophecies might serve to maintain her apparent "outsider" status. (3) Agnes would not be a likely target of imitation, in part due to low peer-group status. She might actually be a model for things *not* to do.

III. (1) For one thing, Stewart would probably be outside the "zone of activity" in a traditional classroom. Otherwise, he might benefit from interactions with "normal" children both in a social and an academic sense, but he might also eventually suffer loss of self-esteem and loss of whatever achievement motivation he has if he continues to lag developmentally. (2) Stewart's distractibility argues against open-classroom instruction, and his age probably does also. It seems clear that he needs a more structured setting. (3) He seems to be off to a good start in terms of popularity, but we might wonder about what will happen if he continues to lag the other children. He will probably not be a high-status member of his peer group, but this does not rule out other children compensating for him along the way. One primary consideration might be how "aggressive" he is toward other children; what form his disruptive behaviors take would be another factor. And he would probably fare better if he is physically attractive.

Applications

I. (1) As discussed in this chapter and in the earlier material on TV, attention-getting aspects are very fast-paced action and myriad special effects. Also note that comedy runs throughout these kind of cartoons, which is by implication another determinant of child attention to TV shows. (2) Effects of cartoons probably depend first on the child's ability to distinguish fantasy from reality, which is in part a function of age. Thus cartoons such as *Roadrunner* might or might not affect children's aggressive behavior, and this is basically a question to be answered by research. Tolerance for "violence," however, might increase independently. (3) With regard to *Roadrunner* cartoons, note simply that the coyote's "aggression" always backfires, teaching that such behavior doesn't pay.

II. (1) Fast-paced movement (perhaps including having the child run from scene to scene) would probably grab attention, along with several changes of scene during the commercial. Also include bright colors, exciting background music, and a thoroughly "enjoyable" setting. (2) As in the "Friendsies" commercial, imply that the child is a high-status member of the peer group, presumably *because of* the candy bar. The message is that you too can be popular, if only you buy a "Friendsies." (3) Whatever the reasons, TV commercials often do attract children's attention at least momentarily away from whatever else they may be doing, including interacting with family, as illustrated in the earlier *Vignette*.

III. (1) Baumrind's authoritative instruction is indicated, in fostering creativity, high productivity, and independent work. Also look for avoidance of physical punishment and negative types of verbal criticism, because of the hostility such methods can foster, as discussed here and throughout the textbook. (2) Effective schools include high standards for individual performance, coupled with encouragement as an emphasized feature. Look for signs of well prepared lesson plans, efficient and "business-like" classrooms, good use of materials, and good teacher morale. (3) Note the indications that the school budget and the total resources and physical plant are not primary factors in effectiveness. Also note mixed findings regarding size of schools and classrooms, use of traditional versus open instruction, and so on, which suggests that these are not primary factors.

FINAL EXAM

1. Developmental psychology is concerned with identifying and explaining the changes people undergo throughout
   a. adulthood
   b. childhood
   c. adolescence
   d. all of the above

2. Developmental psychologists study growth and change in behavior during
   a. the prenatal period
   b. the toddler period
   c. adolescence
   d. all of the above and more

3. Which of the following is best for getting at the actual causes of behavior?
   a. the experimental method
   b. the clinical method
   c. naturalistic observation
   d. all of the above, equally

4. The emergence of a psychology of childhood began with
   a. G. Stanley Hall
   b. Sigmund Freud
   c. both of the above
   d. none of the above

5. In the final analysis, the responsibility for treating research participants fairly and protecting them from harm falls of the shoulders of
   a. ethics committees who weigh benefits and risks and make recommendations
   b. parents, teachers, and school officials who provide informed consent
   c. the investigator who proposes and conducts the research
   d. the federal granting agencies that fund psychological research

6. Theories that do not accurately predict and explain new research findings
   a. violate the requirement that theories must be concise
   b. may still be valuable, through having stimulated the new research
   c. violate the requirements that theories must be precise
   d. have no value whatsoever

7. The issue of whether children are curious explorers or malleable recipients of environmental forces is called the
   a. activity-passivity issue
   b. nature-nurture controversy
   c. question of original sin versus innate purity
   d. continuity-discontinuity issue

271

8. The child is essentially passive and molded entirely by environmental forces in
    a. Bandura's social-learning theory
    b. Erikson's psychosocial theory
    c. Watson's radical behaviorism
    d. Piaget's cognitive-developmental theory

9. When an infant cries to get contact with an adult and to get satisfaction of basic needs for food, etc., the ethological interpretation is that
    a. crying has been learned through conditioning and reinforcement
    b. a crying schema is being accommodated to the demands of the environment
    c. crying is an adaptive behavior that has evolved through natural selection
    d. the child is in the oral stage and libido is invested around the mouth

10. Piaget's work has had the effect of
    a. demonstrating that children's thought processes differ from those of adults
    b. shifting the emphasis in the study of intelligence from content to structure
    c. helping make cognition an acceptable area of study
    d. all of the above

11. The allele for curly hair dominates the allele for straight hair; thus, if two curly-haired parents produce a straight-haired child,
    a. one parent is homozygous, the other is heterozygous
    b. both parents are heterozygous
    c. both parents are homozygous
    d. parental genetic make-up cannot be determined in this case

12. Which of the following does not increase in likelihood as maternal age increases?
    a. Klinefelter's syndrome
    b. the poly-X syndrome
    c. Down's syndrome
    d. diabetes

13. The most basic cause of chromosomal abnormalities is probably
    a. faulty homunculi
    b. uneven segregation of chromosomes during meiosis
    c. aging ova and sperm cells
    d. exposure to environmental hazards

14. Generally, as the kinship quotient increases,
    a. correlations in IQ increase
    b. concordance rates for mental disorders increase
    c. correlations in temperamental characteristics increase
    d. all of the above

15. Due to differing genetic predispositions from child to child, optimal environments to enhance child development are
    a. probably not possible, regardless of the aspect of development
    b. already in effect in many parts of the nation for all aspects of development
    c. possible for intellectual but not personality development
    d. possible for personality but not intellectual development

16. Which of the following normally cannot pass the placental barrier?
    a. teratogens such as viruses
    b. gases such as oxygen and carbon dioxide
    c. blood cells of the child and mother
    d. sugars, proteins, and fats

17. The age of viability begins soon after the end of the
    a. third trimester
    b. second trimester
    c. first trimester
    d. none of the above

18. Generally, the unborn child is <u>most</u> sensitive to the effects of teratogens during
    a. the period of the fetus
    b. the germinal period
    c. the period of the embryo
    d. all of the above, about equally

19. Generally, research indicates that the presence of fathers during labor and delivery
    a. is hard to accomplish, in that most fathers prefer not to be present
    b. distracts the mother and interferes with her concentration on childbirth
    c. is a major obstacle to effective use of medical personnel and procedures
    d. is supportive for the mother and aids in engrossment with the child

20. Natural or prepared childbirth typically does <u>not</u> include
    a. a dimly lit, quiet delivery room
    b. training in relaxation and breathing for the mother
    c. presence of the father during training, labor, and delivery
    d. avoidance of medications during childbirth

21. Which of the following is accurate with regard to neonates?
    a. soon after birth neonates can discriminate tastes of sweet versus sour
    b. vision is present from birth, though somewhat blurred and fuzzy
    c. audition is present from birth, with a preference for listening to human voices
    d. all of the above

22. A crying baby is likely to be
    a. desirous of parental attention
    b. mad
    c. in pain
    d. all of the above

23. Which of the following does <u>not</u> accelerate during the adolescent growth spurt?
    a. motor development
    b. brain development
    c. sexual maturation
    d. muscular growth

24. The motor development sequence of sitting, standing, and finally walking
    a. occurs with no apparent need for practice
    b. is consistent across all children
    c. occurs at the same ages for all children
    d. contradicts the cephalocaudal growth trend

25. A child who experiences short-term malnutrition of a relatively minor nature will probably, when diet later becomes adequate,
    a. remain permanently smaller than normal
    b. be mentally but not physically retarded
    c. experience catch-up growth
    d. develop marasmus or kwashiorkor

26. Generally, it appears that infants begin developing schemata for human faces
    a. within a few days of birth
    b. at about 1 month of age
    c. at about 2-3 months of age
    d. at about 5-6 months of age

27. Differentiation theory, such as that of Bower or Gibson, takes the view that
    a. the senses are separate and independent at birth
    b. intersensory interaction is not present at birth
    c. the senses are integrated at birth
    d. none of the above

28. Which of the following apparently does <u>not</u> improve or increase throughout childhood?
    a. dominance of vision over proprioception
    b. dominance of vision over audition
    c. attention span
    d. selective attention

29. Generally, within the first few days of life, neonates
    a. prefer music to nonrhythmic noise
    b. can recognize the sound of their own mothers' voices
    c. can distinguish between the vowels /a/ and /i/
    d. all of the above

30. Child development is
    a. a genetic process
    b. a holistic process
    c. an enrichment process
    d. a genetic process

31. The idea that most human behavior depends upon its consequences is basically
    a. mere exposure learning
    b. observational learning
    c. operant conditioning
    d. classical conditioning

32. One likely explanation of how parental approval continues to influence behavior even after the child becomes an adult is that parental approval is
    a. an extinguished response
    b. an incompatible response
    c. a generalized secondary reinforcer
    d. an unconditioned stimulus

33. Punishment is a reasonable method of controlling behavior if
    a. it is delivered by a warm and affectionate punitive agent
    b. it is accompanied by explanations of the reasons for punishment
    c. it is not cruel or unusual
    d. all of the above

34. According to Bandura, observational learning mainly involves the child acquiring
    a. associations between conditioned and unconditioned stimuli
    b. stimulus-response habits as a result of reinforcement
    c. symbolic representations of behavoir that are stored in memory for later use
    d. none of the above

35. Learning-to-learn primarily involves
    a. acquiring a concept relevant to solving a problem
    b. acquiring an ability to sit still in classrooms
    c. conditioned habits to specific stimuli
    d. use of image mediators

36. The correct order of infant vocalizations over the first year of life is
    a. crying, cooing, babbling, first word
    b. cooing, crying, first word, babbling
    c. babbling, crying, cooing, first word
    d. crying, babbling, cooing, first word

37. During the holophrastic stage, a child might use the word "car" to apply only to the family car and no others; this would be an example of
    a. expansion
    b. overregularization
    c. overextension
    d. underextension

38. With regard to grammatical morphemes, children typically
    a. start with irregular word forms, then overregularize, then return to irregulars
    b. overregularize nouns but not verbs
    c. learn irregular words early and continue to use them throughout development
    d. use orerregularized word forms until about 9-10 years of age

39. Expansions of a child's telegraphic utterances are often ineffective in aiding language development, but recasts often help; this is probably because
    a. expansions do not parallel the child's utterances
    b. expansions are usually too complex
    c. recasts do not contain additional ideas or information
    d. recasts are novel and maintain the child's attention

40. Evidence in favor of nativist explanations of language development includes
    a. the existence of language universals
    b. the left-hemisphere specialization of language function
    c. the preschool child's tendency to overregularize nouns and verbs
    d. all of the above

41. According to Piaget, the preoperational child's understanding and knowledge of the world is characterized by
    a. compensation
    b. egocentrism
    c. reversibility
    d. all of the above

42. Piaget's intellectual function of "adaptation" is based on the child's
    a. accomodation of schemata to fit new experiences
    b. assimilation of new experiences to existing schemata
    c. both of the above
    d. none of the above.

43. Generally, a child who is in the concrete-operational stage can
    a. solve the "liquid/beaker" problem
    b. solve the "wooden beads" problem
    c. sketch a map of a familiar route from one place to another
    d. all of the above

44. In information-processing theory, "rehearsal" generally refers to the transfer of information from
    a. LTM to STM
    b. sensory register to STM
    c. sensory register to LTM
    d. STM to LTM

45. The infant's habituation to a stimulus provides evidence that
    a. recognition memory is inborn
    b. recall memory is inborn
    c. both of the above
    d. none of the above

46. IQ appears to be stable through development if
    a. it is defined as crystallized intelligence
    b. individual test-retest schores are compared directly
    c. large groups of scores are averaged through test-retest correlation
    d. all of the above

47. Terman's longitudinal study of gifted children indicated that
    a. high IQ guarantees good health and adjustment
    b. child prodigies are frail and poorly adjusted
    c. child prodigies later tend to have disrupted marital relationships
    d. none of the above

48. Which of the following provides evidence that favors the environmentalist's views of intelligence?
    a. adoption studies of disadvantaged children in middled-class families
    b. adoption studies comparing children to biological parents
    c. studies of monozygotic versus dizygotic twins
    a. selective breeding studies with animals

49. The most likely explanation of ethnic, racial, and socioeconomic IQ differences is
    a. the motivational hypothesis
    b. the test-bias hypothesis
    c. the genetic hypothesis
    d. the environmental hypothesis

50. The ultimate goal of compensatory education is to
    a. demonstrate the superiority of White middle-class values
    b. alter the ethnic lifestyles of disadvantaged children
    c. improve disadvantaged children's academic performance
    d. boost disadvantaged children's QI scores

51. Early detection of infants who may be hard to love is best accomplished by
    a. the "strange situations" test
    b. infant intelligence tests
    c. the younger-peer test
    d. the Brazelton Neonatal Behavioral Assessment Scale

52. Early feeding experiences have been assumed to form the basis for infant attachment in
    a. psychoanalytic theory
    b. traditional learning theory
    c. both of the above
    d. none of the above

53. The secure-base phenomenon as an explanation for why stranger anxiety declines during the second year of life is a product of the
    a. psychoanalytic perspective
    b. cognitive-developmental perspective
    c. ethological perspective
    d. social-learning perspective

54. On a long-term basis,
    a. early secure attachment is permanent even if conditions change
    b. early insecure attachment is permanent even if conditions change
    c. both of the above
    d. none of the above

55. Research indicates that the central factor in explaining the effects of impoverished and understaffed institutional environments on children is
    a. social deprivation
    b. maternal deprivation
    c. stimulus deprivation
    d. all of the above

56. Many developmentalists, such as Mead, Mahler, and Piaget believe the infant is born
    a. with a sense of self only in conjunction with others
    b. with a public self but not a private self
    c. with a primitive but relatively complete sense of self
    d. without a sense of self

57. A primary distinction between sociability and emotional attachment is that
    a. sociability does not originate with early caregiver interactions
    b. attachment is directed toward fewer targets and is more intense
    c. sociability is directed toward peers but not adults
    d. attachment is temporary, whereas sociability is enduring

58. Over the preschool period, typically,
    a. instrumental aggression decreases and hostile aggression increases
    b. instrumental aggression increases and hostile aggression decreases
    c. both instrumental and hostile aggression increase
    d. both instrumental and hostile aggression decrease

59. Inductive discipline has the effect of fostering altruism in children because
    a. it encourages social role taking
    b. it enhances the child's altruistic looking-glass self
    c. it models altruistic behavior
    d. all of the above

60. Achievement motivation in children is enhanced by
    a. external locus of control
    b. insecure attachment
    c. positive achievement expectancies
    d. all of the above

61. Research generally indicates that male-female sex-role differences are
    a. determined entirely by learning and environment
    b. determined entirely by genetics
    c. determined by genetics and environment in interaction
    d. nonexistent and entirely mythical in nature

62. Male-female differences such as females being more suggestible and compliant
    a. reflect clear-cut genetic differences
    b. are well established by research
    c. are sometimes found and sometimes not
    d. are entirely mythical

63. Freud's notion of identification is most similar to the social-learning notion of
    a. social reinforcement
    b. imitation
    c. androgyny
    d. direct tuition

64. Young boys who are separated from their fathers early in life tend to be
    a. more emotionally dependent and more aggressive
    b. less emotionally dependent and more aggressive
    c. more emotionally dependent and less aggressive
    d. relatively unaffected in sex-role development

65. According to Bem's view of psychological androgyny, masculine and feminine are
    a. opposite ends of a single dimension
    b. opposite ends of two separate dimensions
    c. two separate dimensions
    d. terms that should be dispensed with in favor of unisexuality

66. Psychoanalytic theorists emphasize the _____ component of morality, cognitive-developmentalists the _____ component, and social-learning theorists the _____ component.
    a. affective, behavioral, reasoning
    b. reasoning, behavioral, affective
    c. affective, reasoning, behavioral
    d. reasoning, behavioral, affective

67. Cognitive-developmentalists and contemporary social-learning theorists agree that
    a. morality is a stable trait across situations
    b. the child is a moral philosopher
    c. moral principles are internalized
    d. none of the above

68. Piaget's theory and Kohlberg's theory share an emphasis on
    a. moral development in an invariant sequence
    b. moral developmetn as a function of cognitive development
    c. stages in moral development
    d. all of the above

69. Most adults function most of the time at Kohlberg's level of
    a. preconventional morality
    b. conventional morality
    c. postconventional morality
    d. none of the above

70. The choice to delay gratification is least likely with
    a. children high in achievement motivation
    b. more intelligent children
    c. delinquent children
    d. older children

71. Inductive discipline is most likely in Baumrind's
    a. authoritative parenting style
    b. authoritarian parenting style
    c. permissive parenting style
    d. none of the above

72. When parents are typically cold and rejecting, their children tend to be
    a. securely attached
    b. high in self-esteem
    c. altruistic
    d. none of the above

73. Research on the impact of divorce generally indicates that
    a. parents should always stay together for the sake of the children
    b. children fare better if the noncustodial parent stays away after divorce
    c. children are much less affected by divorce if the mother is the custodial parent
    d. none of the above

74. In families where the mother is employed outside the home, children tend to
    a. be less independent
    b. hold more stereotyped views of the sexes
    c. be more sociable and outgoing
    d. all of the above

75. A major problem in attempting to eliminate or reduce child abuse is that
    a. it is the right of the parent to use whatever form of discipline seems warranted
    b. authorities are reluctant to separate abused children from their parents
    c. parents who will abuse their infants cannot be identified
    d. most abusive parents have a serious mental illness that is difficult to treat

76. Which of the following has been more or less eliminated from commercial TV?
    a. violence
    b. social and racial stereotyping
    c. sex-role stereotyping
    d. none of the above

77. As an agent for socialization of children, prosocial TV
    a. is basically ineffective
    b. is uniformly beneficial
    c. has both benefits and liabilities
    d. tends to have a brainwashing effect

78. Research indicates that effective schools
    a. have a clear focus on academic goals and standards
    b. employ noncorporal discipline
    c. actively encourage good work
    d. all of the above

79. Research generally indicates that school desegregation has led to
    a. modest but significant gains in academic achievement for Blacks
    b. major reductions in racial prejudice, especially that of Whites toward Blacks
    c. consistently positive effects on Blacks' self-esteem
    d. all of the above

80. Adolescents tend to resolve cross-pressures in favor of parental advice when
    a. academic and scholastic choices are involved
    b. questions of personal identity are involved
    c. friendships are involved
    d. none of the above

FINAL EXAM ANSWERS

1. d	21. d	41. b	61. c
2. d	22. d	42. c	62. d
3. a	23. b	43. d	63. b
4. c	24. b	44. d	64. c
5. c	25. c	45. a	65. c
6. b	26. c	46. c	66. c
7. a	27. c	47. d	67. d
8. c	28. a	48. a	68. d
9. c	29. d	49. d	69. b
10. d	30. b	50. c	70. c
11. b	31. c	51. d	71. a
12. d	32. c	52. c	72. d
13. b	33. d	53. c	73. d
14. d	34. c	54. d	74. c
15. a	35. a	55. a	75. b
16. c	36. a	56. d	76. d
17. b	37. d	57. b	77. c
18. c	38. a	58. a	78. d
19. d	39. d	59. d	79. a
20. a	40. d	60. c	80. a